Staying Local in the Global Village

✳ ✳ ✳

Bali in the Twentieth Century

EDITED BY
RAECHELLE RUBINSTEIN
LINDA H. CONNOR

University of Hawai'i Press
Honolulu

To
Dr. Anak Agung Made Djelantik
and
Professor Frits deBoer (1937–1997)

04 03 02 01 00 99   5 4 3 2 1

Library of Congress Cataloging-in-Publication Data

Staying local in the global village : Bali in the twentieth century /
    edited by Raechelle Rubinstein and Linda H. Connor.
        p.   cm.
    Includes bibliographical references and index.
    ISBN 0–8248–2117–3 (cloth : alk. paper)
    1. Bali Island (Indonesia)—Civilization.   2. Bali Island
(Indonesia)—Politics and government.   3. Bali Island (Indonesia)—
Economic conditions.   I. Rubinstein, Raechelle, 1954– .
II. Connor, Linda, 1950– .
DS647.B2S77   1999
959.8'6—dc21   99–27856
                                                                        CIP

University of Hawai'i Press books are printed on acid-free paper and meet
the guidelines for permanence and durability of the Council on Library
Resources.

Design by Nighthawk Design
Printed by The Maple-Vail Book Manufacturing Group

Contents

Illustrations

Figures

Tables

Maps

Acknowledgments

The chapters in this volume were originally presented at the Third International Bali Studies Workshop held at the University of Sydney on 3–7 July 1995. We would like to thank our co-convenors, Peter Worsley and Adrian Vickers, as well as the other participants at the workshop. We are grateful for funding assistance received from Ansett Australia Airlines, the Australian International Development Assistance Bureau (now AUSAID), the Australian Research Council, and the School of Asian Studies at the University of Sydney.

The Balinese cartoonists Jango Pramartha and Surya Dharma generously made available their original works for use in this book. Our thanks must go also to Putu Suasta for working with the cartoonists on our behalf and providing a wealth of up-to-date photographic and documentary material on the situation in Bali. The Department of Historical Documentation (HISDOC) at the Koninklijk Instituut voor Taal-, Land-, en Volkenkunde in Leiden, Putu Wirata, Leo Haks, Richard Grant, and G. N. Sarjana kindly permitted us to reproduce illustrations.

The School of Asian Studies at the University of Sydney and the Department of Sociology and Anthropology at the University of Newcastle provided important support and assistance at many stages in the preparation of this manuscript. We would particularly like to thank John Couani of the Arts IT Unit at the University of Sydney. Financial support for Raechelle Rubinstein's participation was provided by an Australian Research Council fellowship.

We gratefully acknowledge the suggestions made by the two reviewers for the University of Hawai'i Press and the work and enthusiasm of our editor Pamela Kelley as well as managing editor Masako Ikeda and copy editor Don Yoder. Finally, thanks are due to our partners, Richard Grant and Nick Higginbotham.

A Note on Spelling

The spelling of Balinese and Indonesian words follows the official systems of orthography for those languages. When quoting from a source, however, and in the Chapter 9 appendix, we have retained the original spelling.

A source of confusion in the pronunciation of both Balinese and Indonesian is the letter *"e,"* which represents more than one phoneme. These phonemes are not distinguished here (with the exception of the Chapter 9 appendix), as this is not done in Indonesian, and in Balinese the use of accents to indicate vowel length is customary only in dictionaries and for teaching purposes.

Plural forms are not indicated in Indonesian and Balinese. For example, *"puri"* may indicate one *puri* or several as will be evident from the context.

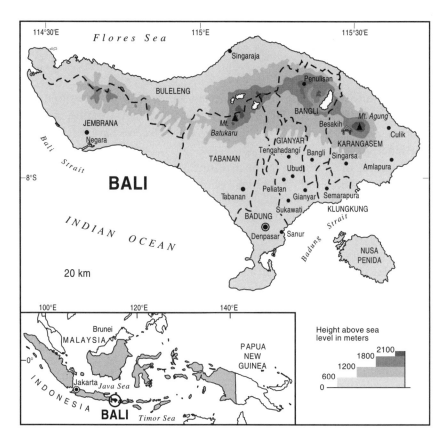

Map 1. Bali: 1998

Introduction

LINDA H. CONNOR AND RAECHELLE RUBINSTEIN

Throughout the twentieth century, Balinese, like other inhabitants of the planet, have ambivalently engaged with global processes that in various ways have been interpreted as opportunities and threats. This book is the result of efforts by Balinese and non-Balinese scholars to understand Bali in the light of recent social theory as the century draws to a close.

The large and diverse international network of scholars interested in Bali, while perhaps not unique (Java and "Borneo" are other contenders in the Southeast Asian region), forms a resource for more intensive and long-standing interdisciplinary exchanges than might be expected in the "area studies" context. This book is one of the fruits of frequent scholarly interchange.[1] It should be seen as part of an ongoing conversation in which Balinese and foreign scholars have been engaged for more than a decade, a conversation that is informed by many other concerns that participants bring to their work—as political activists, journalists, teachers, theorists, performers, and artists.

The original forum for this volume was the Third International Bali Studies Workshop, held in Sydney in July 1995. The workshop, titled "Bali in the Late Twentieth Century: Global Communications, National Identity, and Local Connections," provided fertile ground for the exchange of ideas about Balinese engagement as a minority cultural group with the Indonesian nation-state, as well as the global interconnections in which they are involved. It has been argued that the intense scholarly preoccupation with the "exotic" aspects of one small island has produced an inward-looking gaze that has blinded observers to broad critical and comparative perspectives. Such concerns were expressed by Indonesian dissident and academic George Aditjondro in his keynote address that opened the 1995 workshop. He said:

> By their dominant focus on cultural processes within Balinese society, and their neglect of class, race and social movement issues in the larger national, international and historical context, one can say that in general, most Balinese studies have actually reinforced the "Bali as paradise" paradigm created by the Dutch colonial administration and maintained by subsequent Indonesian administrations. [1995a:12]

But recent years have seen a shift away from the scholarly celebration of the unique, the unchanging, and the exotic in Bali's culture—a shift to a concern with the processes of transformation that link the island to Indonesia and the world beyond. As the chapters in this volume testify, the interaction between scholars of Bali has produced not only an awareness of the value of knowledge that, like Bali itself, transcends the often hackneyed truths of disciplinary boundaries and categories, but also an openness to critical theoretical approaches. The multidimensional engagement with Bali's realities creates an empirical orientation that does not, in these scholars' work, decline into mere empiricism. Rather, their studies have a deep connection with Balinese articulations of tradition and modernity, progress and decline, power and repression, as these issues are specifically nuanced in different contexts of social life. Such dichotomies have in recent years been intersected by a new conceptualization—the global and the local—that points to a growing engagement, on the part of Balinese and outsiders, with the "social movement issues" cited by Aditjondro.

"Globalization" is a vague term. Perhaps this is why it has such wide currency in contemporary social thought. Usage has extended to the far reaches of the social science universe—indeed globalization often occupies a spurious status as an answer (to any number of questions) rather than a question needing to be answered. Some of the term's popularity can probably be attributed to its postulated connection with the demise of the nation-state, which sits comfortably with certain poststructuralist movements in the social sciences and humanities. It also has the whiff of millenarianism about it: a response to the epoch-making imperatives of the 1990s in the dry language of social science. In other words, it is an all-embracing concept that serves the requirement for a grand theory that will encompass the end of one millennium and the beginning of another. In a recent review of economists' arguments for a globalized world economy, Hirst and Thompson suggest that the globalization thesis is "largely a myth" (1996:2). They are referring to a global system in which "distinct national economies are subsumed and rearticulated into the system by international processes and transactions" (p. 10). They argue that there is an integrated "international economy," in which "the principal entities are national economies," linked by trade and investment (p. 8), which shows continuities with economic developments of the nineteenth century and is amenable to governance and regulation.

A further concept of the global that has been popularized in contemporary social thought comes from that prophet of the future, Marshall McLuhan. McLuhan's notion of "the global village" was first imagined several decades ago in relation to the "electronic age" as a new way of perceiving and knowing other human beings. He wrote: "The new electronic interdependence recreates the world in the image of a global village" (McLuhan and Fiore 1967:67). In a book titled *The Global Village*, McLuhan and Powers (1989) developed the idea of the transition of human experience from "visual space" (linear, alphabetic, dominated by the left-brain hemisphere) to "acoustic space," the latter mediated by video technology and electronic communications, in which people find themselves drawing on right-brain capabilities and "relating to information structures which are simultaneous, discontinuous and dynamic" (p. 14).

The reference to the global village in the title of this book is not based on contributors' adherence to the tenets of globalization theory or the idea of the global village. It comes, rather, from the salience that the concept of *globalisasi* has for Balinese themselves as they strive to come to terms with the contradictions and dilemmas posed by daily existence in the "milk-cow" province of Indonesia's tourist industry. In recent years Bali has been the site of at least 2.5 million tourist visits per year (1994 estimates cited in Picard 1996b:53), one of the highest per capita incomes in the country (Warren 1994:1), and a dizzying pace of resort and other tourist-related developments, land alienation, and ecological degradation on many fronts (Aditjondro 1995b). Under such conditions, it is not surprising that the *era globalisasi* is a formulation of contemporary times that is frequently heard in Bali, particularly among the better-educated and more affluent town dwellers who play a large part in the construction of public culture through government rhetoric, mass media, and the officially supported arts institutions.[2] *Globalisasi* seems to have supplanted an earlier awareness of *kepariwisataan* (tourism) as a source of innovation: exciting but potentially threatening. As Michel Picard has argued, "touristic culture" has become thoroughly internalized by Balinese, paradoxically contributing to a reification of that which is defined as authentically Balinese while at the same time becoming "an integral part of a process of cultural invention" (1996b:199). In the 1990s, we find that social critique is increasingly framed in terms of *globalisasi*. The term is not only used to subsume *kepariwisataan* but also suggests a large field of social relations extending beyond the threats posed by Western cultural contact, corruption, and greed of the provincial authorities and Jakarta-based elites to the vertically integrated multinational companies who gobble up land for capital-intensive developments and rake off tourism profits. The custodians of the international capitalist order such as the International Monetary Fund and the World Bank are also implicated.

The popularity of the *globalisasi* concept among Balinese is productive in many senses.[3] It recognizes the scope and variety of internationalized mass media, particularly television, as a source of pleasure and information, most tangibly symbolized by the satellite dishes that sprout like everlasting daisies from urban and rural rooftops. Balinese are, in this respect, enthusiastic citizens of Marshall McLuhan's "global village." *Globalisasi* also signifies a sense of participation in an international order that leaves space to challenge the "national meta-narrative" (Tickell 1994:189) that dominates the mainstream print media, for example. In some discussions, global is almost a synonym for "cosmopolitan." Thus in a recent interview in the daily regional newspaper, the *Bali Post*, outspoken Balinese intellectual and architect I Nyoman Gelebet, in the context of a critique of the famous 1930s study of "Balinese character" by anthropologists Gregory Bateson and Margaret Mead (1942), proclaimed that Balinese will become "the foremost global people of Indonesia, indeed of the world," because of their openness and creativity (*Bali Post*, 11 August 1996, p. 3; see also 20 August 1996, p. 3). For other Balinese exponents of the *era globalisasi* such as medical specialist and environmental activist Professor Ida Bagus Manuaba, interviewed in the *Bali Post* on the theme of rising unemployment, globalization is an exciting challenge, characterized by complexity, competition, and change, an "external factor." Indonesians have to rise to meet the demands of the new era, as only those with high-quality skills and a competitive orientation are going to thrive (*Bali Post*, 10 August 1997).

But other reports construe the *era globalisasi* as having a more somber aspect, which characterizes much of the discourse. Globalization is a theory that lacks historical depth, as Hirst and Thompson (1996:2) point out. Similarly, in avoiding historical interrogation, *globalisasi* sat comfortably with the monologic history of Suharto's New Order, in which only one official version was sanctioned. It is as yet unclear whether the presidency of B. J. Habibie will encourage

Figure 1. Satellite dishes near the main crossroads in Semarapura, Klung-kung's capital. Photo: Richard Grant.

more pluralistic historical interpretations. *Globalisasi* refers to forces that people perceive to be largely out of their control. If the net result is to reinforce political inaction, in this sense it can be seen to support the interests of those who are beneficiaries of the dominant system. The statement that globalization is "a myth that exaggerates our helplessness in the face of contemporary economic forces" (Hirst and Thompson 1996:6) applies as much to certain Balinese versions of *globalisasi* as it does to the economic theory.

In some media analyses, one senses that *globalisasi* has become an acceptable synonym for "westernization" as the values of *globalisasi*—individualism, competition, and perpetual transformation—seem to be those formerly associated with the West. But to point to the West as the source of what amounts to a moral decline is no longer politically correct given that Bali's prosperity in the global marketplace depends on floods of foreign tourists each year. Much of the commodity value of Balinese culture for Balinese themselves is defined in Western terms, therefore, and they have eagerly embraced Western consumption-oriented lifestyles. In other words, reportage in Bali's mainstream print media suggests that in some contexts *globalisasi* has negative connotations, while for cosmopolitan intellectuals like Gelebet and Manuaba it is also an exciting concept.

As the commentaries just cited suggest, in Bali *globalisasi* fosters a looking inward as well as a looking outward. It is in this context that we have used the phrase "staying local" in the book's title. As Michel Picard elaborates in Chapter 1, there is a sense in which, for many years, Balinese have perceived "localness" to have been under siege from many directions. And yet increasingly it is recognized as their primary resource in the international marketplace as well as a source of spiritual values that enhance their lives. These constructions of the local emerge resonantly in a newspaper article on creativity in the performing arts where, at the opening of an art exhibition in Ubud, Urs Ramseyer, Swiss museum curator and well-published author on Balinese arts, was reported to say that "young artists while searching for universal values must maintain their awareness of local values so that their works continue to have distinctiveness *(ciri khas)*" (*Bali Post*, 20 August 1996, p. 3). This theme was taken up by a Balinese artist present, I Nyoman Gunarsa, who was reported as saying that in the era of *globalisasi* "the world is shrinking. But local values and local spirit must continue to exist, and indeed because there is *globalisasi*, artists need a local and national identity."

Many of the chapters in the volume take up this issue of the assertive local stance of Balinese in a variety of different contexts. Tourism has been a significant part of this process on Bali, but it has by no means totally determined the shape of the struggles. Movements of resistance against inequalities of power and status may be taken up by groups who regard other Balinese as outsiders and oppressors. This position is strikingly exemplified by Thomas Reuter's discussion in Chapter 5 of the ways in which highland Balinese villagers reconceptualize their worth in the face of lowland/official attributions of their cultural marginality and again in I Gde Pitana's analysis of commoner groups' struggle against Brahmanic priestly authority in Chapter 6.

Studies from elsewhere in Southeast Asia suggest that this striving to articulate local concerns in the face of change is common to many groups and does not require intensive tourist development for its emergence. (See, for example, Alexander 1989; Houben, Maier, and Van der Molen 1992; Kahn and Wah 1992; Milner 1995.) Recent factory workers' activism in Indonesia (Hadiz 1994)—including a marked increase in the number of strikes and the growth of illegal trade unions—suggests that "local" as opposed to "global" may be defined by protagonists in class terms rather than as a minority cultural identity. It may even be a significant process among advantaged groups, such as the Javanese ruling elite in Indonesia that in various ways perceives itself threatened by the values of Western-style democratic politics. Jakarta's espousal of "Pancasila democracy," in response to its liberal-democratic critics on various human rights issues, is a case in point (see Ramage 1994).

The politics of nation-states and discourses of national unity produce tensions that create alternative modes of action. In the hegemonic discourse of Indonesia's "unity in diversity," diversity is a residual space for commodified, decontextualized, and depoliticized local cultural forms, assimilated into the territorial structure of the Indonesian state as *kebudayaan daerah*, "regional cultures," as Brett Hough argues in Chapter 8. The contestation over the local is partly about forms of agency vis-à-vis oppressive institutions and hegemonic discourses of the nation-state. It is a form of agency that Balinese attempt to assert in many different ways. Michel Picard (Chapter 1), Margaret Wiener (Chapter 2), Brett Hough (Chapter 8), and Mark Hobart (Chapter 9) focus on contemporary cultural practices: new discourses of identity, the creation of local history, the performing arts, and television watching. Putu Suasta and Linda Connor (Chapter 3) examine the way local activists attempt the head-on confrontation with the state through forms of organized political action—a relatively rare phenomenon in the last three decades of Indonesian history until the massive political protests of 1998. Graeme MacRae (Chapter 4) discusses how a traditional elite maintains local ascendancy through a rearticulation of customary social relations in the contemporary context. I Gde Pitana (Chapter 6), by contrast, focuses on the ways in which universalist discourses of the nation can be shaped to address status inequalities between groups within Bali, while Thomas Reuter (Chapter 5) documents the direct challenge that is made by members of a marginal group on the grounds of cultural authenticity. Ayami Nakatani (Chapter 7) explores the strategies of daily living among women experiencing labor intensification in an increasingly cash-dominated economy. In considering the ways in which local actions relate to the imperatives of the nation-state, it is well to remember that for Balinese global processes (such as economics and communication) are mediated through the state.

To term these local struggles "identity politics" is perhaps misleading. What is at stake is not identity in any determinative sense, which is a sociological chimera insofar as it is reduced to cultural identity. People work with a plethora of "identities" (Balinese, Hindu, youth, commoner, Indonesian, worker, student, parent, parliamentarian, and so on) in different situations in complex combinations ("commoner priest," "Balinese Muslim," and "woman intellectual," for example). This field of differences is mobilized in the struggle over resources: land, a clean environment, political rights, religious equality, social infrastructure, economic capital, and the symbolic capital to define the discourse. That the struggle is local is not peculiar to Bali—*lokal* (local) after all does not have only a geographical or ethnic reference; it indexes a strategic positioning vis-à-vis dominant forces that are variously defined by the people themselves. In this book the authors are careful not to construct a generic Balinese identity. Indeed, they specify the conditions under which certain differences—for example, as performing artist, television viewer, political activist, *warga* (clan) member, and so on—become salient for Balinese themselves in "the practice of everyday life," to use de Certeau's evocative phrase (1984).

In taking Balinese concepts seriously as more than the object of analysis, as Mark Hobart argues in Chapter 9, we should perhaps have avoided a westernized temporal construction like "the twentieth century" in the title of this volume. Local conceptualization of time may be crucial in interpreting the significance of major events. For example, ecological disasters such as the fires in Kalimantan and Sumatra in 1997, the collapse of the Indonesian economy, and the growing instability of President Suharto's position preceding his resignation in 1998 may be interpreted in local communities as signs of the *kali yuga*: the "age of chaos" preceding radical change in Hindu cyclical concepts of time.[4] While the Gregorian calendar is indubitably a temporal frame of reference in contemporary Bali, it is by no means the only one. Although several chapters take a historical perspective that broadly speaking covers the twentieth century, they do not necessarily present this frame as a Balinese periodization of events. Balinese may, as the year 2000 approaches, indeed engage in various celebrations centered on centennial or millennial transitions. But the reference to the twentieth century in the title of this book is an editorial imposition intended simply to convey the scope of the work and suggest the historical context of contemporary events that is a feature of many chapters.

At this juncture it may be useful to offer the nonspecialist a synopsis of how Bali has been involved in international and national events of the twentieth century—events that are milestones of the past for Balinese themselves and signal the increasing global connectedness of the island. While northern Bali became integrated into the Netherlands Indies in the mid-nineteenth century, the populous southern Bali kingdoms did not fall under Dutch hegemony until the early years of the twentieth century. The bloody *puputan* ("finishing" through the willed death of ruler and retinue in the face of inevitable defeat) in 1906 and 1908 are a terrible marker of conquest in the kingdoms where they occurred: Klungkung (discussed in Chapter 2) and Badung. Other kingdoms capitulated peacefully and sought whatever advantage there was to be gained under colonial rule.[5] For almost half a century, the whole island of Bali was subjected to Dutch colonial authority: a cog in the international trading empire of the Netherlands. A new intelligentsia was forged through exposure to the colonial education system, Dutch language, and European ideas, as well as employment in the lower levels of the colonial administration (see Chapter 1). By the 1920s, international travelers began arriving in their hundreds each year on the government-owned Royal Packet Navigation Company (KPM), usually to enjoy a three-day tour by hired car (Picard 1996b:23–26). During the 1920s and 1930s, small numbers of influential foreign residents—artists, scholars, and writers—drew international attention to Bali's culture.

A difficult period that is well remembered by all Balinese over the age of sixty was the Japanese occupation of the island during World War II from 1942 to 1945. The hardships of this period—food and clothing shortages, forced labor, the harsh discipline of the Japanese—stand out more vividly in ordinary people's memories than the Pan-Asian nationalism that the Japanese fostered as part of their plan for Asia-Pacific domination. These hardships, moreover, added fuel to the nationalist struggle for independence—the "Revolusi"—that followed in the years 1945–1950, when the Dutch attempted to regain possession of their former colony. The Revolusi was an uneasy period in Bali, not least because of Dutch efforts to weaken the nationalist movement and divide the emerging nation through the formation of Federated States of Eastern Indonesia (NIT), including Bali, in which many powerful Balinese were implicated. But Bali also harbored many republican supporters, many of whom became resistance fighters *(pemuda)* and eventually triumphed in 1950 when the unitary Republic of Indonesia was formed under the leadership of President Sukarno.[6]

The "Sukarno years" of 1950–1965, despite the economic difficulties of this period, are remembered favorably by many Balinese. People admired their leader because of his Balinese mother and his many trips to Bali; they were drawn, as well, to his political charisma. The 1950s were years of parliamentary democracy and an openness to many new ideas: nationalist politics shared the stage with other ideologies such as communism and socialism and rubbed shoulders with Islamic and Christian parties in the most pluralistic period of Indonesian politics. The "Guided Democracy" years of 1959–1965, as Sukarno increased his presidential powers, saw the growth of tensions between the army and the Indonesian Communist Party (PKI), whose land reform policies drew many Balinese to its ranks. These tensions culminated in the abortive generals' coup of 1965 and the subsequent massacre of hundreds of thousands of PKI members and alleged supporters throughout the country. The massacres were widespread in Bali. According to Robinson (1995:274): "An estimated 80,000 Balinese—roughly five percent of the island's population of under two million—were shot, knifed, hacked or clubbed to death in less than a year."

Suharto replaced Sukarno as president of the republic, ushering in a "New Order" of authoritarian politics underpinned by military power and wedded to goals of development *(pembangunan)* on a capitalist model—the main government economic strategy up to the present. In Bali, the tourist industry (initially fostered by Sukarno) has become the mainstay of economic growth. Increasingly capital-intensive development has been initiated from outside the island and an infrastructure of roads, satellite dishes, telephone cables, and the like are transforming Bali from an agrarian society into a service-based tourism and manufacturing economy.

During 1998, as we were revising this manuscript, dramatic political events brought an end to Suharto's presidency. Speculators' raids on the Thai baht in May 1997 precipitated the successive collapse of currencies in the region, most notably Thailand, Malaysia, the Philippines, Indonesia, and South Korea, a situation exacerbated by the stagnant

Figure 2. "Bali hourglass" cartoon by Surya Dharma.

Japanese economy. The weak underpinnings of Indonesia's economy—corruption, nepotism and cronyism, irregular banking practices, and massive unsecured debt—were soon exposed, leading to general economic collapse and a request from the president for International Monetary Fund (IMF) intervention in October 1997. Stringent IMF measures inflamed widespread political unrest, including food riots and the scapegoating of local Chinese businesses as real incomes declined dramatically and the price of essential commodities skyrocketed.

These developments gave Indonesia's pro-democracy movement, which since the mid-1980s had largely been spearheaded by the political ideals of Indonesia's affluent middle class, a new momentum. In the weeks before Suharto's reappointment by the National Legislative Assembly for a seventh term in March 1998 (he was the sole candidate), student protests around the country called for his resignation and an end to the New Order regime in favor of democratic reforms. These protests became increasingly strident and were associated with mass riots of the poor as well as looting and violence on the streets of major cities, especially Jakarta and Yogyakarta. On 20 May 1998, as thousands of students demonstrated outside the national parliament, Suharto resigned in favor of the vice-president, his long-time protégé,

B. J. Habibie. Although military personnel were blamed for fatalities and injuries in earlier demonstrations in Yogyakarta and Jakarta, the military did not carry out any violent actions against demonstrators in the tumultuous days leading up to Suharto's resignation. President Habibie's hold on power is regarded as tenuous by many, and it is unclear whether pro-democracy leaders will be able to maintain a common impetus for a democratically based government or will become fragmented by ideological differences. President Habibie has promised to hold democratic elections in 1999. In November 1998, there was a fresh outbreak of rioting, looting, and widespread student protests in Jakarta, directed at the government's failure to follow through on promised political reforms and the declining economic situation in the country. Military reprisals have been rapid and violent: more than a dozen protestors have been killed so far. Opposition groups continue to mobilize in an attempt to create a more democratic government.

✻   ✻   ✻

The chapters in this volume are based on research carried out in the early to mid-1990s, when Suharto's New Order, presiding over a period of economic growth, still enjoyed widespread legitimacy in Indonesia. Among Balinese, however, political consensus has always been weakened by local perceptions of themselves as an exploited minority: "Jakarta's colony" (Aditjondro 1995b). The plundering of the island's natural and cultural resources by Jakarta-based and international investors over the past three decades sharpened critical awareness of the depredations of state power, at the same time as Balinese have enjoyed some of the fruits of affluence engendered by their participation in the nation-state. As the contributions to this book reveal, the ambivalent positioning of Balinese vis-à-vis the national and the global in recent decades has been played out in many different spheres of life—but usually not in the sphere of institutional politics, which was severely repressed under Suharto's New Order.[7] The chapters take up a number of related themes that give expression to different articulations of the local, providing a bird's-eye view of public culture, local history, definitions of Balineseness, and the politics of place, as well as elucidating specific aspects of Balinese participation in the transformation associated with the tourism-dominated provincial economy, the growth of communications and mass media, and the incursions of the nation-state through its imperatives of economic development and rationalist discourses.

Michel Picard, in "The Discourse of Kebalian: Transcultural Constructions of Balinese Identity" (Chapter 1), documents the initiatives of a small intelligentsia that first began the project of reflexively constructing a modern Balinese identity through their participation in Dutch education and nationalist politics in the 1920s and 1930s. This chapter explores the emergence of Balineseness during the colonial period by providing a historical context for the repeated efflorescence of identity struggles in Bali. A different framing of these issues is developed in Margaret Wiener's "politics of history" (Chapter 2) based on an analysis of the public culture of contemporary Bali using the example of the emblematic and much-mystified Balinese institution of the *puputan*. Putu Suasta and Linda Connor (Chapter 3) analyze struggles in the arena of institutional politics. Scrutinizing the popular protests over large-scale resort developments in Bali, they show how the local momentum of these protests is related to the pro-democracy movement throughout Indonesia.

Graeme MacRae (Chapter 4) uses Bourdieu's metaphor of "symbolic capital" to illuminate the changing practices during this century of the traditional palace elite who continue to exert control over modes of cultural production in the famous "artists' village" of Ubud. In an interesting contrast to MacRae's chapter, Thomas Reuter (Chapter 5) takes up the resilience of highland communities who challenge modernist definitions of their backwardness and poverty with alternative portrayals of themselves as the sacred core of authentic Balinese culture. I Gde Pitana (Chapter 6) writes about challenges of more recent duration to the hegemony of traditional elites posed by the struggles over priestly status that have been fought by commoner groups in Bali. Ayami Nakatani (Chapter 7) makes a fascinating contribution to the much neglected area of women's studies in Bali. Her analysis looks at women weavers riding the crest of a wave of traditional brocade production in response to rising demand from the newly affluent, urbanized elites. The mixed effects on women's lives is tellingly revealed in this chapter.

Brett Hough (Chapter 8) and Mark Hobart (Chapter 9) explore different manifestations of contemporary cultural practices in Bali. Hough argues that the performing arts are a critical domain of government intervention in Indonesia—the more so in Bali because of its high-profile representation of Balinese arts as "Indonesian culture" to a global audience. He uses a number of richly documented ethnographic examples to explicate the sometimes contradictory and challenging ways in which Bali's premier, state-sponsored College of Indonesian Arts participates in the creation of national culture and internationalized representations of Bali while at the same time exploiting the dynamic tension of the national and the local. In a thought-provoking final chapter, Hobart investigates television viewing in contemporary Bali. The critical practices of Balinese viewers he concludes, are the basis for a reconceptualization of overgeneralized and ethnocentric notions of the subject in contemporary theory.

Notes

1. This interchange comprises international workshops held every four or five years, annual conferences held in Bali, and a newsletter *(Bali Arts and Culture News)* that commenced in 1981. The first international workshop, held in 1986, resulted in the publication *State and Society in Bali: Historical, Textual, and Anthropological Approaches,* edited by Hildred Geertz (1991). The second international workshop, held in 1991, led to the publication of *Being Modern in Bali: Image and Change,* edited by Adrian Vickers (1996a).

2. Vickers (1996b) has pointed to similar processes at work with regard to the concept of *moderen* (modern) in Bali.

3. Sometimes the term *"globalisme"* or its Anglicized variant "globalism" is used (as in the cartoon on the front cover). Recently we have noticed an Indonesianized usage, *kesejagadan,* from *"jagad"* meaning "world."

4. Another example comes from Benedict Anderson, who recently commented on a 1997 speech of Suharto in which the leader alluded to his departure from politics in terms of the "succession philosophy" and the cycles of human existence found in stories from the Javanese shadow puppet theater (Anderson 1998).

5. More details on this period can be found in Vickers (1989:33–36).

6. For a detailed discussion of this period see Robinson (1995:chap. 7).

7. It remains to be seen whether the current efflorescence of organized political activity in Bali, mostly student-led, will continue.

Chapter 1

The Discourse of Kebalian: Transcultural Constructions of Balinese Identity

MICHEL PICARD

Religion *(agama)*, culture *(budaya)* and traditional social institutions *(adat)* are indivisible in Bali.

[I Dewa Nyoman Batuan, quoted in Ramseyer 1977:15]

As long as the three main elements of religion, tradition and culture remain intact, Bali will be able to perpetuate itself, its identity will remain intact.

[Ide Anak Agung Gde Agung, quoted in Pratiknyo 1992:8]

In the late 1960s, when the Indonesian government decided to open the country to international tourism, Bali's image as a tourist paradise made it the obvious choice to become the nation's touristic showcase. As a result, the Balinese, faced with the prospect of ever increasing numbers of foreign visitors to their shores, began questioning whether their culture would survive the "impact of tourism" *(dampak pari-wisata)*. Indeed, they were faced with a dilemma. On the one hand, the artistic and ceremonial pageants that had made their island famous the world over provided its main attraction as a tourist destination—thus turning Balinese culture into the most valuable resource *(sumber)* for economic development. On the other hand, the invasion of Bali by hordes of foreigners was perceived as a threat—as cultural pollution *(polusi kebudayaan)*. In 1971, to deal with what they called the challenge of tourism *(tantangan pariwisata)*, Balinese authorities devised the policy of "cultural tourism" *(pariwisata budaya)*. Intended to develop tourism without debasing Balinese culture, this policy aimed at utilizing culture to attract tourists while fostering culture through the revenue generated by tourism (Seminar 1971).

By the early 1980s, it seemed that cultural tourism had successfully accomplished its mission—at least according to the declarations of provincial authorities who extolled tourism as an agent of Bali's "cultural renaissance" *(renaissance kebudayaan)*. The money brought in by tourism was said to have stimulated Balinese interest in their cultural heritage, while the admiration of foreigners for the culture had reinforced pride in being Balinese. By patronizing Balinese culture, tourism had contributed to its preservation, even to its revival, to the extent that it had turned it into a source of both profit and prestige for the Balinese. This is not the place to assess such claims, which are supported by foreign observers who vaunt the resilience of traditional Balinese culture to the encroachment of the modern world.[1] Tourism neither "polluted" Balinese culture nor engendered its "renaissance." In fact the decision to promote cultural tourism elicited from the Balinese a particular form of reflexivity that has made them self-conscious about their culture. It is as though, thanks to tourism, the Balinese have discovered that they "have a culture"—something that is at the same time precious and perishable, which they ought to preserve as well as promote. And just as it was made famous and enhanced by the tourist gaze, their culture became reified, externalized for them, and turned into a separate entity that could be displayed, performed, and marketed for others. In this respect the Balinese are not passive objects of the tourist gaze but active subjects who construct representations of their culture to attract tourists.

Thus tourism in Bali cannot be conceived of apart from Balinese culture: it is inevitably bound up in an ongoing process of cultural construction. This is because tourism—or rather what I would call the "touristification" of a society—is far from being an external force "impacting" on a society from without. Indeed it proceeds from within by blurring the boundaries between inside and outside, between what is "ours" and what is "theirs," between what belongs to culture and what pertains to tourism. It is not surprising then that their identity, which they call their Kebalian—their Balineseness—has become such a sensitive issue for the Balinese, who have been wondering whether they are still authentically Balinese *(asli Bali)*. Indeed, called upon to conform to their image, the Balinese are not only required to be Balinese but, furthermore, they must be worthy representatives of Balineseness: they must become signs of themselves. And all their attempts at affirming their identity are a reaction to this imperative from which they are unable to extricate themselves. Thus the Balinese, enjoined to exhibit their identity in reference to the outside world's view of them, have come to search for confirmation of their Kebalian in the mirror held up to them by tourists.[2] By and large, when debating the issue of Kebalian in seminars and reports, as well as in articles and letters published by the *Bali Post*, the provincial daily, Balinese tend to agree that so long as they are aware of the indivisible unity of religion *(agama)*, tradition *(adat)*, and culture *(budaya)*, their identity will remain intact. My purpose here is not to assess the veracity of such a claim but to elucidate how the Balinese have come to formulate their identity in these very terms.

What we are witnessing here is the expression of a self-conscious Balineseness: a Balinese vision of themselves generated by their dealings with powerful and significant Others. Such a reflexive essentialization of their identity is not unique to the Balinese. Nor is it a specific outcome of the touristic encounter. It appears, rather, to be the common lot of indigenous peoples engaging in a process of self-identification when confronted with an intrusive and dominating force, most often following their incorporation into a modern state whether colonial or postcolonial.[3] Accordingly I contend that the alleged indivisible unity of religion, tradition, and culture, by which the Balinese define their identity nowadays, far from expressing a primordial essence as they would have it, is the outcome of a process of semantic borrowing and conceptual recasting they have had to make in response to the colonization, the Indonesianization, and the touristification of their island.

In this chapter I trace the construction of Balinese identity at the time of the Netherlands East Indies.[4] I do this by investigating how the Balinese have construed their Balineseness in the printed journals that were published on the island during the 1920s and 1930s. (I do not include literary works of fiction but focus instead on publications dealing explicitly with religion, tradition, and culture.) In doing this, I address the expression of Balinese identity as a transcultural discourse. A discourse is both a body of cultural assumptions about reality and a set of social practices that establish and maintain that reality, according to the authority of its authors. Describing Kebalian as a discourse stresses its constructed, historical constitution; qualifying it as transcultural points to its dialogic, interactive character. While the authors of the discourse of Kebalian are Balinese, their discourse is shaped by categories and premises that were imposed on them by outside agencies. In other words, the Balinese are not in a position to choose the terms of their discourse but have appropriated and interpreted them according to their own cultural values and political concerns by means of a process that, following Wolters (1982:52), one could define as "localization."

When I talk about "the Balinese," I refer to the intellectuals—that is, to those among the Balinese who formulate, propagate, and explain contemporary issues and emergent ideas to the rest of the population. Historically these intellectuals are the product of an alien education imposed on indigenous society by the Dutch colonial state. Members of this westernized elite function as mediators between two worlds: traditional and modern, rural and urban, local and global. As such they constitute an "intelligentsia"—in the sense given this term by Robert Redfield (1953:53–54), following Childe and Toynbee—distinguished both from the peasant intellectuals studied by Linda Connor (1982) and from the "literati" who are custodians of a traditional knowledge that is specifically Balinese. Whereas the literati remain entrenched in the village sphere whose worldview and values they uphold, members of the intelligentsia straddle two worlds: the ethnic group from which they originate and the wider (colonial or national) collectivity in which they participate (Benda 1962; Shills 1962).

Dutch Colonial Policy

My purpose in this section is not to summarize Dutch colonial policy in Bali but to focus on the role played by the colonial state in the emergence of a sense of religious, ethnic, and cultural identity among the Balinese people. This was the result of a deliberate "traditionalization" of Balinese society in the guise of a restoration of what was regarded as Balinese "traditional order." (See Boon 1977; Robinson 1995; Schulte Nordholt 1986, 1994, 1996; Vickers 1989; Wiener 1995a.)[5]

The island of Bali was one of the last regions of the Indonesian archipelago to be subjugated by the Dutch. It took no fewer than seven expeditions for their army to conquer the entire island. The kingdoms of Buleleng and Jembrana were compelled to acknowledge this foreign sovereignty from as early as the 1850s. One after the other, the rajas of Karangasem, Gianyar, and Bangli chose to submit themselves and thus conserve a relative degree of autonomy. The remaining independent kingdoms of Badung, Tabanan, and Klungkung were subdued by military force between 1906 and 1908 (Agung 1991; Hanna 1976). The conquest of Bali was not an isolated or incidental event: it was carried out in the course of Dutch territorial expansion throughout the archipelago. This process commenced with the consolidation of Dutch power in Java and saw the transformation of what had initially been a mere commercial enterprise into a colonial state and the replacement of commercial administrators with colonial officialdom. This transition required the political domination of regions still under native rule and reinforcement of the colonial administration. By 1910 the formation of the empire of the Netherlands East Indies was completed. At the time the Dutch were consolidating their colonial empire and expanding its boundaries, moreover, their government adopted its "Ethical Policy," which acknowledged a "debt of honor" toward the people of the Indies. This new policy was to entail a much deeper penetration of local societies by the colonial administration, which felt both obliged and justified in acting to reform them in the cause of peace, order, and welfare.

The Dutch knew little of the Balinese society over which they had stretched their empire. But they had certain ideas about what it should be like, and they eagerly endeavored to make it conform to this conception. Before colonial administrators reorganized Balinese society, it had already been conceptualized by European Orientalists as a living museum of Hindu-Javanese civilization—the one and only surviving heir to the Hindu heritage swept from Java by the coming of Islam (Raffles 1817; Crawfurd 1820; Van Hoëvell 1848; Friederich 1849–1850). In their view, the Hindu religion had been brought to Bali in the fourteenth century by Javanese conquerors from the kingdom of Majapahit, who had imposed a division of society into four castes in accordance with the Indian model (Brahmana, Satria, Wesia, and Sudra). When Majapahit fell to Islam at the end of the fifteenth century, the Javanese nobility who objected to the new faith fled to the courts of their relatives on Bali, where they nurtured the Hindu-Javanese civilization in splendid isolation.

Yet if they were grateful to the Balinese for having preserved Hindu texts and rituals from the depredations of Islam, Europeans in the nineteenth century held divergent opinions as to how far the religion practiced on the island adhered to its Indian model. The Orientalists concurred that the Brahmana priests were genuine Hindus, but they differed in their views regarding the religion of the Sudra. Thus John Crawfurd and Thomas Stamford Raffles (who had spent a short time on the island, in Buleleng only, in 1814 and 1815 respectively) considered that the worship of the common people, as performed in the temples, was mere superstition that could not be called Hindu. But R. Th. A. Friederich (who had accompanied the first military expedition of 1846 to collect manuscripts on behalf of the Batavian Society of Arts and Sciences and had sojourned in the south of the island) was convinced that the religion of the common people was truly Hindu. Whatever the esteem in which the Orientalists held local religious practices, there could be no doubt in their minds that Hinduism constituted the core of Balinese society, the guardian of its cultural integrity, and the inspiration of its artistic manifestations. Accordingly it had to be protected from the intrusion of Islam, which had strengthened its grip throughout most of the archipelago through the enlightened paternalism of colonial tutelage.

Once Buleleng and Jembrana had been brought under direct colonial rule in 1882, the first colonial administrators, chief among them F. A. Liefrinck, emphasized the distinction between Balinese nobility of Javanese descent and commoners of indigenous origin, following the Orientalists. But whereas his predecessors had been mostly interested in the priests and princes (who also happened to be their main informants), Liefrinck directed his attention to villages that he regarded as autonomous communities which had succeeded in protecting their independence from the interference of the courts (Liefrinck 1890). Thus for a brief period after the Dutch had succeeded in extending their control over the whole island in 1908, they considered themselves as replacing the Balinese rulers and left the villages virtually untouched.

To govern the island efficiently the colonial state introduced uniform administration throughout Balinese society, which had heretofore been characterized by local variations. Dutch officials set out to "simplify the village administration and return it to its original state" (Assistant Resident H. J. E. F. Schwartz, quoted in Schulte Nordholt 1986:32). Between 1907 and 1910, a new type of village was created—the "administrative village"—typically consisting of several "customary villages" grouped together under a new name. By introducing a dichotomy between customary authority (which they left to the Balinese) and administrative authority (which they appropriated) the Dutch could rule Bali while purporting to restore its traditional order.

But as the Dutch were reorganizing the village administration of the newly conquered south of the island, they realized that they required the collaboration of the nobility to govern effectively. Thus they fell back on the Orientalist vision of the four castes and decided, in 1910, to "uphold the caste system, as it is the foundation of Balinese society" (minutes of an administrative conference quoted in Schulte Nordholt 1986:28). As a result, the precolonial social hierarchy, which had been variable and mobile, was replaced by a uniform and rigid system that became legally enforceable. It comprised three closed noble castes— the *triwangsa* consisting of the Brahmana, Satria, and Wesia—whereas the large majority of the population were classified as Sudra, "outsiders." Consequently, most of the new village and districts heads were recruited from among the nobility and their power was thus considerably increased to the detriment of the commoners who lost their former positions of political authority. Furthermore, those Balinese acknowledged as belonging to the nobility were exempted from the corvée labor *(heerendienst)* the Dutch had imposed in order to construct their new road network.

During the 1920s, the Ethical Policy lost its momentum when Dutch colonial policy took a conservative turn. This new direction originated in large part from the University of Leiden, where most Dutch civil administrators were trained, and was inspired by Professor C. van Vollenhoven. He opposed the assimilation of the native elite through Dutch education and advocated a dual system for colonial society: the idea was to strengthen indigenous communities through enforcing their own customary law *(adatrecht)* (Van Vollenhoven 1928). In Bali this trend was defended by Resident H. T. Damsté who, in 1923, encouraged the administrator V. E. Korn to conduct research on Balinese customary law (Korn 1932). While Korn made a point of emphasizing local variations within Balinese *adat,* the very fact of codifying in one volume what were in fact flexible rules of conduct, negotiable according to the context, transformed them into fixed legal prescriptions backed by the bureaucratic apparatus of the colonial state.

Korn was also instrumental in promoting the image of Bali as a sanctuary—a world apart, fragile and unique—that should be protected against pernicious foreign influences and the traumatizing impact of modernity (Korn 1925). That such an idea was so willingly accepted by colonial officialdom is not only due to a genuine concern that the uniqueness of Balinese culture might be destroyed by indiscriminate contact with the outside world; it also happened to suit their political agenda. In the 1920s, the Dutch came to regard Bali as the cornerstone of their effort to contain the spread of Islamic radicalism and various nationalist and communist movements that had arisen in Java and Sumatra. To them it was becoming apparent that the Balinese nobility, whom they regarded as the vehicle of the Hinduization of Bali and the pillar of its traditional order, was the strongest barrier against the spread of Islam and the seepage of subversive ideas into Bali. Consequently, they resolved to reinforce the authority of the nobility over the population by reinstating the heads of the former royal houses in the trappings of their previous glory: first as royal administrators in 1929 and then officially as rajas in 1938.

As it turned out, it was not only against nationalism and Islam that Bali had to be protected, but against Christianity as well. In 1925,

Korn had already protested against the project of the Roman Catholic Church to start missionary work among the Balinese. His protest had been successful, but in 1932 the declared intention of a Dutch Protestant mission to pursue evangelizing activities in Bali sparked a heated controversy. The debate was initiated by F. D. K. Bosch, head of the archaeological service in Batavia, and pursued by the language official R. Goris, who was stationed on Bali. While admitting that Balinese society was already being affected by various Western influences such as government, education, and tourism, they opposed missionary activity on the ground that religion and social order form an inseparable whole in Bali. Therefore, by deliberately attacking the religion of the Balinese, missionary work would bring about the collapse of their entire culture. According to both Bosch and Goris, "Hindu-Balinism" should be considered a legitimate part of the world religion of Hinduism, one that could find its regeneration through renewed contact with the spiritual mother country India (Bosch 1932, 1933; Goris 1933). These arguments were disputed by the missionary-cum-missiologist H. Kraemer, who rejected the identification of religion with culture. He contended that Balinese religion evinced only a thin veneer of Hinduism and was permeated by magic and superstition. Furthermore, the island was being subjected to such an increase of foreign influence that Balinese religion was doomed to disappear under the assault of modern secularization. Why then, he asked, should Bali be closed to Christianity alone, while tourism, which reduced the Balinese religion to a mere spectacle, was admitted? (See Kraemer 1932, 1933a, 1933b.) In the end, the Orientalists won the day: the governor-general forbade missionary work in Bali.

Yet it was not enough that the traditional order be rescued from the onslaught of modernization and insulated from disturbing outside influences. The Balinese people, furthermore, had to be taught by their new overlords how to keep on being authentically Balinese. Such was the aim of the cultural-cum-educational policy known as Balinization (*Baliseering*). Conceived by Dutch Orientalists and launched in the late 1920s, Balinization was expected to produce a state-sponsored renaissance of Balinese culture (Te Flierhaar 1941). This policy was intended specifically for native youth who, in the Orientalists' opinion, had to be made conscious of the value of their cultural heritage by means of an education focusing on Balinese language, literature, and the arts.

In sum, then, the colonial "traditionalization" of Balinese society—especially the Orientalist vision of Bali as a Hindu island surrounded by a sea of Islam—was to have long-lasting consequences. By looking for the singularity of Bali in its Hindu heritage while conceiving of Balinese identity as formed through an opposition to Islam, the Dutch established the framework within which the Balinese were going to define themselves. In other words, their colonial policy "ensured that Balinese social and political discourse came to focus heavily on matters of interpretation of tradition, religion, caste, and culture" (Robinson 1995:32). Furthermore, by attempting to preserve Bali's singularity from the rest of the East Indies, the Dutch ended up emphasizing it far more than they had ever envisioned.

Emergence of a Balinese Intelligentsia

To a certain extent the fictions created by the colonial state have become realities. Yet one should refrain from crediting the colonial masters with the exclusive power of making history—as if "the main historical activity remaining to the underlying people [was] to misconstrue the effects of such imperialism as their own cultural traditions" (Sahlins 1993:6). Rather than viewing the colonial encounter in terms of foreign impact, we should identify the active agency of the colonized peoples as they engaged with and accommodated colonial impositions, thereby redefining the terms of that encounter for their own purposes.

If it is true that the Balinese "were not allowed to participate in Western discourses about themselves" (Schulte Nordholt 1994:119), in the sense that they were not asked for their opinions, some of them did in fact write and even publish. Thus we are in a position to elucidate how they perceived and interpreted what was happening to their world. Indeed, while the Dutch wanted to maintain Balinese society in a fixed "traditional" order, Bali actually underwent rapid and profound changes as a result of increasing interference in native affairs by the colonial government. The introduction of a monetary economy, the imposition of taxes and forced labor, the enlistment of the former rajas in the colonial bureaucracy, the access of a minority of Balinese youth to European education—all undermined the relationships that had prevailed between the peasantry and the traditional elites. Specifically, the requirements of a modern administration were instrumental in the emergence of a Balinese intelligentsia, since the colonial state needed bilingually educated natives to mediate between the local population and their European overlords. This intelligentsia strove to make sense of the situation brought about by the opening up of their world at a time when interest in things Balinese was growing among various foreign milieux. At the very moment that disruption of the familiar references which once ordered their lives was compelling the Balinese to ponder the foundations of their identity,[6] the inquisitive gaze of the Other in their midst impelled them to account explicitly for the definition of what it meant to be Balinese in terms comprehensible to non-Balinese.

It was in Singaraja—the capital of Buleleng on the north coast of the island, a harbor town long open to the outside world and seat of the colonial government—that an elite composed mostly of teachers and civil servants educated in Dutch schools founded the first modern Balinese organizations. These organizations were modern in the sense that they were voluntary associations of like-minded people with broad-ranging agendas and highly formalized structures—complete with elected boards, statutes, written regulations, and membership fees. In this respect they differed from the customary organizations that regulated Balinese social relations, such as kinship affiliation groups *(dadia)*, temple congregations *(pamaksan)*, neighborhood associations *(banjar)*, irrigation societies *(subak)*, and cooperatives formed for specific tasks *(seka/sekeha)*.

Besides opening schools and religious foundations, these new organizations started publishing periodicals, a complete novelty for Bali, though already occurring elsewhere in the Indies at that time (Adam 1995). Written in Malay—the lingua franca of the archipelago, adopted by the Dutch as the language of education and administration and soon to become that of Indonesian nationalism—these publications were devoted chiefly to issues pertaining to religion and social order. The use of Malay rather than Balinese to address thoroughly Balinese topics destined for an exclusively Balinese readership (a very limited one, to be sure, a few hundred people at most) indicates that the intelligentsia were conscious of being an integral part of a larger entity due to the incorporation of their island into the colonial state. Thus the same process that prompted the Balinese to question their identity was dispossessing them of their own words by inducing them to think about themselves in a language which was not their own but that used both by their fellow countrymen throughout the archipelago and by their colonial masters.[7]

The history of the founding (and disbanding) of successive or concurrent organizations in the 1920s is rather confused, as the scattered pieces of information one is able to gather from the publications of the time are not only sparse but also contradictory.[8] The first of these modern organizations appears to have been Setiti Bali. It was founded in 1917 by I Goesti Tjakra Tanaja, the *punggawa* (district head) of Sukasada, to counter the Javanese Islamic association Sarekat Islam, which had recently opened a branch in Singaraja. Setiti Bali lasted until 1920 and was succeeded the following year by a short-lived organization called Soeita Gama Tirta, presided over by I Goesti Poetoe Djlantik, member of the Judicial Council for Native Law (Raad van Kerta) in Singaraja and a descendant of the raja of Buleleng. In 1923, the Santi association (also spelled Santy or Shanti) was formed by members of a savings cooperative. Among the founding members were Poetoe Djlantik and Tjakra Tanaja. Ktoet Nasa, another of the founding members, was principal of the primary school in Bubunan. Santi opened a girls' school, provided gamelan music lessons, and furthered the study of religious teachings contained in Balinese palm-leaf manuscripts *(lontar)*, which were transcribed and printed to allow for a wider circulation. A few months after its foundation, the association started publishing its own journal, *Santi Adnjana.*

These three organizations were open to *triwangsa* (nobles) and *jaba* (commoners) alike, but tension appears to have been rife between the two groups, for the *jaba* objected to various privileges claimed by the *triwangsa.* Soon a conflict opposed the leaders of each faction— Tjakra Tanaja and Ktoet Nasa were also joint editors of *Santi Adnjana*—and sometime in 1924 the publication of the journal was taken over by Tjakra Tanaja who changed its title to *Bali Adnjana.* The conflict escalated until a schism between the *triwangsa* and *jaba* grew inevitable. The break finally occurred in May 1925, at a meeting of Santi's members, when Ktoet Nasa refused to change the name of Bali's religion as it appeared in the statutes of that organization: from Agama Hindu (the "Hindu religion") to Agama Hindu Bali (the "Balinese Hindu religion"). In October 1925, Ktoet Nasa started publishing his own journal, *Surya Kanta,* and the following month he established an eponymous organization whose membership was restricted to the *jaba.* The president was Ktoet Sandi, the *punggawa* of Singaraja, and the secretary was Nengah Metra, a young teacher at the Hollandsch-Inlandsche School (HIS, Dutch-Indonesian School) in Singaraja. Meanwhile the membership of Santi was dwindling. It held its last meeting in July 1926 but was occasionally still heard of afterward. The situation became even more complicated after May 1926 with the foundation in Klungkung of an organization named Tjatoer Wangsa Derja Gama Hindoe Bali. Professing to reconcile the interests of all "four castes" (Tjatoer Wangsa)—and discreetly backed by a colonial government anxious to defuse the rising tension—this new organization was in fact controlled by the *triwangsa:* its president was I Goesti Bagoes Djlantik, the ruler of Karangasem; its vice-president was Tjokorda Gde Raka Soekawati, the *punggawa* of Ubud and deputy for Bali to the People's Council (Volksraad) in Batavia; and Tjakra Tanaja was the representative for Buleleng.

The Polemic between *Surya Kanta* and *Bali Adnjana*

The few writers who have commented on these organizations and their publications have tended to stress the conflict between them in terms of a contest between "modernist" and "traditionalist" factions that could be explained by reference to the familiar struggle between the forces of progress and those of reaction. True, the polemic between *Surya Kanta* and *Bali Adnjana* concerned mainly (but not exclusively) caste privileges that had been aggravated by colonial policy. The commoners were challenging the alliance between Dutch interests and the Balinese nobility: their aim was to overturn the archaic feudal order in the name of progress. Yet one should be wary of focusing exclusively on this "caste conflict" *(pertentangan kasta)* at the risk of losing sight of what these two organizations and their leaders had in common— that is, they shared the same opinions on most fundamental issues. Thus, surprising as it may seem, the two journals had the same director, Ktoet Sempidi, until his death in April 1926, and members of both *Surya Kanta* and *Bali Adnjana* kept attending meetings of Santi until it finally disappeared from the scene. The situation was rendered even more unintelligible by the inclination of authors to sign their articles with their initials only and, more often, to hide their identity behind pseudonyms—such as "The Newsman" (I Gatra), "The Worried Father" (Nang Keweh), or "The Full-Blooded Balinese" (Bali Totok).

Attention has focused mainly on *Surya Kanta,* whose positions are more comprehensible today, as they are seemingly "rational" as well as more clear-cut and straightforward than those of *Bali Adnjana,* which tended to be couched in rather ambiguous and allusive terms. Furthermore, *Bali Adnjana* is less accessible than *Surya Kanta,* since the available copies of the journal are scattered, forming an incomplete set, besides being poorly stenciled. And because *Bali Adnjana* was published more frequently and for a longer period than *Surya Kanta,* its contents are wider-ranging and its coverage of issues greater.[9] Published under the leadership of Ktoet Nasa, *Surya Kanta* aimed to raise the position of the *jaba* in Balinese society and defend their rights. Most of its founders and members were teachers or employed in the civil service; a number were former pupils of Ktoet Nasa. For them, Western education had been a means of social mobility. After graduating from the HIS in Singaraja, where they had learned both Malay and Dutch, those who came from better-off families pursued their studies in Java or Makassar—particularly at the teachers' training college in Probolinggo (Java), where they mixed with their fellow Indonesians. The command of Dutch, besides being a marker of status, was for them an opening to the Western world with its values of rationalism and progress, its ideas of nationalism and democracy. Back in Bali, they either found employment as teachers in the schools, which the Dutch were progressively opening in the villages, or else they filled positions in the lower echelons of the colonial bureaucracy. There they experienced frustration from both their own and colonial society, neither of which lived up to their freshly acquired ideals. In particular, they resented the fact that their own access to the higher echelons of the bureaucracy was hampered by a colonial government that favored the *triwangsa*.

According to its motto, "Penjebar kitab-kitab poesaka dan seso-eloeh kemadjoean oemoem" ("disseminator of traditional books and promoter of progress for all"), as well as its statutes, *Surya Kanta* endeavored to enlighten the Balinese people and allow them to partake of the age of progress *(jaman kemajuan)*. The means to this end was believed to be Western-style education, which was expected to equip modern Balinese with both intelligence *(kepandaian)* and character *(budi)*. Thanks to these qualities, the Balinese would be in a position to discriminate among their customs and manners those that they should conserve and those they should reform or abandon in accordance with the demands of the time *(kemauan jaman)*. But first the main obstacle to progress had to be removed—namely caste prejudice and the privileges that the *triwangsa* enjoyed in language, etiquette, cross-caste marriage, corvée labor, and so on. Instead of feeling proud to inherit a noble title from one's father (Ida, Dewa, Gusti), modern Balinese should struggle to obtain academic titles (Ir., Mr., Dr.). In other words, status in Balinese society should no longer be ascribed but achieved. This, claimed *Surya Kanta*, concurred with the teachings found in Balinese *lontar* (such as the *Sarasamuccaya)* as well as in the sacred books of India (particularly the *Bhagavadgita*), which state that a true Brahmana is not someone who is born into a Brahmana family *(keturunan)* but someone who lives up to Brahmana ideals *(dharma)*. Therefore, the aristocrat in the age of progress should be a person whose nobility stems from intelligence and character *(bangsawan pikiran)*. In short, aristocracy should be based on merit, not on birth.

Faced with such virulent attacks, the *triwangsa* attempted to defend their prerogatives as best they could in *Bali Adnjana*. Yet it would be an oversimplification to conclude that this journal was their mouthpiece. Until August 1926, when its motto was removed from the masthead, *Bali Adnjana* was still officially the "voice of Santi"—whose members were mostly *jaba* ("Moeat soera Santi dan kaperloean oentoek oemoem": "containing the voice of Santi and serving the needs of all"). And until that time, which also corresponds to the last meeting of Santi, the opinions expressed in its pages were fairly diverse and often frankly polemical. And unlike *Surya Kanta*, which was avowedly partisan, *Bali Adnjana* was always careful to present itself as neutral in the feud between the *jaba* and *triwangsa*.[10] It was dedicated to the common good of the Balinese people as a whole—that is, to the "four castes" (Tjatoer Wangsa). After the foundation of Tjatoer Wangsa Derja Gama Hindoe Bali, the journal became the unofficial organ of this new organization, and over the years it grew more and more conservative.

Whereas *Surya Kanta* was produced by teamwork, after *Bali Adnjana* was taken over by Tjakra Tanaja it became the undertaking of this one individual. Unlike the leaders of Surya Kanta, who were representative of the "young group" *(kaum muda)* of modernist Balinese who had received a Western-style education, Tjakra Tanaja considered himself a member of the "old group" *(kaum kuno)*, the traditionalists. Born into a family of *punggawa*, a retired *punggawa* himself, he had been educated in traditional Balinese fashion through reading *lontar* (Agung 1974:119–120).[11] The position that Tjakra Tanaja defended was expressed clearly in the issue of *Bali Adnjana* published immediately after the launching of *Surya Kanta*. In this issue he declared his intentions: reconciling the Balinese people *(perdamaian)*, strengthening the religion *(kategoehan berlakoenja Agama)*, changing its outdated customs *(perobahan adat jang soedah koerang baik pada djaman ini)*, and eliminating the oppression of evildoers *(menghapoeskan tindasannja si angkara moerka)* (*Bali Adnjana* 29 [1925] :2). The last goal was aimed at the leadership of Surya Kanta, whom he accused of being motivated by greed and envy in their foolish pursuit to abolish caste hierarchy.[12] Not only did the Balinese inherit that hierarchical order from their ancestors, he argued, but it is based on religious teachings found in *lontar*. And as if to make his point stronger, in addressing his opponents Tjakra Tanaja obstinately refused to substitute the term *"jaba"* for "Sudra," which the *jaba* rejected as derogatory. He also refused to use the term of address "Tuan" (Mr.), favored by the educated *jaba,* alleging that it should be reserved for Westerners.

This became a way for Tjakra Tanaja to criticize Balinese intellectuals *(intellectueelen)* whom he felt had lost their identity. Indeed, he noted that they were no longer able to speak correct Balinese—that is, to use the respectful language prescribed by the customary codes of conduct. Generally he feared that Balinese educated in Dutch schools would look down on their parents as being backward *(kolot)* and would no longer want to engage in farming.[13] This does not mean he denied the Balinese access to modern education. Rather, he considered that it was enough for them to learn how to read and write and, more important, to study the traditional knowledge contained in *lontar.*

Yet for all his hostility against the foreign-educated intellectuals, Tjakra Tanaja often came rather close to the latter's position concerning the necessity of balancing a Western with a Balinese education. Thus one finds in both journals similar admonitions to the effect that the Balinese should emulate what is valuable in Western education without losing sight of their own identity. Moreover, the terms used to refer to each of these worlds—the foreign and the indigenous—are remarkably constant and present a coherent vision that contrasts the material West (*kasar* [coarse], *ilmu lahir* [material knowledge], *ilmu dunia* [worldly knowledge], *sekala* [manifest realm]) with the spiritual East (*halus* [refined], *ilmu batin* [spiritual knowledge], *ilmu akhirat* [external knowledge], *niskala* [nonmanifest realm]).[14] It would be hard to find a more eloquent illustration of this delicate exercise in equilibrium than the image adorning the masthead of *Bali Adnjana* between September 1925 and July 1926: two Balinese men—one dressed in Western garb, the other in Balinese clothes—stand facing each other, separated by a pair of scales on one side of which are piled books *(boekoe)* and on the other side palm-leaf manuscripts *(lontar).*

Religion and Tradition

More interesting for my purpose than the much publicized polemic between *Surya Kanta* and *Bali Adnjana* is the fact that in both these journals, for the first time, the Balinese viewed themselves as a singular entity: as a people *(kita bangsa Bali)*.[15] Of course, one could argue that a sense of pan-Balinese identity already existed through reference

Figure 3. Masthead of *Bali Adnjana*, 10 October 1925. Photo: KITLV, Collection of Oriental Manuscripts (V. E. Korn Collection, Or. 435-283).

to Majapahit, but it is doubtful that Bali could have been apprehended as a totality prior to its integration within the colonial state (Wiener 1994:357). In any case, in these journals the Balinese described themselves as a religious minority—the stronghold of Hinduism threatened by the aggressive expansionism of Islam and Christianity—as well as a particular ethnic group characterized by their own customs. More precisely, they construed their identity—which they called their Kebalian (Balineseness)—as being based simultaneously on religion and tradition ("Kebalian kita berdasar agama dan adat"). The very fact of the Balinese resorting to these foreign terms to define their identity testifies to the conceptual shift occurring on the island after its takeover by an alien power.[16]

To start with, one should bear in mind that *"adat"* is a word of Arabic origin borrowed by Islamized populations in the archipelago to refer to indigenous "customary law" as opposed to imported "religious law" *(hukum, syariah)*. Introduced to Bali by the Dutch, the word *"adat"* replaced a varied terminology for variable local customs *(kerta, palakerta, dresta, catur dresta, sima, tata krama, tata loka cara)*—which had "a field of meanings covering ritual obligation, social institution, legal regulation, and ancestral evocation" (Warren 1993:4) that infused the Balinese sense of communal solidarity in the villages. The advent of this word entailed a twofold consequence. First, it created a new conceptual domain—that of tradition—which initially was contrasted not so much with the domain of religion as with that of administration, especially that which came under the authority of the colonial state. Second, the incorporation of a miscellaneous assortment of local customs into this generic term altered their meaning for the Balinese: what had been, until then, an interplay of significant differences deliberately fostered between villages was becoming the locus of Balinese ethnic identity in the sense of a customary body of inherited regulations and institutions that governed the lives of the Balinese.

Tradition, then, was not clearly distinguished from religion.[17] Indeed, *adat* partakes of the religious worldview of the Balinese in the sense that it refers both to an immutable divine cosmic order and to the social order instituted accordingly by their ancestors—at once describing the ideal order and prescribing the behavior required to achieve that order. Unlike the world religions that have a core of abstract basic tenets and symbols meaningful to people of diverse cultural backgrounds, Balinese religion is highly localized: it consists of rites relating specific groups of people to one another, to their ancestors, and to their territory. Moreover, religion is a customary obligation for the Balinese: participation in its rites is a consequence of membership of a local community as well as membership of a descent group.

Hence it is doubtful that religion was a marker of identity for the Balinese before they started viewing Islam (and Christianity) as a threat. I concur with Adrian Vickers (1987:35) that, in their eyes, religious differences were signs used to differentiate groups seen as having basic similarities. Prior to their colonization by the Dutch, the Balinese did not conceive of a different system of social organization, and so they had no absolute category of the Other; the distinction they made was between people from the same island and people from beyond. From this perspective, Islam was conceived as belonging to the same cultural sphere as Bali. Indeed, even in the two journals cited earlier one finds references to Balinese who embraced Islam alongside those who embraced Hinduism: "The Balinese people profess two religions; namely, there are those who are Muslim and those who are Hindu" (*Surya Kanta* 1[1926]:17).[18]

In any case, defining religion in terms of *agama,* as the Balinese intelligentsia did in their publications, opened a significantly different semantic field. *Agama* is a Sanskrit word that originally had a double meaning: first, "a traditional precept, doctrine, body of precepts, collection of such doctrines," in short "anything handed down as fixed by tradition" (Gonda 1973:499), which brings its meaning fairly close to that of *adat;*[19] and, second, a specific religious doctrine associated with the tantric worship of Siva and Sakti. Over the centuries, it seems that this term came to be related to an Indic model of divine kingship, Sanskrit literature, and Hindu-Buddhist theology in the Indonesian archipelago—in other words, to literacy and power attributed to a prestigious foreign civilization (Atkinson 1987:175). By the eighteenth century, through its association with Islam, the term *"agama"* had taken on the meaning of "religion" (Hoadley and Hooker 1981:61). And indeed, in both Crawfurd's and Friederich's accounts, one finds it used in that sense. But for the Balinese intelligentsia of the 1920s, the discourse of *agama* bore the imprints not only of Islam but of Christianity as well. Proponents of these faiths, by appropriating the term *"agama,"* had shaped new associations for it—mainly an emphasis on a supreme deity, the requirement of conversion to a foreign doctrine whose teachings are contained in a holy book, and an ideal of social progress (Howell 1978, 1982).

If both *Surya Kanta* and *Bali Adnjana* shared a common reference to *agama* and *adat* as the foundations of Balinese identity, the two journals held different opinions as to how their respective domains were linked and how Balinese religion related to Indian Hinduism. And it is this divergence, as much as the more visible "caste conflict," which explains the famous schism within Santi. For the founding members of Santi, things were still unproblematic: its statutes proposed to strengthen the Hindu religion ("meneguhkan Agama Hindu"), as well as to reinforce both tradition and religion ("meneguhkan Adat dan Agama"). Whereas this objective was pursued by *Bali Adnjana,* the leaders of *Surya Kanta* wanted to invigorate *agama* while ridding *adat* of whatever they deemed incompatible with "progress." Thus for the former, Balinese religion was based on the traditional social order ("agama kita wong Bali berdasar adat") within which *agama* was inseparable from *adat* ("adat dan agama tak boleh bercerai"); for the latter, however, religion should be dissociated from a traditional order seen not only as unfair but also as an obstacle to progress.

Reading through their publications, it is clear that the main preoccupation of the Balinese intelligentsia was to ensure that their religion could stand beside Islam and Christianity and thus resist the thrust of their proselytism. Yet they disagreed about what should be done to strengthen their religion. According to *Surya Kanta,* the problem was that Balinese did not really know their religion and were the unenlightened victims of superstitions *(takhyul)* arising from the restrictions placed by Brahmana priests *(pedanda)* on their access to sacred knowledge contained in *lontar (aja wera).* So long as they contented themselves with blindly following the priests who led their ceremonies without understanding the true significance of their rites ("milu-milu tuara nawang"), they would be easy prey to Muslim or Christian indoctrination. Hence the outburst of Ktoet Nasa during the meeting that sealed the fate of Santi, in May 1925, in which he declared that the Hindu religion in Bali was ruined ("Agama Hindoe di Bali roesak") and should be reformed accordingly. (See *Bali Adnjana* 15[1925]:1; see also 18[1925]:3; 30[1926]:5, and 10[1929]:3.) For *Bali Adnjana,* on the contrary, if there was indeed a problem, it resulted from the critical stance adopted by the Western-educated intellectuals toward their own religion and their ensuing intention to transform it as they thought fit.

Viewed from this perspective, the controversy that erupted between the *jaba* and *triwangsa* over the name that the Balinese religion should take makes perfect sense. In defending Agama Hindu Bali (the "Balinese Hindu religion") as the proper name, the *triwangsa* were trying to preserve the religious-cum-social order of yore.[20] In proposing to call their religion Agama Bali Hindu (the "Hindu Balinese religion"), the *jaba* were claiming that—even though their religious practices were corrupted owing to their ignorance of its true nature—the Balinese were in fact real Hindus.[21] Hence one encounters the accusation frequently implied in *Bali Adnjana* that the *jaba* aimed to promote a "pure" form of Hinduism, like the one found in India,[22] to which Tjakra Tanaja opposed the argument that, according to *lontar,* the Balinese religion originated not in India but in Majapahit.

Culture and Art

Surya Kanta held its last meeting in February 1928. At this meeting, which Tjakra Tanaja was invited to attend, it was decided that the organization would henceforth be open to *triwangsa* membership and become more national in its orientation (*Bali Adnjana* 7[1928]:1). But it seems that soon afterward its leaders experienced some pressure from the government; in any case, nothing more was ever heard from Surya Kanta. The year before, in 1927, there had already been calls in *Bali Adnjana* to end the confrontation between *jaba* and *triwangsa* so that the Balinese could unite in the movement for Indonesia's independence. Such petitions notwithstanding, by and large *Bali Adnjana* was more than ever a faithful supporter of the colonial state—the more so as its policy was becoming increasingly conservative. Thus, in June 1929, Tjakra Tanaja declared that his journal no longer had a raison d'être, since the Dutch had made known their intention to restore certain prerogatives to the Balinese rulers and govern Bali according to its *adat (Bali Adnjana* 15–16[1929]:8). Two months later, he hailed the reestablishment of the former Balinese rulers as royal administrators in an editorial titled "The Island of Bali Will Become Bali Again" ("Poelau Bali Akan Kombali Mendjadi Bali") in *Bali Adjnana* 19[1929]:1–4.

The Dutch had valid reason to be worried about the expansion of the national Indonesian awakening and political activism to Bali. One way to defuse that threat was to "culturalize" Balinese identity to prevent it from becoming politicized. In postmodernist fashion, one could say not so much that the Dutch constructed Balinese culture but, rather, that they constructed Bali as a culture. And from the late 1920s onward, one finds growing evidence that Balinese intellectuals were appropriating this construction more and more in order to define themselves in terms of their culture. As a specific topic "culture" (and "art") had been conspicuously absent from Balinese reflections on their identity. In fact, just as the Balinese language has no words for "religion" or "tradition," it also has none for "culture" or "art." In keeping with their marked preference for concrete verbal forms as opposed to abstract concepts, the Balinese have always been concerned with specific activities, inseparable from their contexts, which were therefore not perceived as belonging to domains coming under generic labels such as "culture" or "art." Nevertheless, one begins to encounter occasional references to these topics in both *Surya Kanta* and *Bali Adnjana* shortly after the establishment of the Tjatoer Wangsa Derja Gama Hindoe Bali in 1926. Thus, in *Bali Adnjana,* the phrase *"peradaban Bali"* (Balinese culture) tended to become a substitute for Kebalian. In *Surya Kanta,* one sometimes finds the Dutch term *"cultuur."* Ktoet Nasa even dedicated a whole article to explaining the meaning of that word, which was glossed as the "soul of a people" *(jiwa bangsa)* and understood as including *seni* (art), *adat,* and *agama* (*Surya Kanta* 9–10[1926]:128). At the time, though, "art" was more commonly rendered by the Dutch term *"kunst."*

In 1928, Resident L. J. J. Caron inaugurated a foundation in Singaraja—the Kirtya Liefrinck–Van der Tuuk—named after two great tutelary figures of Balinese studies and dedicated to the collection and study of Balinese *lontar.* In April 1930, his successor H. Beeuwkes, who was also president of the Kirtya, launched the publication of the journal *Bhawanagara,* with the financial support of the colonial state.[23] Its main contributors were former leaders of both *Surya Kanta* and *Bali Adnjana* (but without Ktoet Nasa). Under the leadership of the Dutch Orientalist R. Goris (who was known at times to use the Balinese pseudonym I Made Sweta), these leaders now worked together toward the politically safe goals of education and culture. Finally, in 1932, a long-awaited museum—the Museum Bali—presenting the various forms of the island's material culture was opened. The articles published in *Bhawanagara* were markedly different in tone and content from those in *Surya Kanta* and *Bali Adnjana*. Certainly a significant proportion were in Balinese, as the colonial government had an obvious interest in fostering consciousness of a Balinese cultural identity as opposed to an identity based on caste difference or national unity (Robinson 1995:35). Besides, if there were numerous articles on *agama* and *adat,* it was as if these topics were now more a matter of Orientalist erudition than a crucial question for the Balinese in their effort to reformulate their identity according to the demands of the times. On the agenda was "Balinese culture" as specified in *Bhawanagara*'s motto: "A monthly newsletter dedicated to Balinese culture" ("Soerat boelanan oentoek memperhatikan peradaban Bali").

This Balinese culture *(peradaban Bali)* was portrayed as an entity made up of subparts that were prominently listed (in both Balinese and Malay) in the journal's first issue and commonly referred to in subsequent articles. Thus, for example, Goris presented a lecture at the Batavian Society of Arts and Sciences in which he reviewed the scholarly achievements of Dutch and other European scholars in Bali. Presenting the island as a field of Orientalist study, he constructed his lecture according to the main headings seen to make up Balinese culture: *bahasa* (language), *adatrecht* (customary law), *agama* (religion), *ilmu kitab* (literature), *seni* (art), and *barang kuno* (antiquities). It is noteworthy that, in his eagerness to stress Bali's wealth of cultural riches, Goris commenced his lecture by quoting the opinion of one of his Dutch predecessors, Dr. J. F. G. Brumund, who wrote in 1863: "I went for a one-month excursion to Bali. During all that time I was isolated from the civilized world" (*Bhawanagara* 12[1932]:192).[24] By the early 1930s, Bali had indeed become "civilized" *(beradab)* in the eyes of the Dutch.

This newly expressed interest in Balinese culture would also be taken up in *Djatajoe*, a "social and cultural monthly newsletter" ("soerat boelanan sosial dan cultureel") published by Bali Darma Laksana, an organization born in July 1936 of the fusion of two educational associations, Eka Laksana and Balisch Studiefonds (Putra 1989).[25] Eka Laksana had been established by Balinese students a year earlier in Denpasar with the following aim: "To study and if possible advance

Figure 4. Cover page of *Bhawanagara*, August 1932.

culture and art in Bali and Lombok" ("mempeladjari dan djikalaoe dapat memadjoekan cultuur dan kunst di Bali dan Lombok"). As for the Balisch Studiefonds, it was an association devoted to funding the education of promising young Balinese. According to its statutes, Bali Darma Laksana aimed at enhancing the progress of Balinese culture ("mempertinggi kemajuan kebudayaan Bali").

If the word for religion *(agama)* had been borrowed from Sanskrit and that for tradition *(adat)* from Arabic, the concepts of culture *(cultuur)* and art *(kunst)* were initially acquired from Dutch before being appropriated from Malay. *Bhawanagara*'s motto referred to *peradaban,* and one finds the recurrence of both the terms *"cultuur"* and

⊨| BHĀWANĀGARA |⊨

Soerat boelanan oentoek memperhatikan peradaban Bali.

REDACTIE: I Njoman Kadjeng.
       I Ktoet Widjanegara.
       I Njoman Mas Wirjasutha.

COMMISSIE VAN ADVIES:
  I Goesti Poetoe Djlantik.
  Dr. R. Goris.

Alamat Redactie dan Administratie:
Kirtya Liefrinck- v.d. Tuuk Singaradja

Harga langganan: f 2.50 setahoen
Advertentie: berdamai lebih dahoeloe

ASTA GINA.

Sakadi karangan G. P. Djiwa sané inoetjap ring s. k. Bhāwanāgara no. 2 boelan Juli 1932 sané waoe lintang, wènten manah titiang njamboengin bebaos poenika, saantoekan masoeksema betjik.

Sadoeroeng kaparakang indik sakantjan pakarjan tetoekangan poenika, betjik selehin baosé koena-koena, sané noedoet pakajoenan kemadjoean matetoekangan.

Saking riin piragin titiang wènten baos ASTA GINA, ASTA KOSALA kalih ASTA KOSALI.

Tan wènten goenan ipoen pandjangang marakang artin baos poeniki, saantoekan sampoen ketah. Nanging soekseman ipoen kari makoelit.

Antoek djagaté sakadi mangkin, djanten maboeat maoeroekin indik pakarjan toekang-toekangé, mangda sida betjikan pakarjané mangkin bandi-ngang ring sané koena, oepami indik maoelat-oelatan, ngoekir, mapepoela-san, marada miwah sané lianan.

Ngoeroekang tangan matetoekangan saking alit boeat pisan, mangda biasa tangané makarja, mangda kosala, madroewé geginan. Sadjawining poenika taler boeat kagelisané mapakajoen nempa barangé sané betjik tjara mangkin. Manoet sesoekatan pakarjané koena indik makarja poeri (oemah) kasinahang ring lontar „swakarma" jan sang makarja oemah mang-da nganoetang ring linggah pakarangan raoehing sanggah, mangda masi-koet manoet sesoekatan kadoeloerin banten pangoerip-oerip, pamęlaspas

Figure 5. First page of *Bhawanagara*, September 1932.

"peradaban" in the articles it published. While these terms still figured prominently in *Djatajoe*, they were often replaced with *"kebudayaan,"* a neologism of Sanskrit origin whose root *(budaya)* pointed to the development of a person's reason or character before it took on the meaning of "culture." As for *"kesenian,"* which tended to replace the word *"kunst,"* its root *(seni)* meant "fine," "refined," before becoming understood in the modern sense of "art."

At the same time that Dutch Orientalists and Balinese intellectuals were actively culturalizing Bali, the island's cultural image was receiving an additional boost as well as validation from the development of

Figure 6. Cover page of *Djatajoe*, 25 October 1937.

tourism. As early as 1908, the year that had seen the fall of Bali's last un-
yielding royal house under the assault of superior Dutch military might,
the colonial government had opened a tourist bureau in Batavia with
the aim of promoting the East Indies as a tourist destination. Initially
focusing on Java, in 1914 the bureau extended its scope to Bali as soon
as the army's pacification of the island permitted safe travel. But it was
not until 1924 that tourism really took off in Bali, after the Dutch
shipping company KPM established a weekly steamship service connecting Singaraja with Batavia and Makassar. Visitors would still have
to wait until 1928, however, to find a proper tourist hotel: the Bali

Hotel in Denpasar. From a few hundred tourists visiting the island each year in the late 1920s, the number of tourists visiting the island had risen to a few thousand by the late 1930s.

Along with tourists, the artists and scholars who sojourned in Bali between the wars were instrumental in popularizing the extravagant artistry of Balinese ceremonial pageants. The writings and paintings, photographs and films, they brought back from the island forged a sensational image of Bali, an image that the promotional services of the emerging tourism industry quickly exploited. Not only did they certify and disseminate to the West the image of Bali as paradise. Above all, they identified Balinese society with its culture—which they saw mostly in terms of its artistic and religious activities (Lindsey 1997; MacRae 1992; Picard 1996a, 1996b; Vickers 1989). One example of the pervasive clichés initiated at the time is found in the preface to the first book in English about Bali. There one can read that, thanks to their "wealth and leisure," "the Balinese are the greatest artists of this age, and still more, that every Balinese, man or woman, is an artist"; that the incentive to this artistic disposition is provided by their religion, "a beautiful mixture of Animism and Hinduism"; and that "whether sculpture, painting, music, or dancing, they simply had to produce or to give breath to all these, since they could not help themselves" (Roosevelt in Powell 1930:x–xii).

The Balinese intelligentsia appear to have been aware early on of this newly acquired fame of their island. They reacted in diverse ways. The first references to tourism that I was able to locate, in *Surya Kanta*, were frankly negative. Thus the anonymous author of an article titled "Bali as a Museum of Antiquities" ("Bali sebagai Museum barang koeno") reproached the Balinese for allowing themselves to be seduced by the glamor of their island, for rejecting the image of a "living museum" ("museum hidup") propagated by the Orientalists, and for denouncing the policy of cultural preservation conducted by the colonial government. Zealots of progress, the commoner intellectuals wanted Bali to shake off its archaic reputation and become a modern society (*Surya Kanta* 3–4[1927]:29–30).

Such a critical stance would find no place in *Bali Adnjana* and certainly not in *Bhawanagara*. Indeed, the first articles written by Balinese about their arts in this journal took obvious pride in evoking the artistic notoriety of their island abroad. Thus an article on the modern musical genre *kebiar* opened with this quotation: "For the Balinese are an artistically minded folk; they are born architects, sculptors, actors, dancers, musicians. . . . Such is the opinion of foreigners. We, the Balinese, a people who love art, we have the right to be proud of this quality of ours" (*Bhawanagara* 11–12[1934]:161).[26]

As for *Djatajoe,* the tone was more sober. While appreciating the admiring gaze and flattering praise evinced by foreigners, the Balinese intelligentsia of the 1930s were painfully aware of the difference between the scholarly visitors of yesteryear and contemporary tourists for whom Bali was but a mere spectacle. They resented the attitude of those visitors who assumed that everything on their island was for sale. And they were ashamed of the image circulated by photographs of half-naked Balinese women that had earned Bali a dubious reputation as "The Island of Bare Breasts."

Balinese Religion: From Ethnic to Universal

Whereas the context of Balinese debate in the 1920s remained basically Balinese, during the 1930s it became increasingly Indonesian.[27] At the same time, the old questions concerning Balinese religion—namely its relationship to Hinduism on the one hand, and its links to *adat* on the other, which had been treated in a purely academic fashion in *Bhawanagara*—were reemerging in *Djatajoe* as part of a more urgent agenda. The numerous articles on *agama* published in this journal attest to a notable confusion if not a frank helplessness among the Balinese themselves. This was no longer due solely to disagreement among them, but to the fact that they were at a loss as to how to reply to accusations of paganism by foreigners—not only Dutch administrators (such as Dr. Korn or Resident Jansen, among others) but also Indonesians writing in various East Indies journals.

Illustrative of the Balinese frame of mind at the time is an article bearing the significant title "Our Confusion Regarding Religion" ("Kebingoengan kita tentang agama"). The author explains to his coreligionists that, in the eyes of foreigners, "our religion is based on tradition mixed with all sorts of extracts from Hinduism and therefore cannot be compared to any religion found in India; according to the opinion of foreigners we do not have a religion and do not worship God (Widi), but we are like madmen who worship anything they happen to come across" (*Djatajoe* 4[1937]:98).[28] Faced with such a low opinion of their rites, the Balinese could not help calling into question their religion. They argued over what it should be called and debated the name of its god, as well as the way it related to Indian Hinduism.

Indeed, while a number of changes to Balinese religion had been advocated during the previous decade, no consensus had been reached on the overall direction that reform should take. And despite a tentative agreement to call their religion Agama Hindu Bali (the "Balinese Hindu religion"), the name of the Balinese religion as well as that of its god remained in question.[29] The fact is that, prior to the modernizing impulse of the 1920s, religion for the Balinese had not been regarded as something distinct and in need of a specific name.[30] One could even say that it was not singled out as religion, in the sense of "a set of beliefs and practices that had some kind of systemic coherence and that could be conceptually isolated from other aspects of life" (Kipp 1993:239).

Now a combination of internal changes and external pressures was impelling the Balinese to agree on the true nature of their religion and codify its rites accordingly. Hence the recurring plea in *Djatajoe* urging priests to enlighten their Balinese followers about religious matters: "Our priests and other knowledgeable persons should settle once and for all which religion we should profess, which hodgepodge we should get rid of, which tradition we may still use and which should be discarded as bringing about our decline" (*Djatajoe* 5[1937]:132).[31]

Consequently, during their first congress held in 1937, members of Bali Darma Laksana decided to enlist the help of a council of *pedanda* to compile a holy book *(kitab suci)*. They felt that once the Balinese knew what their religion was actually about, they would be in a better position to defend it against accusations of heathenism by Muslims and Christians alike and would be less tempted to embrace other faiths (*Djatajoe* 4[1937]:114–115). Three years later, however, they were informed that the attempt at composing a holy book had failed. The reason given was that in Bali, *agama* could not be divorced from *adat;* and *adat* differed from one village to the next and from one kingdom to another; hence the priests could not agree on a religious canon valid for the whole island (*Djatajoe* 9–10[1940]:281–282).

This problem would become a crucial issue after Indonesia's independence, for the Ministry of Religion, dominated by Muslims, was to drastically restrict the religions that were officially accepted by stipulating that a religion must be monotheistic, it must have a codified system of law for its followers, it must possess a holy book and a prophet, and, further, its congregation must not be limited to a single ethnic group. Once Bali was integrated into the Republic of Indonesia, the social pressures under which Balinese reformists had initiated their religious inquiries were growing into an undisguised threat and imparting a sense of urgency to debates among the intelligentsia about their religion. The peril was undoubtedly very concrete. For Balinese religion was regarded as tribal by the Ministry of Religion in the sense that its rites were considered to belong to the domain of *adat* and not to *agama*—that is, the Balinese were regarded as people who do not yet have a religion ("orang yang belum beragama"), a label associated with primitive backwardness and parochialism. Consequently, if the Balinese did not want to be made the target of Muslim or Christian proselytizing, they had no other recourse than to reform their religion so that it would be eligible to attain the status of *agama*. In order for Balinese rites to accede to the status of *agama,* they had to be detached from the domain of *adat*.

During the 1950s, the Balinese kept pressing the Ministry of Religion to recognize their religion and a number of new Balinese reformist religious organizations made their appearance. Whereas some reformers were seeking the seeds of regeneration in their own indigenous tradition, the majority of them endeavored to have Balinese religion acknowledged as the local manifestation of a universal religion on a par with Islam and Christianity. They enjoined the Balinese to return to the fold of Hinduism, which they presented as the source of their rites, by renewing their contacts with India. On their initiative, classical texts of Hindu theology were translated into Indonesian; Indian scholars were invited to Bali to teach their religion; scholarships to study in India were granted to a number of young Balinese.

In 1958, the year Bali became a separate province, the main Balinese religious organizations finally succeeded in enlisting the support of President Sukarno to have their religion officially recognized as monotheistic by the Ministry of Religion. The Balinese religion was called Agama Hindu Bali, the name that had been advocated by the conservative faction backing *Bali Adnjana* in the 1920s. The following year, these diverse religious organizations merged into a single representative body, the Parisada Dharma Hindu Bali (Balinese Hindu Council), which became the official liaison body between the Balinese Hindu congregation and the Ministry of Religion. The Parisada undertook to compile a holy book, standardize religious rites, formalize the priesthood, and provide instruction in Hindu religion in schools and universities—all this amounting to a "scripturalization" of Balinese religion, a shift of focus from ritual to text.

While the Parisada's use of the name Hindu Bali implied a clear recognition of the distinctive ethnic component of Balinese Hinduism, its leaders came under increasing pressure to universalize their religion.

At the same time, some Javanese groups, conscious of their own Hindu heritage, began investigating the possibility of associating themselves with Balinese Hinduism, particularly when the Balinese began to introduce their religion to other islands where they moved as transmigrants or civil servants. As a result, in 1964 the council changed its name to Parisada Hindu Dharma (PHD), thus forsaking any reference to its Balinese origins. And when, the following year, Sukarno xannounced the names of the religions that were to qualify for official government sponsorship, it was Agama Hindu and not Agama Hindu Bali that was included (Bakker 1993).

Religion, Tradition, and Culture

Since the incorporation of their island into the Netherlands East Indies at the turn of the century, the Balinese intelligentsia have engaged in formulating their identity in terms of religion, tradition, and culture (cum art). These conceptual categories were intrinsically foreign to Balinese society, however, and had to be imported from abroad. It is not so much, as Bakker (1993:39) contends, that the former unity of religion, tradition, and culture had started to disintegrate due to the colonial occupation of the island. Rather, it was the conjunction of the Dutch-enforced distinction between religious tradition and colonial administration, on the one hand, and the growing urge to dissociate religion from tradition on the part of the emerging intellectual elite of commoners, on the other, that eventually led to the creation of the distinctive categories of *agama* and *adat* as differentiated from the domain of the state. Later on, with the interested approval of Dutch Orientalists and American anthropologists, resident artists and passing tourists, the Balinese added to *agama* and *adat* the categories of culture *(budaya)* and art *(seni)* as components of their identity. Hence, by precipitating a sharper contrast between "our ways" *(cara kita)* and "their ways" *(cara kaum sana)*, the colonial encounter not only helped the Balinese to conceive a notion of themselves as a people *(bangsa)*— a unitary entity—but it also contributed to a further drawing of boundaries between hitherto conceptually undifferentiated domains within Balinese society.

What happened to the components of Kebalian under the New Order regime of President Suharto? As a result of the requirement that the Balinese embrace a duly acknowledged religion—in accordance with the Islamic model of what constitutes a religion—the locus of Kebalian has clearly tipped in favor of *agama*. Here I am no longer referring to the communal identity Balinese could secure from practicing their traditional religion—bound as it is both to a territory and to a descent group—but to its Hindu persuasion, which characterizes the Balinese people as a non-Muslim and non-Christian minority within the Indonesian multireligious nation. This official version of Balinese religion bears little resemblance to everyday religious practices in houseyards and village temples, which are characterized more by orthopraxy than by orthodoxy. Yet it appears that the gap between actual Balinese religious practices and the normative definition of Balinese religion is progressively narrowing. This is the result of the increasing organizational efficiency of the Parisada Hindu Dharma (renamed the Parisada Hindu Dharma Indonesia in 1986), which allows its instruction—endorsed by the state apparatus, in particular by the education system, and conveyed by the mass media—to penetrate Balinese society at village level.

This Balinese investment in religion has occurred mainly to the detriment of tradition, which has consequently become secularized while being increasingly marginalized by the state. In this respect, the New Order regime went much further than its colonial predecessor in the penetration of society by the state. Whereas the colonial state aimed at preserving *adat* with a view to maintaining the traditional allegiance of village communities, the Indonesian state has enlisted *adat* into its policy of national integration, economic development, and public order. In the process, the locus of Balinese tradition has become the province—in effect creating a provincial *adat*.

While Balinese tradition is rendered vestigial and appropriated by the state, Balinese culture appears to be thriving to the point that local and foreign observers alike have felt justified to speak of the island's cultural renaissance. Indeed, the government has spared no effort to promote the visual and decorative aspects of Balinese culture: this is what is called in Indonesian the cultural arts *(seni budaya)*—that is, a conception of culture confined to those aspects that may be made the object of representation and engender aesthetic appreciation. There are two interwoven reasons for this government patronage: the promotion of a regional culture, which has been used to celebrate and legitimize the New Order regime, and the use of cultural performances to attract tourists and thus boost the regional and national economies. In this respect, the state and the tourism industry appear to share a similar conception of culture-as-art.

Now, with their tradition provincialized and their culture folklorized, religion, for the Balinese, has become the emblem of their Kebalian. To the extent that Balinese reformers have endeavored to rework their rites into a universal religion and to shape their ethnic community into a religious congregation, they have come to use Hinduism to mark an ethnic boundary. Thus, somewhat paradoxically, their religion has become the paramount embodiment of Balinese identity even though it gained official recognition precisely under the condition that it not be restricted solely to the Balinese. With the demise of Suharto's New Order and the increasing politicization of Islam in Indonesia, the Balinese are likely to place even greater emphasis on Hinduism as a marker of their identity in the near future.

Notes

This chapter is based on observations gathered during numerous trips to Bali since 1974, particularly research on cultural tourism undertaken between 1980 and 1982. Fieldwork was accomplished under the auspices of the Indonesian Institute of Sciences (LIPI) and benefited from the institutional patronage of Prof. Dr. I Gusti Ngurah Bagus, head of the Department of Anthropology at Udayana University in Denpasar. I am indebted to Linda Connor, Raechelle Rubinstein, and Jean-François Guermonprez for critical comments, as well as to Kunang Helmi for assistance in conveying my French thoughts in proper English. The spelling of Indonesian and Balinese terms conforms to current conventions, except in quotations, where the original spelling is retained.

1. I have dealt with this subject at length elsewhere (Picard 1990a, 1990b, 1993, 1995, 1996b).

2. In 1989, a poll was conducted by the daily newspaper, the *Bali Post*, after a well-known Balinese academic accused his fellow countrymen of losing their Balineseness (Sujana 1988). While 40 percent of the respondents imputed to tourism an erosion of Kebalian, the remaining 60 percent felt, to the contrary, that the growing numbers of tourists visiting Bali each year was the most convincing proof of the enduring authenticity of Balinese identity (Widminarko 1989).

3. Here I am alluding to the literature on the invention of culture and tradition (Wagner 1975; Anderson 1983; Hobsbawm and Ranger 1983; Handler and Linnekin 1984; Sahlins 1993)—specifically, the literature on the relations between culture and colonialism (Dirks 1992; Thomas 1994). A case in point is the politics of cultural construction in the Pacific. (See, for example, Keesing and Tonkinson 1982; Linnekin and Poyer 1990; Jolly and Thomas 1992; Lindstrom and White 1993; Grijp and Meijl 1993.) Several scholars have investigated identity formation among various ethnic groups in Indonesia, such as the Batak (Rodgers 1987, 1987–1988, 1993; Kipp 1993; Perret 1995; Vignato 1998), the Minangkabau (Kahn 1993), the Javanese (Pemberton 1994a; Sears 1996), the Dayak (Sellato 1990; Schiller 1997), and groups

in Sulawesi (Volkman 1984; Atkinson 1987; Antweiler 1993; Adam 1995; Robinson 1995).

4. This chapter is a by-product of work in progress. My intention is to mark out a field of investigations and issues for scholarly debate, both Balinese and foreign. Hence the chapter should be seen as a step in ongoing research.

5. A caveat is in order here. Relying as I do on the work of these authors, I am well aware that the purpose of their research was rather different from mine. To this day no trained historian has investigated the Dutch colonial archives in a systematic fashion. Thus we still do not have an extensive chronological overview and thorough understanding of Dutch colonial policy in Bali. What should be taken for granted, though, is that the colonial state was not a monolithic agent and that colonial policy underwent significant changes during the period under investigation.

6. Balinese writings from that time refer to the precolonial era as "when the world was steady" ("dugas gumine enteg").

7. Ironically, while the editors of the conservative journal *Bali Adnjana* stressed the importance of the Balinese language in sustaining Balinese identity, it did not seem to bother them that they had to resort to the Malay language to convey their point. Nor did this incongruity seem to strike the few Balinese academics who have written about these publications. This is all the more striking as in Balinese, as well as in Malay, the word for "language" has a much broader semantic field than in English, including as it does "the notions of civility, rationality, and truth" (Anderson 1990a:28).

8. The formation and development of these modern organizations in Bali, as well as the contents of their publications, remain largely unresearched. To the best of my knowledge—except for the occasional mention in foreign publications (Bakker 1993:39–44; Connor 1982:265–267, 1996:182–189; Goris 1933:33–36; Korn 1932:46–47, 124–125; Kraemer 1933b:48–50; Robinson 1995:33–36; Vickers 1989:150–155), as well as a few superficial articles and reports by Balinese academics (Agung 1972; Bagus 1969, 1972, 1975, 1996; Kutoyo 1977–1978; Padmawati 1982)—there are only two studies devoted to this topic, both by Balinese historians: Agung (1974) and Atmadja (1987).

9. *Surya Kanta* was a monthly journal published from October 1925 to September 1927. *Bali Adnjana* appeared every ten days from January 1924 to November 1930 (irregularly after June 1929). Issues of *Bali Adnjana* are available only after January 1925; no copies of *Santi Adnjana* seem to have survived.

10. In December 1925, for example, Tjakra Tanaja refused to endorse the project of some *triwangsa* to establish their own organization, Tjandra Kanta, in order to counter the influence of Surya Kanta, for fear of aggravating the schism that had developed between the *triwangsa* and *jaba* (*Bali Adnjana* 36[1925]:1–2).

11. In more than one respect the polemic between *Surya Kanta* and *Bali Adnjana* is reminiscent of the conflict between *kaum muda* and *kaum kuno*

that raged in Java and West Sumatra during the early decades of the twentieth century (Abdullah 1971, 1972; Adam 1995; Kahn 1993).

12. Tjakra Tanaja occasionally went even further in his attack against Surya Kanta, which he accused of being a lair of communists ("S.[arang] K.[ominis"])—an accusation that, especially after the communist uprisings of 1926–1927 in Java and Sumatra and their ensuing repression, was an unsubtle means of arousing the colonial government's vigilance.

13. Tjakra Tanaja's denunciation of the young Balinese educated in Java would find a similar echo a decade later in the concluding remarks in Miguel Covarrubias' *Island of Bali:* "Those young Balinese who have gone to Java to become teachers for the Western-style Government schools have returned convinced that what they learned in Java is the essence of knowledge and progress. They have become conscious of the contempt of Europeans for the native cultures and have been influenced to believe that the philosophy, arts and habits of their country are signs of peasant backwardness" (1997:394).

14. There is, of course, nothing peculiarly Balinese in such a contrast, which appears to be the common lot of native intelligentsias emerging out of a colonial situation. Their predicament is deeply contradictory, as depicted by John Plamenatz, for it involves a rejection—"in fact, two rejections, both of them ambivalent: rejection of the alien intruder and dominator who is nevertheless to be imitated and surpassed by his own standards, and rejection of ancestral ways which are seen as obstacles to progress and yet also cherished as marks of identity" (quoted in Chatterjee 1986:2). One is also reminded of the famous polemic on culture ("polemik kebudayaan"), which led to a split between leading Indonesian intellectuals in the 1930s, concerning the extent to which the emerging national culture should borrow from the West (Mihardja 1948).

15. Besides *"bangsa,"* the authors who wrote in these journals commonly used such terms as *"negeri"* (country) and *"tanah air"* (motherland) to refer to Bali. In this respect, *Surya Kanta* was indubitably more concerned with the island of Bali as a unified entity than was *Bali Adnjana.* Take, for example, the position of Ktoet Nasa in discussing the colonial government's project to grant a representative council to Bali as part of its policy of regional decentralization. He vigorously opposed the idea of establishing local councils, which the Balinese elite favored, as this would divide the island along the lines of the former kingdoms. He instead defended the notion that there should be one council for the whole of Bali in order to develop national sentiment ("perasaan sebangsa") among the Balinese people (*Surya Kanta* 5[1927]:54–57).

16. The problem is that, as early as the 1920s, we are faced with a conception of Balinese identity that is already fully framed in terms of *agama* (religion) and *adat* (tradition). Thus, unfortunately, the investigation of these journals does not allow us to elucidate how the Balinese arrived at this conception.

17. In this respect, the relationship between tradition and religion in Bali was different from the situation that prevailed in Indonesian societies which had been Islamized or Christianized: in those societies the local *adat* was generally perceived as being somehow contrary to the teachings of the universal

religions (Abdullah 1966; Von Benda-Beckmann and Von Benda-Beckmann 1988).

18. "Banga Bali memeloek doea agama, jaitoe: bangsa Bali beragama Islam dan bangsa Bali beragama Hindoe."

19. There is a further twist to the already complicated relationships between *adat* and *agama* in Bali: in the Balinese language of today, *agama* means at once "religion," "law," and "customs and traditions" (Warna et al. 1990:7). Moreover, *agama* is a generic term referring to a collection of law texts of Hindu-Javanese origin whose contents are markedly different from the Balinese *adat*. Hence the confusion created by the Dutch decision to have these texts translated into Balinese and Malay (by I Goesti Poetoe Djlantik in 1918) for use as the basis of a Balinese code of "customary law" by members of the Raad van Kerta (Judicial Councils for Native Law) that had been established in each of the former kingdoms.

20. "The name Balinese Hindu signifies strengthening the Hindu religion as it already exists and is practiced by the Balinese people" ("nama Hindoe Bali jaitoe jang bererti menegoehkan Agama Hindoe jang soedah ada dan dipeloek olih wong Bali") (*Bali Adnjana* 17[1926]:2).

21. In *Bali Adnjana,* one commonly finds both names—Agama Hindu Bali as well as Agama Bali Hindu—the latter appearing to have been the most common appellation during the colonial period. In any case both F. L. Bakker (1993:40–41) and Geoffrey Robinson (1995:34, n. 52), basing their conclusions on Korn (1932:46–47), are mistaken in assuming that the commoners rejected the term "Hindu Bali" because it placed too much emphasis on the Hindu components of Balinese religion and, therefore, also on caste hierarchy.

22. For example: "Surya Kanta, which intends to develop a pure Hindu religion just like the Hindu religion that is practiced in India" ("Surya Kanta, jang bermaksoed mengembangkan Agama Hindoe jang moerni, katanja sebagai Agama Hindoe jang dilakoekan di Hindoestan" (*Bali Adnjana* 20[1926]:4).

23. *Bhawanagara* was published monthly from June 1931 to May 1935. The title of the journal meant "the true situation of the country"—that is, the Residency of Bali and Lombok. In the editorial of its preliminary issue, one could read that even though the journal was published by order of the Dutch Resident, it was not the government's mouthpiece (*Bhawanagara* 1930:5).

24. "Saja pernah bertamasja satoe boelan lamanja di Bali. Didalam waktoe itoe saja terasing dari doenia beradab."

25. *Djatajoe* was published in Singaraja from August 1936 to August 1941 under the leadership of I Goesti Njoman Pandji Tisna, son of I Goesti Poetoe Djlantik, ruler of Buleleng, who had presided over the short-lived organization Soeita Gama Tirta some twenty years earlier. Among the editorial staff one finds the names of former members of *Surya Kanta, Bali Adnjana,* and *Bhawanagara,* such as Tjakra Tanaja among others.

26. "'Want de Balineezen zijn een kunstzinnig volk; ze zijn geboren architect *(sic),* beeldhouwers, tooneelspelers, dansers, muzikanten. . . .' Begitoelah

pendapatan orang asing. Kita bangsa Bali, soeatoe bangsa jang mentjintai seni, berhaklah kita membesarkan hati tentang sifat kebangsaan kita sebagai terseboet diatas."

27. At the 1938 Congress of Bali Darma Laksana, the Balinese intellectual I Goesti Bagoes Soegriwa was criticized for delivering his lecture in Balinese instead of Malay-Indonesian.

28. "Agama kita ini bersendi dari adat dan ditjampoeri oleh bermatjam-matjam sari dari agama Hindoe, jang soedah tentoe tiada bisa dibandingkan kepada salah satoe agama di Hindoe, jang mana pada pemandangan Toean-toean bangsa asing adalah kita tak beragama dan tiada menjembah Toehan (Widi), melainkan kita adalah disamakan sebagai orang gila jaitoe menjembah segala jang ketemoe." This image of the Balinese as heathens who "pray to whatever they first meet in the morning" has a long history, dating back to the first Dutch expedition to the East Indies in 1597 (Boon 1977:12).

29. Thus one commonly encounters in these journals the following names for the Balinese religion: Agama Bali, Agama Tirta, Agama Siwa, Agama Siwa Tirta, Agama Budha, Agama Siwa-Budha, Agama Trimurti, Agama Hindu Bali, Agama Bali Hindu, Agama Hindu. As for the name of its god, it would be difficult to provide an exhaustive list: Bhatara Siwa, Sanghyang Tunggal, Sanghyang Suksma, Sanghyang Widi, Sanghyang Widi Wasa, Sanghyang Widi Wisesa, Sanghyang Parama Wisesa, Tuhan, Tuhan Esa, Allah, and so forth.

30. The following quotation from *Djatajoe* (5[1937]:131) illustrates this point: "Before the boys and girls of Bali started going to school, before there were any newspapers on the island, the Balinese were already practicing this religion, and there was no one who criticized and blamed them; what we heard were only comments like 'the custom in this village is like this, whereas in that village it is like that,' or else 'the people in this area cremate their dead in this way.' . . . Furthermore, one did not speak of religious ceremonies, but rather of village customs. Thus, in short, a proper religion was something unknown; what we knew about were only village customs and Balinese religion, and one did not hear of people who felt ashamed or angry because they had been criticized by Mister . . . so and so" ("Sebeloem poetra-poetra dan poetri-poetri Bali ada jang bersekolah, dan di Bali beloemlah pernah berdiri soerat-soerat chabar, maka keadaan di Bali soedahlah memeloek agama ini, jang mana berdjalan teroes, tiadalah ada mentjela dan menjalahkan, jang mana kita dengar tjoema ada pembitjaraan 'adat desa anoe begini dan desa anoe begitoe,' begitoe poela 'orang dibagian anoe djalan ngabennja begini.' . . . Lantas ini tiada diseboet oepatjara agama, melainkan diseboet adat desa. Djadi ringkasnja agama jang sebenarnja tiada diketahoei; jang diketahoei perbedaannja tjoema adat desa dan agama jang diketahoei tjoema agama Bali, dan tiada pernah kedengaran maloe atau marah ditjela oleh Toean . . . anoe").

31. "Haroes ditimbang oleh para Pandita-Pandita dan orang-orang jang achli mana agama jang haroes dipakai, tjampoeran mana jang haroes diboeang, dan adat mana jang masih boleh dipakai dan mana jang menjebabkan kemoendoeran haroes diboeang."

Chapter 2

Making Local History in New Order Bali: Public Culture and the Politics of the Past

Margaret J. Wiener

In a commonly cited passage, Walter Benjamin presents history as an important site of political struggle:

> To articulate the past historically . . . means to seize hold of a memory as it flashes up at a moment of danger. Historical materialism wishes to retain that image of the past which unexpectedly appears to man singled out by history at a moment of danger. The danger affects both the content of the tradition and its receivers. The same threat hangs over both: that of becoming a tool of the ruling classes. In every era the attempt must be made anew to wrest tradition away from a conformism that is about to overpower it. [1969:255]

It is precisely the way that history may become a "tool of the ruling classes" that is suggested by references to Bali's colonial conquest in New Order public culture. The New Order is the self-designation of the regime that governed Indonesia under President Suharto from 1966 to 1998.[1] By "public culture" I mean the complex cosmopolitan forms of intentional cultural production at the intersection of globalization and state formation in post–World War II nation-states.[2] As Appadurai and Breckenridge (1988:6) have noted, public culture involves, among other things, elite and metropolitan efforts to appropriate and transvalue local traditions and significations. In such forms of public culture, claims about identities and declarations of values are

51

both made and contested. Not uncommonly, these entail assertions about the past.

Allusions to colonial conquest appear in a wide variety of forms of public culture in contemporary Bali—ranging from mass media to memorials, from speeches to street signs. Consider the following description of Denpasar, Bali's provincial capital, from a guidebook for tourists:

> In the centre of town is a large open square called *Puputan Square* after the suicidal battle between the *rajas* of Badung and the Dutch militia in 1906. On one side stands the Museum Bali and the Pura Jagatnatha, a state temple. Across the square is the national military complex. On the third side are the Governor's offices. [Black and Hanna 1973:125]

On and around Puputan Square various sites pertinent to the production of late-twentieth-century Balinese identities are conjoined. The museum, the temple, the square itself—the theme of which is reiterated by another structure located there, not mentioned by the guidebook, the Puputan Badung Statue—represent fundamental aspects of a state-sanctioned Balinese ethnicity. All three were built by state agencies, and all are sites not only for assertions about Balinese tradition but for the rehearsal of new allegiances of citizenship. Objectifying certain visions of Balinese religion, culture, and history, each represents a different strand of the multiple political relations and historical processes that have gone into shaping contemporary Bali.

Before elaborating on the vision of history produced at Puputan Square, let me briefly comment on the sites of cultural production that surround it. As a repository of "tradition," the Museum Bali associates forms of material culture—from prehistoric statuary to palace architecture to contemporary arts and artifacts—with a Balinese identity presumed stable over time and space. Instituted by colonial officials to preserve Balinese sculptural and performing arts, the museum was incorporated into a centrally administered national museum system under Indonesia's New Order government (Solyom 1995). But the museum is figuratively as well as literally a product of colonialism: an instance of a colonizing exhibitionary order that turned practices into spectacles (Mitchell 1988). The temple exemplifies what officially has come to be considered Balinese religion. Commonly used for government ceremonies, its single, centrally placed shrine embodies the totalizing and universalizing disposition characteristic of Parisada Hindu Dharma Indonesia, a state-sponsored Hindu organization responsible for articulating a new religious orthodoxy (Wiener n.d.). All that is missing to fully denote late-twentieth-century "Bali" is the Art Center (Werdi Budaya), where the annual arts festival showcases the glitzy production values that international audiences have come to associate with Balinese music and dance through the Balinese artists sent overseas as cultural ambassadors.

Note that each of these strands of a Balinese ethnic identity is itself hybridized and interpenetrated by state power—the outcome of complex negotiations and contestations rather than an expression of some "authentic" or primordial local voice. When the guidebook description was written, relations between key elements of contemporary Balinese culture and the state were in fact visually coded in Denpasar's urban landscape. Since that time the governor's office—the provincial arm of the state (and a mediating point between Jakarta and Balinese elites)— has moved just south of the city to Renon. But the huge military complex—headquarters for all of Eastern Indonesia—remains a constant reminder of the state's potential for coercive violence. While less fully evident in space than it once was, the juxtaposition of culture and state power is no less consequential. That the description of Puputan Square comes from a guidebook for tourists is even one sign of their relation, just as tourism which has itself reshaped Balinese cultural forms is a cornerstone of an agenda for economic development promoted by the state in alliance with international capitalism.[3]

Contemporary Balinese cultural institutions, in short, are saturated by colonialism and state projects. My main concern in this chapter, however, is not with the museum, the temple, or the military. Rather, it is with the conjunctions of culture and power responsible for naming the square after a particular historical event called *puputan*—and the use of that space for assemblies of civil servants and soldiers as well as for historical commemorations. Puputan Square—and the Puputan Badung Statue—are only two of many allusions to *puputan* in contemporary Bali. What politics of memory and culture is responsible for such allusions?

The idea that there could be a politics of memory returns us to Walter Benjamin and the possibility he holds out for oppositional, even redemptive, uses of the past. That possibility rests on certain insights regarding history. First, the past plays a role (positive or negative) in formulating and realizing visions of the future. Second, in whatever form the past may take—practices understood as traditional, memories of events and experiences, records and registers—it is always actively interpreted and presented in ways that reflect (and implicitly promote) specific values, desires, perceptions, and assumptions. Third, not all interpretations of the past receive equal hearing. While some are widely disseminated, others remain private or become marginal. On the whole, those views of the past that reinforce the status quo—and thus the interests of those in power—are more likely to be heard than those that do not.

This is where the politics of memory comes in. When Benjamin urges that the past be wrested from the control of the ruling classes—that memory may be a resource in moments of crisis—he leaves unsettled the problem of how memories become available to be seized upon in the first place. That is to say, memory itself is not entirely outside the reach of domination. It is those interpretations of the past produced and circulated by authoritative institutions, including schools and the media, those images that become collectively shared, that the Popular Memory Group refers to as "dominant memory" (Popular Memory Group 1982:207–208). Even our most intimate or oppositional memories must contend with dominant memory.

To find new inspiration in the past, to wrest tradition from the ruling classes as Benjamin advocates, it may, therefore, be useful to begin by asking to what extent prevailing accounts of events and customs are effects of power.[4] How is what is included or elided in representations of the past shaped by politics and history? Under what conditions are familiar images formed? How do certain narratives about the past become privileged? What alternative pasts are silenced, lost, or marginalized by dominant memory (including memories of subaltern acts of resistance to power)?

Bali's conquest has been narrativized in different ways by many agents. To trace all the myriad meanings that *puputan* has been made to bear—in newspapers, books, rumors, poems, monuments, paintings, and performances produced by Euro-Americans, by Balinese, and by other Indonesians—would be impossible. Elsewhere I have recorded popular stories about *puputan* in one region of Bali that are in the process of being marginalized (Wiener 1995a). Here I focus on allusions to *puputan* in the forming of dominant memory in New Order public culture. The production of *puputan* as a sign of Bali, however, began with the defeat of Bali's former ruling classes and the construction of discourses about that conquest within the colonial state. As colonialism was contested by a new indigenous bourgeoisie, *puputan* was elaborated through nationalist tropes and themes. Some contents and forms of colonial history remained dominant; others were reworked; still others vanished altogether. Thus in the first part of this study I trace the discursive formation of *puputan* through colonialism and nationalism. Later I turn to the late New Order period in order to explore the role of culture and history in state projects.

The Discursive Formation of *Puputan*

> Yesterday afternoon about 3 o'clock, the capital of Klungkung along with the *puri* [court] was taken, during which almost no resistance was offered. On the arrival of the troops near the *puri*, the Dewa Agung held a little *puputan,* during which he himself, his brother Duma Rabawa [*sic*], the cokorda of Gel-Gel and some other of the most important lords of the realm perished. [Telegram from the Resident of Bali and Lombok to the governor-general announcing the fall of Klungkung, 29 April 1908; quoted in *Java Bode,* 29 April 1908.]

Colonializing History

That *puputan* has become a key theme of Balinese history is in many ways unsurprising. Bali's colonial conquest marked a rupture in the social reproduction of material and discursive practices centered on the hegemony of an aristocratic ruling class. The effect of this rupture on "structures of feeling" (to use Raymond Williams' useful phrase) is evident in the fact that for at least sixty years Balinese have referred to the period before the Dutch conquest as "when the world was steady" ("dugas enteg gumine").[5] The colonial state was concerned by two clusters of incidents—the first occurring in Badung in 1906 and the second in Klungkung in 1908—referred to in reports as *puputan.* That colonial officials used a Balinese term, a nominalization of the root *puput,* "finished," shows that they regarded the actions of Balinese in those places as instances of a generalizable cultural practice. In so labeling these events, colonial officials began a process of reification by turning particular instances of Balinese agency into a fixed cultural form.

Before 1906, *puputan* was only one way among others of describing certain Balinese combat practices. A Dutch history of warfare in the East Indies, for example, published over a decade before southern Bali's conquest, describes *puputan* as an attack by a special front-line squadron whose members dedicated themselves to death and wore white (Hooyer 1895).[6] An earlier history of a campaign against various Balinese rulers in 1849 refers to *puputan* as a "kind of amok" (Weitzel 1859:10), a martial tactic found throughout the archipelago (Reid 1988). Indeed, Balinese nearly deployed it against the Dutch in 1849:

a description of Klungkung plans for an averted "great Amok" (which "would have involved all of [the king's] followers, armed with lances and krisses, throwing themselves on the enemy and seeking death" [Arntzenius 1874:91]) sounds like the definition of *puputan* in Van der Tuuk's Balinese dictionary, published fifty years later: "People [*sic*] who offer themselves up in war for the king" (1897–1912:s.v.). The switch from a vocabulary of amok, which connoted violence and aggression, to that of *puputan* marked a shift in colonial perceptions. This shift produced, and was produced by, dramatic transformations of Balinese practices.

Since Dutch knowledge of terms such as *puputan* came through Balinese functionaries, interpreters, spies, administrators, and clerks, I must explain why I speak of *colonial* reifications, especially as Balinese interlocutors must have participated in the interpretation of the events that transpired in 1906 Badung. Whatever role Balinese agents played, however, in the decision to refer to what happened as *puputan,* it was the inscription of those events in colonial texts that established the dominant mode of inflecting them. In telegrams, dispatches, and reports to the governor-general (head of the colonial administration in the East Indies) and the Ministry of Colonies, and in colonial media and traveler's tales, *puputan* came to refer to a particular set of events. At present *puputan* designates those events for most Balinese. But even now *puputan* is not the only way to refer to them. In Klungkung, for example, people speak of the time when people finished ("dugas anak matelasan") or even of when the country fell apart ("dugas uug gumine").[7]

It was not, of course, just colonialism that reified practices. Nor is the event *not* reified for those who speak of "when people finished," since this phrase too is understood as referring to early-twentieth-century confrontations with the Dutch. But labeling what happened in 1906 Badung and 1908 Klungkung as *puputan* is an example of how colonial power relations refigured practices even for local agents. And the categories so created shape the way these practices continue to be discussed, including their absorption as part of a story about Bali rather than solely about certain polities.

Not all colonial narratives entered into local forms of history making, however, and some colonial tropes play no part in Balinese representations of the conquest. Colonial accounts portrayed these events not only as heroic but as tragic, for example, subsuming them under familiar categories of European aesthetic theory. And as in European dramaturgy, the heroes were all aristocrats: the tragedy is their absorption by futile and feudal pride. In the end such pride was all the more futile because it had little to do with the lives of ordinary people. These, in Dutch accounts, lived in harmony with the cycles of nature in village republics outside of history, their lives marred only by the oppression of despotic overlords. Indeed, given colonial ideologies of progress, the replacement of these despots by enlightened European rule was necessary, however unfortunate the violence of their end.

Such representations of the conquest established the framework for later influential Euro-American discourses about Bali produced in the 1930s, when Bali first began to take its place in European imaginations as an island paradise. Perhaps the decision of the colonial administration to reinstitute indirect rule in the conquered regions had something to do with why most of the accounts of Balinese arts and culture during this period refer to the *puputan*.[8] Beryl de Zoete and Walter Spies, authors of a famous book on Balinese performing arts, are typical. According to them the Dutch "occupation" was completed by 1906 *(sic)* "in a tragic episode known as poepoetan, 'the End.'" They note it made virtually no impression on the people of Bali, thanks to the "tact of intelligent officials" (1973:2).[9] By far the most extensive account of the *puputan*, however, was German author Vicki Baum's novel about the fall of Badung, first published in 1937 and translated into English as *A Tale from Bali*.[10] Still in print, it is widely available in Bali's tourist centers and remains the best-known version of the story among Euro-Americans.[11] Baum reiterated the story generally told in the 1930s: the demise of their rulers and the establishment of colonial administration are peripheral to the lives of the Balinese peasants she describes. Most popular and scholarly Euro-American literature continues to reproduce the categories and stereotypes constructed in a double sense—that is, in representations of Bali and in Balinese practices—by colonialism.[12] For Clifford Geertz (1980), for example, *puputan* exemplifies the politics of the theater-state: ritualized sound and fury, ultimately signifying nothing.[13]

Not only Europeans, of course, recalled these events. At least some Balinese found the massacre of the ruling classes in Badung and Klungkung of considerable concern.[14] About ten years after Klungkung's conquest, for example, a priest named Pedanda Ngurah composed the poem "Bhuwana Winasa" (A World Destroyed) recounting various disturbing events of the previous forty years, including the multiple wars with the Dutch. He writes of omens and amulets and describes the way nature itself seemed to mourn when Klungkung's rulers lay piled "in a mountain of corpses" surrounded by "a sea of blood." His poem ends anxiously: what other things might be yet to come in a "world destroyed"? Other stories circulated orally (at least in Klungkung), though the drama of *puputan* took second place to narratives that sought to make sense of the conquest more generally (Wiener 1995a).

Balinese narratives differed from Euro-American ones in significant ways. For one, they memorialized key participants by name and individuated them by action; but at the same time they did not develop coherent characters, explore motivations, or take a single point of view. Pedanda Ngurah's text, for instance, shifts among numerous persons and situations. For another, the inevitability evoked in Balinese accounts has nothing to do with narratives of progress. Nor is there any sense of tragedy in the European sense, though Pedanda Ngurah chose poetic meters designed to evoke sadness in readers at the appropriate moments. Finally, Balinese narratives offered a broader perspective on these events. Appearing in texts entitled *Uug* or *Rusak* (both translatable by English terms such as "broken," "destroyed," or "shattered"), they belong to a genre concerned with the fall of kingdoms in general, not uniquely through colonial wars.

But during the colonial era Balinese representations of the *puputan* did not circulate in public forums. Orally transmitted or handwritten, rather than mechanically reproduced, they passed along networks of personal relationships. Adding to their invisibility, Dutch was the language of the nascent public sphere. As a topic potentially inspiring unrest, Balinese texts concerned with the conquest may have been subject to monitoring. This would explain why, almost immediately after its composition, Pedanda Ngurah's poem found its way into the possession of a colonial district officer who had a Balinese member of the colonial civil service translate it.[15]

Pedanda Ngurah's poem ends with the traumatic earthquake of 1917; perhaps this inspired him to write of the destruction of the world *(bhuwana)* rather than the end of a specific realm. Perhaps, too, he was inspired by news of peasant rebellions in Gianyar and Karangasem that occurred around the same time. Colonial archives—in contrast to colonial ideologies—suggest that it was not just Balinese aristocrats who found significance in the *puputan*. In 1916 in Karangasem and 1917 in Gianyar (both regions whose rulers had voluntarily accepted colonial rule), there were two incidents of peasant rebellion that, as they escalated, prompted certain villagers to engage in practices reminiscent of *puputan*. The first of these incidents began when villagers in Lodjeh, Karangasem, swore an oath in a temple not to pay taxes or perform corvée labor. The police sent by the Dutch district officer found them armed with krisses and spears and dressed in white. Two were shot dead before the rest laid down their weapons. In another incident a year later, men from Sukawati, Gianyar, refused to perform corvée labor for Gianyar's ruler and then refused to undergo the punishment to which they were sentenced. One of this group's ringleaders also dressed in white and led the group (armed only with the small knives used to inscribe palm-leaf manuscripts) against the authorities who tried to take them into custody. In the ensuing melee, several of the protesters (including the one in white) were shot.[16]

Potentially, this is the kind of history making to which Benjamin refers. Yet given the terms in which Balinese history was inscribed, subaltern defiance could play no part in public memory. Colonial understandings of the *puputan* in Badung and Klungkung as the acts of aristocrats and as final meant that such subaltern acts of insurgency could play no role in images of Bali—despite the presence of what came to be seen as key markers of *puputan* as a practice: people in white, ready to fight to the death; oaths in temples; krisses and spears. Nor were they memorialized in Balinese texts, for peasants had little place in conventional genres of Balinese writing except as (occasionally subversive) comic figures.

Nationalizing Memory

Around the same time that southern Bali (along with other realms throughout the archipelago) was being incorporated into the Netherlands Indies empire, colonial subjects elsewhere in that empire, especially Java and Sumatra, were forging new kinds of identities and organizations centered on religious, cultural, economic, and political activities. By the 1920s these movements had acquired a distinctly nationalist and anticolonial flavor. Thus as Bali was enmeshed in new political and cultural economies, narratives of its conquest began to be relevant to parties that belonged neither to European nor Balinese ruling classes but to an emerging class of Indonesian intellectuals.

Just how or when *puputan* came to the attention of such intellectuals is unclear. One such intellectual—the European-educated Javanese aristocrat who is the main character in Indonesian author Pramoedya Ananta Toer's fictional tetralogy (1990) about the early years of the nationalist "awakening"—reads about *puputan* in letters from a Dutch friend. Certainly those privileged to have had opportunities to attend

Dutch-language colonial schools (as many of the Indonesian national-ists did) could have learned about these events in colonial newspapers. According to Reid (1979), colonial pedagogy itself helped to shape na-tionalist consciousness and, ultimately, nationalist historiography as well.[17] What Dutch textbooks described as the triumphant victory of the colonial state against treacherous or capricious indigenous leaders all over the archipelago some Indonesian students read as testimony of heroic opposition to foreign domination.[18]

Turning colonial historiography on its head solved a problem pre-sented by the diversity of languages and cultures in the Netherlands Indies. Since each portion of the archipelago at some point had been incorporated into the colonial state, each might potentially have its own tales of anticolonial resistance. Through these tales, members of diverse groups could "relate [their] own unique experience of the past with the new nationalist identity" (Reid 1979:294). Nationalists de-ployed such narratives of heroism—as geographically dispersed as pos-sible—to motivate participation in the struggle against colonial rule. By the 1940s *puputan* was being used in precisely this fashion.[19] In his memoirs, nationalist leader Tan Malaka records that during the Japan-ese occupation he helped to stage historical plays in Jakarta with na-tionalist themes, including one on "puputan Bali" (Malaka 1991:180). Like all such plays, it was critical of imperialism. In Benjamin's terms, it aimed to inspire courage in people "singled out by history in a mo-ment of danger." That danger intensified from 1946 to 1949 as na-tionalists fought for independence from Dutch rule and the creation of a unified Indonesian republic. Among those possibly inspired in this ef-fort by narratives about earlier resistance to colonial rule was a Balinese freedom fighter named Gusti Ngurah Rai, killed by a Dutch patrol to-gether with ninety followers at Marga in 1946.[20]

Gusti Ngurah Rai's death became the most famous occasion of Ba-linese participation in the war for independence.[21] More critical for the formation of local history, however, this incident is commonly referred to as a *puputan*.[22] People say that memories of 1906 and 1908 inspired Gusti Ngurah Rai's decision to die with his followers rather than sur-render to the Dutch. Whether or not he intentionally modeled his ac-tions on those of the rulers of Badung and Klungkung—did a memory flash up at the decisive moment?—his acts were assimilated to the cat-egory. This in turn affected what *puputan* could mean when the na-tionalists triumphed and Bali was incorporated into the new Republic of Indonesia. For the victors established a category of "national hero" *(pahlawan)* to honor those who had participated in the struggle, and among those receiving such accreditation was Gusti Ngurah Rai.

In the early years of the new nation, *puputan* increasingly became associated for Balinese with patriotism and opposition to colonialism. A good illustration of this is a booklet published in 1958 by I Wayan Simpen that narrates Badung's past in a nationalist idiom. Not a member of the traditional Balinese ruling class, his authority to narrate the past stemmed from his experiences as a freedom fighter and school-teacher, both highly valued in postindependence Bali. Writing in Indonesian, he titled his pamphlet "History of the War of the Kingdom of Badung Against the Dutch Colonizers from 1820 to 1908" ("Sedjarah Perang Keradjaan Badung menentang kaum pendjadjah Belanda sedjak tahun 1820 sampai tahun 1908"). On the cover Simpen declares his intention to introduce readers to those "heroes" or "patriots" *(pahlawan)* who sacrificed themselves body and soul to defend the motherland *(tanah air)*—phrases that recur throughout the text. Although they provide useful pointers to important events, he suggests that accounts of colonial wars in traditional literary genres (including Pedanda Ngurah's?) are unreliable, given the colonial context of their production, since their authors could not write truthfully. His own narrative returns constantly to themes such as Dutch guile, greed, and lack of human feeling and the mutual love between Badung's rulers and their subjects. At the same time, his mixed rhetoric of royalty and revolution suggests some of the reworkings and displacements necessary to begin to think about Bali's past in a new framework: in a single breath, characters declare their love of the fatherland and their determination to demonstrate their distinction as Satria warrior-kings. In some ways, I Wayan Simpen's text resembles histories being produced elsewhere in the new nation at this time. Composed mainly by scholar-citizens like Simpen, these focused primarily on identifying national heroes, protesting foreign domination, and projecting nationalist ideologies back into the distant past. Something new, however, was in the air: collaborative histories produced under the aegis of the nation-state. Planning for an official "National History" *(Sejarah Nasional)* began in 1957. It did not, however, appear until 1974, by which time new institutions and discourses had shaped the making of history in Indonesia.

Clearly *puputan* emerged from the struggle for national sovereignty as an important trope in a resituated Bali. As nationalist historiography increasingly identified all opposition to Dutch rule with the revolution, *puputan* enabled Balinese to claim a place in the making of Indonesia. Note, however, that the legacy of colonial historiography limited the potential of "Unity in Diversity" (the Indonesian national motto). While Balinese came to read the white clothing worn during *puputan* as a sign of Balinese ethnicity, for example, a similar semiotics of resistance occurred elsewhere in the archipelago: the Minangkabau of Sumatra wore white clothing in confrontations with the Dutch, as well, and colonial officials found large groups of white-clad Javanese alarming.

Note too that nationalist history making did not recuperate the incidents such as the ones in Karangasem and Gianyar. As I Wayan Simpen's booklet indicates, some striking continuities with older forms of Balinese historiography remained. For despite repeated references to the "people" *(rakyat)*, his history is still largely articulated through the characters of individual aristocrats. It is also (or therefore) framed as the history of a kingdom.

Producing History as Culture in the New Order

> We should see historical research and writing in a broad context—that is, in the framework of the construction of culture, including as well a spirit of national union and unity. [Proyek Inventarisasi dan Dokumentasi Sejarah Nasional 1985:iii]

New Order Culture

If *puputan* was formed as an object of memory through colonial rule and its overthrow, under the New Order it was incorporated within wider national and transnational fields of cultural production. History is just one domain in which the New Order attempted to articulate a particular vision of Indonesia as a modern state in a global arena and as a national unity also composed of commensurate and domesticated diversities. The New Order was the product of a sometimes uneasy alliance between transnational and local (often ethnically Chinese) capitalists, the armed forces, bureaucrats, and Javanese elites (Robison 1990). Michael van Langenberg has described its ideological focus as "stability *(stabilitas),* development *(pembangunan),* and modernization *(modernisasi).* It locates the state's legitimacy in a historical process: the state as having rescued the nation from past disorders and as having placed it on the path to future prosperity" (1986:17).

These "past disorders" are attributed to Sukarno, the nationalist leader who became Indonesia's first president (1950 to 1966). According to New Order commentators, Sukarno's tolerance of multiple political parties led to economic collapse, constant conflict, and finally political and social chaos culminating in the murder of six generals (blamed on an attempted communist coup) and the subsequent "spontaneous" massacres of suspected communists in Java and Bali.[23] Indeed these events provide the founding myth through which the New Order ruling class legitimated its authority. Many New Order policies contrasted explicitly with those of Sukarno. Where Sukarno opposed incursions of foreign capital and compliance with U.S. geopolitics as forms of neocolonialism, his successor Suharto welcomed them in the name of development and modernization, concepts devised and promoted by U.S. social scientists and policymakers.[24] Where aristocrats were characterized in the Sukarno years as exploitative landowners with "feudal" mentalities (McVey 1979:345), the New Order recuperated their cultural authority (Pemberton 1994a). And where a discursive emphasis on progress began to mark out a realm of tradition to be left behind as old-fashioned (McVey 1979), certain kinds of heritage became a major element of New Order nation building.

The New Order's interest in culture reminded some of the late colonial state (Pemberton 1994a; Tsing 1993). At the turn of the twentieth century, the Dutch justified colonial rule by an Ethical Policy involving programs of public welfare and education. But when these were blamed for the growth of nationalist and labor movements, new policies in the late 1920s sought to ensure peace and order by encouraging adherence to tradition—interpreted through colonial readings of custom and religion. Faced with a parallel situation (indeed in some ways Sukarno's critique of "feudalism" resurrected elements of the Ethical Policy), the New Order resorted to a similar solution. As Tsing observes: "'Culture' is endorsed as an alternative to 'politics', as *order* is to *disorder*" (1993:24).

But as the centrality of modernization and development indicates, New Order programs combined elements of both colonial policies. The trick is to perform the transformative work of development—much of which is aimed at everyday practices—without disturbing the peace or losing those elements of "Eastern" culture (as constructed in the colonial era) that authorities regard as essential to national welfare. For as the political and economic turmoil of the late 1990s has shown, there are risks in the transnational alliances to which the New Order committed itself. For one, the West is associated with a dangerous and disorderly individualism. If the goal is to become modern, many authorities want this to take a distinctly *Indonesian* form, which means there is considerable effort to develop a national culture. One consequence is the need to clarify the relationship between the emerging national culture and local practices. Another is state attempts to make culture and development compatible: according to New Order rhetoric, it was not just economies but cultures that must be developed.[25]

On the one hand, therefore, the goal was to produce a common subjectivity across the archipelago—to create undifferentiated Indonesian citizens through state projects aimed at the "development" of nearly every aspect of life from diet to family relations.[26] On the other hand, images and discourses of cultural difference abound. The significance of these differences is perhaps best clarified by considering New Order efforts to develop a national culture that could rework tradition to elaborate a shared heritage. Probably the most notorious of these is the controversial "Beautiful Indonesia in Miniature Park" (Taman Mini). A pet project of the late Mrs. Suharto, the park portrays the nation in all its diversity via miniaturized replicas of its islands, ancient monuments, and religious buildings, with twenty-six houses representing the traditional architecture of each Indonesian province (Pemberton 1994a:152).[27] The national motto, "Unity in Diversity," is tellingly interpreted in an exhibit in the park's Indonesia Museum: a diorama of a Javanese aristocratic wedding, attended, as a guidebook notes, "by guests wearing traditional costumes from almost all areas of Indonesia" (Pemberton 1994a:167–168). As guests at a national ritual (marked as Javanese), Indonesians are distinguished largely by their mode of dress.

Or consider cinema, a culture industry owned by members of the ruling class and controlled through state censorship (Sen 1994). Characters in Indonesian films are almost invariably urban and always speak Indonesian rather than the regional languages commonly used for everyday interactions. Ethnicity figures into plots as style and custom rather than as the potentially conflicting subjectivities and experiences produced by particular practices. Invariably custom itself resolves into ritual: films are almost ethnographic in their representations of weddings, funerals, harvest ceremonies, and so forth (Heider 1991:59).

As these examples suggest, Indonesia's identical citizens can wear difference in the form of easily exhibited or performed folk cultures. State projects equate ethnic differences with culture *(kebudayaan)* and tradition *(adat* or *tradisi)*. But these in turn are understood as styles:

of art, dress, dance, music, ritual.[28] On the surface difference is promoted; but the emphasis is placed on local (and marketable) color. As Greg Acciaioli has noted, the New Order regime "has not sought to eradicate diversity, but to emasculate it. Regional diversity is valued, honored, even apotheosized, but only as long as it remains at the level of display" (Acciaioli 1985:161). "Most groups," he adds, "may dance their way to the national goals, each with its own ethnic steps, as long as the underlying ideology, the tune to which the dance is called, is what the state has ratified" (p. 162). In short, the New Order promoted local tradition and culture but only of a certain sort and in certain ways. State-funded cultural displays transform practices into ethnic markers. In turn ethnically marked citizens should be performers of culture, not political agents.

But it would be wrong to see the production of culture only from a Jakartan perspective. It has at least two other sources. First, state projects may be locally contested in the name of culture and tradition. (See, for example, Warren 1993.) Second, national projects of development and nation building are intimately linked to transnational flows of culture and capital. Consider the creation of ethnicity that arises from the objectification of local practices and traditions for the tourist industry (as in Volkman 1987) and indeed is its necessary condition—tourism provides a hefty amount of the foreign exchange needed to fund state modernization programs. Moreover, as David Harvey notes (1990), the production and marketing of heritage is itself a global phenomenon. In fact he suggests it may be a reaction to the constant change generated by capitalism, though late-twentieth-century modes of flexible accumulation can accommodate and even encourage cultural diversity.[29]

History in the New Order

As an important part of the making of national culture, history is a focus of state attention under the aegis of the Department of Education and Culture.[30] The centerpiece of such concern is the official National History, first published in 1974, which is regularly revised and updated. Funded by the government and subject to government directive, the national history serves as the basis for the history taught in schools and indeed is a major part of the curriculum. The Department of Education and Culture also sponsors several ancillary documentary projects, such as the Inventory and Documentation of National History Project and the National Heroes Biography Project. Moreover, the department convenes a National Seminar on History for scholars and officials at five-year intervals on themes such as "contributions of historical research and writing to development" and "using both national and local historical research and writing, we build enthusiasm [*semangat*] for national unity and union."

The public rarely—if ever—sees the results of these activities. More relevant to the kind of history that concerns me are projects targeted at educating citizens. The most important of these, of course, involve the writing of school textbooks. But as elsewhere in the world of nation-states, civic education goes beyond the classroom and is carried out through such media as museums, films on historical themes (Sen 1994:79–107), and commemorative events either attended in person or broadcast through television, radio, and newspapers. Such activities highlight the New Order's master narrative of nation formation. Apart from the event that is the most obvious object of commemoration—the anniversary of the declaration of Indonesian independence—the state celebrates 30 September Movement Day and Power of Pancasila Day (both referring to the events of 1965), Armed Forces Day, even an Integration of East Timor Day. Beginning in the 1970s, the state began to encourage and fund similar projects centering on local and provincial histories. In 1981, the National Seminar on History even devoted an entire panel to the subject (Seminar Sejarah 1982–1983). Everywhere in the archipelago new national heroes were uncovered and celebrations of instances of opposition to colonial domination were instituted. The testimony of anthropologists in Indonesia in that period indicates that these activities frequently provoked controversies and debate.[31]

In Bali, not surprisingly, such history has largely centered on representations of *puputan*. These began in 1973 when the regional government of Badung inaugurated an annual commemoration of Puputan Badung at Puputan Square. Klungkung initiated a Puputan Klungkung Day eleven years later. Similar celebrations occur on the anniversary of Puputan Margarana. New Order representations of *puputan* reproduced some familiar tropes while introducing new ones. On the one hand, *puputan* continued to be construed as instances of anticolonial resistance reflecting the enduring (legitimizing) importance of the revolution in the construction of a national identity. But official discourses also aligned *puputan* simultaneously with claims about ethnic/provincial identities and with state ideologies and nation building.

A speech I heard during commemorations of Puputan Klungkung

in the mid-1980s, for example, unproblematically projected a collective Balinese identity back to the precolonial era. Puputan Badung was declared "Bali's answer to Dutch intervention," and the speaker proclaimed that "Balinese hatred of colonialism was first demonstrated in 1846, when Klungkung . . . sent military aid to Buleleng." Another speech anchored *puputan* to the state's primary projects: development and the production of a unifying national culture: "Bali opposed the Dutch to protect the motherland *(tanah air)*, the nation, and the state. . . . Now we seek to strengthen the people and make the country one through development. . . . This is the era of development, which should be worked for both individually and cooperatively." Speeches also invoked *puputan* as inspiring examples of values and attitudes—indeed, new structures of feeling—crucial to nation building, especially self-sacrifice in the service of national goals and *semangat,* "energy" or "enthusiasm": "We need the spirit *(jiwa)* and energy *(semangat)* of the *puputan* to develop the nation and the state *(bangsa* and *negara)*. *Puputan* shows how to fight with valor, and oppose those who would take away freedom in Indonesia in the years to come." In short, while such statements assert and construct ethnic and (as we shall see) even local identities, they enlist them in state projects. Even the fact that such speeches are always in Indonesian reinforces the sense that local histories are instances of national processes; as in other forms of culture, differences are muted in favor of similarities.

Before analyzing the multiple sites and media through which *puputan* is dispersed to Balinese publics—and the ambivalences and multiple readings these may embody and engender—I want to draw attention to a particularly productive rhetorical trope: the slogan *semangat puputan,* "the spirit of *puputan.*" Officials invoke *semangat puputan* to admonish Balinese about the proper way to respond to government-sponsored projects on occasions both controversial and inconsequential. In 1995, for example, Bali's governor instructed members of a Balinese sports team leaving for a competition to let themselves be "inflamed by the spirit of *puputan.*"[32] More contentious was the suggestion of Indonesia's (ethnically Balinese) minister of mining and energy that the people of Bali respond to an unpopular, Jakarta-backed plan to erect the largest monument in the world in southern Bali "in the spirit of *puputan*" (Warren 1995:386)—a remarkably ambiguous recommendation.

Variously translatable as "energy," "enthusiasm," and "spirit," *semangat* has become one of the New Order's favorite words. No doubt in such usages officials aim to incite passionate determination—to elicit what Durkheim called "collective effervescence" in carrying out civic duty. As an anthropologist I find the conjuring of *semangat* suggestive, however, for *semangat* figured centrally in the colonial anthropology of Malay magic as a nonvisible agency of concern to sorcerers and healers.[33] *Semangat,* claimed the anthropologists, is none other than life force. (Skeat 1965 translated it as "soul.") Healers restore well-being by summoning lost or wandering *semangat;* in a more sinister vein, by stealing a person's *semangat* a sorcerer could gain power over him (Skeat 1965:568–570). In evoking *semangat puputan* are officials recalling the spirit of the past to build the body politic? Or are the constant invocations of s*emangat puputan* in the speeches of government officials efforts to appropriate and control that spirit—a kind of state sorcery?

It would be misleading to imply that a monolithic and unified intention informs these activities. Not only are there inconsistencies in state images of both development and national culture, but the state does not prescribe the forms that public history might take. However much state rhetorics and projects shape public representations of Bali's past, the agents responsible for orchestrating them are Balinese, not bureaucrats in offices in Jakarta. Thus all of the speeches quoted here were made by Balinese administrators at events planned by committees appointed by regional governments.

New Order images of *puputan* were the outcome of dialogues and alliances among state officials and civil servants, artists, and intellectuals (including schoolteachers, university professors, journalists)—roles that often overlap. For example, Indonesia's most prestigious universities are public institutions; thus academic historians are commonly also civil servants and easy to recruit for public history projects. Such projects also drew on the labor of those with a personal interest in *puputan:* Gusti Rai Mirsha, for instance, a historian who worked at Bali's major university and helped to plan Badung's early *puputan* activities, is also a member of Badung's extensive royal clan.

Those involved in *puputan* activities definitely have traits in common: they tend, for instance, to be educated men who live in urban centers. But they also have divergent and changing allegiances— among other things (and to speak territorially) to region, province, and nation. Many would represent themselves as "Balinese" in some contexts, as "Indonesian" in others, and as variously privileged or disenfranchised. While differences in points of view are negotiated through the committee format, conflicting agendas may account for some of the tensions and disarticulations of public representations of *puputan* that will be elaborated in the pages that follow.

Commemorations as National Rites

Annual commemorations are both the most local and the most global forms of making public history: most global because such activities are common and appear to be especially typical of nations born of revolution (Gillis 1994:8); most local because they are bound in space and attended by limited audiences. Thus while *puputan* is discursively about Balinese history, commemorations are held in the capitals of the regions where they took place, not (as with national holidays) at multiple sites. Their audiences, moreover, consist largely of schoolchildren and civil servants—that is, those learning and modeling good citizenship—although other Balinese may be drawn into these commemorative spaces by public performances or through the awarding of prizes to winners of regional civic competitions such as youth groups, neighborhoods, and performing art groups. Sometimes public involvement is encouraged through competitions directly linked to the commemoration, such as best-designed floats.

However local and ephemeral they may appear (though news of them is broadcast in various media), commemorations were at the center of the New Order apparatus producing public history in contemporary Bali. They were, in fact, the hub around which official historiography turned. For it is in connection with annual celebrations that regional governments kick off other history projects: monuments, museums, television broadcasts, new works of art, and so on. And the speeches associated with these events set the tone for all official invocations of *puputan*.

As Robert Foster has suggested, Emile Durkheim's discussion of ritual may describe nationalist celebrations better than it does religious rites. One might see commemorations as calendrical rites by which states seek, through an alchemy of elicited "collective effervescence" (that famous *semangat puputan),* to form a community of citizens (Foster 1991:239, 243)—hence the totemic flags and the prominence of competitive activities that arouse strong emotional responses. Citizenship is embodied on such occasions in characteristic postures, gestures, and movements (Foster 1991:243) that are commonly, as in Indonesia, military: marches, salutes, eyes front, countenance stern.

Commemorations are sites where the sometimes uneasy tensions between national vision and local interests are also played out. Certainly

Figure 7. Children, dressed in white and armed with lances, participate in the Puputan Klungkung commemoration in 1986. Photo: Margaret Wiener.

they are strongly associated with the concerns of the nation-state. For example, public spaces where *puputan* are commemorated serve as sites of other state rituals as well. Indeed, Balinese commentators find all such occasions virtually indistinguishable. Certainly all involve the same repertoire of activities: marches and assemblies, public readings of sacred national texts such as the Proclamation of Independence, exhortations linking patriotism to state projects, and award ceremonies. Yet commemorations also show striking regional differences. Celebrations of Puputan Badung in Denpasar, the provincial capital, for instance, emphasize provincial marks of ethnic identity. These include the performance of "new creations" by Sekolah Tinggi Seni Indonesia (STSI), the Balinese branch of the College of Indonesian Arts in Denpasar, which commonly represents both Bali and Indonesia overseas. (See Hough 1992 and Chapter 8 in this volume.) By contrast, Klungkung commemorations muster up images resonant with local associations (Wiener 1995a and 1995b), marking the greater importance of the past in Klungkung's present. A whiff of rivalry marks these occasions as well—not surprising in a nation whose development plan involves continual competitions for "best village," "best customs," and so on, judged sequentially among districts, then regions, then provinces.

The Infrastructures of Public Memory

Speeches, parades, award ceremonies, even newspaper articles and performances, are ephemeral, themselves events.[34] History is memorialized in more enduring ways as well. Names for public spaces, such as streets and airports and historical monuments, literally insert history into the major thoroughfares of everyday life, especially in the urbanized areas of Denpasar and Semarapura, Klungkung's capital. Those traveling to or from Bali, for example, pass through Ngurah Rai International Airport. As a link to distant places, it is fitting that the airport is named for a national hero who by definition must transcend regional differences.[35] The name marks the site as simultaneously national (Ngurah Rai is a "national hero") and ethnic (he is *Bali*'s national hero). Moreover, an increasing number of spaces named *puputan* mark centers of civic and state activity: Denpasar's Puputan Square and Puputan Road in Semarapura, for example, both memorialize the actual locations in which these events transpired, but there is also Denpasar's Great Puputan Road running between Denpasar and the governor's offices in Renon. Such spaces connect official ceremony to the mundane rhythms of daily life.

It is monuments, however, that truly concretize dominant memory—solidifying significance in fixed points of reference and authoritatively tangible images. While monuments have been built at the sites of all three *puputan*, in the remainder of this section I wish to focus on Denpasar's Puputan Square and Semarapura's Puputan Monument.

The Puputan Statue, erected at Puputan Square in 1979, consists of three enormous bronze figures—a man, a woman, and a child—above a fountain. Armed and dressed in "traditional clothing," their hair loose and flowing, they are frozen in the act of advancing to attack an invisible enemy. Significantly, given that this is a memorial to a historical event, the three are types, rather than historical individuals; there is not even any way to tell if they are princes or peasants. Distinguished only by gender, age, and (as their dress shows) ethnicity, they constitute a virtual invitation to identification.

A brochure produced by the committee responsible for erecting the

Figure 8. Puputan Statue, Puputan Square, Badung. Photo: Linda Connor.

statue confirms that it is meant to be exemplary—to model a form of civic virtue. According to the brochure's author, the statue was commissioned from Javanese sculptor Edhi Sunarso "to honour and show respect for the Heroes of Liberty, including all of the heroes of Puputan Badung" (who even here remain anonymous). But the monument does not merely gesture respectfully toward the past. Its ultimate purpose, asserts the brochure, is to inspire future generations to "imitate their heroic spirit" and "defend liberty through truth and justice." These generations also must "struggle" (a term associated with the revolution)—no longer for national sovereignty but to create "a safe, just, and prosperous society" (Mirsha 1979:10).

This language of mimesis and struggle puts one in mind of Walter Benjamin. As I indicate later, such readings of *puputan* may be becoming increasingly relevant among a new generation of Balinese intellectuals. Until the late 1990s, however, for many Indonesians such phrases were too entangled in official rhetoric to be read as challenging New Order visions of how that society might look. For New Order ruling classes, "safe" implied an absence of political dissension and "prosperous" implied the promised effects of development. As for the statue, its latent populist militancy is perhaps eclipsed by its location on the square dominated by the provincial headquarters of the armed forces: given that context, martial motifs again seem congruent with the alignment of force that marked the New Order.

The choice of Sunarso as its sculptor points to articulations between the production of Balinese and national culture. Sunarso created most of the bronze statuary in Jakarta, including the famous "Welcome" statue before the Hotel Indonesia. He was also an old acquaintance of Ida Bagus Mantra, Bali's former governor and a significant figure in the creation of modern Balinese ethnic identity, having studied with Mantra in India in the 1950s (Mirsha 1979:14–15).

Klungkung's more recent Puputan Monument brings politics and culture together in quite a different fashion. A tall, black stone column, it towers above the horizon at the center of town, next to the offices of the Klungkung regional government and across from Semarapura's main tourist attraction, the remnants of Klungkung's old palace. A Klungkung civil servant told me that the shape was meant to represent "masculinity and courage";[36] a local commentator thought it resembled a dagger or kris. If Badung's Puputan Statue publicly promotes civic mimesis, in Klungkung the object of pedagogy appears to be a non-Balinese public. Inside the monument, in a space mainly traversed by international and domestic tourists, is a set of six more-or-less life-sized

Figure 9. Puputan Monument, Klungkung. Photo: Linda Connor.

bronze statues surrounded by sixteen dioramas set into the monument's interior wall (all designed by Nyoman Gunarsa, a Klungkung-born artist who lives and teaches in Java). Above each diorama is an explanatory text written in both Indonesian and English.

In contrast to Badung's Puputan Statue, in Klungkung two of the bronze figures represent historical personages (who in fact died during the *puputan*, although this is not indicated), both of them unabashedly aristocrats. Ida I Dewa Agung Jambe, Klungkung's ruler at the time of the conquest, sits on a chair in the middle of the group; his son, Ida I Dewa Agung Gede Agung, stands behind him, at his right shoulder. Both the appearance and the posture of these figures are modeled on a precolonial photograph, a copy of which hangs in Klungkung's museum across the way (dedicated at an annual commemoration; its "history room" is also devoted to the *puputan*). The remaining four figures (note that all six are male) are cultural types rather than actual persons.[37] Standing behind the king and his son are two figures whose placards identify them as "Elder Minister" (Patih Lingsir) and "Younger Minister" (Patih Anom), characters ubiquitous in Balinese performing arts. Two other figures seated in the foreground are identified as "lance troop" *(pasukan tombak oncer gada)* and "dagger troop" *(pasukan keris)*, after the weapons they bear. At the risk of overinterpretation, the four figures appear to be precolonial equivalents of key elements of state authority: the cabinet and the army. Rather than types with whom citizens might identify, they are representatives of state authority.

Like the statues, the dioramas highlight actual historical figures, structures of power, and masculinity. But they also present a peculiar chronological narrative about Balinese history. The first diorama is a quasi-ethnographic representation of the timeless "forms of life of Balinese society" (*suasana kehidupan masyarakat Bali*) depicting people preparing a ritual in a village marked architecturally as Balinese. Three scenes from ancient history follow that blend images from performance art with those familiar from New Order discourses about culture and progress.[38] All this is cultural background: history begins in Diorama 5 with the first Dutch military expedition against a Balinese kingdom in the 1840s. Five of the next nine dioramas also depict Balinese-Dutch military engagements up to and including the revolution (the battle at Marga against a painted backdrop of Sukarno reading the Proclamation of Independence).[39] In all but one of these battle scenes, all Balinese are male.[40] The final two dioramas are set in a present explicitly identified with the New Order. Indeed, in the last diorama President Suharto and his wife stand in a Balinese rice field, "cheered by the ripening rice symbolizing that the Indonesian people slowly have achieved increasingly happy lives in developing the Indonesian nation and state."

These dioramas inside the Puputan Monument reflect certain local concerns. There are, for instance, representations of three different engagements with the Dutch in Klungkung (by contrast, the diorama of Puputan Badung presents a scene prior to battle); in addition, there are visual and textual references to phenomena of primarily local significance.[41] Although these dioramas are Klungkung-centered, they identify Klungkung's history entirely with colonial wars. Nothing indicates,

Figure 10. Bronze statues of Klungkung aristocrats who died during the Puputan, accompanied by their "Elder Minister." Puputan Monument, Klungkung. Photo: Linda Connor.

for instance, that this was the kingdom in which Bali's "golden age" polity was centered. Klungkung's nationalist past, not its place in Balinese narratives and practices, is the focus. Absent, too, are other events that figure importantly in Balinese memories. There is not a word about the focal episode of traditional Balinese historiographies: Bali's fourteenth-century conquest by the Javanese empire Majapahit. Nor is

Figure 11. Puputan Klungkung diorama. Puputan Monument, Klungkung. Photo: Linda Connor.

Figure 12. Diorama depicting the dedication of the monument. Puputan Monument, Klungkung. Photo: Richard Grant.

there any reference to the New Order's rise to power. Perhaps most extraordinary of all is the diorama that comments—ironically?—on New Order memorializing practices. The caption notes: "In the present era of development *(pembangunan)* numerous monuments have also been built *(dibangun)* in various regions of Indonesia. One of them is the Puputan Klungkung Monument, dedicated by former Minister for Internal Affairs Rudini."[42] Facing the spectator in miniature is the exterior of the very space in which she stands, complete with a complement of properly reverent citizens.

Performing the Past

Unlike commemorations, which rarely engage public attention, and monuments, which are too everyday to be noticed, historical films on the subject of *puputan* attract large audiences—only appropriate considering that they belong to the sphere of pleasure and leisure. Various commentators, for example, told me how moving they found *Uproar in Semarapura (Gegernya Semarapura),* a film made for TV about Klungkung's politico-military clashes with the Dutch originally produced in 1992 and now broadcast annually on Puputan Klungkung Day.[43]

Although these films constitute popular culture, their production is initiated by government agencies and entail collaborations that involve them in translocal interests and politics. The Klungkung regency provided both economic and cultural resources (including information and locations) for *Uproar in Semarapura,* for example, which was cosponsored by TVRI-Denpasar, the provincial branch of the noncommercial government station. A more ambitious project—a seven-part miniseries about Gusti Ngurah Rai that began shooting in 1995—was cosponsored by the armed forces (the Regional Military Command or KODAM, headquartered on Puputan Square) and Indosiar, one of Indonesia's commercial television stations; the intended audience is Indonesian rather than Balinese.

Apart from their sponsors, the actors are not local either. The cast of *Uproar in Semarapura* came from STSI, an institution indicative of both "Bali" and the nation-state. (STSI performers are often sent abroad on cultural missions representing Indonesia.) For the Ngurah Rai film, movie stars from Jakarta were cast for the key roles. In an effort to show that Balinese interests were not being ignored, daily reports in the newspaper *Bali Post* on the film's progress highlighted matters of local concern ranging from the reactions of Gusti Ngurah Rai's widow to comments by the Jakarta stars about their efforts to master Balinese pronunciation and their reverence for the figures they were portraying. Readers were assured that every effort was being taken to make the film as authentic *(asli)* as possible through historical research and consultations with local experts on Balinese custom. The same concern with authenticity informs the earlier Klungkung film, which was shot on location and in period dress; indeed this was part of what Balinese commentators found appealing.

Like Klungkung's Puputan Monument, *Uproar in Semarapura* interweaves local and national themes. As in other recent official history production in the region, the film emphasizes that Klungkung had opposed the Dutch before the 1908 *puputan*—in a battle in 1849 which, unlike other colonial wars, did not end in a Balinese defeat. The broadcast identifies various historical agents by name,[44] moreover, and shows that members of Bali's ruling class disagreed over the best policy to take toward Dutch aggression, a matter of some controversy among their descendants.

At the same time, New Order ideologies saturate the film. Domestic scenes, for instance, embody New Order dogmas concerning gender roles and family life: the king's only wife is his adviser and helpmate, mother of his children, and model citizen.[45] More important, events are encapsulated within rhetorics of national identity through the all-inclusive Indonesian term *"bangsa,"* which means nation, race, people, class, and group. Thus conflicting points of view pose no real obstacle to a unified Balinese response to colonial aggression. (There never could be *serious* hostilities between Indonesians; see Sen 1994.) In turn the Dutch are presented as a naturally occurring human type: the colonizer *(bangsa penjajah)*.

History beyond the Centralizing State

Writing about New Order Indonesia, Goenawan Mohamad describes the effects of the formulation of national culture in the following terms:

> To those living as mere shadows of a civilization, the prevailing system of verbal communication becomes a means of control, one that defines one's role, position, perceptions, and behaviour. And one is supposed to

accept the world that it creates and one's subservient position in it. What I'm saying is that this verbal imperative can be a source of stress, a form of intimidation. [1993:122]

Public culture in Indonesia under the New Order was dominated by agents of the state whose intimidating and formulaic "verbal imperatives" urged citizens to accept the world that they hope to create. Clearly references to *puputan* in New Order Bali played a key part in efforts to establish the hegemony of values and responses that endorse current relations of power. Official representations harnessed *puputan* to state discourses of development and national unity. Through repetition, those committed to such goals attempted to naturalize their desirability. To what extent, however, did they succeed?

Certainly commemorative activities have had an impact on Balinese. There is plenty of evidence that they have proliferated an awareness of *puputan,* firmly establishing it in Balinese memories, and that the association of *puputan* with anticolonial nationalism constitutes the "dominant memory" of *puputan* for most contemporary Balinese. Apart from offhand commentaries and letters to the editor in newspapers that support this, *puputan* has made its way into Balinese expressive culture. A number of Balinese artists have painted *puputan* canvases. Performers of *topeng* (improvised dance-dramas based on historical incidents) have also taken up *puputan* as a theme: as early as 1980 a group of performers enacted (and recorded) a Topeng Puputan Badung—a theme then taken up by STSI, which occasionally performs its own interpretation at Bali's annual arts festival. Apparently there also has been a Topeng Puputan Margarana.[46] Moreover, forms of public history are shaping the way that Balinese present the past. A descendant of Badung's royal house who composed and self-published a long poem in Kawi about Puputan Badung, for example, coupled it with facing Indonesian translation and bracketed the poem with photographs and an excerpt of an interview with a *puputan* survivor (Konta 1977).

As these examples indicate, however, dominant memory has not succeeded in controlling the meaning of *puputan* or the uses to which it may be put. Many of the examples cited here mix national with local and personal significations. Moreover, as the example of Topeng Puputan Badung indicates, the relationship between official and nonofficial representations is not only one way. Then, too, the fact that bureaucrats may request assistance from ordinary citizens in executing a project may introduce ambiguous themes into the images presented to various publics. Consider, for example, the Puputan Klungkung painting commissioned from an artist named Mangku Mura by the head of the Klungkung government. Like most Balinese artists, Mangku Mura produces art for consumption within national and global arenas. His paintings—in the style now known in Bali as "classic," which is produced almost exclusively by Klungkung artists—are commonly exhibited internationally; at the same time, as a national "cultural asset," he is often called upon—as are STSI performers—to display his work in national and regional exhibitions and competitions. His *puputan* painting, which currently hangs in a conference room in the warren of Klungkung government offices, might be seen as subversive in a number of respects. Certainly he portrays several princes running away rather than participating in the *puputan*. From a late-twentieth-century nationalist perspective, this could only appear as treason; from the perspective of local elites, it highlights incidents that some would prefer to forget. Moreover, several subaltern figures, including his own great-grandfather, occupy the center of the canvas: not heroes but definitely in the thick of things. And finally, while the camouflage uniforms worn by his demonic Dutch soldiers are perhaps simply anachronisms, for most Balinese the immediate referent might be state security forces.

As Mangku Mura's painting suggests, Balinese do not fully adopt official interpretations of the past. Alternative discourses about the past find their way into public spaces as well—sometimes in elusive forms based on local knowledge and communicative practices. It is partly in the form of such knowledge and practices that I see indications of one place we might look to wrest *puputan* "away from a conformism that is about to overpower it." Marginalized memories, and the excavation of what has already been forgotten, form potential sites of resistance, subversion, or obliviousness to official claims about the past. So too do communicative styles such as allusion and allegory, which introduce other potential interpretations of apparently monologic assertions. Elsewhere, for example, I have shown that subterranean tales and themes seep into memorializations of Puputan Klungkung, though only those aware of local traditions might detect the traces they leave in public imagery and discourse.[47] I now wonder whether tales I was told about colonialism and royal power in Klungkung in the 1980s—shortly after the first official commemoration of Puputan Klungkung Day—might have been meant allegorically as oblique critiques of Jakarta hegemony and declarations of local autonomy.

Such interpretations are speculative and perhaps risky. Writing about a Javanese rhetoric of allusion called *semu*,[48] Goenawan Mohamad notes that the meaning of a term or narrative detail "comes from the context in which it is found, from its presence within a certain situation, from its juxtaposition with another expression, or from its relationship to us. However, even then its meaning is not fixed. . . . [An] element of play is at work. And, at the same time, an element of caution, a need for evasion from the deadly grasp of formulaic expression" (1993:120). Recently Nancy Florida (1995) has shown the subtle use of *semu* in nineteenth-century Javanese historical literature. Such arts of allusion are equally popular in Bali and have long informed traditional historiography there (Wiener 1995a, 1995b). Perhaps such communicative practices are even more widespread. State security forces suspect that allusion may be used to critique where direct speech is prohibited: possibly one reason for the banning of Pramoedya Ananta Toer's anticolonial novels was that they may be read allegorically—as being really about the state in New Order Indonesia.

This brings me to another way the past may be seized from the control of the ruling classes—one that may be most important of all since it indicates that even dominant memories may be used to create new visions of the future: ruling class ideologies are vulnerable to recontextualization. Michael Taussig notes that people speak of the past because it "is seen to form analogies and structural correspondences with the hopes and tribulations of the present" (1987:368). This is also, of course, why the New Order regime engaged history; but it was not always successful in controlling where those analogies and correspondences may be found. Thus certain foreshadowings of the widespread discontent with the New Order ruling class prior to Suharto's resignation emerged among a number of younger Balinese intellectuals during the summer of 1994. At the annual meeting of the Society for Balinese Studies they responded to plans by investors from Jakarta to build condominiums and a golf course near the Balinese temple of Tanah Lot (the Bali Nirwana Resort) with cries of *"Puputan!"* Having absorbed from public culture the image of *puputan* as a Balinese response to colonialism that had a place in the making of Indonesia's future, they turned it on its head by equating capitalist speculation not with progressive development, as the state would wish, but with a new form of colonialism.

Revising this chapter in mid-1998—clearly a moment of danger when people throughout Indonesia are trying to articulate new visions of the future—I find myself wondering if in a few years memorializations of *puputan* may themselves become marginalized memories, relics of the New Order state. Since independence, *puputan* has in various ways been entangled with the formation of a Balinese ethnic identity. It is this understanding that informed young protesters' calls for *puputan* to defend Bali from exploitation. At that time, public discontent with official "corruption and collusion" was only just beginning to emerge, and it was not yet clear how widespread that discontent was. What *puputan* will mean to Balinese in the years to come is impossible to say. But in any event, it seems likely to be wrested from the conformism of New Order history making—and freed to flash before the eyes of people in the dangerous and hopeful moments of creating the future.

Notes

1. This chapter was originally written in 1995 at a time when no one suspected that the grumbles of discontent about the existing power structure could result in the ouster of the president and widespread calls for reformation. As this book goes to press, extraordinary events are under way. Whatever their outcome the "New Order" now refers to a historical era—namely, Suharto's thirty-year reign as Indonesia's second president. Whether or not the governments that replace it will differ in more than name is impossible to predict at this time. For this reason, I have not turned all references to the New Order into the past tense.

2. "Public culture" is an awkward phrase, for it implicitly constitutes as its opposite a "private culture"—a contradiction in terms. I use the term because it has come to refer to certain cultural formations.

3. For the complex dialogues that have constructed Balinese culture in relation to tourism see Picard (1996b, 1990a). For an analysis of the political economy of tourism and its role in development in Southeast Asia see Truong (1990).

4. Note that an oppositional history can only be enabled by networks of persons who come to share certain values and interests at particular points in time. As Prakash (1990) suggests in his critique of foundationalism, identities, including ethnic identities, are no more stable than the past itself. What counts as "oppositional," therefore, is necessarily shifting. For example, the events known in Bali as *puputan* are the subject of a kind of oppositional history in a novel written by dissident Indonesian writer Pramoedya Ananta Toer (1990). But to the extent that his narrative use of these events is in the service of a particular understanding of the unity of Indonesia as a nation (and thus to the extent he takes the nation as foundational), his representation of them may remain enmeshed in dominant institutions from certain points of view.

5. The phrase might be older than Williams (1977). Bateson (1973:93), who was in Bali in the 1930s, appears to be the first to refer to it in print.

6. According to an earlier description (Van den Broek 1835), all Balinese soldiers wore white headcloths.

7. *"Telas"* implies "finishing off," depleting some substance, in contrast to *"puput,"* which refers to "finishing an action or process."

8. Such colonial policies depended on seeing these events as safely in the past and insisting that they had no long-lasting effects.

9. For a lengthier discussion of the *puputan* during this period see Covarrubias (1972:32–37), who spoke to survivors of Badung's *puputan,* although his major source was Van Weede (1908). Recent interpretations of what De Zoete and Spies regard as "tact" claim that shock over the *puputan* influenced colonial policies in Bali. Adrian Vickers (1989:91–92) argues that Dutch guilt over the massacres, which were criticized in Europe, led the colonial government to emphasize cultural preservation in Bali. To me these claims appear overdrawn; yet it is certainly clear, as Vickers observes, that Dutch images of Bali changed radically after the conquest. To the degree the Dutch did develop policies of cultural preservation (regardless of any colonial guilt), it must be recalled that since Dutch officials were the ones who decided what was "authentically" Balinese, preservationist policies in fact involved extensive transformations of Balinese practices.

10. The German title was more romantic: *Love and Death in Bali.*

11. Baum based her story on information from a long-time Bali resident: the German painter Walter Spies (who served as an informant for other visitors, as well, including anthropologists Margaret Mead and Gregory Bateson). Baum also submitted a list of questions about Badung's conquest to the government in Batavia, which sent them to Christiaan Grader, who was then serving as a district officer on Bali. I thank Henk Schulte Nordholt for letting me see the questions and Grader's answer. In her novel, Baum pretends she was left notes by "Dr. Fabius," a fictional Bali hand.

12. See Vickers (1989) for more on transformations in European images of Balinese. There was, however, more to this change than a shift in European perception. I am struck by the differences between photographs of preconquest and postconquest Balinese: intense, challenging stares are replaced by the mild and friendly expressions now familiar from countless guidebooks and postcards.

13. In most European narratives, popular or scholarly, *puputan* is described as "ritual" or "mass suicide," as in the guidebook cited earlier. Such characterizations hark back to descriptions of the *puputan* in Badung, where eyewitnesses reported numerous acts of self-stabbing. But "suicide" casts a misleading—even an Orientalist—light on local intentions, bound up as it is in Euro-American discourses of uncontrolled emotion and impotence. For further discussion see Wiener (1995a). I should note, however, some newer images of *puputan* in Euro-American popular culture. The 1989 reprint of Vicki Baum's novel, for example, is subtitled *The Powerful Account of Holocaust in Paradise* (Raechelle Rubinstein, pers. comm.). An intermediary image appears

in the author's note about Puputan Badung that precedes a historical romance set in 1892 Bali (Cartland 1979:5–6). It speaks of sacrifice and offerings to gods (as Balinese motivations) and of slaughter (as characterizing Dutch actions).

14. Indeed, the use of phrases such as *"dugas enteg gumi"* to refer to pre-colonial Bali is evidence of the impact of these events—especially as Bateson conducted research in areas that had not themselves been conquered. The interest taken by ordinary Balinese in those who had died is suggested by a colonial report concerning a Buleleng healer (one of a group of amulet sellers) who claimed to be possessed by Klungkung's dead ruler (V.3 June 1913, no. 45, IIIC9, Ministry of Colonies Archives, Algemeen Rijksarchief (The Hague).

15. The district officer in question was L. C. Heyting, whose copy of the poem is now in the Korn Collection (no. 270) of the Eastern Manuscripts Department in the Koninklijk Instituut voor de Taal-, Land-, en Volkenkunde in Leiden. When commemorations of *puputan* began, Pedanda Ngurah's poem was resurrected by those responsible for researching these events for the regional governments of Badung and Klungkung. Sections of it were even printed in Indonesian translation for a commemoration of Puputan Badung (Mirsha 1975).

16. For the Karangasem incident see Mailrapport 1655 and Mailrapport 1703, both in 1916; for Gianyar see Mailrapports 1104, 1281, 1201, and 1451 in 1917, as well as V.30 May 1917, no. 37, in the Ministry of Colonies Archives, Algemeen Rijksarchief (The Hague). Both events are discussed by Robinson (1995:64–69).

17. There were in fact many forms of colonial knowledge production that provided frameworks for constructing an Indonesian national identity and heritage. See, for example, the discussion of maps, censuses, and museums in Anderson (1991).

18. Colonial textbooks also had something to say about history prior to the arrival of Europeans. Largely Javacentric, here colonial authors focused on the Hindu-Buddhist empires that were a passion of Orientalists. Bali played an indirect role in this historiography, for it was the discovery of a Balinese text called the *Negarakertagama* during the conquest of the Balinese kingdom on Lombok that led Orientalists to speculate that the Majapahit empire (centered in East Java in the thirteenth to fifteenth centuries) once had dominion over most of the archipelago (Supomo 1979); such claims enabled nationalists to project the boundaries of the colonial state back in time to the precolonial past. The Dutch claimed that the cultural and territorial reach of these ancient empires was replicable only by the colonial state; for Sukarno, however, Majapahit became the image of a potentially glorious future. To be sure, not all nationalists were equally enthusiastic about such a heritage: both Muslim and Marxist nationalists found Hindu-Buddhist "feudal" empires a problematic base for their own national dreams (McVey 1979). For more on Majapahit in Balinese and nationalist pasts see Creese (1997).

19. I thank Adrian Vickers for drawing this point to my attention.

20. Books on Ngurah Rai as a national hero appeared in Jakarta in the late 1960s and mid-1970s (Robinson 1995:149–150). Note that Gusti Ngurah Rai was an aristocrat.

21. Indeed, at least compared to Java or Sumatra, few Balinese were active in the struggle for national sovereignty. For a discussion of Balinese revolutionary activity and the conflicts among Balinese that both reflected and affected that activity see Robinson (1995).

22. In fact, his death is specifically referred to as "Puputan Margarana." See Panyarikan (1982–1983), who analyzes *puputan* in general. Asking the question "Why has the opposition [resistance] of our Balinese patriots ended with puputan?" (p. 105), he asserts that *puputan* is not a sign of despair or a form of suicide—the common tropes in Euro-American descriptions. Note the nationalist overtones in the following claim: "Puputan is a traditional Balinese type and style of combat that we are acquainted with [or know] and encounter in the history of the struggles of the Balinese people against domination by foreign races" ("perjoangan rakyat Bali menentang kekuasaan bangsa asing") (p. 125). According to Panyarikan, the followers of Gusti Ngurah Rai went to their deaths shouting "*Puputan! Puputan! Puputan!* For other Balinese perspectives on Ngurah Rai and this battle see Robinson (1995).

23. For accounts of the massacres in Bali see Cribb (1990). This, too, may have been a moment of danger when memories of *puputan* flashed before people's eyes. According to a number of vague rumors, some people dressed themselves in white before being led to their execution. (Such events play no part in official public history.)

24. At least until the political and economic crisis of the late 1990s.

25. For the New Order, then, culture was not timeless. In such spheres of cultural production as the annual arts festival, for example, innovative forms of distinctly Balinese culture are celebrated as "new creations" *(kreasi baru)*. (See Chapter 8 in this volume.)

26. The same projects promoted differentiation—namely by age (the difference between forward-looking youths, *pemuda,* and everyone else) and gender (via the five duties of women advocated through family welfare organizations).

27. Note here an ambiguity in national versions of "locality": often local means provincial, rather than ethnic. Indonesia is divided into twenty-six provinces, but any single province may contain a diversity of linguistic and cultural practices. For example, not everyone living in Bali would identify himself or herself or be identified by others as Balinese; nor do all Balinese live in Bali. On the other hand, Bali (which is, after all, a very small island) is relatively homogeneous compared to, say, southern Kalimantan or central Sulawesi.

28. An emphasis on the superficiality of difference is not distinctly Indonesian—it is, for example, a very American theme. Many Americans who are willing to celebrate cultural diversity never allow differences to disrupt or challenge their views of reality, themselves, or the world.

29. A 1995 advertisement campaign provides an apt demonstration. In each (subtitled) ad, ethnic-cum-traditional-looking people discuss the various uses they might make of IBM technologies.

30. In part this focus may reflect the state's interest in modernization—for as Nicholas Dirks (1990) notes, history, as a recognized attribute of being a nation (and thus a player in the global arena), is a "sign of the modern." Other attributes of nationhood include anthems, flags, and school systems (Foster 1991:252).

31. See Cunningham (1989) for the Batak; Hoskins (1987) for Sumba; Nourse (1994) for central Sulawesi; Volkman (1985) for Toraja; Wiener (1995a:7–9) for Klungkung in Bali. Many of these provincial and local histories were produced under the Research and Registration of Regional Culture Project.

32. *Bali Post,* 5 August 1995.

33. See, for example, Skeat (1965).

34. Technologies of mechanical reproduction make this less and less the case. Thus the museum in Semarapura exhibits facsimiles of colonial newspaper reports of the conquest of Klungkung in its "history room." (Audiocassettes of *puputan* performances were widely available for purchase in the 1980s.)

35. In the same way, names of national heroes dot urban centers throughout the archipelago. Thus Denpasar's position as a regional capital is signaled by the presence of streets named for Sumatran and Javanese national heroes.

36. He added that it was a *lingga-yoni,* a Hindu motif representing male and female energies, an image also used in New Order monuments outside of Hindu Bali to index the nation's ancient Hindu-Buddhist precursors (Anderson 1990b). Elsewhere I discuss the way that Klungkung commemorative activities simultaneously conform to dominant themes and deploy referents of local significance (Wiener 1995b). This monument is no exception. For example, the stone resembles shrines at Besakih Temple; Besakih is a place associated with Klungkung's precolonial rulers (see Wiener 1995a).

37. Significantly, the original photo depicts additional members of the royal family; Gunarsa has copied only their poses.

38. For example, in one scene a figure identified as Bali's first ruler, King Bedahulu, is presented as paradigmatic of a Bali not yet civilized. (The caption above the diorama notes that "religion had not yet developed.") The second scene shows Watu Renggong, ruler during Bali's fifteenth-century golden age, "during whose rule the cultural arts blossomed" and "agriculture experienced some progress." In Diorama 4, dancers and a gamelan orchestra represent the development of Balinese culture and civilization.

39. The battles include the last engagement between the Dutch and the kingdom of Buleleng at Jagaraga in 1846; the Kusamba War in Klungkung in 1849; Puputan Badung; an engagement in Gelgel (also in Klungkung) that immediately preceded the *puputan;* Puputan Klungkung; and Gusti Ngurah Rai's battle at Margarana. In most of these scenes the Balinese are dressed in white. Three additional dioramas represent structures of authority and politically

significant events. Thus in Diorama 8, between Puputan Badung and the outbreak of troubles in Gelgel, Klungkung's king meets with his "staff"; Diorama
10 (modeled after a photograph) identifies Bali's eight Dutch-appointed
rulers by name and region; Diorama 13 represents the Japanese occupation,
during which, according to the placard, Balinese worked hard: indeed, they
made the caves by Klungkung's Bubuh River that tourist buses pass on their
way to and from Denpasar or Gianyar.

40. The exception is the diorama dedicated to Klungkung's engagement
with the Dutch in 1849, called locally the Kusamba War. According to
Klungkung official histories, Dewa Agung Istri Kania, a woman, ruled
Klungkung at that time. The diorama shows her leading Klungkung's army
while brandishing a magical weapon that is the object of many local narratives.
Interestingly, Klungkung official histories suppress the fact that she ruled
jointly with a (lower-ranking) brother.

41. See the preceding note. In addition, the *puputan* takes place at a
Klungkung landmark: the old palace door just across the road, which also
plays an important role in local practices and narratives (Wiener, 1995b).

42. The English caption is slightly different: "Since 1966 Indonesia has
been led by President Suharto. Lots of cenotaphs have been built, this one
included."

43. A video and transcript of this film may be found in the ongoing project
organized by Mark Hobart to archive television shows about Bali or in Balinese: the Balinese Historical and Instructional Study material Archive
(BHISMA). (See Chapter 9 in this volume.) I did not have an opportunity to
ask its director who provided the script or who decided what incidents would
be represented.

44. These agents include Dewa Agung Smarabawa, leader of one of the
factions, whose son survived the *puputan* to become Klungkung's last king,
and Anak Agung Made Sangging and Ida Bagus Jumpung, names that come
up frequently in local narratives.

45. The representation of women in Klungkung commemorations is complex. On the one hand, there is the masculinist flavor of the Puputan
Klungkung monument and the promotion of New Order gender ideologies in
the film. On the other hand, at the time of the Kusamba War, Klungkung was
ruled jointly by a brother and a (higher-ranking and unmarried) sister. In all
references to that war only the sister is identified as ruler.

46. I have been particularly fascinated by representations of the Dutch in
Balinese depictions of *puputan*. In a Topeng Puputan Badung I saw at the arts
festival in 1984, actors portrayed the Dutch as simultaneously dangerous and
comical, goose-stepping across the stage, gesticulating wildly, performing ac-
robatics in which their feet jiggled in the air and they balanced on their hands
(as demons are often portrayed in texts devoted to matters mystical). Similarly,
in *Uproar in Semarapura* the Dutch appear as drunken soldiers and ill-

mannered envoys. Klungkung artist Mangku Mura told me he was actually instructed to paint the Dutch as ogres *(raksasa)*.

47. Wiener (1995a, 1995b). Notably, they are emphasized by persons marginalized in contemporary Bali: priests unhappy about changes in Balinese practices, members of peripheral lines of aristocratic families, and custodians of family memories (especially women).

48. Glossed as "masterfully concealing that which he or she would reveal" in Florida (1995).

Chapter 3

Democratic Mobilization and Political Authoritarianism: Tourism Developments in Bali

PUTU SUASTA AND LINDA H. CONNOR

On 27 July 1996 there was a large demonstration in the city of Jakarta—the first of many internationally reported incidents that were to continue up to the Indonesian general elections in May 1997. Thousands of supporters of Megawati Sukarnoputri, daughter of the former president, Sukarno, and leader of the Indonesian Democratic Party (Partai Demokrasi Indonesia, or PDI), converged on the headquarters of their party, which had been taken over by government-supported political rivals. In their outrage and frustration at the ousting of their democratically elected leader in favor of a government-backed candidate, Soerjadi, they clashed with troops and police who were called in to control the situation. Buildings and cars were damaged, scores of people were injured, an unknown number were killed, and more than a hundred were detained indefinitely by security police. Megawati's growing political popularity, particularly among the young and the poor, was viewed as a threat to the government-backed Golkar Party in the upcoming general elections. Repressive actions against her and her following in the PDI were part of the Suharto regime's strategy to ensure the usual landslide electoral victory for the government.[1]

The Jakarta demonstration was the culmination of more than a month of political turbulence around the country that was precipitated by actions to remove Megawati from the leadership at a government-initiated extraordinary congress of the party that had been held in Medan, Sumatra, on 20–22 June 1996. There were demonstrations in many of the provincial capitals where PDI support was strong, including Denpasar, as well as in smaller population centers (Aspinall 1996:4). The situation stabilized somewhat over the following weeks although protests continued. PDI branches around the country struggled unsuccessfully against pressures to have "pro-Megawati" executive officers replaced by "pro-Soerjadi" officials. In Bali these conflicts were particularly strong and are documented in detailed reportage in the main regional newspaper, the *Bali Post,* throughout July and August 1996. Even before the extraordinary congress in June, the chair of the provincial branch of the PDI in Bali, Ida Bagus Putu Wesnawa, declared that the branch would withdraw from the election if forced to recognize Soerjadi as party leader *(Bali Post,* 10 July 1996, p. 1). But by the end of August, pro-Soerjadi executives had been installed in all the regency branches, and many Megawati supporters had relinquished their membership cards in disgust. Police and security forces intimidated Megawati groups who tried to have meetings outside the officially sanctioned framework. (See, for example, *Bali Post,* 24 August 1996, p. 3, and 31 August 1996, p. 3.) Meanwhile supporters had to defend accusations that they were "fanatics" and adherents of a "cult" of Sukarno's daughter *(Bali Post,* 2 September 1996, p. 3).

These events signaled a change in the relationship between state and civil society in Indonesia—a shift that in many ways had been presaged in Bali several years earlier. The change at the national level had been signaled by the policy of openness *(keterbukaan)* proclaimed in the late 1980s, but it went far deeper into debates over the nature and direction of the government policy of economic development. In Bali the change was manifest in a series of protests and public debates in 1993–1994 that were without precedent since the 1960s. Although others have commented on aspects of these events in relation to changing perceptions of Balinese identity and the role of the media as a political force (Picard 1996b; Warren 1994, 1995, 1998a), the significance of these events in terms of the challenge they posed to the hegemony of Suharto's New Order regime in Bali and the role of Bali's middle-class groups in radical political movements has not been fully examined.[2] This chapter looks at the political implications of protest movements around tourist developments in Bali in 1993–1994 in relation to the national framework, including the economic and political crisis that erupted in late 1997, with particular attention to the role of middle-class activism.

Background to the Demonstrations

Megawati had been elected party leader by a majority vote during another tumultuous PDI extraordinary congress, held in Surabaya between 2 and 6 December 1993 (also specially convened by the minister for internal affairs). The outcome of the regular PDI congress held in Medan in July 1993 had not succeeded in removing Soerjadi from office, despite government machinations to unseat the popular chairman. This turn of events caused the minister to declare the election invalid. Soerjadi was perceived in some government quarters as "too effective in marshalling votes at the last election in 1992" (Van Klinken 1994:2), thus threatening the usual landslide victory of the government party, Golkar, at the forthcoming 1997 general election. At the December extraordinary congress in 1993, Megawati won despite attempts to intimidate the participants to elect the government-backed candidate, Budi Hardjono. A few days later, Megawati was announced as PDI chair during the PDI's national convention held in Jakarta on 13 December.[3]

Megawati's mass support gave new hope to those supporting democratization in Indonesia. Megawati's oppositional stance—for example, her criticism of the banning of the major mass media publications *Tempo, Detik,* and *Editor* in June 1994—was construed by some as the beginning of a meaningful democratic process. The prospect of a successful electoral showing for the PDI in the 1997 general election led pro-democracy activists to the formation of the Independent Election Monitoring Committee (KIPP) in January 1996 to prevent fraudulent manipulation of results by the government (Aspinall 1996:5; Mohamad 1997:5).

In Bali, Megawati had a particularly strong following. This was true for a number of reasons. Before the New Order reorganization of party politics in 1973, Bali was a stronghold of the Indonesian Nationalist Party (Partai Nasionalis Indonesia, or PNI), led by President Sukarno. The PNI was the largest of several nationalist and Christian parties that were amalgamated into the new PDI, and many Balinese carried over their loyalty to the PDI. Bali had always been a pro-Sukarno region. Much of the personal admiration of Balinese for Sukarno can be attributed to his Balinese mother and to the fact that he frequently visited Bali during his presidency. Thus when his daughter Megawati Sukarnoputri became leader of the PDI, support in all the Balinese branches was particularly strong. Moreover, in the early 1990s, with the growth of the Indonesian pro-democracy movement and the search for channels for its expression within the formal political structure, the PDI attracted many pro-democracy groups to its ranks (Aspinall 1996:7). In Bali, as we shall see, the climate of political autonomy that Megawati's leadership represented cannot be divorced from the growing protests over the exploitation of the island for tourist profits by outside investors and powerful government officials.

During the years that Megawati led the PDI, she was widely mooted to be a potential alternative to President Suharto for the 1998 presidential election. As the outcome of the five-yearly presidential election has always been a foregone conclusion, with only one candidate standing, this was an unprecedented challenge to Suharto's leadership. In interviews Megawati was elusive on the topic of her possible candidacy: "Our traditions have a very significant place for the mother. . . . There were Ruling Queens in the ancient kingdoms of Sriwijaya and Majapahit. So why not a woman President?" (Sailendri 1996:3). Megawati's ever-growing popularity forced the government to take action to stop her rise as it occurred during the approach to the 1997 general election and the 1998 general meeting of the House of Assembly (at which the president is elected for a five-year term). In the early months of 1996, the minister for internal affairs declared Megawati's leadership illegal.[4] The government then orchestrated an extraordinary PDI national congress in Medan, to be held on 20–22 June, with the intention of removing Megawati from leadership with the aid of disaffected government supporters within the PDI ranks. There was widespread military intimidation of the carefully screened delegates and the mass media, the more outspoken ranks of which had been decimated by the press closures of 1994.[5] Despite Megawati's palpable support from the party's grassroots, the extraordinary congress delegates removed her and Soerjadi took her place. The choice of Soerjadi—the former PDI chairman whom the government had destabilized in 1993—seems surprising. But as Megawati's leadership presented an even bigger problem for the government, Soerjadi was courted once again (Aspinall 1996:4–7).

In the weeks leading up to the extraordinary congress in June 1996, Megawati's supporters attempted to retain control of the branch offices around the country. Then her supporters occupied the PDI headquarters in Jakarta and held "democracy forums" (public political speeches and debates) on a daily basis until 23 July, when Jakarta's police chief banned them as subversive (Aspinall 1996:5). On 27 July there was violence when pro-Soerjadi followers, later identified as hired troops, invaded the PDI headquarters early in the morning. The armed forces and police then helped the pro-Soerjadi forces to take over the headquarters located on Diponegoro Street in central Jakarta. Attempting to defend the headquarters and engaging in escalating clashes with police and army troops, Megawati's supporters took to the streets in increasing numbers. By midafternoon, thousands of people were fighting the government forces and riots broke out in many areas. It was not until midnight that the riots and violence abated. Further outbreaks ensued the following day, however, and there was a continuing presence of thousands of armed troops in Jakarta for weeks.[6]

According to official statements issued by the government, the 27 July riots were unrelated to the PDI problem. They were due, rather, to agitation by an "illegal" organization, the People's Democratic Party (Partai Rakyat Demokratik, or PRD), which had been formed as an "association" two years earlier as one of a wave of pro-democracy organizations that emerged around the country,[7] all of which had publicly supported Megawati in the weeks leading up to her loss of the leadership (Aspinall 1996:7). Megawati's own analysis of the events, however, revolved around the electoral threat she represented to the government. In an interview on 16 August 1996 she stated: "The earlier elections were calculated on the computer, not in the ballot box. In 1992 we got 56 of the 400 contested seats. But I am convinced that if that election had been truly honest, we could have got more than 80 seats. And that would have been even more obvious in 1997. For this I have been toppled!" (Sailendri 1996:2). The security forces, however, resorted to the familiar scapegoat of communism. They claimed that the PRD was a communist front organization with an ideology of popular democratic socialism. In a predictable and often-repeated response, both the minister for internal affairs and military leaders accused the PRD of trying to spread communism and revitalizing the Indonesian Communist Party (Partai Komunis Indonesia, or PKI), which was banned thirty years ago after an attempted coup and its bloody aftermath in 1965–1966.[8]

In the following months, the threat of communism became a major topic in official political rhetoric. Pro-democracy organizations were suppressed. Their leaders were detained and charged. Labor union leader Muchtar Pakpakhan was again imprisoned after being released in 1995 (Aspinall 1996:6; *Inside Indonesia* 49[1997]:19–21). The office of Women's Solidarity (Solidaritas Perempuan), an organization that defends women laborers' rights, was destroyed, and members of the management board were physically beaten by assailants who claimed they were looking for PRD personnel. The Ministry of Internal Affairs issued decrees and regulations restricting the operations of non-government organizations (NGOs) in rural areas; its avowed aim was to prevent any "communist agitation."[9] NGO leaders described these actions as an effort to silence organizations—such as the Indonesian Legal Aid Bureau (Yayasan Lembaga Bantuan Hukum Indonesia, or YLBHI) and the Indonesian Environmental Organization (Wahana Lingkungan Hidup Indonesia, or WALHI)—that have often criticized the government publicly. Before this policy was instigated, NGOs were receiving anonymous threats. In early September 1996, twenty NGOs lodged complaints with the National Human Rights Committee (Komite Nasional Hak Asasi Manusia, or Komnasham). Pro-democracy activists who had criticized government policies began to feel uneasy. The executive chairman of YLBHI, Bambang Widjoyanto, forecast that over the next two years there would be an increase in the number of people summarily arrested in Indonesia and recommended that pro-democracy activists suspend all activities for a while. A popular phrase among activists describing this situation is *tiarap* (a military term meaning "to lie down" or be inactive).

Limited Openness

The most powerful political institutions under Suharto's New Order government have been the presidency, the government's Golkar party, and the armed forces (ABRI). The military is an integral part of Golkar, as are all civil servants. The Department of Internal Affairs has military support to control all political and social organizations in Indonesia in the interests of economic development *(pembangunan)* and stability *(stabilitas)* (Van Langenberg 1986:14, 19).

The New Order has never based its legitimacy on the prospect of a democratic parliamentary system and future liberalization. A body of institutions and doctrines—the "dual function" *(dwifungsi)* of the military, which legitimates military involvement in civil affairs; a heavily controlled system of political parties; the "floating mass" concept restricting mass political mobilization at the grassroots level; a weak parliament; and the Five Principles of official state ideology (Pancasila) has been the backbone of the state's agenda for the political stability considered necessary for capitalism to grow and thrive (Van Langenberg 1986; Schwarz 1994:chap. 2; Mackie and MacIntyre 1994).[10]

In 1990, however, the government held out the prospect of new democratic rights. Official rhetoric seemed to condone a more liberal po-

litical atmosphere summed up in the widely used term *"keterbukaan,"* or openness (Schwarz 1994:231). The term was first announced on 4 December 1989 by the army chief of staff, Edi Sudrajat. He was quoted in the national daily, *Kompas,* as saying: "Having enjoyed better education our people want differences discussed more openly. As such they want more active participation in the decision making process on national problems and in social control" (cited in Schwarz 1994:231).

Adam Schwarz (1994:chap. 9) documents the vicissitudes of the openness theme. A significant marker was the president's annual Independence Day address in 1990 in which he stated: "Democracy requires a great deal of consultation, discussion, exchange of ideas and dialogue. . . . It is . . . wrong if our vigilance toward security is so excessive that it restricts our own movement" (Schwarz 1994:231). The coordinating minister of political affairs and security, Sudomo, soon followed up with suggestions of more liberal regulations for the print media *(Inside Indonesia* 24[1990]:7; Schwarz 1994:231). In 1990, the government liberalized regulations concerning student organizations by allowing the formation of "senates" on university campuses (McBeth 1993:22). But only months later, politically controversial plays and poetry readings were banned (Schwarz 1994:231–232). And in the arena of institutional politics, by mid-1991, Suharto had moved to block a trend toward greater parliamentary independence by culling outspoken candidates from the parties' lists for the forthcoming 1992 general elections (Schwarz 1994:274).

The parameters of *keterbukaan* were never made clear, but certainly there was evidence of government responsiveness to popular demands. The implementation of new traffic regulations in 1992,[11] which imposed heavy fines on offenders, was delayed because of widespread protests and unfavorable polls (*Tempo,* 18 September 1993). More significantly, the Department of Social Affairs finally responded to mass protests in Jakarta and the provinces—protests that increased in intensity over the years 1991–1993—against the national lottery (Sumbangan Dana Sosial Berhadiah, or SDSB).[12] Student groups who argued the lottery was undermining government programs to eradicate poverty joined forces with Muslims who objected to the lottery as a form of gambling prohibited by Islam. Eventually, in December 1993, the minister for social affairs, Inten Soeweno, announced that the lottery was to be abolished immediately (McBeth 1993:22). Student leaders saw this victory in a wider context. As one representative from Gadjah Mada University stated: "We're thinking about democracy. We have been cool for 15–20 years and we see the SDSB as a starting point to gather student power" (cited in McBeth 1993:22).

Despite such optimism, *keterbukaan* was beginning to lose all meaning by 21 June 1994 when three major newsmagazines in Indonesia—*Tempo, Detik,* and *Editor*—had their licenses canceled over breaches of operating regulations that, according to the director-general for press and graphics, Subrata, compromised national security and political stability (*Inside Indonesia* 40[1994]:2–6). And then *keterbukaan* lost all relevance after the 27 July 1996 riots described earlier. On 17 August 1997, in his Independence Day speech, President Suharto officially declared that *keterbukaan* was over (*The Australian,* 20 August 1997). This announcement coincided with the early stages of what has come to be known as the "Asian financial crisis." Indonesia, with high projected negative growth rates over the next few years, has been the most severely affected Southeast Asian country.

Political Developments in Bali

It is possible to map the trajectory of political openness and its repression in Bali by examining the events surrounding tourist developments that have progressively engulfed the island over the past two decades. Protest movements over resort developments have given form and momentum to widespread feelings of anger and frustration in Bali focused on the exploitation of the island for profit by the intertwined interests of government and private investors.

In 1990, facilitated by the national climate of "openness," criticisms of environmental degradation associated with uncontrolled tourist development began appearing ever more frequently in the *Bali Post* in the form of news reports, cartoons, and letters to the editor (*Inside Indonesia,* 26 March 1991, pp. 26–27; Warren 1994:5). This critical reporting reached a peak in the years 1993 and 1994, when two developments attracted an unprecedented amount of public attention. The case of the Golden Garuda Monument (Garuda Wisnu Kencana, or GWK), as well as the Bali Nirwana Resort (BNR), illuminate the processes involved in local challenges to New Order hegemony.

Garuda Wisnu Kencana (GWK)

The GWK project was announced in June 1993. GWK is a 140-meter-high, gold-plated statue of the Hindu deity Wisnu astride the mythical

Garuda bird, Indonesia's national symbol. This monument, to be located at Balangan Hill south of Denpasar, was to be visible to visitors arriving in Bali by sea and air. GWK, touted as the highest statue in the world and estimated to cost 200 billion rupiahs ($83 million), was to be complemented by a cultural museum, performing arts space, and shopping complex to cater to up to 15,000 people and would be promoted as a leading attraction for tourists to the island.[13] The idea for this project was initiated by the director general of tourism and the governor of Bali in 1990 (*Kompas,* 9 July 1993), and the concept was developed by the Bandung-based Balinese sculptor, I Nyoman Nuarta, renowned for his monumental works elsewhere in Indonesia. Capital for the project came from a variety of sources in the public and private sectors. The central government undertook to provide the necessary infrastructure, and the corporation P. T. Garuda Adimatra assumed a managing role along with the GWK Foundation (*Jakarta Post,* 22 June 1997, p. 14).

From the moment the project was announced there was strong criticism in Bali (*Tempo,* 26 June 1993). A group of concerned citizens issued a press release on 9 July outlining their objections (*Inside Indonesia* 37[1993]:25) on environmental, cultural, and fiscal grounds. Environmental activists argued that the capital investment could more usefully be made in sanitation and water supply, public transport, and improved irrigation. There was concern, as well, that the project would significantly deplete Bali's already scarce water supplies and divert resources from the agricultural sector as many other tourism-related developments have done. It would further exacerbate disparities in wealth in Bali, owing to its location in the tourism-dominated south, and add to the traffic congestion already experienced. Religious leaders too expressed their objections to the monument that, as a secular structure, would be higher than major temples such as Besakih and the nearby Uluwatu Temple.[14] Although these criticisms were expressed in public meetings and in the media during 1993 and 1994, they never reached a point of large-scale mobilization of protesters.

In fact, the GWK project always had a significant amount of support from within Bali—particularly from government and those involved in the domestic tourist industry, for whose customers it is designed to appeal rather than to foreign tourists (Picard 1996b:192). The high-profile minister for research and technology in the Suharto cabinet, B. J. Habibie, lent his support, as well, declaring that the GWK was a "technological wonder" as well as an artistic monument (*Bali Post,* 4 June 1996). During 1997, although sporadic criticism continued, mainly in

Figure 13. "GWK" cartoon by Surya Dharma.

the local press (as in *Bali Post,* 5 June 1996), the project proceeded apace. Indeed, the minister for tourism attended an elaborately choreographed cornerstone-laying ceremony on 8 June 1997 (*Jakarta Post,* 22 June 1997, p. 14). Completion was scheduled for the year 2000. As the more vociferous criticisms had abated, the cornerstone ceremony proceeded without any public demonstrations. In late 1997, however, the project fell victim, not to protesters' demands, but to the economic crisis afflicting the whole country. And as investors' funds evaporated, all construction work ceased.

Bali Nirwana Resort (BNR)

In late 1993, the *Bali Post* was instrumental in bringing the BNR development to public attention. Building on the publicity accorded the GWK, the BNR became a focus for widespread discontent with the government's role in commercial development in Bali. As a mass protest against government policy, the anti-BNR movement ("gerakan anti-BNR"), as it came to be known, caused a reassessment of the assumption made by radical Balinese intellectuals that due to the traumatic experience of the 1965 massacre of Indonesian Communist Party members and suspected sympathizers, as well as other dissidents, Balinese tend to be politically accommodating.[15]

In 1991, the Tabanan regency government approved the develop-

Figure 14. GWK site. Photo: Putu Wirata.

ment application for the Bali Nirwana Resort (BNR) "megaproject" *(megaproyek)* on 121 hectares of land abutting the famous Tanah Lot Temple, one of Bali's major temples, where all Hindus regularly worship. The government had originally approached the Jakarta-based Bakrie Group of companies in 1989 with an idea for the resort development. The plan for the $200 million resort that was approved in 1991 included a luxury hotel, condominiums, and a Greg Norman–designed golf course, all with buildings located within 500 meters of the Tanah Lot Temple (Cohen 1994:30; Kusuma 1994:10).

It appears that as early as 1990, the Tabanan regency authorities started the process of land alienation in this beautiful coastal area of irrigated rice land in response to a request from the Bakrie Group in June 1990 (*Suara Pembaruan*, 11 February 1994). According to a letter the landholders wrote to the head of the provincial parliament on 20 October 1994, Tabanan officials, not the developer, requested that farmers sell their land "in the national interest" in what they were led to believe was a government project (*Inside Indonesia* 43(1995):17–18). Under this sort of pressure, many of them agreed to sell their land. Initially they were patient in their dealings with the authorities. But when they discovered that the land was to be used for a private development, many reversed their decision. As the farmers became more intransigent, the regency government exerted further pressure by cutting off irrigation water to the affected farmers' fields in July 1993—thus threatening to reduce the value of the land as it could be reclassified as much less productive "dry land" *(lahan kering)* (Kusuma 1994:9; Cohen 1994:30).[16]

The farmers began to protest their situation in 1993. In November 1993 the *Bali Post* took up the issue by publishing a series of three critical articles from a local academic and environmental activist (*Bali Post*, 23 November 1993, 4 November 1993, 6 January 1994). In the newspaper coverage that followed, the religious implications of the development emerged as the most salient issue for most Balinese Hindus. While there were already provincial planning regulations prohibiting resort and other developments too close to major temples, these had apparently been ignored when the initial approval for BNR was given by the office of the governor of Bali and the Tabanan regency government.[17] Balinese were outraged that the sanctity of one of their most important temples was to be threatened by a huge tourist development on its very doorstep. Letters of protest from all segments of the population flooded in to the *Bali Post*—a potent indicator of the broad social base of opposition to the development.

During late 1993 and early 1994, the groundswell of protest gained momentum in Bali, mobilizing a number of social groups: environmental organizations, Balinese opinion leaders and intellectuals, and, most important, student groups who were already empowered by the national climate of openness and the growth of pro-democracy organizations around the country (Hearman 1996:9). Protests took the form of petitions and deputations to parliament and the governor's office, media articles and letters to the editor, and demonstrations. During the months of December through February, hardly a day went by when BNR news did not occupy most of the front page of the *Bali Post*. The governor of Bali's pro-development stance was criticized quite openly during this period. Indeed the initials "BNR" also became known as "Botak Nipu Rakyat" ("The Bald One Deceives the People")—a reference to the governor, Ida Bagus Oka, who was bald—and placards bearing this epithet appeared in street marches.

Student groups became particularly active in the growing protest movement. In late December, the Forum of Balinese Hindu Students (Forum Mahasiswa Hindu Bali, or FMHB) sent a deputation to the provincial parliament (Dewan Perwakilan Rakyat Daerah, or DPRD), and to the governor, expressing their rejection of BNR and requesting that the development be stopped (*Bali Post*, 30 and 31 December 1993). The parliamentary spokesperson prevaricated on the issue. The governor himself stated that while BNR's development application

Figure 15. "BNR bulldozer" cartoon by Jango Pramartha.

could not be revoked, no buildings could be erected until the environmental impact analysis or EIA (Analisa Mengenai Dampak Lingkungan, or AMDAL) was completed and approved. Student leaders provided critical comments to the print media at all stages of the conflict and demanded to be included in meetings between the key protagonists. One student leader, Widiana Kepakisan, defined the students' role as follows: "As academics, we feel as if we have to become mediators and facilitate the media dialogues" (*Bali Post,* 5 January 1994).

Student groups and others pressured the Indonesian Hindu Council (Parisada Hindu Dharma Indonesia, or PHDI)—the officially recognized organization representing the interests of Indonesian Hindus to the state—to issue a decree having moral force for Hindus *(bisama)* stipulating the spatial limits of the "zone of sanctity" around major temples (*Bali Post,* 5 January 1994). Despite pressure building since November, the provincial and Tabanan offices of PHDI, largely compliant with government interests, stalled until late January 1994. Finally they issued a decree stating that buildings should not be erected within a 2-kilometer radius of the temple (Kusuma 1994:10; *Inside Indonesia* 43[1995]:16). In fact, the religious decree was vague in its definitions: it used a traditional measure of distance, *apenelungan alit,* "within the near distance of vision," which is usually taken to mean 2 kilometers (*Tempo,* 19 February 1994, p. 94). Cohen (1994:32) describes the decree as "couched in conciliatory language stressing the importance of integrating development, tourism and spiritual needs." After the decree was issued, moves for a compromise position immediately ensued (Kusuma 1994:10; Picard 1996b:194) so that the BNR project could go ahead. Meanwhile, "customary leaders" *(pemuka adat)* in Tabanan regency publicly declared their support for the development (*Bali Post,* 30 December 1993), and the head of the regency, I Ketut Sundria, stated: "The BNR development at Tanah Lot is not going to reduce the sanctity of the temple" (*Bali Post,* 7 January 1994).

There was also a significant level of environmental concern that gave further weight to BNR's opposition. It was not until late December that the public became aware that the EIA had not been completed, even though land clearing had already begun and permits that were theoretically dependent on a satisfactory EIA had already been issued (*Bali Post,* 29 December 1993; MacRae n.d.). The EIA, undertaken by a team from the government-funded Udayana University in Bali, was finally submitted to the provincial government on 4 January 1994 (*Bali Post,* 5 January 1994). At the same time, the *Bali Post* revealed

Figure 16. "BNR bulldozer" cartoon by Surya Dharma.

that 60 percent of the villas planned for the resort had in fact already been sold. One of the main issues for environmental groups, as in the case of the Garuda Wisnu Kencana development discussed earlier, was the depletion of the regional water resources from the resort's accommodation, its extensive landscaped gardens, and above all, its golf course, one of more than twenty planned for the island in addition to the four existing in 1994 (Aditjondro 1995b:6).

The climax of the conflicts was the student-led protests with marches and public speeches in Denpasar in late January. At these demonstrations, organized by the senate of the Udayana University Students' Association, students from all the universities in Bali were joined by students from Malang, Yogyakarta, and Surabaya in Java, as well as by the affected farmers, the YLBHI, the Hindu Youth Organization (Pemuda Hindu Indonesia), representatives of the National Students' Movement of Indonesia (Gerakan Mahasiswa Nasional Indonesia, or GMNI), various NGOs, and prominent Balinese intellectuals. Several thousand people were estimated to be involved (Cohen 1994). These demonstrations had been preceded by a public seminar

Figure 17. Anti-BNR demonstration at the provincial parliament, 1994. Photo: Putu Suasta.

in mid-January by the Society for Balinese Studies, an association of prominent Balinese and foreign intellectuals. The society made a submission to the provincial parliament (Dewan Perwakilan Rakyat Daerah, or DPRD) asking for the project to be halted while a review of planning regulations was undertaken (MacRae n.d.).

Surprisingly, the massive public protests in late January were allowed to proceed. Many activists were encouraged by what they perceived to be the tolerance of the military toward their actions. There was an impression that the local military command was not actively obstructing the protests—despite the usual declarations in an early press conference by the regional military commander, Panglima KODAM Theo Syafei, that the protests were the work of "a small group of agitators" and were "PKI inspired" (*Bali Post*, 19 December 1993). In early January, Syafei asked the PHDI to publicly clarify their stand on the issue of BNR in relation to Tanah Lot Temple because of the negative undercurrents *(arus bawah)* among the population. "In acquiring land," he said, "it is not permissible to pressure or intimidate the people" (*Bali Post*, 5 January 1994). In an interview later the same month for the *Bali Post*, when asked whether he would continue to "back up the people," Syafei responded: "Hopefully this will continue.

It is the task of ABRI to help the people. We are also from the people" (21 January 1994).

Some parliamentarians, too, supported the protest actions. On several occasions in late 1993 and early 1994, the provincial parliament expressed sympathy with the anti-BNR movement.[18] The chairman occasionally conducted dialogues with university students in which they were able to air their concerns, as had happened in the case of the GWK debates some months earlier. It was the DPRD that asked the governor to delay construction on the BNR site until there had been proper consideration and review of the EIA, to which he agreed. The PDI lent its support to the anti-BNR movement, as well, both from the national parliament in Jakarta and from Bali. On 15 January, the PDI section of the national parliament called on the government to cancel the development permit for BNR, because it contravened planning regulations and constituted an insult to a place of worship. On the same day, the PDI members in the provincial parliament pressed the governor to halt the project so that all the issues raised by protesters could be taken into account. "Development of the economy is important," said the deputy secretary of the PDI parliamentary section, Oka Wiratma, "but this does not mean the spiritual aspects can be forgotten" (*Bali Post*, 17 January 1994).

Protesters had begun to hope that the momentum of the opposition and the sympathetic local press coverage might force the governor of Bali to cancel the development permit of BNR. On 25 January, the governor ordered that work on the site be stopped while the EIA and the PHDI decree were considered (MacRae n.d.). In early February, however, the regional military commander, Theo Syafei, was suddenly replaced by Major General Adang Ruchiatna. Syafei was transferred to Bandung, West Java, as chief of the military academy there. Nobody among the general public knew what was really behind the replacement, and indeed such transfers are common. According to some local officials the transfer was caused by the central military command's disapproval of Syafei's lenient stance toward the anti-BNR movement. This theory seems plausible: soon after the transfer the provincial military changed its policy toward the protests.[19] While the district chief commander,[20] Lieutenant Colonel Zaelani Ichsan Ehad, had commented that he would be tolerant of mass action, a few days later, on 12 February, a mass protest at the governor's residence at Jaya Sabha was instantly dispersed by riot police with batons. A few students were injured (Cohen 1994:32).

Figure 18. Anti-BNR demonstration outside the governor's residence, 1994. Photo: Putu Suasta.

Although no one was killed, the use of military force against pro-testers on this occasion weakened the strength of the mass protests. Students and other youth groups split into factions advocating differ-ent positions of compromise or contestation with the resort develop-ment. Even the *Bali Post*, which had strongly supported the anti-BNR movement, became passive; by late February its reporting on the BNR development had declined. Many concluded that the Department of Information had warned the *Bali Post* to stop reporting events. When challenged on this issue by a deputation of students and other activists (including one of the authors), the editors of the *Bali Post* responded that they had stopped reporting on the BNR project because they wanted to report "other important topics," although their statement was never published. It was also noted by many observers that the Bakrie Group investors in the BNR project represented a rich source of advertising revenue for the *Bali Post*. This initial muzzling of the *Bali Post* seemed to be quite a localized phenomenon, for it predated the national press closures mentioned earlier by several months. In the fol-lowing months, however, the English-language section of the paper was closed down—ostensibly for publishing without a full permit, but according to those involved because of a series of critical articles and a cartoon. This closure came at the same time as the Jakarta newsweekly shutdowns.

The governor gave permission for landscaping work to recommence on 21 March. In late March, a letter from the national state secretary, Moerdiono, a close adviser to the president, urged that the PHDI decree should "become the basis for resolving the problem of the hotel and golf development" (Cohen 1994:32). The interpretation of the religious decree regarding the distance of buildings from the temple was never clear-cut, however. While the Tabanan office did publicly consent to a flexible interpretation of the traditional "near distance of vision" measure, the central office in Jakarta never agreed to this (Warren 1998a:250). As landscaping recommenced, opposition on a smaller scale continued—for example, a prayer session led by Gedong Bagoes Oka at Tanah Lot in April (Cohen 1994:30). The PDI members of the national parliament continued to voice their objections on religious, cultural, and environmental grounds (*Bali Post,* 2 March 1994). In March a group of students from the Indonesian Hindu Youth and Students Communication Forum (Forum Komunikasi Mahasiswa dan Pemuda Indonesia, or FKMPHI) met with the head of the National Legal Aid Bureau (YLBHI) to discuss the BNR case (*Bali Post,* 2 March 1994).

On 13 September 1994, the provincial parliament (DPRD) announced that the EIA had been ratified and full construction at the BNR site would go ahead with a number of concessions to protesters. These concessions included an undertaking to relocate resort buildings a little further away from the temple (but not as far as 2 kilometers) and to use the golf course and mounded gardens as a greenbelt that would obscure the view of the resort from the temple and vice versa. Formal undertakings were made to offer jobs to affected landholders (on condition that they drop all compensation claims), and restrictions on water use were agreed (Warren 1998a:250). There were other compromises, as well. Perhaps the most significant was that the developer agreed not to use an image of Tanah Lot Temple as a logo for the resort (Picard 1996b:194).

The parliamentary announcement prompted the Forum of Balinese Hindu Students (FMHB) to write a letter to the DPRD in October outlining their objections to the development and their concerns that it would set a dangerous precedent for other large developments in Bali—"with negligible advantages to the welfare of the Balinese public" (*Inside Indonesia* 43[1995]:17). Ninety-six of the landholders whose fields had been alienated followed up with a letter to the DPRD the next day outlining the injustices they had experienced and demanding that they be given back their land (*Inside Indonesia* 43[1995]:17–18).

Although the farmers have continued to pursue compensation through the legal system with the aid of legal aid foundations, they have met with little success. (See, for example, *Bali Post,* 30 December 1995.) Apart from disagreements about the amount of compensation paid, there was a small group of landholders who refused to sell and whose land was bulldozed before any legal agreement had been reached. Attempts to sue the Bakrie Group have been disastrous for some of the farmers: the court found against three complainants in December 1995, awarding damages of 75 million rupiahs to the BNR company (*Bali Post,* 30 December 1995). In August 1997, the "EIA Monitoring Team" for the development, set up by the Tabanan government, was still dealing with complaints from affected landholders in the "BNR Land Crisis,"[21] as the newspaper called it (*Bali Post,* 14 August 1997). The article cited a letter to the *Bali Post* two weeks earlier in which a landowner "requested that his land be returned. He was sick at heart because his land that had not yet been formally sold had already been leveled by BNR for the hotel and golf course."

In September 1997, BNR received a flurry of media attention around the "soft opening" of the $138 million "Le Meridien Nirwana Golf and Spa Resort" on 3 September,[22] with the "grand opening" scheduled for 14 November (*Bali Post,* 1 September 1997). At the same time, advertisements started appearing in Australian newspapers aimed at corporate customers—"What better place to improve your staff's drive . . . ?" (*Australian,* 5 September 1997)—with a logo featuring a Balinese mask, a dancer, and the words "True Bali." Much of the newspaper coverage in Bali was laudatory in tone, focusing on the economic advantages for the Tabanan government, previously one of the less-developed tourist areas in Bali,[23] and the wonders of the designer golf course, which features productive paddy fields as part of the landscaping. The clear vista of Tanah Lot Temple from the lobby of the hotel (but only the lobby) was also noted.[24] But criticism quickly surfaced. Members of the Society for Balinese Studies met with representatives from the provincial parliament to query the close proximity of the resort buildings to the temple in light of the PHDI decree of 1994. The coordinator of the Indonesian Hindu Youth and Student Solidarity Forum (Forum Solidaritas Mahasiswa dan Pemuda Hindu Indonesia, or FSMPHI) prepared a written statement questioning the benefit of the development for the people of Bali—raising concerns about the

offense to religious sensibilities and the inevitable crisis of water supplies that this and other projects would precipitate (*Bali Post*, 2 September 1997). Further fuel for controversy appeared when it was reported that the governor, the developer, and the contractor were
discussing plans for a huge spotlight to be focused on Tanah Lot Temple (*Bali Post*, 4 September 1997). Intellectuals, student representatives, and religious leaders issued statements deploring such a spectacle
in a religious place. Once more BNR seemed set to become the focus
around which broad public discontent could be aired.[25] By early 1998,
however, the resort was heading toward bankruptcy. Its chief source of
customers—wealthy corporate business executives from Japan and
other parts of Asia—were experiencing the severe contraction of the
Asian economies.

Although the anti-BNR movement of 1993–1994 lost momentum,
it demonstrated the depth of dissatisfaction toward the government's
development policies that favored capital-intensive tourist projects
with little regard for local interests. An interesting question for further
consideration is whether the anti-BNR actions, modest as their
achievements were, point to the growing strength of politically mobilized middle-class groups in Bali. This question cannot be taken up,
however, without considering the nature of economic development in
Bali—a province with a tourism-dominated economy that has been
called "Jakarta's colony" (Aditjondro 1995b).

Economic Transformation and Middle-Class Politics

In formal terms, economic development in Bali can be considered a
success. In the space of less than two decades, the per capita income on
the island moved from below the national average to one of the high-
est-ranking provinces (Jayasuriya and Nehen 1989; Warren 1994:1).
While Bali, like other provinces of Indonesia, has been affected by the
1997–1998 economic crisis, a significant amount of tourism—from affluent countries beyond the region—continues. But however successful economic development may be in crude statistical terms, it is not
without problems. Wage inequities are marked in different sectors of
the economy: in agriculture and handicraft production, for example,
wages remain low compared to those in the urban retail and service
sector (Warren 1994:14).

The economic gaps among regencies of Bali are striking. While the
1992–1993 per capita income for the island was reported to be 1.5

million rupiahs, some regencies, such as Jembrana, average only 900,000 rupiahs whereas the center of the tourist industry, Badung, averages 2.5 million (Warren 1994:14). These inequities have created intense competition among regency governments for tourist developments and have been attributed to the eagerness of Tabanan regency to take on the BNR megaproject at any environmental or social cost (Cohen 1994:28). At the opening of the resort in September 1997, representatives of the Tabanan government were quick to cite the economic benefits that will accrue: jobs for locals, for example, and a boost to the regency development tax income in the order of 100 percent in the 1997–1998 financial year (*Bali Post,* 4 September 1997). Likewise, some of the criticism of the GWK monument from within Bali was on the grounds that it was located in the heavily developed and wealthy Badung regency and would therefore do nothing to spread the wealth from tourism to other parts of the island.

Apart from the regional inequities, development in Bali, mirroring central government policy, places much emphasis on the economy to the detriment of sociocultural dimensions. Yet much of the island's economic success depends on the vitality of Balinese culture and religion as tourist commodities. This has been a perennial concern for middle-class Balinese opinion leaders and has found expression in many forms of rhetoric over the past two decades (Picard 1996b:chaps. 4 and 5). Criticisms of BNR and GWK took the form of concern over

Figure 19. "Bali tourism" cartoon by Surya Dharma.

the social tensions created by the inequitable distribution of wealth from tourism and the fact that the commercial exploitation of Balinese culture would lead to its degradation. Balinese are not alone, however, in articulating their misgivings about the social effects of the Suharto regime's commitment to economic development on a capitalist model—as the protests over the state lottery (SDSB) indicate (a rare instance of successful popular protest where the state capitulated).

While theories about the middle class as a social and political phenomenon in Indonesia are not well developed, the concept of a middle class *(kelas menengah)* is often invoked in both popular and scholarly discussions of social change and "in this sense is as much a cultural as an economic or political category" (McVey 1994:12). The importance of various culturally based evaluations of the social order in the political discourse of Indonesians themselves casts doubt on the usefulness of indicators based only on occupation or source of income (Dick 1990:64). Most analysts argue that the middle class is most usefully conceptualized as a composite of groups such as entrepreneurs, middle-level state functionaries and other salaried workers, professionals, and students, with different groups having varying dispositions toward forms of political mobilization.[26]

Just over a decade ago, a distinguished Indonesian political scientist, Loekman Soetrisno, claimed that a middle class which shares independent political opinions and a strong economic position does not yet exist in Indonesia. More recently, however, a national politician, Soegeng Sarjadi, has argued that Soetrisno's analysis is dated and that a vigorous and growing middle class now exists (Sarjadi 1996). Other analysts have pointed out the negative aspects of this phenomenon in contemporary Indonesia: "the widening gap between the very rich and ordinary Indonesians, the middle class, urban poor and peasantry, in terms of their income levels, assets and control over crucial resources" (Mackie and MacIntyre 1994:3). In Bali itself, a recent newspaper article on "The Conservation of Balinese Culture and the Middle Class" suggests that issues of equity for Balinese intellectuals are articulated through culturalist arguments about the role of the middle class in staving off the moral threat of *"globalisasi"* and the need to sensitively transform Balinese culture in this new global era (Suardika and Warijadi 1996).

Until recently, the growing affluence of middle-class groups in Indonesia seemed beyond dispute. But the question of whether and how this translates into forms of political power is complex. The privatized styles of consumption identified by Howard Dick (1990:64–65), while possibly a unifying value across diverse groups, seem unlikely to provide the impetus for collectivist politics and probably militate against it. Economic growth and a strong middle class are not necessarily accompanied by democratization, as the study of other Southeast Asian societies shows (Mackie and MacIntyre 1994:47). In Indonesia during the New Order, state power grew enormously, particularly the personal power of the president, while the institutions of civil society, such as political parties, NGOs, and various pressure groups, were considerably diminished (Mackie and MacIntyre 1994:3–4). It can hardly be accidental that the protest movements in Bali coincided with the growth of grassroots' power in the PDI, during Megawati's leadership, but the PDI's popular ascendancy too was ultimately suppressed.[27]

It has been argued that Indonesia's middle class is a conservative and consumption-oriented group—politically docile so long as it shares the fruits of affluence (Williams 1997:17) or at least with only a circumscribed commitment to democratization (Liddle 1990). Among the middle class there are many whose interests were protected by social and political arrangements under the New Order, and these groups cannot be seen as a reliable force of political liberalization. But as the Bali protests show, at particular moments, and on particular issues, there can be a broad mobilization of the populace despite the fragmentation and repression encountered in the political arena. Ian Roxborough (1979), in a general work on underdevelopment, has emphasized the importance of a shared vision of change as the main condition for middle-class programs of political action. Drawing on the concept of a shared vision of change, we might say that at certain moments a politically active middle class does exist in Bali—created out of a shared experience of exploitation as an ethnic minority threatened with alienation from land and culture. This experience helped to shape an oppositional political discourse that depended largely on the articulation of common moral values founded in Balinese Hinduism, which could not be readily repressed by the usual forces of state authority.

The groups that mobilized included NGOs, networks of middle-class professionals and salaried workers, and student organizations; other groups, such as certain parliamentarians and the military, provided passive support at least in the early stages. Journalists too played an active role in raising awareness of the issues at stake for the people of Bali. Warren (1994, 1998a) has discussed how the *Bali Post*—an independent newspaper with a history of links to the former Indonesian Nationalist Party—was instrumental in providing critics with accurate information about the contested developments and establishing forums for debate and criticism in the public arena.

The popular mobilization around the BNR project was not exclusively a middle-class phenomenon, however, as the contributions from a wide spectrum of the population in the pages of the *Bali Post* indicate. Among those most directly affected were the farmers whose land had been alienated, but they did not initiate nor even participate in most of the public protests. Through the few facilities available (legal aid organizations and the EIA monitoring team), the more determined among them have continued to pursue just compensation (*Bali Post,* 1 September 1997). Whether they participated in creating a "shared vision of change" seems doubtful at this stage, although their letters to the provincial parliament late in the day, in October 1994, were a strong statement at the time.

The mass protest movement grew as middle-class groups succeeded in defining the common interests of the "Balinese community"—defined both territorially (as residents of the island of Bali) and culturally (as Hindus). According to Saefulloh Fatah, mass protest movements can only exist if the common enemy can be identified and accepted as such by those involved (Fatah 1994). It may be assumed that in the anti-BNR protest the common enemy was identified, not as the developers themselves, but rather as the weak and corrupt provincial government whose elite was seen to be materially benefiting from the capital-intensive, non-Balinese, tourist developments, and therefore refused to curb or control them. Although various members of the middle class involved had different points of view in dealing with BNR, it was generally agreed that the fundamental problem was the predominance of economic factors in determining development policies in Bali. Middle-class groups, through their access to the media and to key state functionaries, saw a role for themselves as articulators of community aspirations in the face of the powerlessness of formal representative institutions. At the same time they attempted to formulate an alternative vision for development policy in Bali.

A Microcosm of Contradictory Forces

The anti-BNR feelings became a trigger for the rise of "people power"—a widely used term among activists at that time, who saw the popular political mobilization in the Philippines as a model to emulate. This kind of political action would have been unimaginable five years earlier. Spurred on perhaps by the fragile opportunity of the openness policy, some groups consolidated a new vision regarding their role in society. At the protest meeting outside the House of Representatives building in January 1994, Gedong Bagoes Oka emphasized that the BNR case opened the community's eyes to the irregularities and injustices in development policies in Bali. She predicted that resistance would continue in the future.

I Nyoman Gelebet, an architect and outspoken intellectual, in a speech at the same protest meeting, articulated a position of expedience in the short term, although it was uttered before the 1994 closures of critical magazines and newspapers. He argued that a heavy-handed government that tends to react violently to criticism of its policies should not be met with head-on confrontation but should be engaged in an accommodating way, facilitated by the middle class:

> Mass mobilization in the present circumstances is irrational. Protest is not a healthy choice. There is another way to carry out resistance: by intensifying open discussion and spreading the word through the mass media. In this way the middle class can consistently interact with the wider community, in order to create a shared vision and common goals on an appropriate path toward development. [From notes taken by Putu Suasta, who attended the meeting.]

Several years after the height of the BNR protests, large-scale resort and shopping mall developments continued apace on Bali, as did unjust land acquisitions and compensation arrangements.[28] In late 1997, two major resort developments on land supposedly protected by customary rights and religious tradition (at Padanggalak beach, north of Sanur, and on the island of Serangan) met widespread opposition not just from the communities affected but throughout the island. The Padanggalak case, in which the interests of Bali's governor, Ida Bagus Oka, and his family were heavily implicated, came to a head when the local *adat* or customary council of Kesiman (where the beach is located) threatened to excommunicate the governor from the council of which he was a member—a fate for a Balinese that has been likened to "social death." Construction has been halted and the earthworks removed. But as in the case of the BNR development, it cannot be assumed that the developers have abandoned their project (Warren 1998b:24–25).[29]

The encroachment of further resort developments has been arrested for the time being by the collapse of the rupiah and the stringent International Monetary Fund intervention in the country's economic governance. Even in times of economic hardship, Balinese have not become indifferent to the land alienation, economic exploitation, and cultural imperialism that tourist developments impose. Some see the current decline of economic growth as offering a respite and opportunity to rethink development priorities. By early 1998, the political landscape had changed dramatically. Economic collapse precipitated political crisis on a national scale. Megawati Sukarnoputri again emerged to prominence, declaring herself prepared to stand for president in the five-yearly election at the general meeting of the House of Assembly. She was supported by Amien Rais and Abdurrahman Wahid, popular leaders of mass Islamic organizations, foreshadowing a new alliance of Islamic and nationalist forces (Budiman 1998:18). But in the event—and despite a ferment of protest demonstrations, food riots, and violent actions toward the Chinese minority in towns and cities throughout the country—Suharto was the sole candidate. His seventh term as president was confirmed at the March meeting of the House of Assembly.

The pro-democracy movement continued to be fueled by student mobilization. Massive demonstrations against the government occurred at universities throughout the country, culminating in a huge student-led gathering outside the national parliament in Jakarta. A number of students were killed by government troops, and many more people were burned to death in fires that ensued from riots and looting in shopping malls. The official response to the student movement has been inconsistent. At the beginning of May 1998, President Suharto announced that "there will be no political reform for at least five years and indicated his government will crack down on attempts to disrupt national stability" (Williams 1998:23). But on 20 May he bowed to the mounting pressure and resigned on the advice of some of his closest advisers. He was succeeded by the vice-president, B. J. Habibie, who has subsequently been acceding to many of the protesters' demands for *reformasi*—the catchword of the pro-democracy forces.

Balinese students were active participants in the demonstrations against the Suharto regime, but other sorts of protests that erupted elsewhere in Indonesia (riots against Chinese shopowners and over food prices) have not occurred on the island. The economic privations caused by the currency collapse and IMF policies have been less marked in Bali, as well, where tourism remains viable (although threatened by even wider political violence across the country in coming months) and the export handicraft industry keeps a lot of people at work. Farmers have fared less well, for a huge rise in the cost of imported fertilizers and pesticides has adversely affected the profitability of harvests. All are affected adversely by rising fuel prices and other austerity measures that are part of the IMF package for Indonesia.

Figure 20. "Megawati . . . Yess" sticker on sale in Bali in 1998. Photo: Raechelle Rubinstein.

Other groups that mobilized against the tourist developments of a few years ago are striving with varying degrees of success for cohesiveness in facing the magnitude of current events. In the first half of 1998, the selection of a new governor of Bali occupied the political energies of many and became a focus for pro-democracy activists at the provincial level. In mid-1998, Megawati Sukarnoputri once again became a focus of popular political mobilization in Bali, engendering the hopes of many that a revitalized PDI might have a future role of significance to play in national politics.

In the 1970s, the development policies of Suharto's regime achieved a broad consensus that was the strength of the New Order's power for two decades. In Bali, by the late 1980s, that consensus could not be maintained because the trajectory of the very development that promised a better future was delivering an unpleasant present. In the early 1990s, *demokrasi* came to represent an aspiration that may be the basis of a new consensus. Its implementation is a fragile process—always subject to the forms of repression that have become institutionalized in the New Order and that may well be perpetuated under the leadership of President Habibie, although in the current volatile environment he has initiated some significant reforms.[30] Not least is the paradox that, in the words of Mackie and MacIntyre, "so many people have a vested interest" in the maintenance of the system (1994:45), including the dissenters themselves, although as economic prosperity disappears, this statement is less valid than it was a few years ago.

This analysis of protest movements in Bali demonstrates a microcosm of contradictory forces at work in Indonesian society—forces that foster dissent and the growth of civil society as well as forces that repress these elements. The events in Bali cannot yet lead us to conclude that the middle class is necessarily the vehicle of sustained democratic mobilization. In the current crisis of legitimacy in Indonesia, it remains to be seen who can shape a new consensus.

Notes

We are grateful to the following people for comments on earlier drafts and assistance with locating sources: George Aditjondro, Ed Aspinall, Rucina Ballinger, Graeme MacRae, Pujastana, Raechelle Rubinstein, Adrian Vickers, Carol Warren.

1. Apart from the PDI, there were two legally recognized political parties at the time of writing: the coalition of former Islamic parties, now known as Partai Persatuan Pembangunan or PPP, as well as the government Golkar (Golongan Karya) Party formed from a coalition of "functional groups" drawn from occupational and government-backed "voluntary" associations such as youth and women's organizations. For an overview of the reorganization of the party system in 1973 see Schwarz (1994:29–33) and Mackie and MacIntyre (1994:12–13).

2. In official Indonesian political rhetoric, the "New Order" (Orde Baru) refers to the period from 1966 until 1998 under the leadership of the second President of the Republic, Suharto. The officially discredited "Old Order" (Orde Lama) refers to the period 1950–1966 under the first president,

Sukarno, after full independence was gained. For an overview of the Old Order period see Schwarz (1994:chap. 1).

3. See Schwarz (1994:264–269) for a concise summary of these events.

4. This was apparently done on the technicality that she had been confirmed as leader by the party at a national convention (held in December 1993), not an official national congress of the party.

5. As Aspinall recounts, the organization of an extraordinary congress by the government, not the party itself, was done by the following means: "From late April [1966], the PDI leadership began to receive reports from the regions that Interior Ministry officials and military officers were visiting party branch officials and instructing them to sign statements calling for an 'extraordinary party congress.' All became clear on June 3, when a delegation of PDI members visited the Ministry of Internal Affairs to seek permission to hold such a congress" (1996:6).

6. For a summary of these events see Aspinall (1996:5–6); for reporting in Bali of the Jakarta demonstrations see *Bali Post,* 29 July 1996, p. 1.

7. The PRD had originally been formed as the Democratic People's Association (Perkumpulan Rakyat Demokrasi) in May 1994. But on 23 July 1996, just a few days before the Medan events, it had declared itself a party, contravening the government's strict controls over the formation of political parties. We are grateful to G. Aditjondro for this information.

8. In the Indonesian context, such statements from the military reviving the communist "specter" have the capacity to evoke strong fears among the populace, given the brutal intimidation of communists and suspected communists dating from the 1965–1966 massacres. For further information on this period see Cribb (1990).

9. In Indonesia NGOs are often quite radical organizations because of their social justice agendas and are thus prone to be labeled "subversive" by the government. For further discussion of NGOs see Lev (1990:33).

10. The Five Principles, as summarized by Van Langenberg, are: Belief in One Supreme God; Humanitarianism; Indonesian Unity; Popular Representation; Social Justice (1986:36).

11. *Undang-Undang Lalu lintas dan Angkutan Jalan,* no. 14/1992.

12. For reports on the protests see *Inside Indonesia* 29(December 1991):1; *Indonesia Business Weekly,* 19 November 1993, p. 10; *Jakarta Jakarta* 384(1993):76–77.

13. For further details of the project see "Bali to Build the World's Tallest Statue to Woo Tourists," *Jakarta Post,* 22 June 1997, p. 14.

14. For further details see "Does Bali Really Need US$83 Million Statue?" *Jakarta Post,* 22 June 1997, p. 14.

15. On the events of 1965 in Bali see Robinson (1995).

16. Members of five *banjar* or village residential wards in the earlier land sales were offered the government rate of about 2 million rupiahs per are (1 hectare = 100 are) (Kusuma 1994:9). Bakrie offered the much higher rate of 5 million rupiahs per are ($2,326) and promised to employ two members

of each household in the resort (Cohen 1994:30). As time went on, those who had withheld selling their land were offered higher prices by the developer, despite assurances that prices would not go up, so that the landholders who had sold earlier demanded that they be paid the difference between the current rate and the former rate (*Suara Pembaruan,* 11 February 1994). These arrangements, perhaps not unintentionally, undermined the solidarity of the landholders vis-à-vis the developer.

17. Approval in principle had been given by the governor of Bali as early as 1988 without any public discussion (*Bali Post,* 31 December 1993).

18. The members of DPRD are chosen by general election and drawn from candidates who are determined by the political parties after close vetting by government officials and the military. Armed Forces members can join DPRD without going through the election process.

19. Such speculations are lent further weight by a recent article in *Tempo* magazine (Special Issue: "Our Parliament Through History," August 1997, pp. 94–95), where yet another transfer of Syafei, from ABRI representative in the national parliament to the Central ABRI Command, was attributed to outspoken comments he had made prior to the May 1997 general election defending the right of people to register informal protest votes.

20. Known as Komandan Distrik Militer, or KODIM.

21. "Kemelut Tanah BNR."

22. The French company Le Meridien joined with the Bakrie Group in October 1995.

23. For example, the projected number of jobs is 1,800 for the whole resort (*Bali Post,* 1 September 1997).

24. As it turned out, the distance of the closest physical buildings from the temple is 400 meters, while the center of the resort is 800 meters distant, according to the general manager (*Bali Post,* 1 September 1997). The temple is clearly visible from the golf course also.

25. For example, see the article titled "Do Balinese Want to Be Known as Robots?"—a phrase taken from an interview with the chair of the Indonesian Hindu Youth Organization (Ikatan Pemuda Hindu Indonesia, or IPHI) (*Bali Post,* 8 September 1997).

26. For example, see Tanter and Young (1990)—in particular the chapters by Dick, Lev, and Liddle.

27. In the 1997 general election, the PDI vote dropped dramatically across the country. PDI members threatened to boycott the election or vote informal (known as Golput or Golongan Putih, the "white/empty group," a pun on the government party, Golongan Karya). In Bali, the proportional percentages, based on the official figures for the formal vote for the 1992 and 1997 elections, were as follows: PDI, 19.72 percent (1992) and 3.5 percent (1997); PPP, 1.99 percent (1992) and 3.28 percent (1997); Golkar, 78.29 percent (1992) and 93.21 percent (1997). The informal vote in Bali was 7.42 percent (1992) and 11.16 percent (1997) (Batubara n.d.). The proportional percentages (rounded) nationwide for the formal vote for 1997 were: PDI, 3

percent; PPP, 23 percent; Golkar, 74 percent (Mohamad 1997:5). The informal vote nationwide was 9.42 percent, higher than in any previous year (Batubara n.d.).

28. See, for example, the cases of farmers in Pecatu, Badung, whose land was taken for another luxury tourist development funded by Tommy Suharto, the former president's son (*Bali Post,* 7 and 9 September 1995), and the residents of Culik, Karangasem, who became refugees from their own village because of factionalized land disputes in which regency officials were implicated (*Bali Post,* 14 September 1996).

29. At the time of writing, work at the Serangan resort has halted because of the developer's insolvency.

30. These reforms include the announcement that democratic elections will be held in 1999 and the release of certain political prisoners (but not Xanana Gusmao, the East Timorese resistance leader).

Chapter 4

Acting Global, Thinking Local in a Balinese Tourist Town

Graeme MacRae

Ubud: a name, a label, given to an entity defined differently by different people for different purposes: tourist destination, paradise of expatriate imagining, administrative village and/or ritual district, ritual village *(desa adat)*, kingdom, palace *(puri)*. All imply bounded unity of some kind. Yet the only boundaries easy to find are the administrative ones on the big, clumsily painted wall map in the district *(kecamatan)* office. "Where are you from?" I ask the blonde woman with the American accent. "From Ubud." "I come from Ubud too," says the seller of bamboo lamp shades in the Kuta sunset. "Whereabouts in Ubud?" "From Tampaksiring." "Where are you going?" I ask my neighbor in Taman, knowing full well she is going to the market five minutes walk away. "To Ubud." "But where are the boundaries of your survey area?" asks the frustrated official trying to process my research permit. "That is a good question," I think to myself.[1]

Global Village

Anthropologyland (Dirks 1994:483) is full of villages like Ubud, places with exotic names and markets and communities about whose local specificity we can say this or that. We all know now that the discreteness, autonomy, and boundedness of these villages that we once took for granted was something of an illusion. It has even been argued

123

that the notion of the village itself was "no more than a colonial construction imposed on an extremely fluid, rural society in which patronage was far more important than communal bonds" (Schulte Nordholt
1991a:2 referring to Breman 1988 and others).[2] Anthropology prefers
now to concern itself instead with "such regional processes as: state formation and disintegration; transnational or multi-state networks; . . .
supralocal and overseas communities . . . or other phenomena of . . .
wide regional scale" (University of Auckland 1994).

The beguiling image of the "global village" was coined in the 1960s
(McLuhan 1968) to suggest the potential of new communication
technologies to shrink the globe into a village-like community. The
1990s term "globalization" draws attention to the other side of this
process: villages supposedly once isolated are progressively integrated
into economic and cultural systems of global scope. Although it has
been promoted in the global tourism supermarket as a traditional
village—the quintessential local product—the development of Ubud
has for over a century been inseparable from links with foreign people
and places. Ubud is now a global village of the latter type: a tourist
boom-town in a tourist boom-island where people, ideas, and money
fresh off aircraft and electronic media from all over the world rub
shoulders with each other and with those of the local village community. While the economic and political events of 1998 have threatened
the boom, they illustrate clearly the three-way link between Ubud,
Jakarta, and the world economy.

Despite all this, the villages have not gone away: people still live in
them and think them. While the people of Ubud act (predictably)
global, they often think (surprisingly) local. Although by no means ignorant of the global economic processes upon which their livelihoods
depend, they tend to speak of their own prosperity, like every other aspect of their lives, primarily in terms of their relationships with the
gods—invisible *niskala* beings and forces of more or less local nature
and not subject to historical change.[3] These various Ubuds may be characterized by opposition not only along the axis between the global and
the local but along a number of polar axes that are related but not per-
fectly aligned: modern versus traditional, changing versus timeless, economic versus religious, visible versus invisible (Wiener 1995a:12–13),
tourism versus culture.[4] While such oppositions are deeply embedded in
the history/structure of anthropological thought, they are also empiri-
cally evident in Ubud and in wider Balinese discourse about conditions
in Bali at present. Understanding Ubud involves understanding the relationship between such multiplex and seemingly contradictory aspects.

The Geo-History of Ritual Practice

Balinese ritual practice seeks to maintain harmonious relationships with a complex pantheon of invisible *(niskala)* beings and forces through a system of ritual works *(karya)* based on sacrificial offerings *(banten)* to such beings. This system is structured within an elaborate ordering of time and space into interconnecting rhythms and contours of spiritual appropriateness. Hours, days, months, phases of the moon, seasons, directions, elevation, hills and valleys, rivers, lakes, and sea are the elements of this system, and their combinations are many and varied.

By locating the main nodes at which ritual resources and labor are deployed and by tracking various connections between them (processions, ritual exchanges) it is possible to construct maps representing what might be described as a *niskala* landscape: invisible to normal human vision but underlying the physical, historical, and social landscapes. The key units of this landscape are not only named institutions such as villages *(desa)*, or even temples themselves, but networks constituted by the links between such institutions. From this point of view, the importance of Ubud lies not in its status as a village but as an important, if somewhat anomalous, node in a network of villages roughly contained within a river valley. In other words, even what appear to be the most local of (ritual) units cannot be properly understood except as part of wider networks.

Figure 21. A procession maps the ritual landscape. Photo: Raechelle Rubinstein.

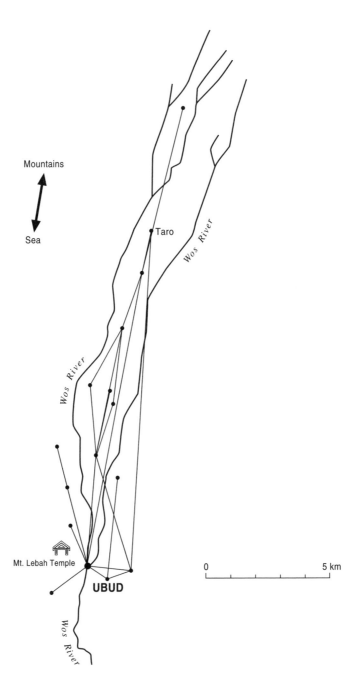

Mountains

Sea

Taro

Wos River

Wos River

Mt. Lebah Temple

UBUD

Wos River

0   5 km

Map 2. Puri Ubud's Ritual Network in the Wos River Valley: 1996

The spatial forms of these networks are misleading—they cannot be understood apart from their constitution through a historical process. Analysis of this process reveals both the agency of the hereditary rulers of Ubud, the *puri*,[5] in creating and maintaining these networks and their links to the tourism economy (MacRae 1995, 1998a:219–264, 1998b). The "Ubuds" that come into focus from attention to global/economic versus local/ritual aspects are neither simple inversions of each other, nor are they the separate worlds they at first appear to be: under careful scrutiny they tend to dissolve into each other or rather into a mass of intermediate levels awkwardly entangled with economic, political, and historical processes. This chapter explores the levels between ritual networks and global tourism and the untidy processes that generate and link them, touching along the way upon a confluence of general concerns of theory and method. Among the venerable and global debates in anthropology, two of the most venerable concern the relationship between the domains of the practical and the symbolic and the proper form and use of historical analysis. Clifford Geertz (1980) has used Balinese material to make significant contributions to both. I offer an alternative view based on specific historical material from Ubud and the use of Pierre Bourdieu's concept of "symbolic capital" as a metaphor for conceptualizing these relationships.

Jean and John Comaroff, in a recent contribution to the debate over history (1992:96–97), argue that the "processes of articulation" that link local communities with larger social, economic, and political environments (such as regional chiefdoms, colonial empires, nation-states, the world economy) give rise to "temporal axes" of shorter and longer duration that are related (not necessarily directly) to the scale of connections in space. These latter are not usefully reducible to the global and the local: there are multiple levels of temporal process corresponding to different levels of spatial connection.[6] The Comaroffs argue for a historical anthropology that takes into account all the elements in this "equation" (p. 98). I think the "equation" is in fact more complex than the Comaroffs allow: the spatial zones and temporal processes of varying term that become apparent depend, at least in Ubud, upon the activities to which we pay attention: the mode of action at the time. In the mode of ritual, certain kinds of spatial order become apparent. Conversely, when I look at historical process, the play of political and economic factors comes to light.[7] There are, therefore, three rather than two dimensions across which both empirical variation and our perception of it occur: spatial (zones), temporal (processes), and modes (of action/perception). To keep track of these dimensions, and more importantly the relationships between them, we must be able to shift our perception within and between all three. The sections that follow trace the twentieth-century history of Ubud in terms of the interplay of factors that become visible at more and less global/local levels of spatial analysis and with the historical processes corresponding to these levels.

The Life, Space, and Times of Ubud

> This all used to be Kerajaan Ubud [the Kingdom of Ubud]. . . . The raja [king] of Ubud owned all the land from the sea at Ketewel to Taro in the mountains.[8]

The Village Becomes a Kingdom

The former kingdom that Puri Ubud is symbolically reclaiming through its program of patronage in the Wos Valley was itself the fruit of a program of expansion by an illustrious ancestor exactly a century previously. Through warfare, diplomacy, and the exercise of personal charisma,[9] Cokorda Gede Sukawati (hereafter Cokorda Sukawati) steered the development of Ubud from the status of a small and peripheral village to the center of a vast (by Balinese standards) strip of land from the sea to the lower edge of the mountain plateau.[10]

While expanding from his village base from around 1880 onward, Cokorda Sukawati was simultaneously developing strategic alliances with the heads (punggawa) of neighboring districts—especially his senior and junior relatives in Peliatan and Tegallalang. These alliances were founded not only on common material interest but ideologically on common descent from the eighteenth-century kingdom of Sukawati, physically long defunct but today still a significant force in the ritual and political geography of the area (Lansing 1983:5–6). While never a guarantee of cooperation, such links through ancestors tend to encourage long-term political cohesion at a local level. Indeed it was through the defeat of Puri Negara, a closely related descendant of Puri Sukawati and a former ally, that Puri Ubud acquired the largest component of its material wealth and confirmation of its kesaktian. An underlying theme of accounts of this episode, however, is the regret of all concerned at being involved in such a fratricidal conflict and emphasis on the divisive role of external (non-Sukawati-descended) elements. At a broader regional level, during this same period Cokorda Sukawati made himself indispensable to the greater king of Gianyar, within whose sphere of jurisdiction his territories fell, and to his western neighbor, the king of Mengwi, thus surrounding himself with allies. As his descent relationships with both inclined more toward conflict than cooperation, such alliances were inherently pragmatic arrangements, unstable over time, which he sought to render more enduring by marriage links.[11]

While relatively isolated from wider patterns of regional trade, all the kingdoms of Bali, by the mid-nineteenth century, were supplementing their local economic bases of agricultural produce and obligatory labor with imports and exports through ports-of-trade managed on their behalf by foreign agents (Agung 1991:4; Hanna 1976:12, 55). Gianyar appears to have had one of the less developed of such trade systems—which may have been a factor in its declining political fortunes in the latter part of the nineteenth century. After gaining control of the small port of Ketewel in 1891, Cokorda Sukawati appropriated a portion of the duties and harbor fees collected there (Schwartz 1900:177–178). He also gained control, after the fall of Mengwi, of its former uphill dependencies, Carangsari and Petang, centers of coffee production and opium exchange, from both of which he gained additional tribute (Schulte Nordholt 1996:197). In addition to a subsistence base spread over a wide area of diverse ecosystems and control over most of an irrigation watershed, Puri Ubud had connections with regional export trade sufficient to ensure a substantial cash income attested to by the amount of gold leaf with which the palace was reputedly encrusted.

The Kingdom Becomes Part of a Colonial Empire

Throughout the period of Ubud's rise to prominence, the Dutch, long established in most of the neighboring islands and in northern Bali (from 1849), were watching the south and awaiting opportunity there. Their southernmost ally, Bangli, played a prominent part in the aggression that maintained a state of chaos in the region, ultimately destroying the kingdom of Mengwi and bringing Gianyar, by the turn of the century, to the point of collapse.

Ubud thus entered the twentieth century wealthy and powerful but poised uneasily between possible destruction in the local (southern Balinese) theater of warring princes and an uncertain future as part of the huge regional empire of the Netherlands Indies with its links to the world beyond. We have no record of Cokorda Sukawati's relationship

with the Dutch during this period,[12] but subsequent events suggest
that he too was watching, waiting, and cultivating connections with
them. It is known that he played a major part in first persuading the
embattled king of Gianyar to offer his kingdom, including Ubud, to
the Dutch and then brokering the subsequent negotiations between
the parties (Mahaudiana 1968:104; Schulte Nordholt 1996:200).
Once the deal with the Dutch was concluded, neither his landholdings
nor his territorial authority were diminished. In fact his power over
them was placed on a long-term basis dependent less on the inherent
wax and wane of his own charisma than on the apparently permanent
and external power of the colonial state. The establishment several
years later, when the whole of southern Bali was in Dutch hands, of a
bureaucratic system of local administration had the effect of freezing at
a certain point a system of constantly shifting alliances of varying size
and duration into a rationalized hierarchy of administrative districts of
decreasing size but supposedly permanent form (Schulte Nordholt
1988:205–208).

Not only was his local economic base and political authority under-
written by the Dutch, but Cokorda Sukawati received from them a
substantial stipend corresponding to the extent of his dominions and
perhaps reflecting the general quality of his relationship with them.[13]
Local perceptions of his charisma may, if anything, have been bolstered
rather than diminished by his association with such powerful and "dangerous" beings as the Dutch.[14] A Dutch visitor to his court in 1902
and 1911 portrays him as a man evidently at home in, and enjoying the
best of, both worlds (Van Kol 1903:470–474; 1914:346–348). While
he attempted to diversify his economic portfolio in accordance with
the changing times by investing in the commercial development in
Denpasar (Hilbery 1979:10), a new system of land taxation in 1913, a
severe earthquake in 1917, and an influenza epidemic in 1918 made
inroads into this prosperity.

A Nineteenth-Century Local Hero and Twentieth-Century Citizen of the World

The death of Cokorda Sukawati in 1919 marked the end of an extraordinary era during which Ubud moved from a local world of seasonal
rhythms and the ebb and flow of kingdoms a few square kilometers in
size—becoming for its moment one of such kingdoms—to absorption
into a vast colonial empire that brought it ultimately into contact with
even wider zones of influence and processes of change. Cokorda

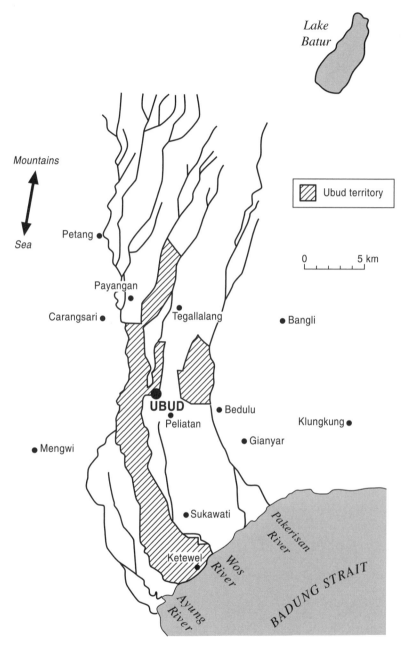

Map 3. Ubud and Its Neighbors: 1900

Sukawati, current fashion in ethnohistory notwithstanding, appears to have been the dominant figure in this process. Indeed, he developed a style of government based on the globally time-honored pattern of politico-military alliance followed by politico-economic alliance, combined with a locally defined charisma, rather than on the ritual display emphasized by Geertz (1980). (See also Schulte Nordholt 1988.)[15] This would come later.

The leadership of the *puri* fell to Cokorda Sukawati's eldest son, Cokorda Raka (Sukawati). Educated in Dutch schools and groomed for the upper echelons of the native civil service, he ultimately became closer to the Dutch than his own family let alone the common people of Ubud (Hilbery 1979:7).[16] His education and contacts enabled him to engineer a subdivision of his father's property favorable to his own interests, while his global approach to the management of local affairs included such cultural innovations as the import of Walter Spies from Yogyakarta in 1927 and a tour of local dancers and musicians to Europe in 1931.[17] Indeed, Cokorda Raka's ambitions were ultimately too global for him to be satisfied with the role of local administrator/prince.[18] After the tour he moved into national politics, leaving his cousin as the official head of the somewhat reduced administrative district of Ubud and his younger brother in charge of the *puri*.

Exposure to Colonial and World Economies

> The insecurities of the world market were . . . greater than those of the traditional local market. [Scott 1977:59]

The subdivision of the inheritance left each of the new sub-*puri* with somewhat reduced landholdings, and the colonial land taxation system introduced in 1922 rendered even this less profitable than before. The former kingdom was shrinking, dividing, and losing its wealth as well as its political dominance. The members of Puri Ubud, however, were not the only ones suffering during this period: for the ordinary people the extraordinarily high rates of taxation were a constant burden. The requirement to pay in Dutch currency forced them into greater involvement in the cash economy, and the world depression of 1932 compounded the situation by reducing the demand and prices of export cash crops such as copra, rice, coffee, and pigs (Robinson 1995:56–57).[19]

Contrary to foreign perceptions of Bali during the 1930s, many of which originated in Ubud (for example, Bateson 1973; Covarrubias

1972), the depression years were a time of real hardship clearly re-membered today by those old enough. Prominent in these memories is the fear of taxation—one of a number of reasons cited for the high incidence of landlessness in Ubud. Farmers, it is said, were afraid to own land because of the tax, preferring to work on land owned by the *puri*, in some cases even voluntarily surrendering their land to the *puri* to avoid tax.[20] Population began to increase during this period (Foley 1987:3.3), as well, and pressure for scarce agricultural land grew with it. It was during this period of economic stress to which Ubud was ex-posed through its dependence on the world economy to pay colonial taxes that the fundamental economic contradiction between the vast landholdings of the *puri* and the hardship experienced by the popula-tion, especially the landless, began to become evident. (Robinson 1995:57–58 points this out for the whole of Bali.)

The world economy began to enter Ubud in other ways during this period. Among the litany of economic decline chronicled by J. B. Bakker, the only sign of growth over the years 1933–1934 was in the number of tourists visiting the island, which rose from 1,795 to 2,139 (1937:290). While the majority of these visitors were on three-day tours of the island, a proportion were longer-term sojourners, many of them visiting Walter Spies in Ubud. Although not great in number, they tended to be reasonably well heeled and lived in a style requiring the employment of considerable amounts of local labor. Sixty years later there are a few old men who remember working for Spies or his friends and several more who were associated with the prominent Dutch painter Rudolf Bonnet who returned to Bali for several years after independence.

Apart from their direct economic impact on Bali, these expatriate residents developed and marketed to Europe and America Ubud's first and most enduring export product: the image of Bali as a natural, so-cial, and aesthetic paradise (MacRae 1992; Vickers 1989:95–130). While the material fruits of this masterpiece of marketing were not har-vested until two generations later, it insinuated into the local cultural economy the distinctly global idea of cultural products as commodities and the notion of culture itself as capital. Once again, the *puri* played a leading role in recognizing and seizing the opportunity. It was Cokorda Raka who, as we have seen, invited Walter Spies to settle in Ubud and who organized the first dance and music tour of Europe.[21] Spies be-came a patron and mentor of local artists; the tour itself introduced the idea of local performing arts as export products on the world market.

After Cokorda Raka moved to Jakarta in 1931, his younger brother,

Cokorda Agung, took over leadership of the *puri* and the cultural development of Ubud. Although he continued to cultivate cultural relationships with foreign expatriates for whom this was something of a golden age, his own account of the period (Hilbery 1979:15–21) confirms a sense of troubles within the *puri* as much as among the ordinary people. The contradiction between the Dutch colonial vision of global/local relations and that of the expatriate glitterati eventually became too great to sustain. The expatriates were forced to leave (Vickers 1989:124–125).

Politics: Global, Colonial, and Local, 1940–1960

In 1941 the great European power of the Dutch was replaced with the (temporarily) greater Asian power of the Japanese. They stripped the resources of the island to support their war throughout the Asia-Pacific region, and people in Ubud remember their lives as being reduced to bare survival (Robinson 1995:75–81; Hilbery 1979:23–26). After the war the Dutch returned and were ultimately ousted again by the Indonesian nationalist movement. The theater of political struggle shifted from a global to a regional scale.

While from a regional point of view the displacement of a European power by an Asian one had significant implications for the nationalist movement (Vickers 1989:155), from a local (Ubud) point of view both were equally nonlocal and relationships with them tended to be mediated by the *puri*. During the Dutch period it was *puri* members whom the occupying power appointed as its local representatives, and it was to the *puri* that people took their problems. A number of Ubud people participated actively in the war of independence and in the struggle to define the way in which the newly won power was to be configured in the region.

Gianyar became the center of a movement for a new, Dutch-sponsored state of Eastern Indonesia. Although Cokorda Raka, through his marriage relationship with Puri Gianyar, supported this movement, the majority of members of Puri Ubud supported the nationalist/republican cause. Puri Ubud became a center of resistance to the Dutch-backed power of Puri Gianyar, and the people of the district divided along lines of affiliation to their respective aristocratic patrons, which coincided roughly with the administrative subdistricts of the time. Nationalists/ republicans from throughout the district, including members of Puri Ubud and neighboring Puri Peliatan, were imprisoned, tortured, and killed by the Dutch/Gianyar coalition (Hilbery 1979:32–33). While this conflict could be seen at one level (spatially large but temporally short) as a struggle of Indonesian nationalism against Dutch colonialism, locally it was seen as a local contest going back generations between the various *puri,* supported by their followers, recruited on the basis of a combination of hereditary ties and active patronage.

The Ubud/Gianyar conflict was ultimately resolved with the establishment of a new state of Indonesia that, from a local point of view, simply replaced the previous Japanese and Dutch regimes. Economic and political instability, however, continued through the 1950s (Bagus 1991; Robinson 1995; Hilbery 1979:2; Vickers 1989:146–173). One of the consequences of this series of political upheavals was the exposure of local communities throughout Indonesia to a range of exotic political ideas and practices and the formation of pan-Indonesian political movements—one of which, communism, was to play a significant part in the following decade.

Cokorda Agung, never a creature of politics like his brother, was increasingly alienated by these problems and withdrew even further: "From that time there were so many political parties here in Indonesia that I was not interested any longer" (Hilbery 1979:41). He was more inclined to see problems in terms of their supernatural *(niskala)* causes (p. 21), and he devoted his energies accordingly to such projects as the restoration of temples and *barong.*[22] He sought also to supplement his income by opening his *puri* to paying guests—creating, in effect, the first hotel in Ubud (p. 40).

Local memories of the 1950s emphasize the priority of survival under the constant threat of unpredictable political violence. In the early 1960s, economic conditions worsened with rodent plagues, the eruption of Mount Agung (1963), subsequent crop failures, and spectacular rates of inflation—especially affecting the prices of basic commodities such as rice.[23] Ubud people over about thirty-five years of age remember clearly having insufficient clothing and food as children, more sweet potato than rice, and often just the fibrous trunk of banana trees. According to local opinion, Ubud was particularly hard hit. Many young men and boys took to the roads during this period, picking up work and food wherever they could find it (see also Robinson 1995:241).

During these times of economic change and hardship the lot of the common people was obviously not easy, yet the *puri* seems to have maintained a position of considerable economic privilege. Unlike other *puri* that turned to business (Geertz 1963:chap. 4), to government, or to academic or professional positions, the main economic base of Puri

Figure 22. *Barong:* child's ink drawing from Bali, 1939. Photo: KITLV, Or. 1462.

Ubud remained its substantial estates of land which, although subdivided, had remained virtually intact since the 1890s.[24] The unequal distribution of land and rural relations of production were, however, obviously factors in the economic suffering of the majority and were becoming a political issue at a national level (Robinson 1995:251–258). The parties of the left—especially the Indonesian Communist Party, the PKI (Partai Komunis Indonesia), with which President Sukarno had considerable sympathy—pushed for a comprehensive land reform program that began in 1960.

The 1960s: Local Effects of National Economics and Politics

Although land reform proceeded slowly and partially, with large landowners all over Bali displaying considerable resourcefulness to retain as much of possible of their estates, it did have the effect of further subdividing the holdings of the *puri* as well as significantly reducing the total areas held.[25] This process forced *puri* members to further diversify their economic endeavors, shifting the emphasis from extraction of surplus from the local agricultural economy to investment and partnerships in wider economic zones. While the newly redistributed lands gave small farmers control over the produce of their lands, spiraling inflation negated much of their gains. The gradual reduction of the sphere of Puri Ubud's economic domain was accompanied by progressive reductions of the administrative district of Ubud and reduction of the formal role of the *puri* in this administration.[26]

The early 1960s mark the point at which the former kingdom of Ubud was reduced politically to the center of an unimportant administrative subdistrict and economically to a poor agricultural village. The relationship between the *puri* and its former kingdom was all but broken by economic hardship and political unrest. These forces strained the internal unity of the local community also, as two new *banjar* (residential village wards) formed along lines of sympathy or opposition to the PKI. In both cases, the new *banjar* were formed around splinter groups that, if not overtly communist themselves, objected to the anti-PKI position of the *puri*. In contrast to other *puri*, however, Puri Ubud did not withdraw from its relationship of mutual obligation to the local community during this period: indeed it was during this period that Cokorda Agung Sukawati began to involve himself in restoring temples and organizing ceremonies not only in Ubud but all over Bali (Hilbery 1979:54–77).

Ubud was less affected than many places by the wave of anticommunist violence that swept the country in the months following the attempted coup in Jakarta in September 1965 and the subsequent downfall of President Sukarno. Although there were active PKI cells in nearby villages, most people in Ubud followed the clear Nationalist Party (Partai Nasionalis Indonesia, or PNI) affiliation of the *puri*. While there were obviously shades of sympathy toward PKI principles, there appears to have been only a handful of active PKI members in Ubud. Estimates of the number of people killed range from nine to around twenty; the majority appear to have been innocent hangers-on or victims of vengeful slander. The role of the *puri* in all this remains a matter of conjecture.[27]

Despite the economic woes of Indonesia, the 1960s was a period of economic growth throughout the developed world, and one of its manifestations was the spread of mass tourism into the Third World. Sukarno had recognized this and, before he was ousted, had taken the first steps to integrate Indonesia into this new movement of global surplus. Bali was chosen—partly as a result of the image developed in Ubud and exported all over the world during the 1930s—as the central locale for this development. Although Ubud had been one of the original sources of the image, the tourist zone was to be concentrated in the coastal area south of Denpasar (MacRae 1992:chap. 2; Picard 1990a:5).

Tourism: The World Comes to the Village

Although geographically peripheral, people from Ubud did participate in this development, which was funded largely by the World Bank and foreign investment (Picard 1990a:5–6). Considerable numbers of people migrated to the coast to work on building projects, some of them staying on as employees in hotels. Traders of batik sarongs, carvings, and paintings took their wares to the tourists in the coastal resorts or to Padangbai, in neighboring Klungkung district, where the cruise ships berthed.[28]

A minority of tourists, however, came direct to Ubud and locals responded by providing accommodation and food and showing them the various cultural resources of the area. This practice developed rapidly into hotels, restaurants, and shops, and by the mid-1980s the economy of Ubud was dominated by a massive inflow of foreign currency and imported products providing for tourist needs and the burgeoning consumer tastes of the new local middle class. While the Dutch monopolized the transport and accommodation sectors of pre–World War II tourism and most visitors to Ubud were associated in one way or another with Walter Spies, after the war Puri Ubud opened the first local hotels and established links with travel agencies in Australia.

The new tourism, however, was different. Unprecedented economic and cultural conditions in Australia, North America, and Europe, as well as the development of cheap mass air travel, resulted in a mass migration of young people traveling often for months on end in search of various combinations of escape and education, pleasure and profit. It was the response of a wide range of local people to these visitors, rather than the projections of government, World Bank, or tourist industry planners, that conditioned the unique form of tourism in Ubud.

Redefining Local Culture

Though Puri Ubud lost its monopoly on tourism, it continued to develop tourism interests—mostly toward the upper end of the market and financed by sales of land and joint ventures with foreign capital.[29] Its members, moreover, occupied positions at all levels of local government. But while these strategies gave them a degree of prosperity and influence, they did not become dominant in either field. What they also did, in striking contrast to other *puri* in Bali, was to reestablish their role as guides and guardians of local tradition and ritual.[30] Throughout his career, Cokorda Agung Sukawati had involved himself in the restoration of temples and their sacred relics *(pretima)* as well as the patronage of the arts (Hilbery 1979). Upon his death, this mantle was taken up by his nephew, Cokorda Agung Suyasa, who has for some years been the elected head *(bendesa adat)* of the customary (as opposed to the administrative) village.

A booklet *(Monografi Ubud)* prepared for the 1983 Lomba Desa, a national competition for civic excellence between villages, provides some insights into Ubud's (official) view of itself at this time.[31] It was prepared by a team representing the local community but consisting almost entirely of aristocracy and dominated by the *puri*. Apart from the (inevitable and interminable) lists of organizations, officeholders, and local statistics, which reflect more the criteria of civic excellence upon which the competition was based than actual local priorities, the book records a version of Ubud history that explicitly links local geography, the pan-Balinese origin myth of Resi Markandeya, and the descent of Puri Ubud from the original aristocratic settlers from the Majapahit empire in Java with a succession of administrations and officeholders down to the present *puri* (Kelurahan Ubud 1983). The essence of Ubud is thus defined not only in terms of its local characteristics but also its place in larger Balinese, Indonesian, and Hindu frames of reference. The links between these frames are articulated by the *puri*.

Puri members speak readily of their role in terms of a sacred duty to maintain "tradition" *(adat/agama)* and provide leadership and guidance to the whole community. Members of this wider community generally concur (at least publicly, to varying degrees, and with a few notable exceptions) with this perception of the ideal role of the *puri*. Outside of Ubud, where such formal avenues linking customary *(adat)* and administrative *(dinas)* spheres were not available to them, especially in areas that had become part of other administrative districts, this role had to be recreated by a program of active patronage.

Cultural Patronage: Recreating a Regional Network

Throughout the upper Wos Valley, a large proportion of villages are linked to the *puri* by ties of ritual patronage. Materially this connection takes the form of Puri Ubud's sponsorship of the artifacts and practices of traditional culture and religion: renovation of temples and sacred objects (especially *barong*), dance troupes and music ensembles, and ever bigger and better ceremonies. In exchange, the client villages invite the *puri* to their ceremonies as well as attending and providing labor for the ceremonial occasions in Ubud and at the *puri* itself. While this relationship involves an ongoing reciprocity of material resources—essentially money for labor—it also involves a less obvious immaterial exchange.

All the projects on which this patronage is built involve the deployment of intellectual as well as material resources: knowledge, decisions, and organization as well as money. The villages linked to the *puri* in this way ask for and defer to the advice of the *puri* on such matters, which often extend to interpretation of local tradition and history. A recurring reply to my questions in these villages was: "We don't know anything here. If you want to know, ask that *cokorda* in Ubud." While the terms of the material patronage obligate the villages to provide labor to *puri* projects, the terms of the intellectual patronage mean that the control of local knowledge is gradually being centralized in Ubud. When villages ask for help with a temple or *barong*, this is rarely (if ever) refused. But it comes in a package including interpretation of local mythohistory that usually emphasizes their integration into the network of which Puri Ubud is the focus (Supartha 1994, 1996). The Wos Valley is replete with examples of local traditions appropriated to the grand narrative told by the *puri*. One that illustrates most eloquently the extent to which tradition is being rewritten to conform to this narrative is a negative one, an example of appropriation by exclusion, from a village outside the main network.

Among the distinctive features of the Wos Valley network is a pattern of reversing the normal orientation of *bale agung*. A *bale agung* is a raised open pavilion—linear in form and conventionally oriented with its head *(ulu)* uphill *(kaja)*—in which village members and ancestral gods assemble. Most of the *bale* in the valley are oriented with head facing downhill. There are, however, a few doubly anomalous *bale* outside the valley that are also oriented in this way. In mid-1994, I asked Cokorda "A" of Puri Ubud to explain these patterns. Although he had an explanation for the reversal within the valley, he seemed to share my mystification by the exceptions outside the valley.[32] In one of these villages, the temple in which the *bale agung* was located was being renovated with funds donated by the *puri*. Two years later when I next visited this village, the *bale* had been rebuilt—with its orientation returned

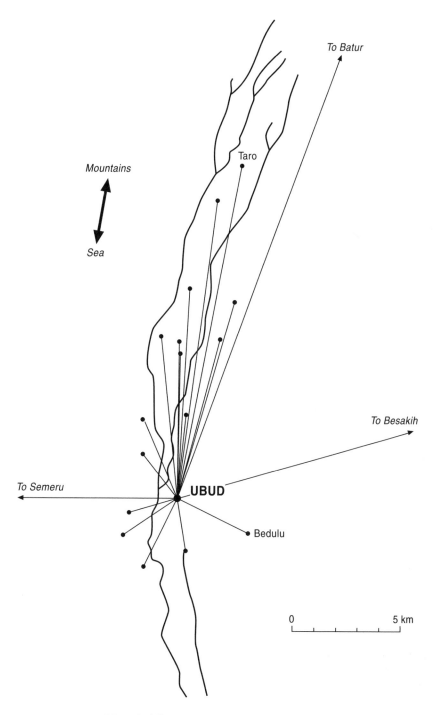

Map 4. The Patronage of Puri Ubud: 1996

to the conventional. The local ritual leader *(bendesa adat)*, a young man I knew from his frequent presence in Ubud assisting with ritual matters at the *puri*, was there again and I asked him about it. The previous (reversed) orientation, he said, had been wrong: it was appropriate only in the Wos Valley. This had been explained to him by Cokorda "A" who had offered to "help" them rebuild it the right way round.

Negara Ubud

We are back where we started, perhaps, but with a better understanding of what is going on. Puri Ubud (or at least some of its more prominent members) are engaged in a program of what might be described as cultural (re)colonization. The kingdom that their grandfather built by military conquest and diplomacy a century ago has been whittled away by the successive incursions of historical processes of wider geographical compass. Most of the *puri* in Bali have responded to this process by simply shifting their focus from traditional forms of local leadership to activities more in keeping with the times such as trade or government. Puri Ubud, however, has sought to manage the articulation of Ubud with these processes by entering wider arenas of trade and politics while simultaneously retaining its local authority through ideological dominance backed by material patronage.

Until recently, this has been little more than a holding operation— a losing battle against the inevitable commercialization of the economy, secularization of belief, and centralization of political power, all of which have increased the prestige and authority of other parties vis-à-vis the *puri*. Since the 1980s, however, while these very processes have intensified, the *puri* has been able to turn the local consequences to its own advantage by a skillful blending of material and ideological strategies. While by no means dominant in the local tourism economy, it has developed a strong economic base in tourism-related businesses, much of which has been financed by sale, lease, or joint ventures using the remainder of its hereditary landholdings. Instead of reinvesting the proceeds of these enterprises in a conventionally capitalist manner, it has used a significant portion to radically upgrade the level of its cultural/religious sponsorship.[33]

The traditional form of this patronage has had the effect of reestablishing the sentiments (if not the forms) of traditional patron/client relations. While it receives no direct economic return from its clients, the *puri* receives deference, respect, and loyalty to a concept of hereditary lordship. Its moral authority is imbued with a supernatural *(niskala)* dimension associated with the local deities with whom it becomes identified in the process of rebuilding temples or sponsoring ceremonies. By recreating this moral authority in a large number of places and explicitly linking them via *niskala* connections to each other and to itself as the central node, the *puri* is recreating a kingdom more or less coterminous with its old one. This kingdom is not constituted in military, political, or economic terms. It is a *negara* (state) of hearts and minds supported, on the one hand, by material patronage and, on the other, by reactivation of traditional beliefs in divine legitimacy.

My use of the term *"negara"* refers obviously to Geertz's (1980) celebrated and idiosyncratic use of it to characterize his idealized model of "the nineteenth-century Balinese state" constituted by ritual dramaturgy rather than orthodox technologies of power.[34] A number of writers have expressed reservations about this formulation. (See, for example, Schulte Nordholt 1981, 1996:6–7; Tambiah 1985; and Wiener 1995a:10.) But the history of Ubud in the late nineteenth century offers a particularly succinct empirical critique in the form of a kingdom whose rise from nowhere was clearly based on a combination of military and political skills of the most mundanely material kind.[35]

Figure 23. Puri Ubud's *cokorda* on the march: members of Puri Ubud lead a procession, 1996. Photo: S. N. Sarjana.

In a nicely ironic twist, however, as the twentieth century has pro-
gressed, Ubud has come increasingly to resemble Geertz's vision of the
nineteenth century: polities constituted in cultural rather than material
terms. There are, however, important differences. While the visible
manifestations of Puri Ubud's project are cultural/ritual/performative
in the sense Geertz describes, it is clearly based on a process of patronage fueled by the transfer of substantial material resources to the client
villages. These resources are paid for by the proceeds from business enterprises, especially tourism and land transactions.

Accounting for the Symbolic

> It is easy to see why the great families never miss a chance (and this is
> one reason for their predilection for distant marriages and vast proces-
> sions) to organise exhibitions of symbolic capital (in which conspicuous
> consumption is only the most visible aspect). [Bourdieu 1994:175]

No accountant could discern the rationale of this extravaganza of patronage: the direct economic returns to the *puri* are negligible in relation to the expenditure involved, and a magico-moral authority over a
few dozen farming villages does not amount to very much in either the
globalized economy of tourism or the political arena of modern Indonesia. And yet it would be stretching credulity to accept at face
value (as many of its village clients appear to do) the official *puri* version of this program as simply a cultural imperative: the exercise of its
hereditary and sacred responsibility to provide the spiritual and moral
guidance, leadership, and welfare its people need and expect.

To make sense of it requires that we expand our notion of purposive
action to take into account its symbolic as well as material dimensions.
What Puri Ubud is doing is sacrificing material resources within a cultural context in which it receives, in exchange, the nonmaterial goods
of supernatural merit and sociocultural prestige. There is nothing particularly mysterious or unusual about this: it is the universal form of
patronage—"a kind of 'politics of reputation' in which a good name is
conferred in exchange for adherence to a certain form of conduct"
(Scott 1985:185). There are, however, more than reputations at stake,
and the exchange is as much economic as political. The "form of conduct" consists of substantial economic outlay, and the supernatural
merit acquired in addition to the good name creates the appearance of
a conventional ritual exchange with the gods.

This patronage is clearly an act of exchange. And as Mauss (1990:3) insists of exchange (and Balinese economic theory agrees), it must, if the relationship is to be sustainable, be (or at least appear to be) reciprocal. That is, the giver must, sooner or later, receive something in return, and the receiver must likewise give. From a local point of view, this requirement is satisfied at a material level by the respect and obedience of the client villages, and at a *niskala* level by the beneficence of the deities. Yet the respect of a few villages is in itself inadequate return for the outlay involved, I would argue, and the *niskala* rewards may (with due respect to both the people and the deities) obscure a further level of material reciprocity.

Bourdieu, writing of a similarly obscured interface between gift and monetary exchanges in North Africa and drawing upon both Mauss and Marx, refers to nonmaterial assets of this kind as "symbolic capital" and argues for an inclusive "economics of practice" encompassing both material and symbolic capital: "The only way in which such accountancy can apprehend the indifferentiatedness of economic and symbolic capital is in the form of their perfect interconvertibility" (1994:173). While there are problems with Bourdieu's formulation (Smart 1993), it offers a useful metaphor with which to begin thinking about the *negara* of patronage in the Wos Valley: it may be seen as a kind of capital asset of Puri Ubud constituted by the conversion of material (monetary) capital into the symbolic capital of sociopolitical prestige and *niskala* merit. For such an economics of practice to work, however, it is essential that the symbolic capital thus created be reconvertible back into material capital as required by its owners/controllers.[36]

The symbolic capital embodied in the neo-*negara* of the Wos Valley network is reconverted and reinvested in a number of ways—most graphically in the symbiotic relationship between tourism and traditional culture. While it is the material capital accumulated through tourism that is being converted into the cultural forms of the *negara*, it is precisely the reputation for conservation and development of traditional cultural forms that is the symbolic capital upon which tourism in Ubud was founded and is maintained and developed (Vickers 1989:140–142). Thus it is the returns, through tourism, from the investment of symbolic capital that create the ongoing material profits which in turn enable further reinvestment in symbolic as well as material capital.[37] The ideological force of this material symbiosis is reinforced in local belief by its symmetry with a *niskala* symbiosis expressed in terms such as: "All this prosperity has been given to us by the gods. Therefore the least we can do is to offer back to them as

much as possible by looking after their temples and making the best offerings and ceremonies we can afford." Or: "The gods have been gen-
erous to us because of the diligence with which we make offerings to
them and adhere to our traditions." This understanding of the material and symbolic foundations of current prosperity—and the pivotal
role of the *puri* in maintaining it—legitimates its privileged status and
defuses most criticism and virtually all resistance to its position and
activities.[38]

The returns from this program of investment in the symbolic have
not been limited to the Wos Valley nor to the economic sphere. Symbolic capital is a form of accumulation or credit whose currency is, like
that of monetary capital, inherently translocal. Puri Ubud, although by
descent not the senior branch of the Sukawati lineage,[39] has assumed a
kind of de facto precedence within the clan—most visibly evident in its
renovation of the Sukawati family subtemple at Besakih in the Ubud
style recognizable for its liberal use of carving, red paint, and gold
leaf.[40] This precedence enables it to reclaim a kind of symbolic authority over the area once "owned" by Sukawati: between the rivers Ayung
and Pakerisan and from the sea to Mount Batur. Pura Batur, the main
temple of this mountain, and Pura Er Jeruk, a temple associated with
the origins of Sukawati, are two sites at which Puri Ubud has recently
chosen to make substantial material investments.[41]

Since the collapse of the kingdom of Sukawati in the mid-eighteenth
century, both political control and symbolic precedence in this area
have been contested between its descendants and the rulers of the
emergent kingdom of Gianyar. The combination of the economic and
cultural prominence of Puri Ubud is now such that its members cannot be ignored at a formal political level. And while the leadership of
the district of Gianyar remained, until the early independence period,
in the hands of Puri Gianyar and has since then nominally rotated
among the various subdistricts, the heads *(bupati)* since 1983 have
been from Puri Ubud. This shift of the center of gravity of symbolic
authority and the effectiveness of the conversion of material into symbolic capital were recently tested on the occasion of a major ceremony
at Pura Samuan Tiga—an important temple predating either *puri* and
situated at Bedulu, a village of independently ancient tradition but historically the site of conflicts between Gianyar and Ubud/Sukawati.
Both *puri* contributed to the ceremony in an effort to associate themselves symbolically with the *niskala* power of the temple. When I arrived at the climax *(puncak)* of the ceremony, important offerings in

the form of sacred dances were being performed by a *cokorda* from Ubud. A local resident asked: "So do you know now which *puri* won the battle?"[42]

In a larger arena again, Puri Ubud has become well known for its role—in partnership with both the symbolic capital of Pura Batur and Parisada Hindu Dharma Indonesia (the Indonesian Hindu Council, official umbrella organization of Indonesian Hinduism) and the material capital of a prominent Balinese businessman—in the conception, development, and maintenance of a Bali-Hindu temple at Mount Semeru in East Java. This mountain is associated both with the origins of Balinese cultural/religious tradition and with the Indian origins of pan-Indonesian Hinduism. By identifying itself with this temple, Puri Ubud has achieved a symbolic capital asset of the highest order and widest currency. The means by which it has achieved this asset has been largely through direct investment of (reputedly large amounts of) material capital and through reconversion of symbolic capital around Ubud into the form of busloads of ritual labor and truckloads of offerings to each major ceremony at Semeru Temple.[43]

In the mountain area around Semeru, where most of the local population practice a form of Hinduism that they (and Balinese) believe to be a somewhat attenuated branch from the same (Majapahit) root as Balinese religion, Cokorda "A" has begun another local program of sponsorship of temples. Because of the area's poverty and a degree of religious demoralization in the face of growing Islamic dominance, this program has provided an enormous boost to local Hindu communities who seem only too willing to embrace Bali/Ubud versions of temple form and ritual practice and interpretations of their own history. Recently the cultural influence of Puri Ubud has expanded further to eastern Kalimantan with the planning of another temple at Kutai: allegedly the site of the first Hindu settlement in Indonesia.[44]

Concluding Movement

A quality of Balinese dance that sets it apart from the more Indianized forms of much of Southeast Asia is a dynamic asymmetry derived from constant shifting of the dancer's center of gravity from one foot to the other and from higher to lower.[45] In less elegant but somewhat analogous manner, we have tangoed between spatial zones, temporal processes, and modes of thought/action, creating a cotillion of connections that, I trust, tell their own story. Between the steps I have endeavored to advance an argument that makes general points at several levels.

First, locally and ethnographically, what the various parties refer to as "Ubud" is an entity perceived in various forms according to their point of view. A holistic understanding recognizes not only all of these viewpoints but their constitution through processes of local, colonial, national, and global scope, as well as ritual, economic, and political mode. Ubud is thus a series of dissonant unitary conceptions but also a polyphony of pattern and process that deconstructs these unitary conceptions while simultaneously linking them.

Second, this notion implies that the polarized terms of the "village studies debate" (Breman 1988; Kemp 1988) may be overconceived. While Ubud is an exceptionally complex and globalized village—this point is inescapable—all villages are, to a degree, artifacts constituted at the intersection of similarly multiplex processes. Villages are not merely the machinations of colonial, academic, and touristic imaginations, however, but empirical realities, physical, social, economic, ritual, and administrative, for the people involved in them. The village is dead: long live the village.

Third, Balinese studies have historically been skewed toward the ritual, performative, and aesthetic aspects of Balinese culture. Only a minority have addressed economic and political matters. In very few cases have attempts been made, let alone successfully (Lansing 1991 and Warren 1993 being notable exceptions), to consider them in relationship. By using the metaphor of symbolic capital, I have attempted to show here the deep and systematic interpenetration of the domains we label the material and the symbolic—and the need to consider them as aspects of socioeconomic form/process rather than independently. This point need not be reiterated for anthropological method in general where it is more widely recognized. It remains, however, in disguised form in the problematic relationship between history and anthropology. This, too, has tended to polarize into approaches that would reduce historical process to transformation of timeless cultural structures (as in Biersack 1991) in which cultural forms are seen as the momentary reflections of underlying economic processes.

This study suggests that different modes of social practice are rendered more visible as a consequence of attention to spatial and temporal patterning. Conversely, attention to different modes of social practice (such as those conventionally designated ritual and economics) draws attention differentially to spatial pattern and temporal process. A properly anthropological history or historical anthropology must take into account multiple levels of spatial zone and temporal process and, furthermore, the modes of practice through which they are related.

Notes

Field research was carried out in 1993–1994 and 1996. I am grateful to Lembaga Ilmu Pengetahuan Indonesia for organizing the necessary permits, to Dr. N. Erewan of Fakultas Ekonomi, Udayana University, for his sponsorship, to the University of Auckland for funding assistance, to Max Rimoldi, Steve Webster, and the editors and reviewers of this volume for their comments, and to Balinese too numerous to list here for hospitality and patient instruction.

1. Tampaksiring is only some 10 kilometers from Ubud, but it is a village, court center, and administrative subdistrict in its own right. Taman is one of the constituent neighborhoods *(banjar)* of Ubud, only a few minutes walk from the center. The Indonesian state, despite much rhetorical emphasis on national unity, is administered through a hierarchy of clearly bounded spatial units.

2. I refer here to debates over the status of "the village" or "the (closed corporate) community" both as empirical entity and as analytic concept, which have been conducted at the level of Bali studies (Guermonprez 1990; Warren 1993:3–5), Southeast Asian studies (Breman 1988; Kemp 1988), and peasant studies (Greenberg 1995; Wolf 1957). The debate concerns a set of assumptions about the discrete, autonomous, bounded nature of the village that provide the theoretical foundation for the research practice of "village studies" as a central tool of anthropology, rural sociology, and, to a lesser extent, other disciplines. For a particularly concise summary see Ruiter and Schulte Nordholt (1989).

3. At least they said this is how they understood it. And their actions—in the form of ritual labor and expenditure—add weight to this impression. For general discussions of the importance of the *niskala* domain in Balinese life see Warren (1993:40) and Wiener (1995a:49–50).

4. The existence of these alternative Ubuds recalls Hauser-Schäublin's notion of the two "worlds" of tourism and "Balinese" life in Sanur (1995:8), as well as more generalized anthropological oppositions between communities integrated spatially and temporally into wider spheres of exchange and historical processes, on the one hand, and those supposedly isolated from them on the other. These alternative Ubuds are, of course, only two among the many ways in which Ubud is variously constituted by groups including the tourist industry, the expatriate community, the national administration, immigrant laborers, and Balinese from other areas.

5. *Puri* means "palace" (or "court") in the English sense of house, family, and political institution. For the etymology of the Balinese term see Wiener (1995a:394); for aspects of its social, spatial, and symbolic construction see

Geertz (1980), Lansing (1983:37–41), Schulte Nordholt (1991a), and Vickers (1989:48). While I refer here to Puri Ubud as if it were a monolithic institution, it is, like the palaces of Western history (not to mention the tabloid press), a complex of individuals, families, alliances, and factions characterized as much by the private divisions between them as by its public unity.

6. Similar points have been made by Roseberry (1989:152) and in several of the essays in Biersack's collection (1991).

7. I emphasize here that by ritual (or economics or politics), I mean both a mode of Balinese action *and* an analytic category by which I order my observations of Balinese activities.

8. This was a typical response to my questions throughout the Wos Valley as to the nature of local relationships with Puri Ubud. This section summarizes a more comprehensive history of Ubud based on a synthesis of local oral accounts, manuscripts, and published sources in Balinese, Dutch, and Indonesian. (See MacRae 1998a.)

9. "Charisma" is used here as a gloss for a peculiarly Malay constellation of personal qualities and attributes of leadership of which invisible/spiritual power *(kesaktian)* is believed to be the foundation. In the case of Ubud, the *kesaktian* of the *puri* was, and indeed still is, associated with the possession of certain heirloom regalia *(pusaka),* the earliest of which Cokorda Gede Sukawati inherited from his father, also a leader of some *kesaktian.* The only Western account of Cokorda Sukawati, by H. H. van Kol (1903:470), who was probably ignorant of Balinese notions of *kesaktian,* stresses a personal quality best summarized as "charisma." For a thorough discussion of *kesaktian* see Anderson (1972); for a discussion of the role of *pusaka* see Errington (1983).

10. The configuration of this land, most of it within a single watershed, and the history of its acquisition conform nicely to Geertz's (1980:19–24) insightful model of the topographic and hydrological factors shaping the political geography of southern Bali.

11. Descent ties seemed in general to become less binding at larger regional levels, and indeed Cokorda Sukawati's deepest enmity was with his relatives (through pre-Sukawati descent) in Puri Klungkung.

12. Although I have not yet had the opportunity to systematically search the Dutch archives for such evidence, none is reported by researchers. The only exception is Van Kol's (1914:33) reference to having met Cokorda Sukawati in 1881.

13. According to Robinson (1995:60), an allowance in the range 15–50 guilders per month was made to district heads (in Bangli, Gianyar, and Karangasem) to compensate for the removal of their rights to exact corvée labor. A Dutch report of 1914 (Mailrapport 1360), however, mentions that the *punggawa* of Ubud received the "maximum salary" of 50 guilders but also an additional 18,409.77 guilders per annum that appears (the paper is damaged at the critical point) to result from his collection of various other levies, taxes, and rentals. His total income from the Dutch was more than three times

as much as the combined salaries of the other six Gianyar *punggawa* and two other officials from Bangli. His son, Cokorda Agung, recalls his annual salary, probably around 1915–1919, as having been 2,200 ringgit (the Malay unit of currency equal to 2.5 guilders and subsequently 2.5 rupiahs) per month (Hilbery 1979:3, 10)—an extraordinarily high figure. Despite the inconsistency of these figures, they lend support to the widespread popular perception of Cokorda Sukawati as having been very wealthy and a beneficiary of the Dutch.

14. Balinese perceptions of the Dutch were at best ambiguous. Balinese often "carried on as if the Dutch were not there" (Vickers 1989:73), and Wiener's account (1995a:275–300) stresses the Balinese perception of Dutch impotence. Artistic representations of the Dutch tended to portray them as "rapacious but comical" and with "low status in Balinese eyes" (Vickers 1989: pl. 9 caption; see also illustrations in Covarrubias 1972). Other accounts, however, suggest they were seen as having the character of *niskala* beings of the lower orders: gross and uncivilized but powerful, unpredictable, and therefore dangerous.

15. Ubud—and indeed what I know of other precolonial Balinese kingdoms—seems to conform more to Milner's (1982) model of the Malay *kerajaan* than to Geertz's model of the *negara*. Geertz's *negara*, apart from downplaying the role of realpolitik, is essentially spatial and static in its conception, while Milner's *kerajaan* is a processual model taking into account the dynamic balance of a wide range of factors.

16. I could find among contemporary members of his own family and the general public of Ubud only one person with fond memories of Cokorda Raka—a former employee, a *parekan* (retainer) of exemplary loyalty but diminished critical faculties. The turbulent carriage of the Cokorda's corpse, borne reluctantly by the local community to its place of cremation, bears witness to this reputation. He is remembered on a larger stage primarily as a political opportunist, collaborator with the Dutch, and instigator of repressive violence against his own people (Robinson 1995:169–178).

17. In a sense, he was merely continuing the tradition of his father's and other Balinese courts in attracting artists from other kingdoms. It is typical of Cokorda Raka's vision and contacts, however, that he chose a foreigner from beyond Balinese shores. The story of Walter Spies has been told often enough (see Boon 1986; Rhodius and Darling 1980; Vickers 1989:105–124) to obviate any need to repeat it here.

18. In this respect his career bears a striking resemblance to that of his maternal uncle, Gusti Putu Mayun in Blahkiuh, another Dutch-trained local aristocrat. The resemblance ends here, however, as Gusti Mayun chose to pursue the local rather than global potential of this combination (Schulte Nordholt 1991a:141).

19. Statistics from this period paint a consistent Bali-wide picture of declining exports, imports, prices, and tax payments from the late 1920s

through the 1930s (Bakker 1937; Van der Kaaden 1938:44–45; Robinson 1995:58). Scott (1977:chap. 4) describes similar patterns throughout Southeast Asia.

20. The relationship between Puri Ubud and the Dutch over matters of taxation is obscure, and its effects on local land tenure are complex. They are discussed in detail in MacRae (1998a:330–335, 369, 375–377).

21. It was in the course of this tour that he initiated the practice, now popular among princes and peddlers alike, of importing wives from all over the world.

22. This has been the official position adopted by Puri Ubud toward politics ever since. Indeed, it has been a factor in a culture of indifference or even antipathy toward any kind of translocal politics—the dominant political orientation today.

23. The price of rice rose from 3.50 rupiahs per kilogram in 1956 to 30 rupiahs by the end of 1962 and then to 125 rupiahs before the end of the following year (contemporary newspaper reports quoted by Robinson 1995:238).

24. The branches of Puri Ubud, in fact, varied considerably in this respect: some members, particularly those of less well endowed branches, entered all these fields. This was not, however, done systematically or, with a few exceptions, with outstanding success.

25. Twenty-one members of Puri Ubud and related *puri* with the largest landholdings reported total holdings in excess of 1,000 hectares (1 hectare = 100 are) of which some 425 hectares had been redistributed to local farmers by July 1996.

26. Both the Dutch and Indonesian governments reorganized administrative boundaries several times with the subdistrict of Ubud shrinking on each occasion. Despite their loss of formal authority, members of Puri Ubud usually occupied the position of district head *(prebekel)* until 1981, when Ubud became a *kelurahan* (a village administered directly by the state) with a head appointed from above.

27. Most people are reluctant to speak of this period, preferring to forget it altogether, and in most cases actually knowing little and understanding less of what happened. The widow of one of the alleged PKI "leaders" in Ubud, herself a woman of some education and intelligence, insists that she had no idea of what her husband was involved in until he was arrested and to this day does not really know what it was all about. The accounts of those who are prepared to talk are vague but follow a consistent pattern (see, for example, Hilbery 1979:79), varying mainly in the role attributed to the *puri*. For a general account of this period in Bali see Robinson (1995:273–303).

28. For a general account of this development see Picard (1995); for its effects in Ubud see MacRae (1992).

29. The well-known Hotel Campuan, for example, although established in the 1950s by the *puri* on the site of Walter Spies' old house, was revived in the

late 1990s by an Australian journalist who leased it for $100 per week, employing local people as staff and running it in combination with travel agencies in Bali and Australia.

30. I do not mean to suggest that other *puri* are not involved in ritual but, rather, that none has done so on such a scale or so publicly. Geertz (1963:99–120) records the move of Puri Tabanan to commerce in response to the loss of its traditional role. The closed gates and high walls of Puri Gianyar reflect its (lack of) relationship with both the local community and tourism. Members of this *puri* are, like those of Karangasem regency, prominent in politics, academia, and professions such as medicine. Puri Bangli, in Bangli regency, has developed very modest tourism interests; I believe the minor *puri* of Krambitan, in Tabanan regency, has done likewise.

31. Lomba Desa is a national competition in which villages compete in terms of several criteria of civic excellence defined by the central government in accordance with New Order development ideology. It has now been overshadowed (replaced?) by Adipura, an annual competition between larger administrative units, which reflects a more contemporary urbanized vision of the image Indonesian villages should aspire to.

32. For a detailed discussion see MacRae (1995).

33. The fraction involved is impossible to estimate, but I describe it as significant because the *puri*'s publicly known contributions to temple renovations and ceremonies frequently run into hundreds of millions of rupiahs and often far outstrip the combined (cash) contributions of the villages involved.

34. Balinese rarely refer to their own political forms, past or present, as *negara*. For palaces or courts they use the term *"puri"*; for the kingdoms controlled by *puri* they use *"kerajaan."*

35. One of the conclusions that may be drawn from this is that Geertz's model, although supposedly "historical," is actually a synchronic model composed of fragments observed here and there at various times. Had he taken into account the actual historical processes by which the very kingdoms from which he draws his evidence came into being, rose, and fell, he might have been forced to different conclusions.

36. Bourdieu is not the only one to address the relationship between the symbolic and material dimensions of human intention. Others who in various ways enter into this "dialogue with the ghost of Marx" (Wolf 1982:20) include Clifford Geertz (1980), Stephen Lansing (1991; introduction), Marcel Mauss (1990), William Roseberry (1989:chap. 6), Marshall Sahlins (1976), and Michael Taussig (1980). This is not the place to pursue the dialogue: my choice of Bourdieu's formulation is provisional and reflects more than anything its nice fit with the facts as they present themselves in Ubud.

37. Obviously not all the economic fruits of tourism flow directly to the *puri*, but they benefit the *puri* in symbolic terms by association. It is also tourism that has made possible the spectacular capital gains in the form of inflation of land values of which the *puri* has been prime beneficiary. And it is

indeed through very lucrative land/tourism deals that the program of patronage has been largely financed.

38. In Bourdieu's words: "The endless reconversion of economic capital into symbolic capital, at the cost of a wastage of social energy, which is the condition for the permanence of domination, cannot succeed without the complicity of the whole group" (1994:189).

39. Puri Ubud is a branch of Puri Peliatan, which is in turn the senior branch, albeit arguably, of the tree long since uprooted from its native soil at Sukawati, which was itself a cutting (root division?) from one transplanted from Majapahit to Gelgel.

40. Besakih, a mountain temple of great importance for the whole of Bali, is associated with the ritually foremost kingdom of Klungkung. It contains many subtemples and shrines including those of a number of kingdoms subsidiary to Klungkung.

41. Pura Batur refers here to the large temple on the rim of the crater of Mount Batur, rather than Pura Ulun Danu Batur at Songan. There is a rivalry for symbolic precedence between the adherents of the two temples (Lansing 1991:106–108; Reuter 1996:92), in which Pura Batur has some advantage by virtue of its own program of conversion of material into symbolic capital.

42. Ubud may have won this battle, but I suspect the war is not yet over. Given the undoubted historical importance of this temple and a local intention to see its status as a major pan-Bali temple (Sad Kahyangan) formally reestablished, I would expect both rival *puri* to be prepared to make substantial further investments here over the next few years. While I have no record of the material resources invested by Puri Ubud, these were obviously significant and were particularly evident in the Ubud-style restoration of a shrine with which it claims association. I would also expect Ubud's future claim to the temple to involve mobilizing the symbolic capital stored in the (fact of the) proximity of the former residence of the last king of Sukawati. My knowledge of Bedulu, Pura Samuan Tiga, and the politics of this ceremony (Karya Penyejeg Bumi) is largely anecdotal. I am, however, grateful to Garret Kam for illuminating comments reflecting profoundly local knowledge.

43. The full name of the temple is Pura Mandaragiri Semeru Agung. Mount Semeru is said to be the peak of the sacred Mount Mahameru in India relocated to Java, just as the great mountains Batur and Agung in Bali are relocated fragments of Mount Semeru. I am grateful to Freek Bakker for copies of some material on Semeru Temple.

44. Further research is planned in the Semeru area. For a comprehensive description of the Hindu communities around Semeru and their religious and political-economic conditions see the writings of Robert Hefner (1985, 1990). I have not yet had the opportunity to visit the Kutai temple.

45. I am grateful to a dancer, Ross Logan, for this observation and to another, Rucina Ballinger, for confirming it.

Chapter 5

People of the Mountains, People of the Sea: Negotiating the Local and the Foreign in Bali

Thomas A. Reuter

Indonesia's recent economic crisis and political turmoil are ample evidence of how the globalization of economic interdependence between nations may affect the lives of people in the developing world. Their participation in a global market together with advanced technologies of communication and transportation also confronts modern Indonesians with foreign commodities, ideas, and values. We cannot predict what consequences these changes may have for the cultural diversity of human civilization—particularly for the future of disempowered societies at the margins of the global system. Possible trajectories will be shaped, among other things, by the processes of cultural negotiation that transpire at the conceptual boundaries between the foreign and local, between the self-representations of people in marginal societies and the discourses of those who control the world around them, regardless of whether they are global, national, or regional elites. This chapter examines such conceptual negotiations and mutual representations in a remote part of the island of Bali. Like many island cultures of the Southeast Asian Pacific region, Balinese have lived in anticipation, between hope and fear, of whomever would arrive next from across the sea to trade or invade their shores. Traditional strategies for negotiating the inward passage of the culturally "foreign" toward the heart of Balinese society have been developed in the course of this political history.

155

Late-twentieth-century modernity is but the latest layer in the patina of the culturally foreign that surrounds a hypothetical "Balinese" core. Thus the relevance of earlier strategies for incorporating the foreign is worthy of consideration.

If we wish to examine how the encounter with global influences is negotiated locally, at the margins of the modern world, it is instructive to look beyond nations such as Indonesia, or even provinces like Bali, as representative of the local. Far from being merely at the receiving end of global changes, the political and economic elite of Indonesia are by now as modern and cosmopolitan a group as most other national or regional elites on the globe. Moreover, they are engaged quite deliberately in a modernizing mission of their own, both at a national and provincial level. The Enlightenment ideal of progress has long been domesticated, and it is reproduced inwardly with a passion. The torch is carried from the national capital Jakarta to provincial centers, and ultimately meets its challenge at the local margins of state power and at the fringe of the web of economic interdependence. In the modernization and development discourses of the political and economic elite, people in geographically remote areas who are administratively inaccessible and have little technological sophistication are identified as a "problem."

In ethnographic terms this chapter concerns an apparently marginal people who dwell in the remote mountainous interior of the island. Though some of them are situated at the coast, the inhabitants of these villages are commonly identified as "Bali Aga" or "mountain Balinese." This chapter is based on field research carried out in 1993–1994 in more than sixty of their villages, most of them located in the mountain district of Kintamani in Bangli regency. These are not isolated communities. Patterns of ritual alliance around regional temples unite clusters of villages into ritual domains *(banua)*. In Bali there are approximately one hundred villages that I would classify as Bali Aga on the basis of their local social organization.[1] I estimate that about 80,000 people live in these communities, or between 2 and 3 percent of the island's total population.

Mountain villages differ in appearance from villages in lowland Bali. Characteristic are long parallel rows of wooden houses with bamboo shingle roofs and a unique interior design, but much of the traditional village layout and architecture is now disappearing. Typically the mountain villagers' subsistence was based on dry rice agriculture and mixed gardens, not on irrigated rice as in the lowlands. Nowadays cash crops including citrus, coffee, and cloves and the sale of cattle, pigs,

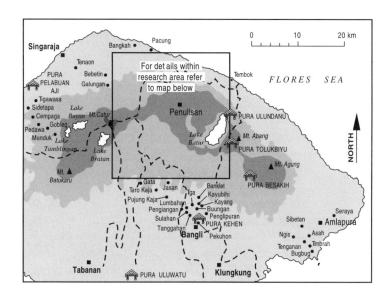

RESEARCH AREA

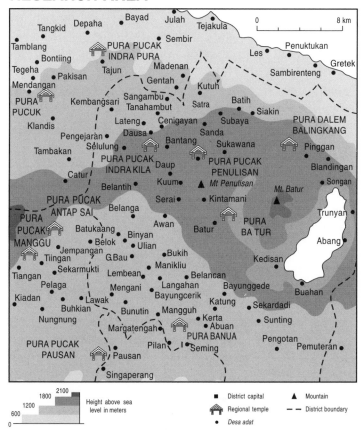

Map 5. Distribution of Villages with Bali Aga Traditions in Contemporary Bali

and chickens have become the main source of income. Most rice has to be purchased.

That the Bali Aga can be located simultaneously in "the interior" and at "the periphery" of Bali presents an admonition that the spatial metaphor of marginality cannot be regarded as a natural category. By defining a people as marginal, anthropologists are in danger of elevating a global materialist interpretation of society to hegemonic status. The use of such a metaphor may endorse a spatial perspective in which power is the center of all concerns and fragile culture perches precariously at the margins. The sociological identification of a "marginal group" may also legitimize the kind of political and economic centralism that is cultivated by national and regional elites in Indonesia.

While the people of the Balinese mountains may appear marginal when viewed from the centers of national and provincial power structures, their conceptual status in the fabric of Balinese identities is far more ambiguous. I believe that Balinese representations of society are focused on a balance between the powerful and the sacred, the foreign and local. This duality of values allows room for an alternative perspective on the cultural heritage of the politically marginal highland Balinese. In some contexts, at least, they come to represent the most venerable, central, and sacred layer of Balinese identity and civilization.[2]

Balinese identities do not simply rest on a static distinction between "us" and "them." They are based on an idea of transforming the other

Figure 24. Parallel house rows in the Bali Aga village of Belantih. Photo: Thomas Reuter.

into the self and the self into the other. Balinese narratives depict order as the product of a historical sequence of changes, rather than a static system, and celebrate the tensions between the local and foreign, the old and the new, as the very essence of a living and "fertile" society.[3] Perhaps the most widely known Balinese narrative of origin involves an encounter between local and foreign people: between a minority of autochthonous "Balinese of the mountains" (Wong Bali Aga) and the majority of Balinese who call themselves "descendants of legendary immigrant kings and nobles from the Hindu-Javanese kingdom of Majapahit" (Wong Majapahit) and who populate the lowlands.

In the narrative of the dominant lowland groups, it is claimed that while the majority of the indigenous Wong Bali were subjugated and culturally transformed by the more civilized newcomers, some retreated from the newcomers into the mountains to remain the Bali Aga and retain their original traditions. Whether this Balinese representation of their own history is historically true is unknowable. Although there is reason to be skeptical about the claim that the arrival of nobles from Majapahit marked a radical break in Balinese cultural history, it is highly significant that it is portrayed as such. The label "Bali Aga" is disliked by the mountain people because it is often employed in a derogatory fashion. Villagers I worked with regard themselves simply as "the Balinese," although they grudgingly accept the designation "Bali Aga" by focusing on the term's favorable connotation—namely, that all Balinese consider the mountains to be the abode of the gods. Following this line of interpretation and as a counterdiscrimination, the Bali Aga sometimes sarcastically refer to the "newcomers" as Wong Bali Dataran or Wong Bali Kelodan, "the people who dwell on the plains" or "nearer the sea"—hence the title of this chapter. So that the reader may appreciate this sarcasm fully, it should be mentioned that Balinese generally regard the sea as a repository of pollution and the dwelling place of demonic beings.[4] It is not my intention to argue that the Bali Aga/Bali Majapahit distinction is the only dimension of Balinese identities worth exploring. Nevertheless, this theme is central to an understanding of how Balinese conceptualize the inside and outside, the familiar and foreign, the traditional and modern. When it comes to understanding how Balinese position themselves in an interconnected global system, it is imperative to examine how they structure the internal boundaries between the local and foreign within their own social world.

The relationship between Bali Aga and the descendants of Majapahit is interpreted in this chapter with the help of a comparative framework—that is, by focusing on the cultural theme of dual authority. Ethnographers have frequently commented that a dual division of authority—political and ritual—between original inhabitants and newcomers forms part of the shared cultural heritage of Austronesian-speaking societies and is evident in narratives of origin from Madagascar to Bali and all the way across the Pacific. There may even be scope for extending this comparative field beyond the confines of linguistic affiliation to a level of shared history and cultural heritage. This would include non-Austronesian-speaking societies in South Asia and mainland Southeast Asia where this theme of dual authority can also be observed.

My first aim, therefore, is to promote an alternative interpretation of Balinese identities from the perspective of a comparative ethnology of the Asia-Pacific region.[5] I also wish to examine whether the indigenous idioms that proclaim a sharing of authority between original inhabitants and "the descendants of strangers" remain relevant to an analysis of the social and political dimensions of contemporary relationships. The Bali Aga are no longer faced with the politics of precolonial kingdoms and their Majapahit identity: today they face the modernist discourses of a Balinese elite who represent national state authority at the provincial and local levels. An analysis of modern processes of Balinese identity formation must touch on "discourses of marginalization" and "the politics of cultural borderlands"—themes that are becoming popular in anthropological studies of politically marginal societies all over the world. Nevertheless, I remain critical of such explanatory models insofar as they fail to accommodate indigenous idioms of authority and perpetuate a materialist discourse on the centrality of "the modern."

My second aim, therefore, is to establish how "global" the societies are that anthropologists nowadays study and to discover at what point a globalist perspective may fail us in the analysis of local identities. The specific question is this: to what extent is an indigenous notion of dual authority in Indonesian societies, based on a categorical insider/outsider distinction, still relevant to the contemporary political narratives of the nation-state? To answer this question we must determine in which contexts the theme of dual authority is being transformed or displaced by modernist representations of Balinese society.

Dual Identities in Traditional Balinese Narratives

It is somewhat surprising to observe that an increasing majority of contemporary Balinese, even though they are proud of their separate Bali-

...ider themselves to be
...dominant myth of Ba-
...ginated from the leg-
...a and invaded the is-
...General Gajah Mada.[6]
...d other parts of the
...ajapahit descendants
...ral legacy of this epic

...ilitary intervention in
...ry by portraying it as
...just rule of their in-
...bed as an atheist and
...supported and thus
...said to have been ne-
...the *Babad Dalem*, a
...feat the king of Ma-
...lung in Bali, eventu-
...restore order in that
...and other spiritually
...lished a new dynasty
...l palaces *(puri)* were
...f Bali to serve as the
...cracy *(anak jero,* "in-
...came to be known
...ide, that is, from the

...ter, the new elite es-
...Pura Besakih (Stuart-
...oting the innovative
...ion, foremost among
...med ancestors of the
...*nda)* still officiate at
...nts of former ruling
...ed in textual sources:
...the newcomers to an
...ir rule. In their quest
...leadership began to
...rs of a new civil soci-
...ilders of temples and
...The Bali Aga were
...rder.

Narrative accounts of the ori...
means singular and uncontestec...
conquest of Bali, for example, te...
as illegitimate rule. This perspec...
tion of the tale of Raja Bedahul...
"the king with a different head...
danawa, Raja Bedahulu was a s...
his head from his torso and eleva...
practice. On one occasion, the...
anxious attendant to place a pig...
upon the unjustified fear that the...
Thus the royal head was perm...
body.[9] Mountain people interpro...
rule. The ghastly animal head...
japahit extraction, an unrefined...
come to rule the civilized huma...
elsewhere constructed as a missi...
an attempt to replace an already...
the installment of the foreign "h...
described as irreversible in the n...

While they give little credence...
called descendants of Majapahit...
authority of ancient Bali in their...
in annual festivals that include i...
directed toward the guardian de...
ber of ancient sanctuaries in th...
Batur and Pucak Penulisan. Th...
ritual authority of the Bali Aga...
contemporary lowland worship...
Aga conceal the embarrassing...
priests of non-Majapahit origin...
devotional acts" (mabakti) as o...
(for financing and maintaining t...
pretation suggests that they at l...
ity of the deities at temples like...
of fertility and irrigation (Lansi...
noted in this context that the te...
ancient Balinese kings whose sta...
tum and whose identities have...
Pucak, "the king of the mount...
thus remained in the heavens, ar...
is acknowledged by worshiping...

Figure 25. Stone statues of pre-Majapahit Balinese rulers dating from the eleventh to thirteenth centuries. Photo: Thomas Reuter.

Even this brief extract from a complex body of Balinese origin narratives reveals that they locate the origin of political power and its human representatives at an external source—a concept that strikes cultural resonances across the Southeast Asian and Pacific region. In societies as widely separated geographically as Hawai'i and Sumatra, the theme of a powerful outsider who arrives at the shore and gradually begins a symbolic journey toward the interior is a paradigmatic feature of origin histories. By means of powerful heirlooms, magical efficacy, cleverness, or sheer prowess, the outsider gains political control over an autochthonous community. Subsequently the newcomer may or may not challenge the original inhabitants' special ancestral relationship to the land or their role as ritual leaders in the worship of the divine protectors of the land. This in turn is related to the presence or absence of further waves of immigrants.

In view of the underlying distinction between political and ritual forms of authority, the pattern has been referred to as "dual sovereignty" (Van Wouden 1968) or "diarchy" (Cunningham 1965; Needham 1980; Valeri 1991). Others have highlighted the dominant position of the outsider in this dyad by focusing on the notion of "the stranger-king" (Sahlins 1985), or "the power of strangers" (Barnes 1996), or the precarious and variable processes of "installing the outsider on the inside" (Fox 1994). This variable terminology is not simply a matter of semantic preference or interpretation. Rather, the different labels presented in these ethnographies reflect the different outcomes of historical struggles for authority between "the two parties" in various societies.[10]

The observed diversity among societies in the Southeast Asia–Pacific region at the representational level can be attributed to their specific political histories—most importantly to the amount and form of resistance offered by the original inhabitants. A study of the Balinese way of constructing and managing insider/outsider relationships must therefore not only identify one further conceptual variation on a cultural theme but illustrate how thematic representations of authority were actualized under the specific conditions of Balinese history. In the Balinese case, the outsiders installed themselves at the inside—namely, at the original political center in Pejeng or Bedahulu. To erase the moral blemish of this violent act, they gradually established alternative ritual and political centers free from the authority of the original inhabitants.[11] The dominant myth of Majapahit kingship in Bali thus departs significantly from Sahlins' description of the stranger-king in Polynesia:

> Kingship makes its appearance from outside the society. Initially a stranger and something of a terror, the king is absorbed and domesticated by the indigenous people. . . . The draconian feats by which they [kings] come to power are foreign to the conduct of "real people" or "true sons of the land," as various Polynesians express it. . . . Power is a barbarian. [Sahlins 1985:73, 78–79]

In Bali's dominant myth, the strangers from Majapahit, no matter how violent their arrival, are claimed to have been on a civilizing mission—to have invaded the center of a barbaric autochthonous society by bringing the monster Mayadanawa to his justified death.[12] Only the Bali Aga counternarrative of Raja Bedahulu shows elements of the into the self and the self into the other. Balinese narratives depict order as the product of a historical sequence of changes, rather than a static system, and celebrate the tensions between the local and foreign, the old and the new, as the very essence of a living and "fertile" society.[3] Perhaps the most widely known Balinese narrative of origin involves an encounter between local and foreign people: between a minority of autochthonous "Balinese of the mountains" (Wong Bali Aga) and the majority of Balinese who call themselves "descendants of legendary immigrant kings and nobles from the Hindu-Javanese kingdom of Majapahit" (Wong Majapahit) and who populate the lowlands.

In the narrative of the dominant lowland groups, it is claimed that while the majority of the indigenous Wong Bali were subjugated and culturally transformed by the more civilized newcomers, some retreated from the newcomers into the mountains to remain the Bali Aga and retain their original traditions. Whether this Balinese representation of their own history is historically true is unknowable. Although there is reason to be skeptical about the claim that the arrival of nobles from Majapahit marked a radical break in Balinese cultural history, it is highly significant that it is portrayed as such. The label "Bali Aga" is disliked by the mountain people because it is often employed in a derogatory fashion. Villagers I worked with regard themselves simply as "the Balinese," although they grudgingly accept the designation "Bali Aga" by focusing on the term's favorable connotation—namely, that all Balinese consider the mountains to be the abode of the gods. Following this line of interpretation and as a counterdiscrimination, the Bali Aga sometimes sarcastically refer to the "newcomers" as Wong Bali Dataran or Wong Bali Kelodan, "the people who dwell on the plains" or "nearer the sea"—hence the title of this chapter. So that the reader may appreciate this sarcasm fully, it should be mentioned that Balinese generally regard the sea as a repository of pollution and the dwelling place of demonic beings.[4] It is not my intention to argue that the Bali Aga/Bali Majapahit distinction is the only dimension of Balinese identities worth exploring. Nevertheless, this theme is central to an understanding of how Balinese conceptualize the inside and outside, the familiar and foreign, the traditional and modern. When it comes to understanding how Balinese position themselves in an interconnected global system, it is imperative to examine how they structure the internal boundaries between the local and foreign within their own social world.

The relationship between Bali Aga and the descendants of Majapahit is interpreted in this chapter with the help of a comparative framework—that is, by focusing on the cultural theme of dual authority. Ethnographers have frequently commented that a dual division of authority—political and ritual—between original inhabitants and newcomers forms part of the shared cultural heritage of Austronesian-speaking societies and is evident in narratives of origin from Madagascar to Bali and all the way across the Pacific. There may even be scope for extending this comparative field beyond the confines of linguistic affiliation to a level of shared history and cultural heritage. This would include non-Austronesian-speaking societies in South Asia and mainland Southeast Asia where this theme of dual authority can also be observed.

My first aim, therefore, is to promote an alternative interpretation of Balinese identities from the perspective of a comparative ethnology of the Asia-Pacific region.[5] I also wish to examine whether the indigenous idioms that proclaim a sharing of authority between original inhabitants and "the descendants of strangers" remain relevant to an analysis of the social and political dimensions of contemporary relationships. The Bali Aga are no longer faced with the politics of precolonial kingdoms and their Majapahit identity: today they face the modernist discourses of a Balinese elite who represent national state authority at the provincial and local levels. An analysis of modern processes of Balinese identity formation must touch on "discourses of marginalization" and "the politics of cultural borderlands"—themes that are becoming popular in anthropological studies of politically marginal societies all over the world. Nevertheless, I remain critical of such explanatory models insofar as they fail to accommodate indigenous idioms of authority and perpetuate a materialist discourse on the centrality of "the modern."

My second aim, therefore, is to establish how "global" the societies are that anthropologists nowadays study and to discover at what point a globalist perspective may fail us in the analysis of local identities. The specific question is this: to what extent is an indigenous notion of dual authority in Indonesian societies, based on a categorical insider/outsider distinction, still relevant to the contemporary political narratives of the nation-state? To answer this question we must determine in which contexts the theme of dual authority is being transformed or displaced by modernist representations of Balinese society.

Dual Identities in Traditional Balinese Narratives

It is somewhat surprising to observe that an increasing majority of contemporary Balinese, even though they are proud of their separate Balinese identity within the Indonesian nation, consider themselves to be the descendants of outsiders. According to the dominant myth of Balinese origins, the ancestors of these outsiders originated from the legendary Hindu kingdom of Majapahit in East Java and invaded the island of Bali in A.D. 1343 under the leadership of General Gajah Mada.[6] Following the introduction of Islam in Java and other parts of the archipelago, the Balinese who claimed to be Majapahit descendants came to regard themselves as the heirs to the cultural legacy of this epic Hindu empire.

The initial violence of Majapahit's presumed military intervention in Bali is legitimized in literary sources and oral history by portraying it as the liberation of the Balinese people from the unjust rule of their indigenous king, Raja Mayadanawa of Pejeng, described as an atheist and a demonic tyrant.[7] The expedition was magically supported and thus legitimized by the gods, whose proper worship is said to have been neglected and prohibited by this ruler. According to the *Babad Dalem*, a dynastic origin narrative, after Mayadanawa's defeat the king of Majapahit, acting on the request of Minister Patih Ulung in Bali, eventually sent the nobleman Sri Kresna Kapakisan to restore order in that troubled land, equipping him with a magical kris and other spiritually potent regalia. The victorious outsiders thus established a new dynasty of kings. A succession of major and lesser royal palaces *(puri)* were constructed in the irrigated plains and foothills of Bali to serve as the new political centers for a ranked hereditary aristocracy *(anak jero,* "insiders"). The majority of Balinese commoners came to be known metaphorically as "outsiders" *(anak jaba)*—outside, that is, from the perspective of the palace.[8]

To further their claim of representing the center, the new elite established a ritual order based on the state temple Pura Besakih (Stuart-Fox 1987) and other sanctuaries, as well as promoting the innovative teachings of legendary priests of Javanese extraction, foremost among them Mpu Kuturan. These priests are the presumed ancestors of the Balinese Brahmana clans. Brahmana priests *(pedanda)* still officiate at most temple ceremonies sponsored by descendants of former ruling houses or the state. A general trend can be observed in textual sources: from initial praise of the extraordinary prowess of the newcomers to an increasing emphasis on the civilizing effect of their rule. In their quest for the symbolic center of Balinese society, the new leadership began to construct themselves not only as the potent bearers of a new civil society but as the champions of a ritual order: the builders of temples and protectors of fellow immigrant Brahmana priests. The Bali Aga were officially irrelevant to the new ritual and secular order.

Narrative accounts of the origins of Balinese civilization are by no means singular and uncontested. Bali Aga versions of the legendary conquest of Bali, for example, tend to interpret the Majapahit invasion as illegitimate rule. This perspective is epitomized in their interpretation of the tale of Raja Bedahulu, Bali's last indigenous king, literally "the king with a different head." Unlike his demonic double Mayadanawa, Raja Bedahulu was a saintly personage capable of detaching his head from his torso and elevating it to the heavens during his yogic practice. On one occasion, the prolonged absence of his head led an anxious attendant to place a pig's head on the royal shoulders—acting upon the unjustified fear that the king would otherwise meet his death. Thus the royal head was permanently prevented from rejoining its body.[9] Mountain people interpret this myth as a metaphor for foreign rule. The ghastly animal head represents the Balinese king of Majapahit extraction, an unrefined and potent but alien power that has come to rule the civilized human body of the Balinese people. What is elsewhere constructed as a mission of civilization is herein portrayed as an attempt to replace an already civilized Balinese ruler. Nevertheless, the installment of the foreign "head" at the apex of an organic unity is described as irreversible in the myth.

While they give little credence to such Bali Aga discourses, the so-called descendants of Majapahit implicitly acknowledge the religious authority of ancient Bali in their ritual practices. Thousands participate in annual festivals that include islandwide harvest and fertility rituals, directed toward the guardian deities of land and water, held at a number of ancient sanctuaries in the mountainous interior such as Pura Batur and Pucak Penulisan. These temples have remained under the ritual authority of the Bali Aga and their non-Brahmana priests. Some contemporary lowland worshipers at these temples who are not Bali Aga conceal the embarrassing truth of this ritualized submission to priests of non-Majapahit origin by construing their visits as "voluntary devotional acts" *(mabakti)* as opposed to "carrying the responsibility (for financing and maintaining temples)" *(nyungsung)*. But this interpretation suggests that they at least acknowledge the spiritual authority of the deities at temples like Pucak Penulisan and Batur in matters of fertility and irrigation (Lansing 1991; Reuter 1996). It should be noted in this context that the temple of Penulisan was a state temple of ancient Balinese kings whose statues are still venerated in its inner sanctum and whose identities have merged into that of the deity Ratu Pucak, "the king of the mountain peak." The severed royal head has thus remained in the heavens, and the sacred authority of ancient kings is acknowledged by worshiping their deified manifestation.

theme in which "power is a barbarian" who installs himself at the apex of a preexisting social order.[13] By contrast, it is a remarkable similarity, to name but one example, that when Sahlins reflects on Fijian origin narratives and describes how "the stranger wanders into the interior where he is taken in by a local chieftain whose daughter he eventually marries" (1985:79), he may just as well have been describing the origin narrative of the Bali Aga villages of Sukawana (Reuter 1996:207) or Trunyan (Danandjaja 1980:40). These myths narrate how the son or royal emissary of a foreign king is sent to Bali, where he encounters and marries the daughter of already civilized original inhabitants. This example illustrates, too, that a number of Bali Aga clans consider themselves "outsiders" in a local context in that their immigrant ancestors are said to have moved to the inside of an even earlier society.[14] In short, Bali Aga need not look toward lowland Balinese as the outsider when it comes to representing the more subtle polarities within their own local and regional politics. At the same time, lowland Balinese generally do not need the Bali Aga as the representatives of ritual authority, given that their Brahmana priests can adequately fulfill this role.

To comprehend the origin of such specific variations and contradictions, it is necessary to turn to the particularities of Balinese political history insofar as it can be reconstructed. The picture we find in Bali is one where the outsider's journey to the ritual center of society did not entirely succeed. There is evidence suggesting that the Bali Aga were recalcitrant to political and economic control from the very beginning. Their unwillingness to accept the sovereignty of the immigrant rulers led to several military expeditions in the times of Sri Kresna Kapakisan and to numerous raids by later kings such as Panji Sakti of Buleleng (Worsley 1972).[15] In the *Babad Pasek*, the chronicle of the Pasek clan, it is reported that

> after the noble warrior families from Java had settled in Bali, it became obvious that the leaders of the Bali Aga were not content to see them rule and hold power in Bali. They expressed their displeasure by rebelling against the new government and trying to destroy the state. The rebellion arose in the villages of Batur, Cempaga, Songan, Serai, Manikliyu, Bonyoh, Taro, Bayad, and Sukawana, the headquarters of the rebellion. [See, for example, Sugriwa 1957:63a][16]

The Bali Aga villages reported to have resisted the initial invasion are among those that even today are tightly organized in interconnected ritual domains or *banua*. The alliances of Bali Aga villages within such domains, as I have discussed elsewhere (Reuter 1996), allowed them to show a unified front to the newcomers. Although the Bali Aga were repeatedly violated, they resisted eradication and cultural absorption.[17]

According to the *Babad Pasek*, it was only after the new king had sponsored a ritual in the Bali Aga temple of Penulisan that a truce was established. The terms of this truce clearly show a distinction between secular and ritual authority—if only in a context of limited and uneasy interaction between the two parties. Despite the mutual tensions, ceremonial interactions have always taken place and have followed this established division of authority. The apparent irrelevance of the Bali Aga to lowland centers of power, as we have seen, is contradicted by the fact that they have retained their ritual authority as the custodian of some of Bali's most important agricultural temples. Although lowland Balinese have their state temples and Brahmana priests, tens of thousands participate in the festivals of these Bali Aga temples; the Bali Aga people, however, normally refuse to accept Brahmana priests and recognize no obligation to visit temples established by the descendants of Majapahit.[18] By the same measure, the Bali Aga have never succeeded in establishing a secular kingdom of their own and have nominally accepted the authority of the newcomers.[19]

Thus while each group has in one sense its own social reality and inner polarity, there have always been limited but important interactions between the two parties that reveal a mutual recognition in terms of dual authority. The preservation of a residual non-Majapahit category of Balinese was not only a logical necessity in the legitimization scheme of Majapahit but also the product of a fierce and enduring desire for some measure of independence and special status among the Bali Aga. I have gathered evidence suggesting that endemic power struggles among lowland rulers in precolonial times led them to appreciate the politically neutral mountains as a refuge following a military defeat (Reuter 1996). Just as these rulers' legitimacy required the Bali Aga as evidence for their own proclaimed status as outsider, it also required the perpetual threat of renewed invasion from the outside—whether the invasion of the neighboring Islamic sultanates or a cholera epidemic. When this threat became a reality with the arrival of the Dutch, the balance of authority had to be renegotiated. The lowland courts first ceased to represent the political center of Balinese society under the Dutch. Their privileges were further diminished, as we shall see, after Indonesian independence.

Modern Balinese Identities and the Narratives of the Nation-State

The question remains how traditional notions of the autochthonous and the foreign are affecting Balinese identities in the present and the recent past. Bali has been changing so rapidly that the relevance of traditional representations of society to contemporary life is open to question. The accelerated pace of change began with Bali's colonial experience, but it has continued throughout the twentieth century with the nationalist struggle, the Japanese occupation during World War II, the massacre of communists in 1965–1966, and the growth of the tourist industry—to name a few milestones well recognized by Balinese themselves. Evaluating the relevance of "traditional" representations to contemporary society is a difficult task and poses a risk of becoming caught somewhere between the twin dangers of romanticism and cynicism—of lamenting dying traditions and proclaiming the gloomy dawn of a global monoculture. As a methodology for investigating the relevance of dual authority and other traditional cultural themes in contemporary Bali, I therefore suggest a hybrid approach: applying a general social theory of marginality in the modern state while remaining alert to culturally specific idioms of Balinese self-representation such as those described earlier.

Contemporary sociological or anthropological studies of minority groups within modernizing societies often focus on their social or political marginality. Such studies have emerged in the wake of a postcolonial or postmodern critique of writing ethnography, itself inspired by the changed research conditions in a postcolonial Asia and elsewhere. The most significant insights offered by this approach are that marginality is culturally constructed, not a mere reflection of geographic, economic, or political conditions, and that the construction is mutual insofar as the underprivileged minority group may object to a dominant discourse or resist practical interventions. The better of these studies have not just romanticized the heroic struggle of noble natives against an evil empire of international capitalism but have studied in ethnographic detail the processes of negotiation between the representations of the centers and margins: the powerful and the fringe dwellers of modern Asia.

A prominent example of this work is Anna Lowenhaupt Tsing's study (1993) of the autochthonous people of the Meratus Mountains in southern Kalimantan and their relationship to the coastal people of the provincial capital and former kingdom of Banjar. The Banjarese, in turn, claim that their ancestors were immigrants from the empire of Majapahit. Tsing employs the notion of "cultural borderlands" to capture the process of negotiating regional ethnic identities—negotiations that take shape at the in-between spaces and through boundary crossings between ethnic categories. Moreover, she emphasizes the need to situate these regional negotiations of identity within the larger question of how the Meratus Dayak and Banjarese relate to the Indonesian state. As in Bali, it is a coastal and urbanized elite in Banjar who predominate as the local participants in the economy, administration, and political organization of southern Kalimantan. The marginal Meratus, like the Bali Aga, are portrayed as primitive, disorganized, and recalcitrant traditionalists in state narratives about the desperate need for development *(pembangunan)*. They are seen as impediments to the national agenda: an agenda informed by global discourses on economic growth and modernity, just as it in turn informs the political strategies of the local Banjarese elite (Tsing 1993). Tsing strives to juxtapose negative external portrayals of Meratus Dayak with her own observations of Meratus responses to encounters with the outside world. She demonstrates that they are not at all passive or rigidly defensive of "tradition" but imaginatively blend strategies of appeasement, subversion, and appropriation of the strangers' discourses and practical interventions.

Such minority studies examine the rhetoric of modern marginalizing discourses, particularly state discourses, and this same method can facilitate an analysis of political processes in contemporary Bali.[20] In modern Bali the term "Bali Aga," in its pragmatic usage, carries connotations of physical, historical, and cultural remoteness. Bali Aga people inhabit the remote mountains. They are regarded as survivors from a distant past before the dawn of civilization. And their continuing adherence to different customs—presumed to be "primitive" or "animist"—is taken as evidence of their exclusion from a civilizing process that has produced a refined courtly culture under the banner of Majapahit in other parts of Bali. Lowland Balinese typically deem them to be impoverished, uncouth, and uneducated hill dwellers ignorant of the sophisticated process of Balinese wet rice agriculture, awkward in their use of refined language, without literature or literacy, and ignorant of Brahmanic ritual.[21]

These views from the political, economic, and administrative center of Bali perpetuate the marginalization of the Bali Aga. The elite of lowland Bali have constructed cultural remoteness, not upon the results of observation or analysis, but upon an act of selective amnesia. The historic significance of the mountain region in the development of Balinese civilization has been systematically ignored. And yet there are hundreds of royal inscriptions *(prasasti)* that bear testament to the centrality of Bali Aga communities for some six hundred years before the presumed Majapahit invasion—a period in which Hindu Balinese dynasties had already established a sophisticated civilization on the island (Goris 1954; Reuter 1996). The category "Bali Aga" is thus built on the fallacious notion that a vast cultural chasm divides "the Bali before the mythical conquest" from "the Bali thereafter"—a discourse in which the physical remoteness of their misty mountain home is nothing but a trope for the temporal, economic, and educational classification of the Bali Aga.[22] Although they are quietly acknowledged as the first settlers and custodians of the most ancient temples on Bali, the mountain people are not acknowledged as the true founders of its civilization.

Knowledge about the details of current "Bali Aga traditions" is severely limited among their fellow Balinese. And most often such knowledge is conveniently phrased as a negative description: "The Bali Aga do not cremate their dead. They do not acknowledge caste. They do not consult Brahmana priests. They do not use Sanskrit mantras (sacred formulas) in their ceremonies." These are typical stereotypes held by lowland Balinese. In short, any known difference between the traditional practices of the two groups is interpreted as a deficiency on the part of the Bali Aga—an absence of important elements of "appropriate ritual procedure" as defined by the literature and expert opinion of the Brahmana priesthood. There is no acknowledgment of Bali Aga traditions more elaborate than those in lowland Bali.

Another way of distinguishing the Bali Aga is to select them as the most appropriate targets for government-sponsored reform projects. Indonesian tertiary students, for example, are required to take part in a compulsory community service internship (Kuliah Kerja Nyata, or KKN). These internships are a means by which the government seeks to proliferate progressive ideas at a local level wherever development is seen to be retarded. In Bali it is the communities of the Bali Aga that are labeled the "undereducated" sector of society in that they enjoy the dubious status of most-favored KKN target. (See Chapter 8 in this volume.) In recent years, Bali Aga villages have also been identified by local authorities as the appropriate targets in Bali for a nationwide government initiative for the advancement of Indonesia's economically and socially most backward communities: its *desa tertinggal,* "villages left behind" by progress. In some Bali Aga villages, for example, people have had to destroy their traditional bamboo houses and build concrete structures instead on the pretext that the new houses are more hygienic. Low-interest government loans were provided for building new homes, but ultimately the affected families were left with few other choices but to sell land in order to pay for a lifestyle they could not sustain. The only real beneficiaries were members of a village elite who could redirect such "housing loans" toward various high-profit investments.

Bali Aga marginality, therefore, is not merely a matter of forgetting ancient Balinese history and the dynasties of pre-Majapahit kings. It is reproduced through an ongoing reinterpretation. These lowlanders' reinterpretations are framed in terms of a state discourse—with "education" *(pendidikan)*, "development" *(pembangunan)*, and "progress" *(kemajuan)* as its key phrases—rather than in terms of a juxtaposition to an earlier civilization subsumed under the hegemony of Majapahit. Majapahit is now regarded as a precursor to the current Indonesian nation-state and is evoked in order to illuminate that the national motto of "unity in Diversity" has always meant a unity maintained and defined by the Javanese. The ancient religious traditions of Hindu Majapahit are somewhat of an embarrassment to a predominantly Islamic Jakartan elite—a sentiment not necessarily shared by the modern elite of Bali.

The distancing devices, denial of history, negative description, negative targeting, and other marginalizing strategies directed toward Bali Aga tradition by the Balinese elite may eventually legitimate the systematic and deliberate eradication of the Bali Aga. The interventions regarded as most detrimental by the Bali Aga themselves are those involving tradition *(adat)* and religion *(agama)*. They are implemented through the manipulation of provincial and local branches of state-controlled institutions such as the Badan Pelaksana Pembina Lembaga Adat (or BPPLA, the Agency for the Development of Customary Institutions) and the Parisada Hindu Dharma Indonesia (PHDI), the Brahmana-dominated religious organization that officially represents all Hindus in Indonesia.[23]

The concepts *adat* and *agama* are central to nationalist discourses concerning Indonesia's future. On the one hand, the outside forces of modernity are to be tempered and civilized by promoting an indigenous heritage of "Indonesian tradition" as a kind of filter. On the other hand, tradition and religion are perceived as obstacles to progress and national unity unless they are reconstituted according to the needs of the modern state. The state thus gains a mandate to intervene in the traditional and religious affairs of local groups—particularly those in marginal and "disorderly" *(belum diatur)* regions—and to eliminate the extremes of cultural and ethnic diversity they seem to represent. The power of this nation-state presents itself to the Bali Aga with a Balinese face, as it is wielded by local state representatives and administrators. Although the latter are members of an urban Balinese elite, many of them are also the children of the former traditional elite and still have a stake in the myth of Majapahit.

While the Bali Aga regard many state interventions as originating from an old opponent under a new cloak, they now occasionally have the opportunity to compete with other Balinese in the borrowing of national state power. Continuing calls by modernist elements within PHDI for a simplification of ritual procedure, for example, have been welcomed among them. Bali Aga attitudes to ritual have long been opposed to what they describe as the unnecessary pomp of lowland Balinese ceremonialism. The casteless Bali Aga also claim to have far more democratic customary institutions than lowland Balinese, and they cite the egalitarianism of the official state ideology, Pancasila, in criticizing lowland society.

State discourses and interventions elicit a wide range of local responses: from accommodation, appeasement, and opportunism to noncooperation, subversion, and public protest. Some ethnographic examples of Bali Aga responses may illustrate how these negotiations unfold. Over the last two decades, the Balinese offices of the BPPLA have tried to impose changes on the traditional village organization *(desa adat)* of mountain communities, which consists of a council of paired elders *(ulu apad)* ranked in order of seniority (Reuter 1996). Bali Aga customary leadership is commonly criticized for not being based on aptitude and qualifications—such as literacy in Indonesian, the language of national identity and bureaucracy. Little credit is given to the fact that a senior position in these councils can be obtained only after a lifetime of experience and training as a junior council member. The real concern may be that the seniority system of succession in these councils is impervious to manipulation by institutions like the BPPLA, which elsewhere "approves" and "educates" elected customary leaders. Village communities in lowland Bali are headed by a single customary leader *(klian adat)* and his assistant rather than by a large council of paired and ranked elders. These customary leaders must be literate in Bahasa Indonesia and during Suharto's presidency had to support the ruling Golkar Party before being approved by the authorities. Thereafter they must regularly attend meetings and educational sessions chaired by the BPPLA offices in the district or regency capital.

Suggestions of dismantling the councils of village elders have been uniformly rejected. Such attempts at intervention are discussed by the leaders of Bali Aga villages during ceremonial and informal gatherings at regional temples. Frequently, locals respond to pressure from government officials by evoking their regional religious identity. The BPPLA, in turn, has recognized this unity as a problem by officially declaring its determination to force the Bali Aga into line. In a formal statement of the program for the future, a report of the provincial committee states its aim: "to integrate the social structure, culture, and Hindu religion of old Balinese [Bali Aga] villages into that of the appanage villages [*desa appanage;* lowland villages], so that in the long run the cultural difference between them becomes less acute" (MPLA 1993:item 3, p. 35, my translation).[24] The text leaves little doubt who is to be integrated and who is to provide the blueprint for this vision of a culturally homogenized Bali.

Bali Aga responses have not always taken the form of undiluted resistance. Many villages accommodate by electing a customary leader as well as maintaining a council or by allocating the office of customary leader to an elder of a particular rank. Other villages have indeed decided to disband or modify the council of elders itself. Such changes are rare, however, and often indicate serious internal factional conflicts rather than a collapse under external pressure.

A different set of interventions has originated from the PHDI—an organization that seeks to rationalize and homogenize Hindu religion and ritual practice in keeping with the strictures imposed on Hinduism as a state-approved religion under the Indonesian constitution. Their national agenda has inclined PHDI leaders to be critical of the wide diversity of religious practices in Balinese communities. And again the Bali Aga have been identified as those with the greatest diversion from the norm.[25] One issue relates to temple architecture. Many Bali Aga villages did not meet the official requirement of having "three essential village temples" *(kayangan tiga,* that is, a *pura dalem, pura bale agung,* and *pura puseh),* although many have renamed their sanctuaries to create an appearance of conformity. Their temples also do not always contain all the shrines deemed essential in lowland Bali. To name but one case, the leaders of the temple committee in Penulisan have suffered repeated criticism because this temple has neither a *meru* (tall shrine with a multitiered roof) nor a *padmasana* (stone seat dedicated to the paramount Hindu deity Sang Hyang Widi). PHDI has promoted the inclusion of both in response to the monotheism requirement under the Indonesian constitution.

Perhaps the most contentious religious issue for the casteless Bali Aga is the use of *pedanda* priests—that is, outsider priests of Brahmana extraction. In one incident, the important Bali Aga regional temple of Pura Penulisan was visited by a PHDI-organized delegation of worshipers under the ritual leadership of a *pedanda* from Bangli. The visitors were unwelcome but had the support of the head of Bangli regency, who belonged to the same Brahmana family as the *pedanda*. Local leaders were outraged by this attempt to ritually appropriate their domain. The visit by the *pedanda* was constructed as a "defilement"— particularly since the PHDI delegation had brought a sacrificial pig, an offering despised by the local deity. Immediately after the conclusion of the festival, the thirty thousand members of the temple's congregation responded by holding a massive three-week-long purification ceremony. The ceremony included a journey to a seaside temple maintained by Sukawana's ritual clients in Tejakula on the north coast. There the polluting influence was finally returned to the sea by ritually bathing the deities of Penulisan temple. This public ritual protest caused a huge embarrassment for the unwelcome visitors, who have never returned.[26] In another Bali Aga village, the dominant faction under the leadership of the village administrative head *(kepala desa)* invited a *pedanda* to officiate at a number of village rituals. Since the *pedanda* was none other than the relative of the Brahmana head of Bangli regency, the faction gained the latter's favor. As a reward, this faction's hold on the office of village administrative head has since become virtually unassailable, as candidates need the regency head's support for successful appointment.

Efforts to passively involve the Bali Aga in modern versions of religious state ritual have led to considerable resentment among them. In one case, the administrative head of a mountain village reported to the elders during a new moon meeting how he had been ordered to Bangli in order to receive *tirta* (sanctified water) from the sacrifice *(taur agung)* held there and in other regency capitals on the day before *nyepi* (the lowland Balinese festival of the new year). "Where did you throw it?" they asked in puzzlement—given that *nyepi pemerintah* (the government-decreed islandwide *nyepi* festival) is not customarily celebrated in Bali Aga villages and none would have use for such *tirta*. "With respect," answered the village head, "I just opened the bottle, put it on the kitchen shelf, and let it evaporate!" Yet government pressure does not evaporate quite so easily, and the excessive laughter in the assembly over this small victory only accentuated the gravity of the situation. The village head later urged the council to order villagers to show consideration to the authorities by not working or commuting too much on the day of *nyepi* when, officially, everyone in Bali is supposed to refrain from work and stay home.[27]

The cultural autonomy of the Bali Aga is thus precarious, but perhaps no more so than the future of the Balinese within a national context. The notions of the autochthonous and the foreign are acquiring a new meaning as Bali is swept by a new wave of outsiders—including an increasing number of Muslim economic migrants and wealthy investors from Java who have sought their fortune in Bali's tourist industry. (See Chapter 3 in this volume.) In one sense, mainstream Bali's romance with Majapahit is itself a metaphoric border crossing: a borrowing of power from the outsider, that is, from a political authority that once again resides in Java and beyond.

To fully appreciate the current relationship between Bali Aga and the lowland descendants of Majapahit, one must recognize that it has been affected, if not transformed, by the advent of colonial rule and, later, by the establishment of an independent Indonesian nation-state. With the violent arrival of the Dutch, Balinese rulers became political figureheads under colonial control. Finding themselves at the receiving end of a new political order, at first colonial and later national, these rulers had two options: strive for a position in the new elite (borrowing or subverting external power to suit their own purposes) or gradually move toward a position of traditional or religious power. The inward motions of "the outsider" in the colonial and national contexts have led to a renewed assault on the residual authority of the Bali Aga, an assault now fought with the institutional and ideological authority of the modern state.

The Local, the Foreign, and the Future

This discussion of the relationship between the people of Bali's remote mountains and the increasingly urbanized political and cultural elite of the Balinese plains, between Bali Aga and the descendants of Majapahit, and nowadays between those who face and those who wield the borrowed power of the state, has revealed a glimpse of the transformations and continuities in Balinese identity. Indigenous narratives of origin already construct a complex, multilayered, and contested political history and eventually blend with the narratives of colonialism, nationalism, and global modernism. An emphatic continuity of Balinese political history resides in the experience of perpetual exposure to

outside forces and a conceptual preoccupation with the control of encounters between "the Balinese" and "the foreign."

Balinese notions of identity are not unique in this sense. Indeed they
are comparable with notions of dual identity and authority observed in
other Austronesian-speaking societies. In a recent article, James Fox
(1994) provides a preliminary list of thematic features based on an
analysis of origin narratives from Fiji, Timor, Roti, Palembang, Be-
semah, and Bali. He emphasizes that various combinations of the following possible outcomes occur: (1) a stranger from across the sea encounters autochthonous inhabitants; (2) a king is requested from
abroad by the original inhabitants to restore order; (3) the male outsider moves "inward" by marrying the daughter of insiders; (4) the
stranger is installed as ruler, but original inhabitants retain control over
land and fertility—thus a permanent compact or diarchy is established;
(5) the outsider violently usurps the insider's authority over the land
and enters into a dichotomous relationship with a new wave of outsiders to whom he is wife giver; (6) the new ruler is immobilized at the
center; (7) the outsider creates a new organization for the domain and
the insider disappears; (8) the original inhabitants are explicitly said to
have been chased out.

If these themes are examined in light of the information presented
in this chapter, it appears that the Balinese case, while it strikes many
resonances, is difficult to interpret. A dual categorical distinction between secular and ritual authority is clearly significant, but it has been
actualized within a specific historical struggle for the control of symbolic resources—an open-ended process with unpredictable outcome.
The original people of the island, the Bali Aga in this case, have managed to retain their separate identity and a role in an enduring but con-
textually limited diarchic relationship with "the newcomers," as represented by lowland Balinese, who see themselves as descendants of
Majapahit.

With Bali's incorporation into the Indonesian nation and the shift
from a rice-growing to a tourism-dominated economy, traditional categories of the autochthonous and the foreign are acquiring new meanings and new social representatives. In contemporary Balinese society
the position of the Bali Aga as the "original people" is open to question, as is the lowlanders' position as powerful strangers. Struggling to
survive at the margins of an increasingly internationalized economic
system and under the coercive power of a modern nation-state, the descendants of lowland Bali's courts are faced with limited options: either
engaging in a competitive appropriation of state power or seeking an

alternative form of authority in the now distinct spheres of customary institutions *(adat)* and religion *(agama)*, sometimes at the expense of the Bali Aga. Some of the old Majapahit-derived elite have been successful in establishing themselves as leaders in a modern political context. But they compete for such power and for material wealth with modern elites who do not have a prestigious Majapahit pedigree, and their traditional status is no longer constitutive of their power. And yet there is continuity in the discourse of elite groups in Bali. As functionaries of the state and the economic system, they construct the Bali Aga as the most traditional and backward sector of Balinese society in order to emphasize their own modernity. Rural areas in general tend to be targeted, and Bali Aga villages are singled out as particularly recalcitrant to "social progress" and "economic development." Old and new notions of the foreign and local thus merge in the thinking of modern elites and in the modern experiences of the Bali Aga alike.

For the time being, at least, indigenous concepts of dual authority relating to a wider Austronesian cultural heritage continue to inform Balinese strategies of negotiating historical or constructed encounters with "the foreign" and remain relevant as the possible foundation for an interpretive model of Balinese society and identity. Even in the discourses of the modern Indonesian nation-state, the global/local or modern/traditional duality reveals a system of complementary values, though the value represented by a foreign-oriented elite is portrayed as superior to the value represented by local traditional societies. This is no different from the claims of Bali's old elite. Nor is it a discourse that can utterly silence or socially dispense with the local.

Notes

1. Only a few of these mountain villages depicted in Map 5 have achieved fame in lowland Bali as exemplary cases of a distinct Bali Aga culture. Other than the inhabitants of adjacent villages, most southern Balinese have no detailed knowledge about which villages in the mountains do or do not adhere to Bali Aga traditions. Exploiting this ambiguity, some of these villages would themselves be hesitant to openly proclaim themselves "Bali Aga" to outsiders in view of the term's derisive connotations. The foregoing figures therefore reflect my own tentative definition of what a Bali Aga community may be. This is a complex matter, but perhaps the most important criterion of my classification is that the villages of the original Balinese all maintain assemblies led by paired elders *(ulu apad)* ranked in order of their seniority as council members. In other Balinese villages, the members of the assembly are unranked and led by an elected representative.

2. A general ethnographic account of the social organization in the mountains of Bali, from the level of kinship and alliance to village communities and regional ritual domains *(banua)*, has been presented in an earlier work (Reuter 1996). In this chapter I am not particularly concerned with the content of the traditions maintained by mountain Balinese or with comparing these traditions to those of other Balinese. There are enough significant cultural differences to lend credibility to the hypothesis that they represent a separate ethnohistorical layer within Balinese society. It is futile to debate whether or not they represent a separate society; they do in some ways, but in more important ways they do not. Even the observed ethnic distinctiveness of the mountain Balinese is as much a cultural construction as it is a product of a separate historical heritage. Furthermore, the distinction is not easily defined on empirical grounds, for many villages reveal both Bali Aga and lowland Bali characteristics.

3. A transfer of notions such as "fertility" from the conceptual domain of gender to that of social organization and cosmology is particularly common in Bali.

4. The paired categories of "mountain" and "sea" are but one manifestation of a complex Balinese system of dual classification. A similar distinction is contained in the paired terms *bali mula/bali majapahit,* that is, "original Balinese/Balinese of foreign Majapahit ancestry," or *wedan/pendonan* meaning "people of the trunk/people of the leaf" (Reuter 1996). Both pairs suggest a notion of the local, autochthonous or old versus the foreign and new. The botanical metaphors also suggest a temporal process of transformation. "Leaves" move closer to the trunk of a growing tree just as newcomers to a society may become locals with the arrival of new immigrants.

5. I am critical of the way in which indigenous spatial metaphors have been interpreted by some Western researchers (see Tooker 1996). The self-representations of Indic polities in Southeast Asia in particular tend to be interpreted as a spatial mandala, with an "exemplary center" and a lusterless fringe. (See, for example, Geertz 1980.) As opposed to interpretations based on a notion of dual authority, such studies are center-biased and tend to reproduce unwittingly the viewpoint of indigenous cultural elites.

6. There are many versions of this myth, written and oral, and what I present here is what most Balinese know about these mythohistorical events. For an inventory of different published versions see Geertz (1980:144, nn. 14–17); for an example of a Balinese written version see Creese (1997).

7. It is remarkable that a similar accusation of atheism supported the legitimation for the government's violent purge of so-called communists in 1965–1966.

8. The original Majapahit settlers on Bali must have been few in number. It is only through the "Majapahitization" of the Balinese who are not descendants of Majapahit that the majority of Balinese now claim to be of Majapahit descent. Even some Bali Aga people have "discovered" their Majapahit origins during the last two decades, usually with the help of a trance medium *(balian).* They jokingly refer to themselves as "Pasek Peras Penyeneng." The

Pasek are a large and prominent Balinese clan, many of whose members proclaim their Majapahit origins (see Chapter 6 in this volume). *Peras penyeneng* is an offering brought for the consultation of trance mediums. The expression "Pasek Peras Penyeneng" refers to the fact that some Bali Aga clans have changed their supposed *kawitan* (origin group affiliation) several times, following misfortune, each time confirming their choice by consulting a medium. They tend to highlight or conceal their status as Majapahit descendants (Pasek) or Bali Aga depending on the social context. When pressed to explain the contradiction, they just smile and argue that Pasek are really the descendants of original Balinese kings—as was Sri Kresna Kapakisan himself!

9. I am presenting a brief and popular oral version of this narrative of origin as known to most mountain Balinese. For other Balinese it merely serves as a possible explanation of how King Mayadanawa acquired his demonic shape and disposition.

10. In many cases, "the two parties" may indeed be descendants of earlier and later arrivals, who simply have chosen to define themselves in those terms by means of a constructed history.

11. The former courts of Puri Gelgel and Puri Klungkung are relevant examples of the establishment of "new" political centers, but the pattern is less obvious with the ritual centers established and maintained by Majapahit descendants. It is uncertain, for example, whether Besakih Temple was established or merely appropriated and transformed to become a state temple of the Gelgel and Klungkung dynasties.

12. In fact, the portrayal of Majapahit's civilizing agenda is remarkably similar to the self-justifications of "benevolent colonialism" concerned with eradicating the "barbaric" aspects of native society—in other words, its political powers.

13. It is well know that a bodily form with both human and animal elements is commonly attributed to demonic beings in Balinese narratives and art. These demonic beings can be described as manifestations of raw, untempered power or efficacy *(kesaktian)*.

14. A distinction between Wong Bali Aga and Wong Bali Mula (original Balinese) is sometimes employed to distinguish between these layers of "original" Balinese.

15. It is uncertain whether Panji Sakti (ruler of northern Bali from about 1599 to 1680 according to Sastrodiwiryo 1994) and his successors conducted these raids on behalf of the paramount ruler in Klungkung or for reasons of their own (but with his approval nonetheless). References to "Panji Sakti" in Bali Aga oral histories may also refer to other military leaders. In later times, the rulers of the northern kingdom of Buleleng sought alliances and received military aid from Bali Aga villages (Sastrodiwiryo 1994:75; Rubinstein 1996).

16. An Indonesian translation of the *Babad Pasek* was published by Sugriwa (1957), and this translation, so far as the preceding passage is concerned, corresponds with other manuscripts of this text at the Gedong Kirtya, Sin-

garaja, and at Pusat Dokumentasi Bali, Denpasar. The *Babad Pasek* is a text that must be considered with caution, for it may have been written in the political context of the Pasek movement. (See Chapter 6 in this volume for the struggle of *jaba* clans for status equality.)

17. There have also been sporadic military alliances between lowland kingdoms and groups of Bali Aga villages. One example is the traditional ties that exist between the village of Bayung Gede and Puri Bangli, the Bangli court (Reuter 1996).

18. Although mountain people may visit lowland temples to pray *(mabakti)*, neither this nor support of the temples constitutes a formal obligation.

19. According to narratives I have recorded in the Bali Aga villages of Batur and Selulung, a small Bali Aga kingdom around Lake Batur was destroyed by a ruler named "Panji Sakti." After this victory, Panji Sakti publicly demonstrated his continuing respect for the ritual authority of the priests of the defeated kingdom by offering a gift of atonement at the temple of the lake goddess at Batur.

20. This approach can also help to reveal how foreign ethnographers who have conducted research in Bali have contributed to the marginal status of the Bali Aga.

21. These stereotypes do not reflect the opinion of all Balinese. Those who come into regular contact with Bali Aga people tend to maintain much less stereotypical views. Some urban Balinese may even look with romantic admiration at the presumed "cultural authenticity" of the Bali Aga.

22. It should be noted that this geographical trope is not entirely correct even if its meaning is taken in the immediate descriptive sense. Several Bali Aga villages are situated on or near the coast rather than in the mountains—for example, Julah, Pacung, Les, and Tenganan.

23. A predominance of Brahmana is still evident among the ranks of the PHDI, but this may change in the near future. (See Chapter 6 in this volume.)

24. The term "appanage villages" was first used by the Dutch researcher V. E. Korn (1932:77) in order to distinguish Balinese villages that had come under the cultural influence of the Majapahit courts from those that had not, most prominently the villages of the Bali Aga. Korn saw the latter as illustrative of the autonomy of original Balinese village republics—autonomy that had been lost elsewhere due to the oppressive rule of exploitative petty kings of Majapahit descent. This hypothesis may be linked to the legitimization of colonial rule: Bali was to be restored as a unified realm in which villages could once more enjoy their local autonomy.

25. Initially some members of the PHDI may have had a genuine interest in "enlightening" the Bali Aga with their newfound knowledge of contemporary Indian religious philosophy and practice, but in recent years this institution has become more and more a vehicle for the "anti-ethnic" campaign of the national government.

26. Not everywhere has there been such well-organized and potent resis-

tance. For example, some Bali Aga villages in the western part of Buleleng regency have deliberately changed their customary religious practices and treat their Bali Aga identity as a thing of the past. For this reason I was forced to abandon my original plan to conduct field research in these villages in favor of the Kintamani district.

27. A local version of *nyepi (nyepi desa)* is celebrated in these villages at different intersections of the Balinese lunar/solar calendar, sometimes up to three times a year. To be fair, it should be added that the specific traditions of some non–Bali Aga villages are just as unique and suffer equally from the cultural homogenization mission of the state.

Chapter 6

Status Struggles
and the Priesthood
in Contemporary Bali

I GDE PITANA

In July 1994, I attended a major ceremony at Ulun Danu Batur Temple in the village of Songan, Kintamani, in Bangli regency.[1] In addition to thousands of the faithful, the ceremony was attended by high-level civil servants such as the governor of Bali, the regent of Bangli, representatives of all the other regents in Bali, the chairman of the Indonesian Hindu Council (Parisada Hindu Dharma Indonesia, or PHDI, the officially recognized organization representing the interests of Indonesian Hindus to the state), and the chairman of the Council for the Development of Customary Institutions (Majelis Pembina Lembaga Adat, or MPLA).

Eight *sulinggih* or "twice-born priests" officiated at the ceremony. Interestingly, these priests came from different clans and represented nearly all the clans that have their own priests. They included a priest from the Pande clan, a priest from the Arya Wangbang Pinatih clan, a priest from the Pasek Sapta Rsi clan, as well as three priests from the Siwa branch of the Brahmana clan and two priests from its Boda branch. A Bhujangga Waisnawa clan priest had also been invited to officiate but was unable to attend. The officiating *sulinggih* performed their rituals simultaneously, seated at the same level, facing the same direction. Such broad priestly representation at a ceremony is uncommon in the religious practice of Bali's Hindus, let alone at a high-status public temple like Ulun Danu Batur.

At the height of the ceremony, a PHDI officer and member of the

Brahmana clan, Ida Bagus Uttara,[2] approached a temple priest *(pemangku)*, Jero Mangku Raka, and quietly instructed him that the holy water used for the *pedagingan,* the most important set of ritual ingredients at the ceremony, had to be the holy water made by a "real Brahmana" *(brahmana jati)*. He meant a priest from the Brahmana clan, not any of the other priests. While Mangku Raka nodded his head, a younger temple priest, Jero Mangku Rai, who overhead the conversation, spontaneously asked Ida Bagus Uttara, "What do you mean by a 'real Brahmana'?" He emphatically answered himself: "All of these *sulinggih* are 'real Brahmana' . . . they have all undergone the 'twice-born' *(dwijati)* ceremony, and all hold a certificate acknowledging that they are 'twice-born' priests, issued by you people, the *Parisada*. Do you want to ignore the truth? Who are you trying to deceive?"

While the temple priest was speaking, a number of people, including members of the organizing committee, hastened to the scene. I saw from their expressions that all supported the young priest. Aware of the situation, Ida Bagus Uttara quietly left, red-faced.

The *Warga* Movement

Most literature about Bali that mentions the Hindu priesthood states that it is the monopoly of the Brahmana clan—both its Siwa and Boda branches—which implies that all Balinese use the services of Brahmana priests who are known as *pedanda*. While this is true in general, evidence reveals that some *jaba* clans, such as the Bhujangga Waisnawa, have never used Brahmana priests. Instead they use their own priests who are known as *rsi bhujangga*. The same is true for many members of the Pande clan from Buleleng, Tabanan, Gianyar, and Jembrana regencies, who not only use their own priests known as *sri mpu* but also maintain that they are not permitted to accept the purifying holy water made by *pedanda*. Following their example, members of other *jaba* clans have begun to question the monopolistic role of *pedanda* in religious practice. This grassroots reaction to Brahmana domination has intensified in recent times, and the desire for status recognition and equality in religious and customary matters has caused many *jaba* clans to formally constitute themselves as *warga* or clan organizations.[3] These *warga* organizations are characterized by their ownership of a common ancestral temple or temples, an internally agreed origin myth and founding ancestor, an accepted body of rules of conduct *(warga sesana)*, and the claim to possess supernaturally powerful religious regalia, in particular for the performance of death rites. Moreover, each *warga* organization generally has a written genealogy/history or *babad*. There are well over thirty *jaba* clans in Bali at present, and many have established formal organizations for their members.[4] Their increasing visibility and vocalness has made the "*warga* movement," as I term it, a potent force for religious and sociocultural change in contemporary Bali.

The background of the *warga* movement can be traced to social changes that occurred after Indonesia gained independence in 1945. For a religion to be recognized by the state it had to conform to the following framework: it had to be monotheistic; it had to have a unified holy book, a codified system of law for its followers, and a prophet; and its congregation had to extend beyond a single ethnic group. To fulfill these requirements and gain equality with other recognized religions, such as Islam and Christianity, Balinese were forced to "rationalize" their religion (Forge 1980; Bakker 1993; see Chapter 1 in this volume). Eventually, in 1958, after a long struggle, Balinese religion was officially recognized by the state. A consequence of this rationalization and Indonesianization of Balinese Hinduism was the fostering of a recognition that all human beings are equal before one god and, hence, that everyone should be entitled to attain the highest level of religious authority—that of the "twice-born" priest. This led the PHDI, which had been established in 1959,[5] to formulate as policy, at its second general meeting held in 1968, that all Hindus are entitled to undergo the "twice-born" ritual in order to become priests and that all priests are equal in status.[6] For some *jaba* clans, such as the Bhujangga Waisnawa and Pande, this decision was merely the codification of a situation that already existed.

The existence of *jaba* priests in Bali today is an interesting phenomenon. While their recognition is a consequence of the rationalization and modernization of Balinese Hinduism as well as the adoption of the official state ideology of the Five Principles of the Pancasila—belief in a single, supreme god; humanitarianism; unity; democracy; and social justice—and the increasing homogenization of diverse societies and cultures throughout the Indonesian archipelago, the seemingly rigid hierarchy of the Balinese social structure into *triwangsa* and *anak jaba* continues to undermine true egalitarianism in the religious domain: *jaba* priests are treated as second-class priests. This conflict within the priesthood, backed by the continuing establishment of new *warga* organizations, gives us a lens for viewing the transformation of status relations in Bali and forms the focus of this chapter. After surveying the priesthood in Bali, I want to discuss the contestation of status between *pedanda* and *jaba* priests.

There are degrees of priesthood in Bali: two major categories are recognized by the PHDI and adherents of Hinduism. The first category of *pinandita* comprises people who have undergone a special consecration ceremony *(pawintenan)* that does not involve the step of "spiritual death," so that these people are not considered "twice-born" but "once-born" *(ekajati)*. This category includes temple priests *(pemangku), jero kubayan,*[7] *jero gede,*[8] exorcist shadow puppeteers *(mangku dalang),* traditional healers *(balian),* and female temple attendants *(prasutri).* Although the PHDI has limited the authority of priests who are *pinandita*—they may only officiate at certain ceremonies—this ban does not hold in practice. Priests who are formally categorized as *pinandita* tend to officiate at all ceremonies, particularly those held by *warga* organizations that do not have their own priests and at ceremonies held by predominantly *jaba* village communities.

The second category of priest is the *sulinggih* or *pandita*—namely, priests who have been consecrated with a complete set of "twice-born" rituals *(dwijati* or *padiksan),* chief among which are spiritual death *(amati raga),* rebirth, and changing one's name *(amari aran).* Depending on the clan to which they belong,[9] these priests are known by different titles. Ideally, *sulinggih* function as *patirthaning sarat,* that is, as a place for people to seek "the water of life"—*tirta* or purifying holy water—and spiritual well-being (Purwita 1993; Titib 1993). Most *sulinggih* make holy water, which they dispense to their followers and perform ceremonies, also taking charge of the preparations. But there are also *sulinggih* who undergo the *dwijati* ceremony to increase their own holiness without any intention of officiating at ceremonies.[10]

Contesting Hierarchy

Most Balinese, if asked, would venture that all *sulinggih* are of equal status. In keeping with the PHDI's pronouncement that all *sulinggih* are equal in status, duties, and rights, they would say there is no group of twice-born priests who are higher or lower than another. My research findings, however, suggest that in practice most people consider the twice-born priesthood to consist of a two-tier hierarchy with Brahmana priests *(pedanda siwa* and *pedanda boda)* occupying the top tier and *jaba* priests the lower tier. *Triwangsa,* in particular, consider *jaba* priests to be inferior to *pedanda* and contend they are not twice-born but merely once-born. Most *triwangsa* invite *pedanda* to officiate at their ceremonies; very few of those I encountered in Kuta, Denpasar, and Mengwi use *jaba* priests. The selection of priests to officiate at public temples demonstrates the same pattern: *pedanda* are usually appointed. And when Bhujangga Waisnawa priests, the *rsi bhujangga,* are included,[11] they are invariably relegated to a subordinate position, sitting at a lower level and to the south of their Brahmana counterparts, a sign of their lower status. This practice negates the acknowledgment of equal status and angers the *jaba* clans—particularly the large, powerful clans who have formed *warga* organizations and have their own priests, such as the Pande, Pasek, and Bhujangga Waisnawa.

Hildred and Clifford Geertz state that "*homo hierarchicus* and *homo aequalis* are engaged in Bali in war without end" (1975:167). This is not only true of the society at large but also of the priesthood supported by the various clans from which they come. The struggle to achieve equal status for *jaba* priests and the reactions encountered are demonstrated by the following cases. Some of the data were obtained through participant observation; most were obtained through interviews and documents (letters, the minutes of meetings held by *warga* organizations, and photographs).

Case 1: Tribhuana Ceremony, Besakih

The Tribhuana ceremony is associated with the Ekadasa Rudra ceremony, the largest propitiatory rite involving the entire island, which is performed at Besakih, the most inclusive temple complex where Balinese Hindus gather to worship at periodic ceremonies. An Ekadasa Rudra ceremony was held for the first time in a number of centuries in 1963. Although it was successfully concluded, disputes erupted over its timing. As a result, a further Ekadasa Rudra ceremony was performed in 1979 (Stuart-Fox 1987; Lansing 1983). It was followed by Tribhuana and Ekabhuana ceremonies, whose main aims are the restoration of harmony and welfare in the universe.

During the Tribhuana ceremony held in 1993, three *warga* organizations—the Maha Samaya Warga Pande, the Keluarga Besar Bhujangga Waisnawa, and the Maha Gotra Pasek Sanak Sapta Rsi—insisted that their priests be included as officiating priests at the central ceremony. The organizing committee rejected their proposal, however, arguing that traditionally only three priests—called *tri-sadhaka,* comprising a *pedanda siwa, pedanda boda,* and *rsi bhujangga*—are permitted to officiate at major ceremonies in the temple's main complex. In support

Figure 26. A *pedanda* and *rsi bhujangga* perform a ritual. The *pedanda* (left) is seated above the *rsi bhujangga* (right). Photo: Goris and Dronkers (1952).

of their stance, the committee members resorted to terms documented by David Stuart-Fox in his dissertation about Besakih, "Pura Besakih: A Study of Balinese Religion and Society" (1987). These terms dichotomize "*pemangku* ceremonies" on the one hand and "*pedanda* ceremonies" on the other, the latter being ceremonies that may only be performed by twice-born priests from the Brahmana clan. The *warga* organizations challenged this explanation: they questioned the meaning of the word "traditional" and asked the committee to clarify the situation before the arrival in Bali, around the fifteenth century, of Mpu Dwijendra, the Javanese priest and alleged progenitor of the Brahmana in Bali, since Besakih Temple is known to have existed well before his arrival. They then proceeded to challenge the committee's interpretation of the *tri-sadhaka* doctrine. They contended that the term *"tri-sadhaka,"* which is mentioned in old documents associated with Besakih Temple *(Raja Purana)*, denotes "priests from three sects." These priests, they argued, can be any priests, not only a *pedanda siwa, pedanda boda,* and *rsi bhujangga.*[12]

When the organizing committee, dominated by members of the Brahmana clan, was unable to respond adequately to these questions and charges, the dispute was referred to the governor of Bali, himself a Brahmana and adviser to the ceremony. His adjudication took into account the ceremony's smooth passage and successful outcome, unmarred by "social problems" that could jeopardize its efficaciousness. On 19 March 1993, an agreement was finally reached at a meeting held between the governor, the organizing committee, and the three *warga.* The governor advised the *warga* organizations to be tolerant of the existing arrangements and promised that at future ceremonies (such as the Ekabhuana in 1996), their own priests would be included.[13] This promise, however, was later broken. At the Ekabhuana ceremony held at Besakih Temple in 1996, *pedanda* presided over the rituals for the general public with the assistance of one priest from the Bhujangga Waisnawa clan. Priests from the other *jaba* clans merely officiated at their respective ancestral compounds *(padharman)* at Besakih.

Case 2: The Inauguration of Jagatnatha Temple, Singaraja

A new temple, Pura Jagatnatha, was erected in Singaraja, capital of the regency of Buleleng. The main objective in its construction was to establish a public temple that accommodates all Hindu worshipers in the north of the island—regardless of geographical boundaries or people's ancestral background and occupational status. In this respect, the temple would replicate another Pura Jagatnatha Temple that had existed in Denpasar in the south of the island since 1963. Planning of the temple in Singaraja—its layout and design—was discussed at meetings attended by, among others, *sulinggih* from all clans, officials of the PHDI, and civil servants from the provincial Office of Religious Affairs (Kantor Agama).

After the temple had been built, an inaugural purification ritual (*plaspas*) was scheduled to be held some time between the auspicious dates of 19 June and 11 July 1993. An organizing committee, responsible for determining the ceremony's detailed events, provided that each clan would be represented by its priests. Apart from *pedanda* from the Siwa and Boda branches of the Brahmana clan, there would be a *sri mpu* from the Pasek Sapta Rsi clan, a *sri mpu* from the Pande clan, and a *rsi bhujangga* from the Bhujangga Waisnawa clan. The proposed agenda was accepted except for the important matter of the *sulinggih*. The chairman of the Buleleng branch of the PHDI, himself a *pedanda siwa*, and a number of other *pedanda* rejected the participation of the *jaba* priests. They delivered an ultimatum: if *jaba sulinggih* were involved, the invited *pedanda* would boycott the ceremony. After learning of this ultimatum, a number of *sri mpu* and *rsi bhujangga* retaliated by declaring the ultimatum was so insulting that they would not participate at the ceremony even if were they invited. One of the *sri mpu* asked: "Should priests, these so-called holy men, behave like that? Why should I sit with such arrogant men?"

The regent of Buleleng and his staff, the committee members, and the PHDI officials were faced with a huge dilemma. After hot and lengthy debate, as well as skillful diplomatic work on the part of the committee members in approaching individual *sulinggih* and their *warga* organizations, the committee finally decided that only one non-Brahmana *sulinggih*, a *rsi bhujangga*, would officiate during the main part of the ceremony and only *pedanda* would be invited to officiate during the rest of the ceremony. For future annual festivals, however, all *sulinggih* would be given an equal chance to officiate by taking turns. This has indeed happened: at the 1994 annual ceremony, a Pasek clan priest, Sri Mpu Dwitantra, officiated.

Case 3: Laying the Cornerstone at Jagatnatha Temple, Negara

A Jagatnatha temple was constructed in Negara, Bali's westernmost regency, in 1993. The first set of ceremonies for this project involved laying the cornerstone. The regent of Jembrana, who was a Brahmana, was aware of the strength of the *warga* organizations and their priests in his regency. This led him to decide, from the outset, that all priests in Jembrana would be invited to officiate.

At the ceremony that took place in October 1993, eighteen priests participated: two *sri mpu* from the Pasek clan, two *sri mpu* from the

Pande clan, two *rsi bhujangga,* two *pedanda boda,* and ten *pedanda siwa.* (The number of Brahmana Siwa priests in Jembrana was much larger than for any other clan.) The priests performed their rituals in three areas of the temple: the outer or profane court *(nista mandala);* the middle court *(madya mandala);* and the innermost or most sacred court *(uttama mandala).* In determining who should perform their ritual where—which signifies relative status—the priests discussed the matter among themselves and reached a unanimous decision that *jaba* priests should be represented in all three courts.

There are a number of reasons why these priests were able to cooperate. First, clan hierarchy is not as rigid in Jembrana as elsewhere in Bali. Second, the use of *jaba* priests is relatively common there. Finally, the chairman of the Jembrana branch of the PHDI was a member of a *jaba* clan, the Pasek Sapta Resi, and was also vice-chairman of the Jembrana branch of the Pasek *warga* organization known as the Maha Gotra Pasek Sanak Sapta Rsi.

Case 4: Purification Ritual at Ulun Danu Batur Temple

Ulun Danu Batur Temple, one of the island's most important temples, as noted, underwent major renovation during 1993 and 1994. Upon its completion an inaugural purification ceremony *(plaspas)* was scheduled. To broaden the temple's worshipers to encompass members of all clans while promoting the renovated temple throughout the island, the organizing committee proposed to obtain the services of priests from the various clans to officiate at the ceremony.[14]

The idea was initially rejected by the Brahmana regent of Bangli and the Satria chairman of the Bangli branch of the PHDI, who declared it was not common practice for several priests from different clans to perform a ceremony together. One Brahmana priest officiating alone would be sufficient, they asserted. These two powerful officials also argued that if *jaba* priests were to be used, *triwangsa* would refuse to pray at the temple. The *jaba* chairman of the organizing committee, however, Putu Mahayuna, argued strongly against this view:

> Ulun Danu Temple is a public temple, not a *warga* organization temple, hence its officiating priests must be representative of the public. If the regent does not agree, it does not matter, because the committee has the right to decide—we must keep the temple and politics separate. If the PHDI rejects the presence of *jaba* priests, we will make this position known to the public, and it will rebound on the PHDI, since we know that it has declared all twice-born priests to be equal. It is the PHDI that

examines *sulinggih* candidates before the twice-born ceremony and issues certificates of priesthood to them. . . . Moreover, if it is true that *triwangsa* do not want to worship at a temple at which *jaba* priests officiate, we are not worried at all by that. The *triwangsa* constitute only about 10 percent of Balinese . . . we will appeal to the remaining 90 percent. [Interview, 29 July 1994]

After the issue was resolved in favor of the organizing committee, a fresh challenge was issued by a number of Brahmana priests who as a demonstration of their superiority, refused to sit on the same platform and at the same height as their *jaba* counterparts. To overcome this problem, the committee offered to construct separate platforms for each priest, all of the same height, an idea that met with acceptance from the invited priests.[15]

As mentioned in the opening vignette in this chapter, eight priests from various clans eventually officiated at the ceremony.[16] They were divided into three groups corresponding to the temple's three courtyards. In determining who should perform their ritual where, the priests decided among themselves. Such was also the case for a ceremony at Patirthan Temple—a smaller temple that is the source of holy water for the main temple—where three of the priests were to officiate. They decided that seniority in the priesthood would determine where they would sit. Thus Sri Mpu Santapala, the Pande priest, sat in the north, the direction of greatest purity customarily reserved for *pedanda;* Sri Mpu Dhaksa Samyoga, from the Pasek Sapta Rsi clan, sat in the center, and Pedanda Gede Ketut Sebali Tianyar Arimbawa,[17] a Brahmana Siwa priest, sat in the south.

Case 5: Cremation Ceremony, Baluk

In September 1994, a large cremation ceremony *(ngaben)*, at which 109 dead from various clans were to be cremated, was planned for the village of Baluk in Jembrana regency. At a village meeting, the organizing committee proposed that three priests would be invited to officiate: a *pedanda*, a *sri mpu*, and a *rsi bhujangga*. There was no problem—everyone agreed. But the invited *pedanda*, Ida Pedanda Sigaran, initially refused to officiate at a ceremony alongside his *jaba* counterparts. The committee then explained to him that his position was unacceptable and that it would seek another *pedanda*. He was given three days to consider the matter.

For fear of losing his followers and after lengthy discussions, the *pedanda* finally accepted the invitation. Thus three priests from different clans officiated at the cremation: the Brahmana Siwa priest Ida

Pedanda Sigaran, the Pasek priest Ida Sri Mpu Dharma Ekashanti, and the Bhujangga Waisnawa priest Ida Rsi Bhujangga Tegalcangkring. They sat on the same platform, their positions determined by their seniority in the priesthood, and their holy water was used by all members of the village.

Status Contestation via the Priesthood

These five cases illustrate status contestation—the conflict between ideologies of equality and hierarchy—held by different groups in present-day Bali. Not only are clans that were traditionally considered to be at the bottom of the hierarchy now openly challenging those at the top, but their struggles are being channeled through the priesthood. The involvement of the priesthood in this contestation stems from the *jaba* protagonists' perception that equality among clans can only be realized when *jaba* priests are recognized as having equal status to Brahmana priests through their participation at important public ceremonies. The involvement of the priesthood in status contestation has a firm basis, for equality of the priesthood was declared explicitly by the PHDI as early as 1968. As one informant told me, this formal acknowledgment gives power to *jaba* clans with their own priests because "to say that non-*pedanda* priests are lower than *pedanda* is insulting to the PHDI."

The PHDI, as the representative body of Indonesian Hindus that is formally recognized by the state, does not question the ideology of equality. Nonetheless, the organization continues to be dominated by Brahmana, and some PHDI officers have privately done their best to keep *jaba* priests from officiating at ceremonies held for the general public—as, for example, occurred at Ulun Danu Batur Temple. Even when *jaba* priests are used, efforts are made to minimize their roles. This ambivalent attitude is associated with a conflict of interest experienced by *triwangsa* who have traditionally enjoyed high status but now, like everyone else, have to demonstrate that they are supporters of Pancasila, the egalitarian state ideology. But as is usually the case, people who enjoy high status are not willing to renounce their status and privileges in order to promote equality with others.

Perceptions of *Sulinggih* Status

The preceding examples demonstrate that people's perceptions of the relative status of twice-born priests depend on their social status, education, occupation, and, most important, clan affiliation. In this section I canvass a variety of viewpoints to illustrate the diversity of positions held.

The late Ida Dalem Pemayun, head of the royal family of Klungkung—traditionally Bali's highest spiritual authority and a Satria priest in his own right—represents the conservative view of priestly status. He explicitly told me that only Brahmana priests and *sulinggih* from the Satria royal family of Klungkung are entitled to officiate at public ceremonies. *Jaba* priests, he said, are only entitled to officiate at small family ceremonies.

Ida Pedanda Gede Ketut Sebali Tianyar Arimbawa, a forty-nine-year-old Brahmana priest from the conservative area of Karangasem with somewhat of a reputation as a maverick, holds a diametrically opposed view. He said to me:

> In what manner are *pedanda* superior to non-*pedanda sulinggih,* such as *sri mpu, rsi bhujangga,* or *dukuh*? Are *pedanda* more *sakti* (supernaturally powerful)? I am a *pedanda,* but not *sakti.* Does God love *pedanda* more than the others? Are a *pedanda*'s invocations more powerful than others? The answer is categorically *no....* Moreover, who is the ancestor of Bali's *pedanda*?... There were no *pedanda* before the era of Mpu Dwijendra. So only those who are stupid and narrow-minded will think that *pedanda* are superior ... and will behave accordingly.[18]

A more moderate view was expressed by Ida Pedanda Nyoman Pidada, a Brahmana and former chairman of the Karangasem regency branch of the PHDI. So long as a priest holds a certificate of authorization from the PHDI, he says, the priest's rights and duties are equal to the rights and duties of other priests. He warned that this issue must be dealt with cautiously in practice, however, because it is a "new" development and most people still regard *pedanda* as the highest *sulinggih.* He continued: "Let the people decide who they will use; and those who are not chosen should accept the situation with an open heart and try to improve their abilities, their credibility, their respect, reliability, and so forth."

A similar perception is shared by the Brahmana priest Ida Pedanda Nabe Padangkertha from Singapadu, Gianyar, whose late father, the priest Ida Pedanda Gede Kutri, consecrated several *jaba sulinggih.* Ida Pedanda Nabe Padangkertha believes that his father had certain fundamental reasons for teaching and consecrating them. "Priesthood is not for pleasure, nor is it a means of attaining worldly pleasure," he told me. In his opinion, people do not join the priesthood unless there are sufficient grounds for doing so—including a strong personal motivation to attain a higher spiritual life—since priests face a variety of complex problems. "And do not think that being a *sulinggih* is easy. It is a very tough life abounding in prohibitions." So far as the use of priests from different clans is concerned, he maintains that the matter should be left to each individual to decide, so that the existing "harmony" will not be affected and the "flow of concentration" required to perform rituals will not be obstructed. The same view was espoused by Ida Bagus Oka Punyatmadja, a Brahmana who, from 1968 to 1993, served in a prominent capacity in the PHDI.

Leaders of the Pande, Pasek Sapta Rsi, and Bhujangga Waisnawa *warga* organizations maintain there are no higher or lower *sulinggih*. They consider *pedanda, sri mpu, rsi bhujangga,* and *dukuh* to have equal status and regard their different titles and ritual regalia as merely a difference rather than symbolizing a hierarchy. Colors were commonly used as a metaphor to explain this difference to me: red, blue, green, yellow, white, and so forth, though different colors, are not superior to each other; they are merely different. I Ktut Soebandi, a leader of the Warga Pasek Sapta Rsi, also told me: "The uniform of the army is green, while that of the navy is white; brown is for the police, and blue for the air force. Which one is higher? No one! They are different, but all are equal. It's just a difference."

The promulgation of the concept of difference, which is nothing other than a denial of hierarchy, is very evident in the struggle to have *jaba* priests officiate at public ceremonies or in public temples. Despite some failures, there have also been significant successes, as we have seen, in gaining equal status for *jaba* priests on several occasions.

An Episode of Sociocultural Transformation

I have described at length an arena of significant sociocultural change that is taking place in contemporary Bali. For it was not until the late 1960s that people began to talk openly about equality between *triwangsa* and *jaba* priests, let alone invite both to officiate at public ceremonies on an equal basis. My interviews with elderly priests from the three main *jaba* clans that have their own priests—the Pande, Pasek, and Bhujangga Waisnawa—indicate that it was then, for the first time, that *jaba* priests began to challenge the status of *pedanda* at public ceremonies with the backing of their *warga* organizations. Prior to that, it seems they had never attempted to place themselves on an equal footing with *pedanda* or sought to officiate at public ceremonies over which *pedanda* presided.[19] They merely accepted that *pedanda* were higher in status. They did in fact have struggles, but those struggles were internal conflicts involving their *warga* organizations whose members, they felt, should utilize their own priests rather than outsiders. In the case of *rsi bhujangga* who customarily officiated alongside *pedanda* at public ceremonies that were purificatory or exorcist in nature, they were (and sometimes still are) content to be seated in a separate pavilion, at a lower level, and to the south of their Brahmana counterparts, signifying lower status (Hooykaas 1973, 1976).

When placing the contested status of priests in a broader context, it is useful to consider theories of sociocultural change—in particular Anthony Giddens' theory of structuration (1984). Giddens says we must recognize the active process of agents in interaction because people do not automatically follow a system of codes, and our actions are both structured and structuring. People's capacity to reflect, monitor, define, and decide on their actions must be seriously considered. He also contends that the concept of "structural contradiction" is crucial in explaining sociocultural change. But Giddens does not concentrate exclusively on contradiction. He also holds a view of "conjuncture," which emphasizes that historical variations influence the transition of societies (Cohen 1989). Sociocultural change must be studied against the background of the involvement of a preexisting society in a broad context of intersocietal relations. In other words, endogenous and exogenous circumstances must be taken into consideration.

With respect to sociocultural changes occurring in present-day Bali, the role of specific agents in defining the path of these changes is obvious. Leaders of *warga* organizations, particularly the Pande, Pasek, and Bhujangga Waisnawa, have a clear agenda for change. From their sociodemographic characteristics we see that these leaders are mostly members of new elites that gained their social and economic status through modern (formal, Western-style education) and not through status ascription by birth. These new elites have tried to overcome the structural injustices they encounter in their society by using the cultural capital of their educational status. Both endogenous and exogenous factors have been important in their efforts to reshape Balinese Hindu society.

Access to the Indian sources of Vedic teachings—many of which have been brought to Bali by Balinese who received their tertiary education in India and have been published by them or the PHDI—has become an important means for *warga* organizations to legitimize their common agenda for a more egalitarian social order. It is becoming increasingly popular among educated *jaba* Balinese, many of whom have the ability to read and understand languages other than Balinese or Indonesian, to cite passages from holy books such as the *Rg Veda, Arthava Veda, Bhagavadgita,* and *Sarasamuccaya,* which promote equality. According to contemporary readings and interpretations, such holy books implicitly and explicitly mention the equal position of people before God.[20] And if there are differences in society, they are based on individual talent and achievement (*guna* and *karma*). The expression *"tat twam asi,"* loosely translated as "you are me," has become one of the most popular quotations in Bali in this regard, because it declares that all human beings are the same. Another popular quotation that derives from the *Rg Veda* (I.80.1) declares that "everyone must recognize everybody else's independence and dignity." The most popular quotation used to defend the equal status of *sulinggih* is from the *Yajur Veda* (26:2): the notion that learning the Veda is everybody's right, not that of a particular group only. Activists from the Pasek, Pande, and Bhujangga Waisnawa *warga* organizations also display a fondness for citing passages from the great *Mahabharata* and *Ramayana* epics showing that many famous priests were not Brahmin born. For example, Maharsi Vasistha was born of a prostitute woman; Maharsi Vyasa, the compiler of the Veda, was the son of a fisherwoman; Maharsi Parasara's mother was a *candala,* an untouchable.

Complementing the universalistic messages culled from these texts, certain *warga* organizations draw on their own *babad* or written genealogies as the most common source for claiming status and priestly equality. In particular, parts of the *babad* called *bisama,* "sacred ancestral messages," are frequently cited. A *bisama* from the Pande clan's *babad,* for example, the *Prasasti Pande Besi,* presents the injunction "Do not seek holy water from Brahmana,"[21] stating instead that "Pande are entitled to give holy water for death rituals" (p. 10).[22] A *bisama* found in the Pasek Sapta Rsi clan's *babad* alludes to a similar point. It states that members should always remember their duties and obligations, including the duty to be a good priest (Soebandi 1991:11).[23] The *bisama* found in the *babad* of the Bhujangga Waisnawa clan, the *Bhujangga Dharma,* supports the existence of their priests. It mentions that they cannot be tainted by ritual pollution, a situation that also pertains to Brahmana priests, which means they may always make holy water and perform ceremonies (Ginarsa et al. 1979:35).[24]

Exogenous discourses are also appropriated by groups struggling to improve their status—in particular the global issues of human rights, equality, and social justice. At the national level, clearly the state ideology of Pancasila, which recognizes equality for all, is a powerful factor. Nobody would openly dare to reject it (Warren 1993). The PHDI organization is also used effectively. Though often severely criticized,[25] it is undeniable that its influence on the religious life of the Balinese has been of enormous significance, a situation that *warga* organizations have sought to use to their advantage. In particular, with regard to equality in the priesthood, people of *jaba* descent frequently quote the PHDI. I have often heard members of the Pasek Sapta Rsi, Pande, and Bhujangga Waisnawa clans, for example, state that *sulinggih* do not belong to any clan or *warga* organization but are the *sulinggih* of all Hindus because they have been given a certificate of authorization by the PHDI. Consequently they are *"sulinggih Parisada,"* and the PHDI must accord them protection and treat them fairly.[26]

Giddens contends that "all social life is episodic" (1984:224). By this he means that every society undergoes changes and a society's situation is merely an episode in a process of continuous change. So too for Bali. The current situation is merely an episode within the flow of sociocultural change. Even so, I would not dare to speculate that *"homo aequalis"* will soon win the war over *"homo hierarchicus."* They are still, as Hildred Geertz and Clifford Geertz (1975) put it, locked in an intense struggle. If one of them does win, it will take generations to do so. Past and present trends show that *homo aequalis* has been gaining ground.

Status conflict between the *triwangsa* and *anak jaba* can be traced back to at least the 1920s, when the colonial education system established new elites among *jaba* groups. One such group in northern Bali established an organization named Surya Kanta, which had among its goals the abolition of discrimination based on birth as well as the privileges enjoyed by the *triwangsa* (Bagus 1969; Agung 1974; Connor 1996). There is no evidence that *jaba* groups at the time attempted to elevate their priests to the status that *pedanda* enjoyed, however, although pressure among the Pande in certain areas of Bali to use *sri mpu* rather than *pedanda* appeared to intensify. Certainly arguments for and against them appeared in the *Surya Kanta* newsletter and that of its pro–status quo *triwangsa* rival *Bali Adnjana* (no. 35, 1926). In November 1926, for example, when a group of Pande families from Mengwi in Badung regency planned to hold a cremation ceremony performed by a Pande *sri mpu* from their village, other villagers blocked the road connecting the Pande house and the cemetery and refused to let the ceremony proceed. Prominent members of the clan who were also activists in Surya Kanta then requested official protection. The potentially violent situation was defused only when the district head and other officials intervened. A compromise was reached: a *pedanda* officiated, but the Pande were permitted to use the holy water made by their own priests (Connor 1996:183–184).

Eventually, after further decades of struggle, the *jaba* majority of Balinese achieved a significant victory in the 1950s when the government of Bali formally abolished the prohibition of marriage between people from certain clans, notably *triwangsa* women and *jaba* men.[27] Likewise, as we have seen, another important development promoting status equality among Balinese was the PHDI's pronouncement that every Hindu in Indonesia, regardless of the clan to which they belong, is entitled to undergo the twice-born ceremony in order to become a priest: all Hindus are of equal status. And this formal recognition, as we have seen, has now been implemented in some cases.

Local and Global Dialogues

Balinese society and culture have been increasingly exposed to international influences over the past two decades—particularly through mass tourism to the island (Picard 1990b; Pitana 1992, 1995; Lanfant et al. 1995). Thus one might expect that so-called homogenizing global forces would have dissolved status relationships and left "irrational" practices behind. (See, for example, Giddens 1984, 1991; Haferkamp and Smelser 1992.) This, however, has not occurred. Despite the existence of other status indicators, such as modern education and material wealth, traditional forms of status rivalry over clan hierarchy and priestly precedence are still prevalent in Bali today. Globalization and localization occur simultaneously. Hand in hand with the exogenous modernizing processes, the local processes, such as traditional networking based on membership of *warga* organizations, are also strengthening. And these, in turn, are used to support a modern, egalitarian outlook.

I have endeavored to show that in their struggle for status *jaba* clans use the priesthood—one of the main pillars of the Balinese Hindu religion—and that the struggle within the priesthood is channeled through public temples. Temples in Bali are not merely places to worship God, and gods, or other spiritual forces. Their functions embrace things far beyond this: they are a source of legitimation, a source of power, and the nexus of the social web. In Stephen Lansing's words, temples are "the very backbone of the social order" in Balinese civilization (1983:51). In pointing this out, I wish to emphasize that acceptance of *jaba* priests to officiate at ceremonies in public temples, as well as acceptance of the holy water made by *jaba* priests for use by all Hindus, is a potent indicator of the wave of transformation occurring in social and cultural life in contemporary Bali.

In strengthening their appeal for equality, the *warga* movement oscillates from local to national to global. *Warga* members engage with the national discourses of Pancasila, equality, and development; with global issues of social justice and human rights; and with local discourses of a rationalized and universalized Hindu religion, as well as ancestral worship and sacred ancestral messages *(bisama)*. The appeal for equality is a strong appeal for social change. In an effort to accelerate change—particularly the elimination of discrimination based on birth—discourses of modernity at the national level have been drawn into the traditional arena to support the ideology of equality while traditional Balinese sources, Indian-derived Vedic teachings, and other literature are eclectically selected and reinterpreted as a means of legitimation.

Notes

I am grateful to Raechelle Rubinstein and Linda Connor for their critical comments and for polishing my English. I also wish to thank Helen Creese, Drs. Wayan Pastika, Drs. I Gusti Ngurah Putra, and Drs. Jamhari for their comments on the original version of this chapter.

1. There are two rival temples named Pura Ulun Danu Batur. One is located in the village of Songan; the other is in the village of Batur. Each claims to be the real Ulun Danu Batur Temple. Expert opinion is divided on this issue.

2. Pseudonyms are used for the most part in referring to specific individuals in this chapter.

3. The term *"warga"* derives from Sanskrit *(varga)*, where it means "a separate division, class, set, multitude of similar things (animate or inanimate), group, company, family, party, side" (Monier-Williams 1956) or "a separate division, class, group, company, family" (Zoetmulder 1982). Badudu and Zein (1994) translate this word as "members, family, clan, citizen." In present-day Bali, *warga* commonly refers to a form of social organization based on kinlike relations, whether true or presumed. Members of a *warga* trace their common ancestry to a figure, whether historical or mythical, as their "origin point," who is worshiped in their ancestral temple known as *kawitan* ("the origin").

4. The *warga* organizations include: Maha Samaya Warga Pande, Maha

Gotra Pasek Sanak Sapta Rsi, Keluarga Besar Bhujangga Waisnawa, Maha Se-
maya Warga Pande, Keluarga Besar Arya Tegeh Kori, Pasemetonan Keturunan
Arya Pengalasan, Maha Gotra Pasek Sanak Sapta Rsi, Keluarga Besar Arya
Kepakisan Dauh Bale Agung, and Maha Gotra Catur Sanak (Pasek Kayuse-
lem). All of these organizations state their main objectives as strengthening
the unity of their members in accordance with "sacred instructions" *(bisama)*
passed down by their ancestors and maintaining clan temples. For a detailed
discussion of the Warga Pande see Guermonprez (1987); for the Warga Pasek
in Tabanan see Boon (1979).

5. It was originally known as the Parisada Dharma Hindu Bali.

6. Kep. no.5/Kep/PHDP/1968.

7. In Balinese villages that adhere to "old" traditions of customary governance *(desa Bali kuna)*, the *kubayan* is the highest official in religious matters. The *kubayan* officiate at all ceremonies in these villages; priests from outside are never used. For further discussion of the priesthood in such villages
see Reuter (1996 and Chapter 5 in this volume).

8. The *jero gede* is the highest priest in certain temples in "old" Balinese villages *(desa Bali kuna)*. For example, Jero Gede Batur, Jero Gede Duuran, and
Jero Gede Alitan are the titles given to the priests of Ulun Danu Batur Temple.

9. Priests from the Arya Sidemen and Arya Pinatih clans are known as *rsi*
or *reshi;* priests from the Bhujangga Waisnawa clan are known as *rsi bhujangga;* priests from the Pande clan are termed *sri mpu;* priests from the Pasek
Sapta Rsi are called *sri mpu* or *pandita mpu;* and priests from the Boda branch
of the Brahmana clan are known as *pedanda boda,* while those from the Siwa
branch are known as *pedanda siwa.* Until his death in 1998, there was just one
priest from the Satria Dalem clan in contemporary Bali—who was given the
title Dalem by his consecrator—but he was not permitted to perform all the
ceremonies that other *sulinggih* perform. Priests from the Arya Gajahpara clan
appear to be known as *dukuh.* This title is also assigned to ascetics who reside
in remote hermitages *(padukuhan* or *asrama)* usually located in the forest
(Hooykaas 1974, 1976). (See note 14 for further discussion of *dukuh* in Bali
today.) Because this variety of priestly titles makes it difficult to converse with
priests and address them collectively, proposals were put forward at general
meetings of the PHDI to call all priests by a single title, whether *sulinggih* or
pedanda. While these proposals were initially rejected, at the general meeting
held in Solo in September 1996, it was finally agreed that all priests should be
called by the title *pandita.* Nonetheless, this decision has not been well received by society at large, and the other term, *sulinggih,* appears to be gaining
ground as the title for twice-born priests. The term *(su + linggih)* literally
means "good seat" and signifies that priests hold an esteemed position in
Hindu Balinese society. It must also be noted here that the name given to a
new *sulinggih* is the prerogative of the consecrator *(nabe)* and is negotiable.

10. Two priests, the late Ida Dalem Pemayun (see note 9) and the late Ida
Sri Reshi Anandakusuma, both from Klungkung, belonged to this category.

11. Traditionally, *rsi bhujangga* (also known as *sengguhu*) were called upon

to participate alongside *pedanda* at purificatory or exorcist rituals. They also sat at a lower level and closer to the sea *(kelod)*.

12. There are numerous "sects" *(paksa, sampradaya)* within Hinduism that are chiefly differentiated on the basis of the deity or deities worshiped. In Bali today, the dominant sect is Sivaism (or Siva-Siddhanta), which worships the *trimurti:* the three gods Brahma, Wisnu, and Siwa as equals. Apart from Sivaism, the Boda and Vaisnava sects are found in Bali.

13. For further discussion, see Pitana (1998:chap. 8 especially).

14. *Dukuh* were not on the organizing committee's invitation list. I discovered that the committee was unaware that *dukuh* exist in Bali—an understandable situation since their number is extremely small. I know of only four *dukuh*, not all of whom actively participate at such ceremonies.

15. The organizing committee did not invite the individual *jaba sulinggih* but sent invitations to their *warga* organizations. The committee left it to the discretion of the organizations to select the *sulinggih* who would officiate. They sent invitations directly to the Brahmana *sulinggih*, however, because Brahmana have no equivalent organization that represents the clan Bali-wide.

16. As mentioned, the Bhujangga Waisnawa's priest was unable to attend.

17. As I explain later (see the section "Perceptions of *Sulinggih* Status"), Pedanda Gede Ketut Sebali Arimbawa is known as a modern or progressive *pedanda*. He is outspoken in his crusade for equality in the priesthood.

18. This is an extreme view for a Brahmana priest. While one could argue that this *pedanda* is not representative of the majority, his viewpoint demonstrates that some *pedanda* do espouse equality within the priesthood.

19. Some public temples in Bali have always used their own temple priests *(pemangku)* or the higher-status *jero bayan (kubayan)* and *jero gede* (see notes 7 and 8).

20. It must be noted here that the Hindu Veda is a large corpus of accumulated knowledge and hence is not comparable to the Koran or Bible (Titib 1993; Wiana and Santeri 1993). Because of their nature, Vedic teachings can be interpreted in a diametrically opposed fashion—depending on the passages selected, the books in which they occur, and the era when they were composed. Although the *Sarasamuccaya*, one of the most famous religious books known in Bali, supports hierarchy, some of its stanzas also speak of equality. Naturally, *anak jaba* only quote verses in favor of their vision of social equality. Within the framework of the national discourse of Pancasila, citing such stanzas is viewed sympathetically.

21. "Aywa nunas tirta ring Brahmana."

22. "Wenang sira Pande mangentas-entas."

23. "Kengetakena ling ning tithi gagaduhan, mwang pandita paramartta. . . ."

24. "Sira Sang Bhujangga Waisnawa tan keneng cuntaka, apan sira mraga suku mwah cecek, wenang nyiwa boda."

25. For criticism of the PHDI see, for example, a series of articles in the *Bali Post,* 16–18 September 1996.

26. All certificates authorizing members of the priesthood are nowadays issued by the PHDI. These certificates are the same. They mention the name of the *sulinggih,* the name of the consecrator *(nabe),* and the priest's right to perform particular ceremonies.

27. Peraturan Daerah Tingkat I Bali no. 11/1951.

Chapter 7

"Eating Threads": Brocades as Cash Crop for Weaving Mothers and Daughters in Bali

AYAMI NAKATANI

Every Balinese girl must learn to weave and in every house there is at least one loom. Particular proficiency or artistry is admired. With about 200,000 looms Bali could even be called one big weaving mill. [Goris n.d.:181]

To buy food, I have this [weaving]. I eat threads. I'm lucky to have such skills. In times of financial necessity I just don't sleep and carry on weaving to earn money. [I Dewa Ayu Puspa, 19 October 1992]

Over the past two decades, scholars have begun to devote increasing attention to the problems of rural women associated with economic development in Southeast Asia.[1] This interest seems to have grown out of concern with the effects on women's lives of the region's rapid transformation through capital-intensive development, urbanization, commercial agriculture, and mass production. The declaration of the United Nations Decade for Women (1976–1985) did much to stimulate scholarly research in this area as well. The major problems revealed by this growing body of literature can be summarized as follows: a decline in female employment in rice cultivation due to changes in agricultural technology and harvesting methods; a displacement of women from traditional small-scale production; the negative effect of gender ideology on the evaluation of women's work; and state intervention in formulating policies of national development—policies that not only

203

determine the general orientation of the industrialization process but characterize the nature of women's roles within state-defined frameworks. (See Grijns et al. 1994 and White 1991.)

We can observe two concurrent changes with regard to the demarcation of male and female spheres of activity in these development-oriented economies. First, the position of women is marginalized and their work in the labor market underestimated by recourse to the notion that women are primarily wives and mothers and hence only secondary income-earners (Grijns 1987; Ong 1987; Robinson 1988; Wolf 1992). This rhetoric is further intensified by the gender ideology of the state: for example, the Indonesian government clearly characterizes women's roles as "dual" (both productive and reproductive) and simultaneously emphasizes that motherhood and wifehood should come first (Smyth 1993; Wieringa 1985). This conceptualization has framed the activities of Pembinaan Kesejahteraan Keluarga, or PKK, the Family Welfare Movement of Indonesia, and has confined the scope of its development programs for women to such narrowly circumscribed spheres as housework, child care, and handicraft production. Second, male and female roles have been rigidly separated, with women associated with the domestic domain. Yet this process has been accompanied by increasing gender fluidity in spheres of production that were traditionally restricted to men or women only. In the Javanese batik industry, for example, the wax pen *(canting)*, traditionally defined as a "female" tool, has been used by male artists since a new form of batik called *batik lukis* (batik painting) was introduced to the tourist market. Other crafts in Java, such as metalwork or hand weaving, conventionally associated with one gender only, have also begun to involve members of the other sex (Joseph 1987).

These changes brought about by increasing capitalist penetration appear to have produced a single outcome: deterioration in the position of women as producers both inside and outside the home. This is a well-documented problem throughout the world. (See, for example, Benería 1982; Boserup 1970; Etienne 1980; Mies 1982a.) Consequently, a number of case studies from Indonesia exemplify widespread phenomena such as the "domestication" of women (Rogers 1980) and "housewifization" (Mies 1982b). It must be noted, however, that case studies in Indonesia concentrate heavily on Java: we know little of women's situation in other regions. While industrial capitalism has wrought great changes throughout Indonesia, particularly under Suharto's New Order government, which came to power in the late

1960s, the process of development and its effect on women's work may differ greatly from region to region. Given the geographical proximity and shared topographical traits of Bali with Java, as well as Bali's distinct historical and cultural background, the island presents an interesting contrast to accounts of Indonesian women and their work, particularly in Java. Moreover, surprisingly little exists about this issue in the large corpus of scholarly literature about Bali.[2]

This chapter presents a case study of a small-scale weaving industry. My intent is to illuminate the complex interplay of economic and social forces in both local village and regional developments while differentiating the status and working conditions of the female textile workers. For women of different generations, traditional cloth production has different meanings and values. Yet nearly all women engaged in hand weaving experience increasing pressure to supplement the household's income through their labor. Ironically, this pressure is often the result of newly created needs that arise precisely because of their engagement in the relatively profitable hand-weaving sector. I begin by examining major changes in the economy of the village that was my main research area, "Singarsa." In subsequent sections I describe the growth of cloth making as a major cottage industry in this village and the systems of production. In the final section I present three case studies that illustrate how women organize their time and labor for producing textiles while continuing to meet other culturally prescribed obligations.

The Village Economy

The village of Singarsa, where I carried out fieldwork between 1991 and 1993, is located in the central eastern part of Bali. Although it is included within the regency *(kabupaten)* of Karangasem, it has better transportation connections with the neighboring regency of Klungkung. Indeed, a regular minibus service operates between Singarsa and Semarapura, Klungkung's capital, located 12 kilometers to the south. From Semarapura, a major market town, one can travel by long-distance bus to other villages and towns, including Denpasar, Bali's capital. Singarsa, with the second largest proportion of irrigated rice fields (46.4 percent of the total area), is relatively well off among the villages in Karangasem. The total population of this village was 9,131 in 1991. At the time I conducted this research, foreign tourists were becoming an increasingly common sight in the village though their numbers remained limited. A scenic drive from Karangasem to Klungkung via Singarsa had begun to attract tourists exploring the island in rented cars or on motorbikes. Many would stop at the roadside shops to purchase locally produced textiles.

People from all status categories *(warna)* reside in Singarsa. These categories, which local people designate as Brahmana, Satria, Wesia, and Sudra, have terminological correspondences with the so-called caste system found in India. The Balinese hierarchy lacks certain key features of the Indian system, however, in particular the formalized division of labor according to caste. Moreover, the *warna* are not exclusively associated with certain occupations. The high-status groups—the Brahmana, Satria, and Wesia, collectively known as *triwangsa* ("three peoples")—comprise a small proportion of Bali's total Hindu population, accounting for less than 10 percent, as compared with the majority Sudra who are more commonly termed *(anak) jaba*. In Singarsa, Brahmana houses *(gria)* are located exclusively in one area and form a separate *banjar* (residential village ward). Similarly, most Satria houses are built close to the former palace of the local overlord, from which they claim to originate. While the vast majority of Singarsa's residents are Hindu Balinese, a Muslim enclave numbering less than seven hundred people exists.[3] These residents also form a separate *banjar*. Singarsa's Hindu and Muslim populations appear to maintain an amicable relationship, although they hardly mix with one another in everyday life. The notable exception occurs at the morning market, where many of the sellers are Muslim.

Following the general trend throughout the island, agriculture no longer provides the predominant source of income or work in Singarsa, though it remains a major productive activity.[4] The agricultural sector includes both wet rice cultivation and the farming of dry land. In the late 1970s, all of the irrigated rice fields *(sawah)* in the village were forced to undergo intensive cultivation by the local government as part of the nation's Green Revolution. By the early 1980s, however, the realization of inherent problems with the new rice-producing technologies had induced many local *subak* (irrigation associations) to return to the traditional system of rice farming. Farmers prefer traditional farming methods that enable the cultivation of profitable secondary crops after the rice harvest—chilies, garlic, and shallots, for example, which can be easily transported to the major markets in Semarapura and Denpasar due to improvements in roads and transportation. The dry land on the mountain slopes is planted with market crops such as coffee, vanilla, and cloves as well as traditional dryland crops like sweet potatoes (a staple food supplementing rice until the mid-1970s), bananas, and coconuts.

In the nonagricultural sector, hand-loom weaving experienced a remarkable growth as a home-based industry during the 1980s. According to the 1988–1989 census conducted in Singarsa, the weaving sector absorbed 35 percent of the workforce, exceeding 34 percent for agriculture, whereas in 1982–1983 people engaged in cloth production accounted for only 18 percent of the working population compared with 34 percent in the agricultural sector (*Monografi Desa "Singarsa"* 1982, 1989).[5] The sharp rise in the percentage of cloth producers compared to the relative stability of the agricultural workforce can be explained by the involvement of many more women than men in the hand-weaving sector. Table 1 shows the occupational pattern for women in one *banjar* of Singarsa in 1992. While the traditional economic activities of village women have ranged from assisting their husbands with farming and petty trading of local produce to raising livestock, chickens, and pigs, the vast majority of women of all ages are now devoted to textile production, which provides them with a relatively large income.[6] Consequently, the number of women who engage in farming even as a secondary occupation has diminished dramatically, although women in rice-farming households still assist their fathers, brothers, and husbands with the harvesting of secondary crops, which must be completed on time to fetch good market prices. As for the rice harvest, it is now commonly carried out by agricultural laborers from the vicinity of Singarsa. Similarly, with the exception of their locally produced cloths, market trading is no longer a prominent activity for (Hindu) women from Singarsa.

Some women run shops on Singarsa's main street. Those who do not like to weave but have little capital opt for selling homemade snacks or drinks, factory-made sweets, slices of fruit, and the like at *warung* (small food stalls) in alleyways. Other women, who perform various kinds of low-paid work, often do so in addition to weaving. While some women who marry into the village quickly pick up weaving skills, others never master the craft and turn to alternative work where available. Although women clearly dominate the workforce with respect to textile production, participation in the textile industry has become an important employment option for younger men, as well, as indicated by Table 2. Sons nowadays often refuse to take over share-

Table 1
Women's Occupations by Age in Banjar Tengah, Singarsa: 1992

Occupation	Age 15–30	%	Age 31–40	%	Age 41–50	%	Age 51–60	%	Age 61<	%
Textile production	101	89.4	37	80.4	28	84.8	25	64.1	19	71.0
Civil service and other office work	1	0.9	1	2.2	0	0	0	0	0	0
Animal husbandry	1	0.9	0	0	0	0	3	7.7	1	3.7
Trading	8	7.1	4	8.7	3	9.1	7	17.9	2	7.4
Agriculture	0	0	3	6.5	0	1.4	1	2.6	1	3.7
Other[a]	1	0.9	1	2.2	2	6.1	3	7.7		
Unemployed	1	0.9	0	0	0	0	0	0	4	14.8
Total	113	100	46	100	33	100	39	100	27	100

Source: Household survey conducted in the residential ward of Banjar Tengah, Singarsa, 1992.

Note: Those who do not work because of illness or old age are excluded from this table.

[a]Drivers, offering specialists, and coconut oil producers.

cropping contracts from their fathers and seek off-farm employment. The well-educated migrate to cities, especially to tourist areas, while those who remain in the village engage in a variety of occupations as schoolteachers, government officials, carpenters, tailors, drivers, manual laborers, and textile workers.[7]

These changes in the structure of the labor force for both men and women parallel—and in turn accelerate—transformation of the overall village and regional economies. The cash inflow to the local economy has increased since the late 1960s, for example, with the expansion of the civil service (local administrators, schoolteachers, medical specialists, policemen) (Cole 1983:162–165, Edmondson 1992:6). With the prospect of acquiring stable, white-collar jobs in the government sector, parents increasingly aspire to better education for their children—hence the need for increased cash income. Even though there is no tuition fee for primary school, there are many related expenses. Enrollment in secondary school requires a monthly tuition fee (2,100 rupiahs in 1993, or about $1) and additional expenses for uniforms, textbooks, and school excursions. To send children to high school and university in the cities is a far more expensive venture because of the costs of lodging and transport. Medical consultations and treatments (including childbirth) at modern clinics require cash, whereas tradi-

Table 2
Men's Occupations by Age in Banjar Tengah, Singarsa: 1992

Occupation	Age 15–30	%	Age 31–40	%	Age 41–50	%	Age 51–60	%	Age 61<	%
Agriculture	6	6.4	18	38.3	15	50.0	25	67.6	22	71.0
Textile production	28	29.8	6	12.8	1	3.3	0	0	1	3.2
Civil service and other office work	21	22.3	8	17.0	4	13.3	2	5.4	1	3.2
Skilled labor (tailoring etc.)	2	2.1	4	8.5	3	10.0	0	0	3	9.7
Manual labor	6	6.4	1	2.1	3	10.0	2	5.4	0	0
Household-based manufacture	12	12.8	2	4.3	0	0	2	5.4	0	0
Trading	1	1.1	1	2.1	2	6.7	3	8.1	1	3.2
Other[a]	9	9.6	4	8.5	2	6.7	3	8.1	3	9.7
Unemployed	9	9.6	3	6.4	0	0	0	0	0	0
Total	94	100	47	100	30	100	37	100	29	100

Source: Household survey conducted in the residential ward of Banjar Tengah, Singarsa, 1992.

Note: Those who do not work because of illness or old age are excluded from this table.

[a]Drivers, *adat* (traditional law) functionaries, healers, and priests.

tional healers *(balian)* receive remuneration in kind. These trends have coincided with commercialization in the agricultural sector—namely, the shift from subsistence-dominant production to market-oriented production (Edmondson 1992:9).

History of *Songket* Production

Presently two types of handwoven cloth are produced in Singarsa: *songket,* which is supplementary-weft ikat using golden thread made on traditional backstrap looms *(cagcag),* and *endek,* which is single-weft ikat made on treadle looms (Alat Tenun Bukan Mesin, usually abbreviated to ATBM). This chapter focuses on *songket* production.[8]

Songket is traditionally used for special ceremonial attire and is worn in the form of wraparounds *(kamben* or *wastra)* by both men and women,[9] men's outer cloths *(saput* or *kampuh),* women's sashes *(slendang),* and men's headcloths *(udeng* or *dastar).* It is also used for

Figure 27. Posed photograph of weaver and backstrap loom, ca. 1930. Photo: KITLV, Or. 5573.

decorative purposes at ceremonial venues. Because of its high price, wraparound *songket* (both *kamben* and *saput*) tends to be worn only on special ceremonial occasions, such as hair-cutting, tooth-filing, and wedding ceremonies, though less expensive *slendang* or *udeng* may also be worn on less important occasions. In recent years, primarily in urban areas, the wearing of splendid *songket* at official parties and graduation ceremonies where participants are required to attend in traditional costume *(pakaian adat)* has gained widespread popularity. As *songket* is unsuitable for further processing and washing, its sale is largely confined to the Balinese domestic market.

The weaving of *songket* developed as an aristocratic craft. Traditionally it was an activity pursued by women at court at a time when women were not permitted to move beyond their confines (Ramseyer and Nabholz-Kartaschoff 1991:34). Miguel Covarrubias describes the situation in the 1930s as follows:

> Weaving is the main occupation of the women of caste who feel above doing heavy house labour, but they are not lazy and take to weaving with tenacity. In our house the wives and aunts of our host, all noble women with servants to do the housework, remained all day glued to their looms and often continued working into the night by the faint light of a petrol lamp. [1972:100–101]

This account seems to apply to *triwangsa* women in the old days in Singarsa. Yet not every *triwangsa* woman practised weaving. Indeed, the number of weavers was reportedly very limited until the Japanese occupation of Indonesia (1942–1945). Even at the local palace it appears that few women engaged in cloth making in previous generations. Those who wove *songket* did so not so much for their own use as for selling to the rich, including members of various royal houses, who placed their orders in person.

The restricted nature of *songket* production in the past can be attributed to limited demand. The materials for *songket*—gold and pure silk threads—were so expensive and difficult to obtain that only extremely privileged people could afford to weave and purchase them. There was also a greater number of women, both *triwangsa* and *jaba,* who wove other types of textiles such as plain or checked cotton garments. Such clothing was more likely to be worn by the weaver or by members of her family. Some weavers also produced special cloth used exclusively as an ingredient in offerings to the gods (Hauser-Schäublin et al. 1991).

A drastic change in cloth production occurred during the Japanese occupation. Due to a serious shortage of material for clothing throughout the occupied Dutch East Indies, the Japanese civil administration promoted cotton cultivation and processing (Office of Strategic Services 1945; Robinson 1995:79). All the women in Singarsa were ordered to weave or perform other stages of cloth production. It was during this period that most Singarsa women took up weaving for the first time in their lives. Young, unmarried women were called up to work in the workshop *(gudang)* set up by the Japanese for spinning cotton yarn *(ngantih),* spooling *(ngulak),* and warp winding *(nganyinin).* School-age children too worked there for low wages. Married women were provided with backstrap looms to weave plain, coarse cotton cloth *(blacu)* at home.[10] Because the costly materials were no longer available, the weaving of *songket* and other traditional textiles had ceased.

During the years of political turmoil that followed Indonesian independence, cloth production was limited to the manufacture at home of plain white cloth for daily wear.[11] When the political and economic situation began to improve in the mid-1950s, the weaving of *songket* and other types of cloth such as multicolored, checked cloth *(blekatan)* was taken up again. *Songket* weavers, in particular, gradually increased in number. The rise of *songket* production in Singarsa is strongly related to the general transformation of the Balinese economy, especially the improvement of infrastructure throughout the island. In the late 1950s when the materials for *songket*—imported from Java and overseas—became more readily available, a few villagers of means started to provide weaving materials to local people and sold finished cloth in Denpasar and other cities. Singarsa became better connected with other parts of the island around the mid-1960s; accordingly the numbers of weavers and traders of *songket* increased especially in the 1970s and 1980s. At the same time, with the increased importation of cheap, machine-made batik cloth from Java and the introduction of "Western" clothing, the hand weaving of other types of textiles for daily wear ceased.

The truly remarkable growth of *songket* production as a rural cottage industry was spurred by "the increased democratization of Balinese society" (Ramseyer and Nabholz-Kartaschoff 1991:37), which weakened the traditional and exclusive link between *songket* and people from high-status groups. In 1980, Ida Bagus Mantra, then governor of Bali and a Brahmana, encouraged the local population to buy Balinese traditional textiles for their ceremonial attire (Ramseyer 1987:4; Ramseyer and Nabholz-Kartaschoff 1991:37). The governor's appeal further undermined the prerogative of the *triwangsa* to produce and wear *songket*.[12] Although *songket* was still prohibitively expensive for most of the population, rising incomes, connected among other things with the development of the tourist industry, created more and more well-to-do Balinese who increasingly chose *songket* for their ceremonial wardrobes. As the market for *songket* expanded, so too did its production. Concurrently, government programs extended funding through PKK and the local village cooperatives (Koperasi Unit Desa, or KUD) to support women *songket* producers in the early 1980s. By the beginning of the 1990s, *songket* production had spread throughout the village and its vicinity.

As this craft spread to the wider population of Singarsa, a high degree of specialization in production ensued. In former times, *songket* producers were generally involved in the entire process from start to finish. In other words, they were all independent weavers who controlled every stage of production including marketing of the finished cloth. Today, however, the emergence of dealers who have taken over the role of organizing the production process has led to a marked differentiation of tasks and remuneration among *songket* producers. At present, as we shall see, *songket* production allows for a wide variety of production relations depending on the capability, financial means, and time available to its participants.

Figure 28. Exclusive handwoven *songket* worn by a bride and groom in Puri Payangan. Photo: Raechelle Rubinstein.

The System of Production

The process of making *songket* can be divided into three parts: the preparation of the warp beam *(papanen)*, pattern programming, and weaving. Few women are engaged in all of these tasks today. Even when all the tasks are carried out in one house compound, usually a division of labor is implemented to ensure greater efficiency.

Commonly the preparation of warp beams (Table 3, stages 1–5) is organized by *songket* dealers who employ a piece-rate system *(borongan)*. Those who perform these tasks are provided with yarn and receive payment for their commissioned work. Some specialize in these

Table 3
The Process of *Songket* Production

1. *nyikat:*	preparing warp threads	
2. *ngulak:*	winding bobbins	
3. *nganyinin:*	winding warp	
4. *nyuntik:*	threading warp threads through the reed	
5. *nyasah:*	winding the warp onto the warp beam	
6. *nuduk:*	pattern programming	
7. *nguun:*	setting up additional heddle rods for patterns	
8. *ngunda:*	transferring supplementary patterns to the warp	
9. *ngliying:*	winding weft threads onto spools	
10. *ngecob:*	winding supplementary weft threads onto spools	
11. *nunun:*	weaving	

preparatory jobs while others combine it with daily weaving. Typically a dealer has a stable relationship with a group of workers who take regular commissions from her. These piece-rate workers are often, though not always, related to the dealer by kinship ties. Bobbin winding (*ngulak,* stage 2) and warp winding (*nganyinin,* stage 3) are more often performed by young men than women, whereas the other stages are almost exclusively women's work.[13] Of the entire production process, pattern programming (*nuduk,* stage 6) requires the greatest skill of all. Very few specialists are capable of it: at the time of research, there were just fifteen programmers (*tukang nuduk*) in Singarsa. Seven of them were women from *triwangsa* families that had practiced *songket* weaving for generations; the others were *jaba* women who had learned the craft in recent years. Because of the scarcity of pattern programmers, they are never short of work. It must be noted, however, that except for these pattern programmers, workers who undertake the preparatory stages of *songket* production are invariably of noble origin—a situation reminiscent of the traditional link between the *triwangsa* and *songket* production.

When the warp beam is completed, it is sent to a pattern programmer and then passed on to a weaver. The preparatory work, prior to weaving, takes ten to fifteen days. This period may be prolonged if, for example, all workers are busy with major temple ceremonies or a pattern programmer falls ill. The final four stages (see Table 3) are normally performed by individual weavers. The length of the warp in a set of warp beams is 12 meters, sufficient for weaving six half-pieces (*arirang*) of wraparound. In other words, two half-pieces are sewn to-

Figure 29. Pattern programming. Photo: Ayami Nakatani.

gether to make one wraparound; three complete wraparounds are produced from each warp beam.

The amount of time required for finishing *songket* varies greatly, depending on the type of cloth, the motif, the skill of the weaver, and her working conditions. It takes a skilled, unmarried weaver around twenty days to finish a piece of *kamben bek* (two half-pieces with gold supplementary-weft thread running the full length, which are sewn together to make a wraparound) using yarn of the highest quality. Provided that she could work without interruption, her daily remuneration at the time of research ranged between 4,000 and 6,000 rupiahs.[14] But due to their involvement in multiple pursuits, married weavers require far more time to complete a wraparound. With regard to the means of production, backstrap looms and other implements essential for *songket* weaving are produced locally; a brand-new set cost around 35,000 rupiahs at the time of research. In most cases, daughters inherit the looms that belonged to family members who have stopped weaving. Upon marriage, a wife brings her own loom to her husband's house or uses her in-law's loom if it is available. Because they are valuable tools, these looms are presented with small *canang* offerings on ritual days. But because of their strong association with femininity, they are deemed polluting *(leteh)* for men.

Songket weavers can be classified into two types. Both categories own their looms and other necessary implements but can be distinguished on the basis of ownership of the materials they use. The first category comprises independent weavers who pay for their own warp and weft threads. Since no dealer is involved in their weaving, they are free to choose the market for their finished products. Sometimes they accept orders from outside Singarsa through their family or other connections; sometimes they travel alone to the market in Klungkung with their woven cloth. More often, however, they sell their cloth to traders in the village for the sake of convenience. They make their own decisions about the type of cloth to weave, the color of the warp and weft threads, and the motifs. Some of them commission each stage of the warp beam preparation to their family members or neighbors. Others buy a ready-made warp beam and materials from the shops owned by *songket* dealers. They then take the warp beam to pattern programmers who set up motifs for them. The second category consists of weavers who work for dealers on a piece-rate basis. These weavers receive all the materials for weaving from their *bos* (employer): the prepared warp beam, the weft yarn, and supplementary-weft threads. They get paid for each piece of cloth they finish. The cost of the materials and preparation of the warp beam is deducted from the total price of all the pieces of cloth made from one warp beam. As a rule, the dealer controls the sale of the finished cloth.

A piece-rate weaver can become independent if she saves enough money to buy her own materials. Conversely, an independent weaver may become dependent on a dealer if her savings run out and she cannot buy a new warp beam. In many cases, however, piece-rate weavers are closely linked to dealers—not only because the dealers own the weaving materials but also because the weavers are paid a cash advance by the dealers. Particularly during the months when many religious ceremonies take place, women weavers tend to request advances from their *bos* in order to buy the ingredients for temple offerings and gifts. Consequently, the final payment they receive for their finished work is useful only in liquidating the debts they owe to their *bos* for weaving materials. And once again they find themselves without capital—a situation that leads to further reliance on their *bos* to provide another warp beam and yarn so that they can continue weaving, making it difficult to break the cycle of dependence. Even so, many married women prefer to work on a piece-rate basis because they have less time for weaving than single women and often bear greater financial responsibility in their households. Even within families, one finds unmarried

Figure 30. Preparing the warp beam. Photo: Ayami Nakatani.

daughters working as independent weavers while their mothers work as piece-rate weavers.

Songket Weavers as Mothers and Daughters

Today throughout Singarsa, except for the Muslim *banjar* and the village's remoter parts, women from different generations work on back-strap looms side by side in the open space of their house compounds. Typically several looms are located on the elevated ground of an open pavilion *(bale)* or on the veranda outside walled rooms. Some women

Figure 31. Women weavers working together, ca. 1900. Photo: KITLV, Or. 5570.

may operate wooden tools for bobbin winding or spool winding next to their mothers, sisters, or friends who are busy with their weaving. Many women weave inside their own rooms.

Girls normally start to learn *songket* weaving at the age of ten, commencing with the simpler, shorter sashes. By the time they leave primary school, at about age twelve, they are already full-fledged weavers producing proper wraparounds like their mothers and elder sisters. Those who still go to school sit at their looms in the afternoons and on Sundays. Most weaving daughters pay their school fees and personal expenses from the income they earn from weaving; nearly all of them contribute to the household economy. Unmarried women who have become full-time weavers literally work all day long. Many of them carry on weaving until late into the night, while some relax in the evening to enjoy talk with friends at the roadside stalls. Married women normally start to weave around noon after cooking midday meals for their husbands and children. They, too, resume weaving after the evening meal and work until late at night.

One of the major problems for *songket* weavers in Singarsa today is the fluctuating amount of time available to them for weaving. Women in general, and married women in particular, are involved in a range of other activities that compete for their time: preparation of offerings, taking gifts to other house compounds on ceremonial occasions, and attending life cycle rituals year round, not to mention their daily household chores (see Nakatani 1997:733–735). It is practically impossible for them to continue their cloth production when there are temple ceremonies for the community or large-scale rituals in their own compounds. Furthermore, *songket* weaving is subject to a number of taboos at different times in the Balinese calendar. During the Galungan-Kuningan period, for example, weaving must cease five days prior to Galungan when the souls of ancestors descend to their family compounds. From then on weavers may not sit at their looms until the day following Kuningan, that is, fifteen days later.[15] In many households, backstrap looms are dismantled and stored away so that the space they occupy can be put to use for the massive task of making offerings. On the days of the full moon *(purnama)*, the new moon *(tilem)*, and the other auspicious calendrical conjunctions that account for four or five days every (Gregorian) calendar month, the weaving of *songket* is not allowed. Moreover, many rituals tend to take place on these days of the month. The following case studies illustrate the ways in which *songket* weavers organize their work under different circumstances.

Case 1

I Dewa Ayu Puspa, an unmarried Satria woman in her early twenties, is an independent weaver. She buys all her weaving materials and organizes every stage of cloth production, although she performs only the last three stages herself. She commissions *(mupahang)* preparation of the warp beam and pattern programming from three different people. If ritual activities do not disrupt her weaving, it takes about twenty days to complete two half-pieces of *songket,* which are then sewn together to make one wraparound. The preparatory work for every three wraparounds (made from a single warp beam) takes fifteen days. This means that she must plan ahead and organize the preparation of a new warp beam before completing the one she is working on—otherwise she would waste time waiting for a new warp beam. With the interruptions occasioned by the Galungan-Kuningan period and other major rituals, the completion of one warp beam typically takes longer than eighty days.

She usually sells her finished cloth to a *jaba* woman in the village who trades *songket* in Denpasar. Sometimes special orders for her *songket* are placed with her relatives in Denpasar; in that case, the finished cloth may be expensive. She is a skilled weaver and her cloth sells well. The cloth she weaves is *kamben bek* using yarn of the highest quality. At the time of research, she was selling each of these wrap-arounds for 140,000 rupiahs on average, so the net profit from one warp beam was as much as 266,500 rupiahs. She is also aware of her strong bargaining position vis-à-vis the commoner *songket* trader, due to the high quality of her work as well as her Satria status.

Living with her parents and three unmarried brothers, Ayu Puspa contributes part of her earnings to the household income to meet daily needs and ritual expenses. She also helped to support the schooling of her younger brother, who has remained unemployed since graduating from a local high school in 1991. Although most domestic chores are undertaken by her mother, Ayu Puspa performs a number of ritual du-ties such as presenting family offerings at temples *(maturan)* when an-nual celebrations *(odalan)* take place and presenting ceremonial gifts to her neighbors and extended family members residing in other house compounds.

Her father is a dryland farmer who tends a shared inheritance with his three brothers. But he spends most of his time performing duties incurred by his official position as customary head of the residential ward *(klian adat)*. Ayu Puspa's mother had been weaving *songket* for many years, but less efficiently than her daughter. Unlike Ayu Puspa, the mother worked for a dealer on a piece-rate basis. For her it was a more suitable arrangement because it took her a long time to complete a cloth due to other tasks she had to perform. At the time of my re-search she had stopped weaving because of failing eyesight.

Case 2

Ni Made Sayang, aged forty-two, is a married *jaba* woman with two un-married sons. Her daughter is already married and lives in a different part of the village. Made Sayang has been weaving for two *songket* deal-ers so that she can obtain the ready warp beams she requires without delay. Unlike I Dewa Ayu Puspa, who weaves cloths with full motifs, Made Sayang mainly weaves *kamben pinggiran* (a wraparound with a motif on one edge only) using lesser-quality yarn. The price of such cloth is lower: at the time of research, each finished wraparound was priced at 60,000 rupiahs; after the costs of the materials were deducted by the dealer, her profit was 107,000 rupiahs per warp beam. It takes her thirty to forty-five days to complete one warp beam, depending on the amount of ritual work required during this period. Busy with multiple tasks as a married woman, needing cash for her household's daily subsistence, she prefers to work on lower-quality materials that can be finished more quickly even though the profit may be smaller. In any case, without sufficient capital she has no other option but to work as a piece-rate weaver.

Her husband, a part-time tailor, contributes all of his income to the upkeep of their house. Made Sayang is therefore the sole provider of expenses for daily food, religious offerings, and ceremonial gifts. While her older son, a local high school student, does not contribute to the household economy, her younger son works for a village tailor, running errands and performing other tasks, and pays his own secondary school fees from the money he earns.

Made Sayang regrets that her only daughter has left the household: not only has she lost her work companion but she now has less help in supporting the household financially. Moreover, the absence of any other females in the household means that she alone is responsible for the entire range of domestic and ritual obligations. Although her husband and sons wash their own clothes, other tasks such as shopping and cooking are undertaken by Made Sayang herself. In addition, all the ritual obligations associated with the family temples, communal temples, ritually significant days, and honoring ceremonial ties between households *(makrama desa)*—obligations that require the participation of a woman from each household—are her responsibility. When the daytime hours are taken up with these activities, she must get up at five in the morning to get some weaving done before going to the morning market. She resumes her weaving after the evening meal and works until ten or eleven at night.

Case 3

I Dewa Ayu Raka, a Satria woman in her early sixties, is an elder sister of the present heir of the local palace of Singarsa and has never married. She started to weave *songket* when she was around twelve years old, learning the craft from her mother. They bought undyed yarn in Klungkung or Denpasar and applied natural dyes that they themselves made. It would take her months to complete one wraparound, for she performed all the tasks herself, from the very beginning to the end, including pattern programming. Though she rarely weaves these days, she still is known as a skilled weaver. She used to receive personal commissions from aristocrats in different parts of Bali. Even the prince of

Gianyar commissioned her to make *songket* for him. Although she earned money from her weaving, she wove not so much for economic return as for her own satisfaction and pride. In any case, in earlier years she was not free to leave the house compound and was thus forced to fill in the time at home by weaving.

Although her younger sisters know how to weave *songket,* they are unable to perform the entire process. Ayu Raka finds it a cause for regret that the younger generation of *songket* weavers knows nothing but weaving and is incapable of undertaking other stages of production. Not only that, she says, but they are too economically oriented. According to Ayu Raka and other Satria of her generation, Singarsa women nowadays think only of money: every act and aspect of "beating reeds" means rupiahs.

The Triple Burden

I Dewa Ayu Puspa (case 1) and Ni Made Sayang (case 2) come from different status groups and differ in marital status as well. Yet they share a strong concern with the time that is available to them for weaving, which they negotiate vis-à-vis other time-consuming activities both domestic and religious. A serious dilemma faces female weavers during ritual periods: they inevitably spend their money purchasing ingredients for offerings and gifts, yet they cannot weave: they spend but are not earning. Women in Singarsa, both married and unmarried, are unanimous in recognizing this problem as a source of constant anxiety.[16] The case of I Gusti Agung Sri, an unmarried girl in her early twenties, illustrates this point. When I went to visit her one day, she was at her loom although she had been sick the two previous days. As she looked tired and weak, I asked her, "Why don't you take a rest? You are so sick!" She replied, while continuing her weaving, "I cannot. I must finish this cloth before Galungan." Galungan, I should point out, was twenty-three days away.

I had similar conversations with many other women during my fieldwork. When major rituals or ceremonial days approach, every woman works especially hard to ensure she has enough cash in hand before she must stop weaving. Another young woman, frantically trying to finish a wraparound, complained: "If I had not been obliged to help with the preparations for my cousin's wedding, I could have finished this cloth by now. But it will take me another day to complete it because I am going to attend the ceremony later today. This cloth has taken so long because I was busy helping out with this wedding. There are always obstacles *(halangan)* like this." That day, early in the morning, she had visited the house compound where the wedding ceremony *(semayut gede)* would be held and had then come home. She planned to work on her loom for two hours before the ceremonial feast *(magibung)*, which she was obliged to join.

Commenting on the intensity of these *songket* weavers, a Satria woman in her early fifties remarked: "When I was still single, staying with my parents, I was much more relaxed than unmarried girls are these days. I often played sport or engaged in some other activity. Well, yes, I did weave *songket*, but not in a demanding way. Nowadays, all girls force themselves to work hard. They weave and weave only, to such an extent that their lower backs turn black. Their bottoms must also be very hard, because they sit all day long. They leave their looms only to eat."

The experiences of contemporary weavers in Singarsa certainly contrast with those of I Dewa Ayu Raka (case 3). Representative of traditional *songket* weavers, she has always taken pride in weaving a cloth of truly high quality, the entire production of which she controls. Time has never been an issue for her. Nor have "market trends" affected her weaving: she has always endeavored to create acclaimed pieces. Although skilled, independent weavers like Ayu Puspa do draw a sense of satisfaction and pride from their weaving, the most important point in selecting motifs and colors is whether their products will sell well *(laku)*.

These young, independent weavers are always keen to keep up with the latest colors and new motifs. Likewise, *songket* dealers look for samples of new motifs from the former palaces of Klungkung and Gelgel, where women still create original *songket* designs. They then commission local programmers to set warp beam patterns according to the samples. Dealers try to limit the number of weavers they commission so that cloths featuring new motifs will fetch a higher price because of their novelty and exclusiveness. Such motifs are of course bound to be copied by others and become widespread within a month or so. At one point during my stay in Singarsa, many women were weaving *songket endek*, combining predyed warp (like *endek* cloth) with supplementary golden weft. Some months later, everyone was turning to a different pattern called *sajak*, which was a revival of a classical motif.[17] Indeed the pressure to produce something trendy or, better still, something new is mounting in the face of a sharp rise in the number of weavers in and around Singarsa and the resulting surplus of cloth. As a consequence, the price of *songket* has dropped since 1992. When business is slow everywhere, only high-quality cloth can fetch good prices. It is piece-rate weavers who suffer most from this recent development, for they inevitably accept whatever price is offered by dealers. Moreover, they are likely to be married women who are unable to maximize their time and labor because of competing demands.

Another indication of pressure on *songket* weavers in this increasingly competitive environment is that married weavers feel they are under an obligation to augment their own incomes. A woman with three small children lamented that she could hardly sit at her loom because her children were all sickly and demanded her attention constantly. Indeed, it had taken her two months to complete just half a piece of wraparound. Without any other grown women in the household, she spent most of her time engaged in child care, household chores, and, every now and then, ritual activities. Apart from financial difficulties (her husband was a dryland sharecropper), she was particularly concerned with what others would think of her: "If I don't work, I feel ashamed in front of my family [a reference to her neighbors from the same status group] *(lek teken sameton tiange)*. They all weave. I just look after my children. I look as though I am idle, as though I do nothing."

Although village women often affirm that their family's daily subsistence depends on their weaving, their earnings are spent on many other things as well. From the accounts of villagers and outside observers it is clear that the standard of living in Singarsa has improved dramatically since the early 1970s. As noted earlier, the growth of textile production into a major village industry coincided with the rapid monetarization of the village economy, the gradual decline of the supremacy of wet-rice agriculture as a means of subsistence, and expanding job opportunities in the civil service. The improvement of infrastructure, such as roads and transport, and a booming tourist industry created demand for prestigious, handwoven cloth and widened the marketing network for it. While the number of village males who could obtain secure positions in the public sector was limited, more and more women were drawn into the growing textile sector to satisfy their increasing need for cash income. Their economic returns further stimulated the expansion of their household consumption beyond subsistence level as they strove to provide better education for their children (more so for sons than for daughters), better clothing, modern household utensils, and modern housing.

One also observes a general tendency to hold more costly rituals at all levels of society, coupled with commercialization of making offerings. (Villagers now market and purchase ready-made offerings; see

Nakatani 1995a:sec. 4.7; Poffenberger and Zurbuchen 1980.) In fact, changes in the village economy have had two effects on religious activities. On the one hand, as the financial status of most households has improved, people have started to spend more money and host more elaborate rituals. This trend is particularly noticeable with regard to ceremonial clothing and the amount of money spent on entertaining guests. On the other hand, villagers, especially women, have become busier and more time-conscious. When engaging in obligatory ritual work, not to mention household tasks and child care, they think constantly of their unfinished cloth and how much longer it will take before they can complete and sell it.

Juggling Working Hours

The development of textile production has been part and parcel of structural change in Singarsa's economy at both regional and village levels. And the emphasis placed on the role of women in economic activities, as we have seen, is connected to their access to the cash economy through weaving.

Although women had already engaged in income-generating activities prior to the development of textile production in Singarsa, villagers interviewed at the time about the major occupations of their mothers readily identified them as housewives ("She cooked") or as their husband's helper ("She helped my father"). The most characteristic reply, however, was that they were unemployed ("She did not work": *tan magae*). Such descriptions do not apply to the women of Singarsa today. Women involved in the weaving industry invariably identify themselves as weavers *(tukang nunun)*. Likewise, no villager today would say of a woman who weaves at home that "she does not work" or "she just does housework." Clearly, then, women's extensive involvement in the weaving industry has made their productive work more visible.

This point differentiates the present study from much of the literature on women's work elsewhere in Indonesia and in many other parts of the developing world. Elsewhere observers have noted the increasing identification of women with, or confinement to, the domestic sphere. This process of domestication has been discussed in the framework of colonialism and the penetration of the capitalist economy (Boserup 1970; Locher-Scholten 1987; Mies 1982a, 1982b; Robinson 1988; Rogers 1980; Standing 1991). One implication of this process for women's work is that many productive activities which women perform at home are not perceived as work by women themselves and are not classified as such in official censuses (Boserup 1970:163; Casey 1989:45; Mies 1982b:54; Moir 1980:5–6; Ram 1991:12; Rogers 1980:chap. 4). In Singarsa, however, women's productive activities, carried out in domestic space, are clearly perceived as work, both by themselves and by other villagers, largely as a result of the development process. Insofar as Bali's economic growth, as a whole, has paved the way for the development of textile production, it may be said that the women of Singarsa have benefited greatly from the development process.

Yet they experience a dilemma. On the one hand, the conventional associations of *songket* weaving with femininity and aristocracy have enabled them to retain leading roles in this industry. On the other, precisely because of their increasing responsibilities in the economic sphere, these women weavers are now facing the problem of having to constantly juggle their working hours in order to fulfill their multiple obligations in different domains. Furthermore, with increasing competition among *songket* producers, a wider discrepancy is emerging between married women, whose weaving activity is constrained by competing interests, and their unmarried daughters who have more time on their hands and whose weaving, therefore, is more productive. As the economic value of *songket* production has increased, the household itself has become the site of intensification of women's labor through the interaction of the domains of housework and child care, ritual obligations, and weaving.

During a brief visit to Singarsa in August 1998, I learned that local weavers had been hit by the Asian financial crisis, which has been experienced most severely in Indonesia. Despite my expectations, the sale of *songket* was not badly affected: part of the Balinese population actually benefited from a steep rise in the value of foreign currency and has continued to stage large-scale rituals, creating demand for luxury cloth. The rise in price of weaving materials, however, most of which are imported, exceeds by far a markup of the end product. As a result, weavers are making smaller profits than before and have been forced to cope with hyperinflation of daily necessities. I was told that a number of female weavers, particularly those who live on the fringes of Singarsa and only recently joined the *songket* production industry, have deserted their looms and returned to farming or petty trade. At the same time, other weavers are producing *songket* using cheap thread. Consequently there seems to be a widening gap, in terms of income and working conditions, between a limited number of independent weavers pro-ducing high-quality cloth and piece-rate weavers.

Unlike other Balinese handicrafts such as silverwork and woodcarv-ing, handwoven cloth produced in Singarsa is not directly connected with the tourist market and, hence, would seem less vulnerable to the fluctuating demands of international tourism. Nevertheless, this situa-tion demonstrates that Singarsa's weaving women, like other Balinese, cannot remain untouched by national and global events.

Notes

This chapter is a revised version of the paper I presented at the Third Interna-tional Bali Studies Workshop at the University of Sydney, 3–7 July 1995, an earlier version of which has been published (see Nakatani 1995c). The field-work on which this study is based was conducted between 1991 and 1993 under the auspices of Lembaga Ilmu Pengetahuan Indonesia and Pusat Penelitian, Universitas Udayana, Denpasar. The research was made possible by financial assistance from the INPEX foundation (Tokyo) and the WOM/ACT Fund administered by the Royal Anthropological Institute (London). The au-thor gratefully acknowledges the extensive help of the administrative person-nel at these institutions and the unlimited hospitality and friendship of the people of "Singarsa." The name of this village as well as the names of individ-uals in the text are pseudonyms.

1. See, for example, Chandler et al. (1988), Heyzer (1986), Locher-Scholten and Niehof (1987), Manderson (1983), Ong (1987), Sajogyo (1984), Stivens (1996), Stoler (1977), Suratiyah et al. (1991), and Wolf (1992).

2. Notable exceptions are Branson and Miller (1988) and Connor (1983).

3. These Muslims are, for the most part, the descendants of Sasak people who originally came from Lombok. They also include Javanese migrants who settled in the community on a temporary basis in order to work as food vendors.

4. In 1990, when the latest census figures were available, agriculture re-mained the biggest source of income for the province as a whole, although its share of the regional income fell sharply from 55 percent in 1970 to 35 per-cent in 1990 (Jayasuriya and Nehen 1989:333; *Statistik Bali* 1991).

5. *Monografi Desa "Singarsa"* (1982, 1989), from which these figures are taken, defines the workforce as the population from fifteen to fifty-two years of age.

6. The average land size cultivated by Singarsa farmers, including both landowners and tenants, was 0.37 hectare in 1992. The annual harvest from such land (39.7 kilograms per 0.01 hectare) did not meet the daily consump-

tion requirements of a family comprising four or five members. Given that most sharecropping farmers cultivate less than 0.2 hectare, the yield from their rice fields alone is insufficient to support an entire household. Edmondson's findings for a village located to the north of Singarsa indicate that agriculture contributed only 20 percent of the annual income for upper and lower socioeconomic groups, despite the positive gains from new rice technologies (Edmondson 1992).

7. Recent developments in home industries that supply the tourist market include the production of *jukung* (miniature wooden boats) and *komik* (*lontar* palm leaves engraved with Hindu epics and drawings), which are sold at tourist sites in Karangasem and Klungkung and at Sanur.

8. See Nakatani (1995b) for an extensive analysis of systems of cloth production including *endek*.

9. Balinese wraparounds are slightly different from what has come to be known in English as the sarong. While a sarong is a piece of tubular cloth, a *kamben* or *wastra* is a piece of rectangular cloth, 2.5 meters in length, whose ends are not sewn together. Men wrap it around the lower part of the body, from right to left, and pleat the end that falls at the front. Women start with the left end of the cloth and wrap it clockwise around themselves. Although men normally wear sarongs (or trousers) in everyday life, they must wear *kamben* for religious or formal social occasions. A woman always wears *kamben* (unless she opts for Western-style dress).

10. *Blacu* is "coarse, unbleached cotton cloth" (Barber 1979:27, 42). The cloth produced during this period was also called *kain Jepang* (Japanese cloth). This product was taken by the Japanese administration in return for wages; villagers themselves did not have access to it (Robinson 1995:79). Villagers complain they did not have decent clothing at that time. They made their own clothes from coconut fiber, pineapple leaves, sisal hemp, and banana stalks (see also Dinas Pendidikan dan Kebudayaan 1986:141–142).

11. Villagers from the older generation recall the persistent shortage of clothing materials during the 1950s and 1960s. Women in their forties remember that they had only one set of clothes for every occasion. A plain cotton cloth called *tapih*, worn under their wraparounds, was also woven with a backstrap loom. Javanese batik cloth, which is nowadays the most widely worn type of wraparound cloth for everyday use, remained scarce until the 1950s.

12. Christian Pelras (1962:230) reports that in some places where *songket* production had become a specialty, *jaba* women had started to practice this aristocratic craft as home workers shortly before the time of his research. This means that democratization of *songket* production had already begun in the early 1960s in some parts of Bali.

13. Traditionally the cultural definition of weaving as women's work prevented men from engaging in cloth-related activities, except for the manufacture of weaving implements such as reeds and looms. The rapid expansion of the weaving industry, however, combined with a high degree of youth unemployment in Singarsa, has encouraged male labor to participate in the

preparatory stages of cloth production. In fact, since the early 1990s a small number of young men have started to weave *songket,* although this is generally frowned upon by villagers who believe that weaving males will become impotent or even effeminate *(bancih).* The increasing male participation in textile production and its implications for female cloth producers are analyzed in Nakatani (1995a, 1995b).

14. An example is I Gusti Agung Sriasih, an unmarried weaver, who wove three pieces of wraparound with full motifs in just one and a half months. At the time of research, the warp beam cost 50,000 rupiahs, including the cost of the warp threads and the commission paid to the preparer. She paid 7,000 rupiahs to the pattern programmer and bought golden threads for 75,000 rupiahs and weft yarn for 21,000 rupiahs. Thus the materials for three wraparounds cost her a total of 153,000 rupiahs. Her finished wraparounds were each sold for 150,000 rupiahs, making her profit 99,000 rupiahs per wraparound, on which she spent twenty days. Her daily earning, therefore, would have been 4,950 rupiahs—considerably higher than the daily wage of full-time tailors (3,000 rupiahs) or piece-rate weavers at *endek* workshops (2,000 to 4,000 rupiahs), for example.

15. This taboo was explained to me as a precaution against disturbing the homecoming of ancestors by the loud noise of beating reeds. The operation of ATBM for *endek* weaving, however, which is even nosier than backstrap looms, is not subject to such prohibition (see Nakatani 1995a).

16. Unstable production rates, due mainly to prescribed religious activities, is one of the major reasons why a small-scale credit scheme designed specifically for handicraft production did not work in Singarsa. Most women could not earn as steadily as envisaged by the scheme and thus failed to keep up the monthly payments (see Nakatani 1995a:sec. 6.4).

17. Villagers themselves acknowledge that their cloth is of lesser quality because weavers in Singarsa try to weave as quickly as possible. The weavers of Klungkung and Gelgel, by contrast, are said to weave each cloth much more slowly and attentively. In Gelgel, most *songket* producers still engage in the entire process, obtaining help from family members (Subagyo 1991:156), although the overall number of weavers is much smaller than in Singarsa. A similar situation appears to exist in northern Bali: a handful of weavers in Bratan are said to make highly acclaimed cloth; in Jineng Dalem, where nearly every woman practices *songket* weaving, coarser cloth is produced.

Chapter 8

Education for the Performing Arts: Contesting and Mediating Identity in Contemporary Bali

Brett Hough

An information brochure produced by the College of Indonesian Arts in Denpasar announces the following institutional aims:

> To form Indonesian man in accordance with the principles of Pancasila [the Five Principles of the official national ideology] and the Constitution, capable of performing his work in a pluralistic society professionally, skilfully and creatively as an expert in the arts, with a presence and competence that is scientific, responsible, and aware, with love for and desire to develop his culture in the context of duty to the development of his society and dedication to God. [College of Indonesian Arts 1988:1][1]

The aims clearly demarcate the College of Indonesian Arts (Sekolah Tinggi Seni Indonesia, or STSI) as a site for the development and dissemination of national Indonesian culture—both in the broad sense of language, values, and identity and in the specific sense of artistic practice. Couched in the rhetoric of nationalism, no mention is made of STSI's role as a center for the development of regional culture other than the reference "in a pluralistic society." The rhetoric effectively obscures STSI's position as the premier arts institution in Bali in the nexus between regional and national culture. Indeed, STSI simultaneously engages in the process of developing an Indonesianized Balinese artistic culture as well as contributing Balinese elements to national Indonesian culture through its inclusion in cultural missions to other parts of Indonesia and abroad and the staging of major performance spectacles.

Here I wish to examine aspects of this nexus between the local and the national in order to understand the ways in which STSI acts as a site of mediation and contestation between, on the one hand, the contemporary (re-)creation and promotion of a local Balinese identity and, on the other, a national Indonesian identity within the context of a modern nation-state that is unitary in nature and committed to development *(pembangunan)* at any cost. My main concern is to locate STSI within the wider context of Indonesian cultural production and through a body of literature that is concerned with the political use of culture in present-day Indonesia. I use the term "culture" not in the broad anthropological sense of "all-encompassing worldview" or "beliefs and practices" but rather the narrow sense denoted in Indonesian by the term *"kebudayaan"* (culture), which refers to specific attributes such as language, customs, traditional arts, and architecture.[2] A related subset of attributes is encompassed by the term *"kesenian"* (or *seni budaya*), which refers specifically to the arts—performing, literary, and plastic. In official rhetoric, *kebudayaan* and *kesenian* are often conflated, with music, dance, and theater treated as the constituents of culture. Culture in this sense entails efforts by the national government and the bureaucracy, among others, to promote a supralocal Indonesian culture that informs and mediates contemporary local identities.

In the first section I examine the discourse of national and regional culture in order to indicate why culture is considered to be an appropriate and, indeed, essential domain of government intervention. I then survey the national education system, especially its role in creating Indonesian citizens and disseminating national culture throughout the vast Indonesian archipelago. In the final section I focus on STSI, examining aspects of the interaction between its staff and students as well as their relationship with the traditional village artists they are gradually displacing.

Culture

In Indonesia, culture is ideologically and constitutionally held to be an appropriate domain of government intervention. The Constitution explicitly states that the "government will advance national Indonesian culture" (Zurbuchen 1990:133; Yampolsky 1995:701). Consequently, there is not only a strong nationalist commitment to include culture within a government ministry but also a constitutional imperative to do so. Indeed, the underlying assumption is that culture is too important to the project of nation building and ensuring unity in diversity for it to be left alone (see Yampolsky 1995:708). Culture—national and regional—must be directed and controlled.

Culture and Government Policy

Nation-states, such as Indonesia, had from the outset of their establishment set up government portfolios for culture. Indeed, the speed at which this occurred "indicates the importance placed on culture in establishing nationhood" (Lindsay 1995a:658). Moreover, debate in Indonesia regarding cultural heritage and national identity had continued for several decades before independence was gained (p. 658)—as was evident, for example, in the 1928 "Youth Pledge" (Sumpah Pemuda) of "one nation, one people, one language." But as Jennifer Lindsay points out: "The debate never questioned the basically accepted premise of the educative values of culture itself as a civilising agent of human behaviour, and, as such, a source of pride and sense of identity" (p. 659).

The creation of a national culture and language has been central to the nationalist project's efforts to unite the diverse communities of the archipelago. The nationalist intelligentsia originally envisaged national culture as something new, not bound by a single regional culture, but rather an amalgam of many elements. Most of it was to be modern, not "feudal" or "primitive"—a reflection of the new age (McVey 1996:12–13, 19). Control over the meanings assigned to "national culture" has, therefore, been essential to its realization. Throughout the New Order period under Suharto's presidency (1966–1998), maintaining control was also in the interest of elite groups within Indonesia, thus ensuring that it was their vision of the nation that remained ascendant. This control entailed "instituting homogeneity or commonality as normative" (Verdery 1996:231), allowing the state to set the criteria to include and exclude, to demarcate what is acceptable behavior, and to assign tasks and roles for its citizenry in accordance with an official vision of national culture. The assignment of culture to a government ministry, Depdikbud (Departemen Pendidikan dan Kebudayaan, the Department of Education and Culture) has ensured that culture has been consistently accorded attention by government officials and bureaucrats. Moreover, throughout the New Order period under Suharto, this was considered imperative to ensure the success of national development (Zurbuchen 1990:133; Yampolsky 1995:708).

National Culture

There are two main referents of "national culture" *(kebudayaan nasional)* in Indonesia. The first referent is encapsulated by the national motto of "Unity in Diversity" (Bhinneka Tunggal Ika). The motto's underlying assertion is that all regional cultures *(kebudayaan daerah)* can be subsumed under the appellation "national" or "Indonesian," as they all constitute one culture sharing common attributes that are Indonesian in character.

The second referent, and the one I am concerned with here, is national culture that is transmitted throughout the archipelago via the bureaucracy and the education system. It is characterized by the use of Bahasa Indonesia, the national language, and is manifested in literature, theater, film, and popular music (Yampolsky 1995:710) and disseminated through the modern mass media (television, radio, cassette recordings, newspapers, and magazines). On one level it has been viewed as a largely urban middle-class culture centered in the larger towns and cities across the country.[3] Certainly members of the urban middle classes are more likely to come into contact with national Indonesian culture as consumers of films, music, newspapers, and magazines. Moreover, many of these people are transmitters of national Indonesian culture through their roles as government bureaucrats and, to a far less extent, as active participants in the creation of literary works, music, films, and so on. Consequently, national culture may have very little practical day-to-day meaning for the majority of the population who still live in rural environments that are demarcated by the use of regional languages and cultural practices.[4] In other words, for those urban Indonesians whose main language of communication is Indonesian, national culture may in fact be their primary culture and locus of identity; for those who speak Indonesian as a second language, however, the associated cultural attributes are more likely to represent secondary markers of identity.

Nevertheless, national culture can be seen to coexist with regional cultures and thus represents for most Indonesians another part of their identity to be mediated and negotiated alongside that of their regional identity. These two identities constitute different epistemic frames within which people live and upon which they draw to varying degrees in their daily lives, depending on the context.[5] Institutions like STSI represent one arena within which the two interact. Although most of the staff and students who teach and study Balinese arts are Balinese, for example, the culture of pedagogy and administration is Indonesian.

Regional Cultures

Just as national culture has more than one referent, so too does regional culture *(kebudayaan daerah)*. The first refers to the specific ethnolinguistic communities that exist throughout the archipelago. There are approximately three hundred groups that are quite distinct in anthropological terms. The second referent is the specific designation of regional cultures as belonging to one of the twenty-seven provinces that Michel Picard (1996b:176–179) calls "provincial differentiation."[6] In official rhetoric, regional cultures are considered to be the source *(sumber)* from which national culture draws its diversity. It is specifically the "peaks of regional culture" *(puncak-puncak kebudayaan daerah)* that are held to contribute to the notion of national culture as a plurality of cultures encapsulated in Pancasila (Hughes-Freeland 1993:89; Picard 1996b:171–179). But as Felicia Hughes-Freeland points out, while the rhetoric of Pancasila promotes diversity "it is the unifying powers of [the] ideology which are given priority" (1993:89). Or to put it as Philip Yampolsky does, within this discourse there is no sense of any conflict between regional past and nationalist present, as "national culture subsumes the regional cultures without replacing them" (1995:708).

While at the level of rhetoric/discourse there may be no conflict, at the level of lived reality there may be considerable tension between people's identification with their ethnic roots and loyalty toward their own regional community, on the one hand, and "the political need to forge 'unity and oneness' *(persatuan dan kesatuan)* within a diverse population, on the other" (Zurbuchen 1990:133). The overriding consideration is, however, that such identification and diversity should not undermine national unity. Any disruption to this living dynamic of "Unity in Diversity" that threatens the strategy of national development invites the active intervention of the state (Zurbuchen 1990:133; see also Acciaioli 1985:161).

Apart from the nationalist ideal and the constitutional imperative, two assumptions underpin contemporary government intervention in regional cultures. First, national (Indonesian) culture is invariably associated with the modern whereas regional cultures are associated with the traditional; second, as culture is seen as intrinsic to national development, it is modern Indonesian culture that is held to be the appropriate culture of development.[7] Regional cultures (or more precisely specific elements of regional cultures) may also be employed in furthering national development, but only after being modernized through a process termed "upgrading" *(perkembangan)* or "guidance" *(pembinaan)*.

At this point, it is useful to differentiate between two domains of national and regional culture. The first can be designated as an *official* domain that is characterized by a high degree of rhetoric which informs policy decisions and constitutes the reference point for direct state intervention. This official domain is physically manifest in the major displays held to mark national holidays and in cultural theme parks such as Taman Mini Indonesia Indah (Beautiful Indonesia-in-

Figure 32. "Modernism–Tradition" cartoon by Surya Dharma.

Miniature Park) outside of Jakarta. The second is an *autonomous* domain that represents the specific identities of the people themselves anchored in their own languages and cultural practices which remain beyond the reach of official intervention. This autonomous domain is heterogeneous in character and open to a diverse range of local and global influences.

Depdikbud: The Department of Education and Culture

The promotion of *official* national (and regional) culture occurs in two major ways: through the education system and through direct bureaucratic intervention. The government department directly responsible for both education and culture is Depdikbud.[8] Within the department there are three directorate generals responsible for education and one for culture (Table 4).

Education

The education system is the key means at the government's disposal for transmitting *official* national culture throughout the vast archipelago as well as instructing the population in how to be "citizens." As the majority of Indonesians undergo at least six years of formal education during their lifetime, while increasing numbers spend twelve to eighteen years within the system, control over the education system and the content of its curricula is therefore crucial to ensuring that the vision of those in control is implemented.

Barbara Leigh indicates that from the outset the nation-makers of Indonesia saw education as providing the means of "deepening the national consciousness and strengthening the unity of Indonesia." And she contends that this has remained "the overarching objective of Indonesian education" ever since (1991:17). Indeed, this possibility had already been realized during the colonial period, when government schools "created a self-contained, coherent universe of experience" through their use of "uniform textbooks, standardized diplomas and teaching certificates, [and] a strictly regulated gradation of age-groups, classes and instructional materials" (Anderson 1991:121). The underlying logic is that national culture, as the culture of modernity and development, is the culture essential to being a modern Indonesian citizen whereas the teaching and socializing of inhabitants from diverse

Table 4
Administrative Structure for Depdikbud

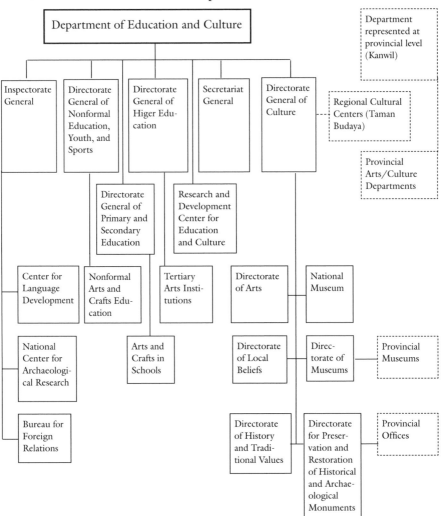

Source: Lindsay (1995b:58).

regional backgrounds to be Indonesian citizens is, likewise, essential for national culture to be successful as the culture of unity.

The principal means of achieving these aims is through the exclusive use of Indonesian in the classroom and the use of standardized curricula. Indonesian is the language of pedagogy: all textbooks, instruction, and classroom interaction are required to be in Indonesian. The body of knowledge conveyed to students is determined in Jakarta by senior bureaucrats in the curriculum branch of Depdikbud, who are often required to "respond to ministerial 'initiatives' with regard to new subjects or new subject matter within existing subjects" (Leigh 1991:17). The guiding principle behind such ministerial intervention, Leigh contends, "has been primarily to achieve the goal of state consolidation and nation unity" (p. 17). To this, of course, one must add the goals of national development. Teachers, parents, and students have no input into the curricula (Parker 1992a:48). Both Lyn Parker (1992a) and Leigh (1991), in their analyses of textbooks used in primary and secondary schools, comment on the overwhelming emphasis that is placed on the promotion of Pancasila—not only in the subject "Moral Education in State Principles" (Pendidikan Moral Pancasila, or PMP) but in other subjects as well. They also highlight the overall lack of material in the curriculum that focuses on regional culture. The emphasis is always on national Indonesian culture; regional examples are either Indonesianized or placed in a national context. In other words, any regional specificity is diluted or refracted through the prism of national culture, resulting in the portrayal of "a single, 'normal' culture, the Indonesian culture, not a multiplicity of cultures" (Parker 1992a:59).

Both Leigh and Parker note a strong emphasis on the rote learning of information contained in textbooks, the unquestioning acceptance of such information, and the authority of the teacher. Leigh contends that as "schooling is concerned with learning correct knowledge," there is an emphasis in the examination process on right versus wrong or on true or false answers to all questions. "The political implications of this educational emphasis," she suggests, "are a devaluation of critical analysis and students' reduced ability (or often inability) to evaluate action from alternate perspectives" (1991:37; see also Parker 1992b:101).

Directorate General of Culture

The same overall messages—of uniformity and correct knowledge—are conveyed to society at large by the Directorate General of Culture through diverse activities focused on active intervention in regional cultures at all levels, in particular the arts. These activities include "registering performers, inventorying genres . . . monitoring content, suggesting technical or stylistic changes in performance, selecting individuals and groups for financial assistance, producing festivals and competitions, commissioning performances for visiting dignitaries and state occasions, subsidizing appearances on local television, and even arranging travel to Jakarta to perform at the national theme park, Taman Mini" (Yampolsky 1995:710).

There is a threefold thrust to Depdikbud's activities: first, to control the political content of performances and exploit the potential for introducing government messages into them; second, to control the moral content of performances so they do not offend members of other groups on religious or moral grounds; and third, to upgrade the artistic quality of performances (Yampolsky 1995:711–712). Yampolsky believes that underlying Depdikbud's intervention is the fundamental premise "that there is something wrong with the arts as they stand, and usually what is wrong is that they are too rough, too crude; not respectable" (p. 711). In other words, regional arts need to be upgraded, improved, and modernized in order to be in step with the times ("sesuai dengan irama zaman"; p. 712).[9]

The two elements crucial to the process are the evaluative criteria employed by officials and the performance contexts for implementation. The former element Yampolsky terms "the aesthetic of respectability," which requires "art that is neat and orderly, disciplined, inoffensive, attractive or impressive to look at, pleasant to listen to." The latter consist of the many festivals, competitions, and commissions sponsored each year by all levels of government administration. These contexts enable the showcasing of specific forms and allow Depdikbud officials the opportunity to exert a powerful influence on how this is done (1995:712).[10]

There are compelling reasons why many performers throughout Indonesia are willing to comply with Depdikbud directives concerning the upgrading of their artistic practice. As Yampolsky suggests: "Satisfying the local Depdikbud can lead to invitations to bigger events—competitions or festivals at the district, provincial, or even national level—or to a lucrative spot on the tourist circuit. In hopes of these rewards, performers do not seem to mind subordinating the local aesthetic to Depdikbud's" (1995:713). Jennifer Lindsay (1995a, 1995b) and Hughes-Freeland (1993) discuss the importance of government patronage to performers and the kinds of obligations entailed by the relationship. Others may be intimidated by the status of an official directive and the presence of authority figures, such as the *camat* (local district head), and feel they have no alternative but to comply.

The changes wrought by government intervention have often been detrimental to regional art forms. Research undertaken by scholars in

Figure 33. "Dancing for rupiahs" cartoon by Surya Dharma.

various locations throughout Indonesia has documented these effects.[11] The ministers and bureaucrats who determine policies in
Jakarta are usually not artists themselves nor from the areas affected by
their decisions. Consequently they may have no direct experience of
the specific regional culture or any emotional attachment to the art
form. With little or nothing at stake, other than perhaps the advancement of their careers, they are unlikely to perceive any harm in their directives—particularly in the context of an unquestioning commitment
to development and a pronounced bias against *kampung* or "rural"
culture.[12] As for the local artists who are subject to bureaucratic intervention, Yampolsky says they may not be "conscious that something
still more basic is also at risk: the communal dimension of regional art.
The changes Depdikbud promotes nullify the aspect of meaning that
depends not on the sounds, words, movements, and symbols deployed, but on who is performing, who is observing, and what the
local significance of the performance is" (1995:713).

An important coda might be added to this point: as outside observers, we must be careful not to see the entire process as Machiavel-
lian in intent (1995:714). Indeed, my own observations and discussions with various people in Bali have led me to conclude that the

process is much more mundane and bureaucratic—and for that reason potentially more detrimental. Most artists at STSI with whom I am acquainted are committed to the overall process of developing the arts. Some question specific aspects of it; others accept the wisdom of policymakers without reflection; still others exploit the system to promote their own self-interest. But all have to work within a system that is highly centralized, thoroughly bureaucratic, and substantially underresourced in terms of financial and intellectual capital.

Depdikbud, however, is not always successful in its attempts to control and regulate. Many scholars have documented the ways in which locals respond to government intervention, indicating that there is often potential for subverting directives and asserting of a local agenda.[13] In other words, locals may not only participate in implementing changes to a local cultural form but may also resist heavy-handed intervention that fails to take into account local needs. Strong regional groups—such as the Javanese, the Balinese, the Sundanese of West Java, and the Minangkabau of Sumatra—are in a better position to resist than those with no institutional base or recognized cultural capital.[14] Significantly, these four regions constitute the locations of the former conservatories and the present-day performing arts academies, colleges, and institutes.[15] Although they come under the jurisdiction of Depdikbud and are bound to implement government policies, they nevertheless assert local identity through their focus on regional art forms and mediate national demands through direct input into policymaking as part of the overall bureaucratic structure. It is this nexus between the local and the national that I wish to discuss next. As we shall see, the situation is by no means straightforward but involves competing agendas and unforeseen outcomes.

STSI: The College of Indonesian Arts in Bali

As an institution, STSI is informed by the intertwined discourses of nationalism, modern education, and development evident in its statement of aims quoted at the beginning of this study. And as we have seen, the overarching aim of tertiary education is to continue the process of creating Indonesian citizens in the regional context of Bali that is carried out at primary and secondary levels. STSI's chief role in this process is achieved through professionalization of the arts, modernization of artistic production through the use of "modern" or "scientific" methods, and training students to become expert in the arts. The guiding imperative is dedication to God—congruent with the first principle of Pancasila—and the motivating force is the selfless duty to contribute to national development through the development of culture.

Its aims confirm the importance of STSI as a site for the cultural production of Indonesia in the regional context of Bali. In conflating regional with national in the phrase "his culture" ("Kebudayaan Nasional bangsanya"), the aims refer to the discourse surrounding Balinese artistic culture itself: what it consists of, how it should be preserved and developed, and who has the right and authority to speak for Balinese artists.[16] STSI has the authority to decide all of these matters, for it is able to draw on the resources of the state to ensure that it carries out the compelling nationalist and development agenda.

STSI, located next to the Art Center in East Denpasar, originally began as Akademi Seni Tari Indonesia, or ASTI, the Academy of Indonesian Dance. Established in 1967 through local initiative, it was brought under the control of Depdikbud in 1969. In 1988, it was upgraded from an academy to a college, enabling it to confer its own degrees. (Until then it had been associated with a sister institution in Yogyakarta that conferred all degrees.) The change of its status to a college reflects a general expansion of the institution over the last decade in terms of the courses that are offered, the facilities available, and the qualifications of the staff. There are currently two faculties offering five course streams. The Faculty of Performing Arts (Seni Pertunjukan) consists of Dance (Seni Tari), Gamelan Music (Seni Karawitan—musical forms that have a pentatonic scale), and Shadow Puppetry (Seni Pedalangan); the Faculty of Fine Arts (Seni Rupa) consists of Painting (Seni Lukis) and Carving (Seni Kriya).

Like similar arts institutions, STSI comes under the administrative jurisdiction of the Directorate General of Higher Education, but it also assumes a significant role in implementing the policies of the Directorate General of Culture. All national tertiary education institutions are bound by the Tri Dharma Perguruan Tinggi: the Threefold Tasks of Tertiary Education Institutions, namely, education, research, and community service. The Threefold Tasks set structural parameters within which STSI is required to work and, moreover, ensure that its institutional identity remains Indonesian with "Balinese color" rather than the other way around.[17] In keeping with the agenda of the Directorate General of Culture, STSI's staff members take an active part in the many festivals and competitions held each year—participating as members of organizing committees, as teachers of community groups, and as judges. STSI also documents and stores records of the various performance styles and techniques, costumes, and musical instruments found throughout Bali and among Balinese communities on the neighboring island of Lombok. Staff and students are frequently called upon to participate in welcoming ceremonies for visiting dignitaries, the official opening of hotels and conferences, and cultural missions to other parts of the archipelago or overseas.

Originally arts academies were part of the Directorate General of Culture.[18] But after an internal restructuring of Depdikbud in 1976, they were transferred to the Directorate General of Higher Education, known by the acronym Dikti.[19] The significance of this reorganization for the institutions concerned, which included STSI's forerunner ASTI,[20] was a change from a conservatory style of education under the Directorate General of Culture to a tertiary style of education under Dikti.[21] This fundamentally changed the focus of these institutions, the content of their curricula, and the way they were funded. Incorporation into the financial and administrative jurisdiction of Dikti means that STSI is subject to the same policy decisions that affect tertiary institutions throughout the archipelago. Although it is recognized that STSI, as an arts institution, has special curriculum requirements, its ad-

Figure 34. STSI students participating in the opening parade of the Bali Arts Festival in 1991. Photo: Brett Hough.

ministrative structure, bureaucratic organization, and adherence to an overall national curriculum are the same as in other tertiary institutions. Consequently, it experiences many of the problems that afflict the entire system.[22] These problems are in turn compounded by what many critics of STSI regard as its overbearing position in setting the artistic agenda and monopolizing resources in Bali.[23]

The Threefold Tasks, as noted, determine the parameters governing tertiary institutions. Education, the first of these, occupies most of STSI's time—teaching undergraduates and providing opportunities for teaching staff to undertake further study to obtain postgraduate qualifications (either from an overseas institution or an appropriate local institution). When the college was opened in 1967, there were twenty-nine students enrolled in the one program. Almost thirty years later, STSI regularly enrolls one hundred and fifty students across five programs.

Under the 1994 national curriculum guidelines, students are required to take units from the following four groups: General Studies (Mata Kuliah Umum), Foundation Studies (Mata Kuliah Dasar Keahlian), Specialization Studies (Mata Kuliah Keahlian), and Local Studies (Mata Kuliah Lokal). The Local Studies component is a recent addition to the curriculum and permits input from regional institutions in determining course content. In effect, its existence is the department's acknowledgment of regional specificity. The overall parameters, however, are still determined by the department's guidelines. Whereas local content may be included in units of the other three groups, the national curriculum specifically mandates its inclusion in Local Studies. The curriculum, therefore, represents a mixture of prescription and flexibility allowing for "local color" defined within a national framework.

The following observations are based largely on my experience participating in and documenting activities associated with STSI's Dance Program (Jurusan Tari) during the period July 1989 to July 1991. Here I wish to highlight three areas: the role of village artists in dance classes; the national community service programs; and the examination process for final year students.

Village Artists

Students who enroll in the Dance Program are required to learn both male and female dance styles so that they will attain proficiency in both for teaching and choreography. Typically they also specialize in male or female genres depending on their physical build, ability, and temperament. Most of the classes I attended were conducted by up to four instructors simultaneously. One of the instructors would demonstrate a section of a dance in front of the class; then students would copy the movements.[24] Large groups were divided into smaller groupings, each taking turns to go through the piece while other class members watched from the side or chatted with each other. Some correction was undertaken, but the number of students made it impossible to provide the kind of intensive, "hands-on" tuition a student would receive from a village dance teacher. Most of the classes were of two hours duration, though often less than half of that time was actually devoted to practical instruction.[25] For non-Balinese students like myself and those from other parts of Indonesia, practical classes were often frustrating as very little allowance was made for those who were unfamiliar with a dance—it was assumed that everyone was already able to perform it.

Some of the practical classes were enlivened by the addition of honorary instructors *(tenaga pengajar tidak tetap* or *tenaga luar biasa)* who were invited to teach a particular dance, such as the Batuan style of Gambuh or a classical form of Baris. These village artists, or *seniman alam* as they are now known, are widely acknowledged as experts in specific dances and local styles yet lack the formal qualifications that would enable them to become permanent instructors *(tenaga pengajar tetap)* at STSI. The appellation *"seniman alam"* was coined after the advent of formal arts education. Prior to that, such artists were designated by various terms indicating the performance genres in which they specialized.[26] Nowadays, however, a distinction is made between those who have undergone formal education in the arts (designated *seniman* or "artists") and those who have not received any formal education (referred to as *seniman alam* or "natural artists"). The word *"alam"* connotes "nature," "natural," and "world" or " realm"; hence the appellation implies both a style and a domain of practice. The continued involvement of the *seniman alam* in practical classes is an attempt by STSI to maintain links with village practice and harks back to the extensive input of such practitioners during its early years when there was only a small cohort of students and a significant number of *seniman alam* teaching there. Graduates at that time received a more thorough training (particularly in classical forms) than it is now possible to provide—given the constraints of time, the larger number of students, and the demands of the curriculum.

I Nyoman Sedana, a graduate of shadow puppetry at STSI and now a member of the teaching staff, makes the following observations about the *seniman alam:*

> Before graduates of SMKI [Sekolah Menengah Karawitan Indonesia, the High School of Traditional Indonesian Music] and STSI started teaching, the bulk of the instructors were village artists. To this day, the best village *dalang* [puppeteers] are more skilled than we graduates with our official credentials. It seems ironic, therefore, that village *dalang* who teach at the academy receive smaller salaries and are not eligible for the research funds that we, their students, may receive. Nor are these village artists always credited for information given us during our research. Understandably, village *dalang* become frustrated once they realize their subordinate position, and attrition of these expert instructors from the schools back to the villages is symptomatic of the problem that arises when the best artists, for lack of academic credentials, are given a lower status. One of my teachers, for example, has often threatened to quit his job, saying that my peers and I are already capable of running the department. [Sedana 1993:96]

Sedana questions whether the next generation of students will be deprived of the expertise of these *seniman alam*—an issue that today's educators will have to resolve. One factor militating against its resolution is that many of the *seniman alam* have already reached their twilight years and will die within the next decade or so. Their positions as artists within their communities will be filled increasingly by others (often their own children) who have undergone formal education and graduated from SMKI or STSI. The nature of performance will undoubtedly change as this occurs. Sedana himself confidently notes that with the creation of artist-scholars such as STSI is producing, "the twentieth century may well see a new type of Balinese *dalang*—one who can perform *wayang* [shadow puppet theater] and explain it for the modern world as well" (1993:97).

The surviving *seniman alam* appear likely to remain marginal to the system for two reasons: first, without formal qualifications, they cannot be incorporated into the various levels and pay scales of the bureaucracy; second, they are not a product of the arts education system and would find it difficult to become a permanent part of it.[27] On numerous occasions I witnessed direct or indirect expressions of the frustration mentioned by Sedana as well as resentment toward the formal education system that some *seniman alam* perceive as a threat to their economic and social position in the wider community.[28] At the same time, however, many *seniman alam* now put their own children

Figure 35. Village dance performance, ca. 1930. Photo: Courtesy of Leo Haks.

through STSI as they recognize the necessity for them to gain academic credentials.

Community Service Programs

Another area in which STSI's students and staff can be seen to be taking over, or at least encroaching, is the third of the Threefold Tasks—community service, that is, teaching local communities, a role traditionally undertaken by village artists. This involvement in local commmunities occurs in a number of ways. The community service program I focus on here is the national Kuliah Kerja Nyata (KKN), in which students in their final years are obliged to spend up to three months in a village applying their skills in the arts to assist the community.[29]

STSI's KKN program differs from the national standard in that students spend only two to three days per week in the assigned localities, thus enabling them to continue to attend class as well as any extracurricular activities. There are national and institutional guidelines for conducting the program. Staff are supposed to provide initial information about the program and explain fieldwork methodology to the students. Then, throughout the period of KKN, they are supposed to provide ongoing supervision of their activities. At the end of the three-month period, there is usually a closing ceremony at which members of the local community, with the aid of the students, demonstrate the skills they have acquired. But these guidelines are not always implemented effectively.

Although KKN is a compulsory component of all tertiary degree programs, it also serves an important role in STSI's "community service responsibilities" *(pengabdian pada masyarakat)*. Moreover, the program disseminates STSI's influence at the village level—often to villages that are isolated and, by Balinese standards, artistically impoverished. In such contexts, it is generally an STSI style of dance or music that is taught by the students.[30] STSI's program is somewhat akin to the traditional practice of village artists traveling to other communities as guest teachers. In the past, established performers were invited by other communities and gamelan groups to teach and in some cases even traveled around Bali offering their services to communities or the local nobility *(triwangsa)*. Of course, a major difference is to be found in the way that STSI's KKN program is effected. Moreover, the old practice of village artists teaching other communities resulted in the diffusion of particular artistic styles from one part of Bali to another whereas nowadays, by contrast, STSI's students propagate officially sanctioned, standard dance versions—local variation is "controlled." And while, in the past, long-term relationships were often established between village artists and the communities they taught, students generally have only short-term contact with the communities they visit. Another significant difference between former practice and STSI's KKN program is the program's institutional and, by extension, political context. The students represent STSI and, therefore, the Indonesian state. Consequently, political considerations often enter into the program's organization. For example, a community may be targeted by a regency government to receive a KKN contingent due to its involvement in an upcoming customary village competition (Lomba Desa Adat). This can result in the promotion of the arts to communities that have no performing arts tradition or do not really care to develop one.[31]

One of the KKN sites I visited during the 1990–1991 program was located on the southern slopes of Mount Abang in the regency of Bangli. Well off the tourist track that ascends into the Penelokan–Kintamani region, the village of Abang Soongan is fairly spartan, bisected by a dirt road, and surrounded by vegetable and fruit gardens. It was one of the villages targeted by the regional government for "special attention" and simultaneously played host to a KKN contingent from STSI and the private Warmadewa University in Denpasar. A group of eight STSI students was initially assigned to the regency and, on the basis of meetings with the *camat* of Kintamani district, it was decided that they would split into two groups of four and devote their energies to two villages (Daup and Bantang). After conducting the requisite investigative visit *(penjajagan)* to the two communities, they were informed that the head of Bangli regency had requested that they proceed to three entirely different villages. The group consequently decided that five of them (three dancers and two musicians) would cover the villages of Abang Soongan and Batur Tengah while the remaining three (dance students) would focus on Belantih.

I visited the first group both at Abang Soongan, where they spent the mornings, and at Batur Tengah, where they taught on Friday and Saturday afternoons. As both villages were about to participate in arts festivals, the students were asked to provide instruction in several popular dances (Panyembrama, Margapati, Pendet) and the accompanying music. A further reason that Abang Soongan requested KKN assistance was that community members intended to perform some of the dances at the ceremony to mark the start of an agricultural extension program for school dropouts (Penyuluhan Pertanian bagi Remaja Putus Sekolah) that the governor would attend. Some days after the governor's visit, the KKN program was brought to an abrupt end due to the mysterious disappearance of the village head. (His dismembered body was found several days later.) The students felt that he had been an authoritarian figure who insisted that villagers always attend the weekly practice sessions.[32] Without ongoing support from the students in his absence, it was open to question whether or not the community was able or indeed willing to continue the sessions.

Although I could cite many examples of communities that have enthusiastically embraced and benefited from KKN assistance, the preceding case highlights some of the problems faced by the national program as a whole. Many critics question the usefulness of a nationwide program that fails to take into account local variations and needs. Others say that KKN places an undue burden on poor communities that have to host the students throughout their three-month stay; often the sole testimony of the community's generosity is a small memorial *(tugu peringatan)*. Moreover, some students regard the entire exercise as just another compulsory requirement. In other words, the program's heavy-handed imposition tends to work against the establishment of truly cooperative, organic links between villagers and students and may be of little long-term benefit to either group.[33]

Another major problem appears to beset the program and certainly dogged STSI in 1990–1991: the inadequate practical and psychological preparation of students.[34] This is further compounded by insufficient time and resources once they have moved to the assigned communities. Unlike village artists, who enter other communities because of their acknowledged expertise, most students have only their status as STSI students on which to rely and, of course, they have not had the same degree of life experience as the older village artists. Although the program's underlying intention is laudable, its implementation requires modification to transform it into a relevant interface between the two spheres.

Examinations

At present, KKN is one of the many practical units that students have to complete during their degree course. It is one that exposes them to the roles for which they are training. But the most important test of their skills and the one that ultimately validates them as "expert in the arts" is the Bachelor of Arts Examination (Ujian Sarjana Seni).[35]

The examination involves the production of a performance piece (generally of fifteen to twenty minutes duration), an accompanying written script, and an oral examination. The two examinations I witnessed during 1989–1991 each involved approximately eighty students, divided into two rounds, each of three nights duration, during mid-December and early January. Eight to ten performances were presented each night. Most of them were proficiently executed, but only a small percentage could be considered outstanding.[36] Indeed, the panel of examiners seated in the middle of the packed auditorium faced quite a challenging task in maintaining their attentiveness each night as they watched numerous variations on similar themes. Students are free to choreograph or compose a piece that is classical *(klasik)*, a new creation *(kreasi baru)*, or contemporary *(kontemporer* or *masa kini)*. Apparently there is no preference for any particular style. Moreover, the examiners possessed expertise in all three styles. The highest mark awarded in 1990 went to a dance student who choreographed a new creation; in 1991 the top mark went to a student of shadow puppet theater who composed a contemporary performance that made use of a range of hand-held lights to illuminate the screen. Most dance pieces were based on Balinese stories, local historical events, and episodes from the Hindu epics. That the dominant themes of these performances remain overwhelmingly Balinese, some eighteen or so years after the integration of the arts into the national education system, indicates the strength of regional identity. On the one hand, this fact highlights one of STSI's important institutional roles: strengthening local identity in the face of the homogenizing tendencies of the national education system. On the other hand, most of the performances are variations on set themes and movement vocabulary and therefore tend to be artistically bland. In effect they confirm the system's success in emphasizing appearance over content, conformity over innovation.[37]

The degree awarded to successful candidates legitimates their status as "expert in the arts" and differentiates them from village artists.[38] In fact, the appellation *seniman alam* only has meaning when juxtaposed against *seniman,* "practitioners with formal qualifications." On a practical level, the degree enables (though by no means guarantees) access to employment within the bureaucracy. For a few people each year there is the possibility of gaining a position within STSI itself. For the majority, however, it inevitably means working in other depart-

Figure 36. "Shadow puppet play with overhead projector" cartoon by Surya Dharma.

ments at the national, provincial, or regional levels, either in Bali or other parts of Indonesia, or else establishing their own dance foundations to teach or put on tourist performances.[39] The advantages of becoming an STSI staff member are many, including the possibility of undertaking overseas performance tours, receiving sponsorship to pursue further study (usually in the United States), and gaining access to project funding. Each year students who attain the highest results in the final year examination are encouraged to become full-time staff members.[40]

Into the Next Century

In 1998, a number of developments took place that will influence STSI for years to come. The most significant was the appointment of I Wayan Dibia to the position of *ketua* (director), replacing I Made Bandem who had held the position for the previous sixteen years (1981–1997).[41] The importance of the changeover for STSI lies in their contrasting personalities—hence style of leadership—and in their artistic and professional vision for the arts in Bali. Both men were born into performing arts families in the village of Singapadu in Gianyar: Bandem in 1945 and Dibia in 1948. From childhood they were exposed to the performance genre of *arja* through their parents, and they were among the first cohort of students to attend the newly established KOKAR in Denpasar in the early 1960s and ASTI when it began in 1967. Bandem and Dibia were also the first two graduates of ASTI to undertake M.A. and Ph.D. study, respectively spending a total of eight years in the United States.

Bandem was hand-picked to pursue ethnomusicological studies in order to develop expertise in Western theory. Early on he was designated to be the successor to I Wayan Mertha Suteja, the military-appointed director of ASTI (1967–1981). Since his return from doctoral studies in the United States, he has pursued a scholarly and bureaucratic trajectory. He has published articles and books extensively, has been an active member of Golkar, the government-sponsored political party under the New Order, as well as an appointed representative for Bali in the national parliament (MPR). While occupying the directorship for some sixteen years, Bandem was enfolded by the elite world of the national bureaucracy. He was at ease with its language and frequently involved in policy deliberations within the Directorate General. Moreover, as he worked tirelessly toward the upgrading and expansion of the institution, he maintained close personal and professional links to senior officials at both the regional and national levels of government. In 1998 he became a candidate for the position of governor of Bali, although he did not make the short list.

Dibia, by contrast, has pursued a performance-oriented career path undertaking postgraduate studies in choreography and performance. He is still actively engaged in creative endeavors. Well known as a choreographer throughout Bali, he has maintained close links with the community at large and appears much more at ease among fellow performers than among bureaucrats. In his former position as a deputy director, he was involved intensively in day-to-day interaction with students. Although a member of various committees that influence national education policy, he has continued to spend time with artists outside the formal system.

In conversations both men seemed conscious of problems with STSI and both had clear views on how the institution should develop in the years to come. For Bandem, the major priority was to upgrade academic standards and develop the campus infrastructure. Dibia, by contrast, wishes to change the internal emphasis so that village artists can develop those spheres they have always excelled at while leaving STSI to concentrate on the modern domain that represents its area of expertise. The task ahead, of course, will be the degree to which Dibia can reshape the internal culture, given that the structural parameters are still set by the ministry in Jakarta.

On the national level, two recent developments have the potential to affect STSI: the Asian economic crisis and the establishment of a new ministry, Depparsenbud (Departemen Pariwisata, Seni dan Budaya, the Department of Tourism, Art, and Culture). The ministry's specific role and responsibility remain unclear at this stage, particularly as it overlaps with areas of responsibility already covered by the Directorate General of Culture. On the surface, however, it appears to be the logical outcome of the differentiation process discussed by Michel Picard (1996b). Seni (Art) and Budaya (Culture) have been abstracted and commodified to the point of representing products that can be marketed along with Pariwisata (Tourism), hence requiring a separate ministry.[42] The term *"kebudayaan"* in the title of Depdikbud presumably now encompasses culture in the residual sense of (regional/provincial/ethnic) identity.

With respect to the economic crisis, there are two areas of concern: its effect on the tourist industry and the drying up of government funds to finance further expansion of STSI. Until now, the tourist industry has been one of the main areas of employment for graduates as well as a key source of nongovernment funding for STSI. Consequently, any downturn in the industry will limit the opportunities for graduates to earn a living on the basis of their expertise. It will also deprive STSI of extra revenue at a time of considerable constraint on government funds. In a more positive light, however, the crisis may also result in a rethinking of institutional priorities and a decline in the number of students enrolling in courses. High student enrollment in the dance and music programs over the last decade or so has made it impossible to pursue the intensive tuition that characterized the early days of both KOKAR and ASTI. Whatever the eventual outcome, the potential for rethinking STSI's direction has increased due to internal change and the local effects of external forces that are dramatically reshaping Indonesian society.

At the close of the twentieth century, education for the performing arts in Bali offers both threat and potential, control and liberation, stultification and renaissance. The teaching staff and students of STSI—as well as arts practitioners, both graduates and village artists, outside the institution—are caught up in processes they can only partly direct, processes in which they make choices, follow particular career paths, devise and implement agendas, and follow or circumvent bureaucratic procedures. Here I have sought to demonstrate some of the ways in which this occurs and to locate the discussion within the broad Indonesian context.

Performing arts production in Bali has changed substantially over the last thirty years. Since the 1960s, the Indonesian state has made its presence felt through its provision of infrastructure and an ideological framework for study of Bali's various performing arts within the supralocal space of Indonesia. The presence of state-sponsored arts institutions has provided a conduit through which to mold, direct, and control artistic production in accordance with the nationalist agenda of creating an Indonesian culture. Likewise, it has ensured that Balinese have a means to assert their presence in the national arena in a way that few other Indonesian communities have available to them. By encouraging and sponsoring local arts in a controlled environment, the government ensures that local identity has an outlet through its display. While this policy stems from a genuine desire to maintain regional diversity, it is based on the premise that it should not threaten national unity. The compelling logic of the Indonesian nationalist project requires that diversity should always be curtailed in the interest of unity and, under the New Order government of President Suharto, the demands of development. Consequently, the state has employed a range of strategies from concession to suppression to maintain the status quo. In the case of Bali, one of Indonesia's most prosperous and high-profile provinces, the strategy has been to control local identity in order to prevent its emergence in a subversive agenda (as has occurred in separatist movements in Aceh, East Timor, and Irian Jaya).

As a result, Balinese performing artists are now working within an increasingly bureaucratized society dominated by tourism development. The challenge they face, along with graduates of STSI, is to maintain the vitality of their heritage while building upon it to advance the arts. The danger lies in allowing the tradition to stultify through unquestioning adherence to an agenda that seeks to direct artistic production in line with nationalist and development goals. Institutions such as STSI are significant sites for the assertion, mediation, and contestation of local and national demands. It remains for Balinese artists to harness its potential to overcome their structural and historical constraints and take the performing arts into the twenty-first century.

Notes

This chapter is based on research carried out from June 1989 to June 1991 and from December 1994 to January 1995. I gratefully acknowledge funding support provided by an Australian Postgraduate Research Award, a travel grant from the Centre of Southeast Asian Studies at Monash University, and a Darmasiswa scholarship from the Indonesia Department of Education and Culture. I also thank Linda Connor, Raechelle Rubinstein, and Barbara Hatley for their invaluable comments and suggestions on earlier versions.

1. "Membentuk Manusia Indonesia Seutuhnya yang berkepribadian Pancasila sebagaimana tercantum dalam Undang-undang Dasar 1945, mampu menjalankan pekerjaannya dalam masyarakat bineka secara profesional terampil dan kreatif sebagai tenaga ahli seni yang memiliki sikap serta kompetensi ilmiah, penuh rasa tanggung jawab, sadar, mencintai dan bertekad untuk mengembangkan Kebudayaan Nasional bangsanya dalam rangka pengabdian pada perkembangan bangsa dengan bertakwa kepada 'Tuhan Yang Maha Esa'" (Sekolah Tinggi Seni Indonesia 1993:19). It is intriguing that the English translation makes no attempt to convey the nongendered sense of the phrase "manusia Indonesia" but rather has opted for the gloss "Indonesian man." It is also revealing that "Kebudayaan Nasional bangsanya" has been rendered as "his/her culture" rather than "national culture," as the phrase implies. Use of the unqualified "culture" in English indicates the hegemonic status of national (Indonesian) culture in official rhetoric. In other words, the

terms are interchangeable and subsume all other distinctions. Throughout this chapter, however, I will render the phrase as "national culture" to refer to a supralocal culture that coexists with regional cultures.

2. Economics and politics are explicitly excluded; religion *(agama)* and customary law and practice *(adat)* are treated as two separate domains within the broader classification *kebudayaan*. The process of demarcating and defining *agama* and *adat* as domains of government intervention began under the Dutch (see Chapter 1 in this volume). Similarly, broad political and economic concerns were demarcated and defined as administrative matters *(dinas)* and considered by Dutch colonial administrators to be their specific domain. This overall scheme was adopted and extended by the postcolonial polities. See Warren (1993) for a detailed discussion of the history of state intervention in local communities in Bali.

3. In 1963, Hildred Geertz put forward the phrase "Indonesian metropolitan superculture" to describe an emerging urban-based culture characterized by "the colloquial everyday use of the Indonesian language, and directly associated with this language are the new Indonesian literature, popular music, films, and historical and political writings. . . . The prime external symbols of adherence to the superculture are the acquisition of higher education, facility with foreign languages, travel experience abroad, and Western luxury goods such as automobiles. . . . As with any cultural standard only a privileged few have the ability or resources to model the whole of their lives according to its tenets" (cited in Schiller 1996:101). Jim Schiller observed some twenty or so years later that the "'metropolitan superculture' or at least elements of it [as described by Hildred and Clifford Geertz] have spread far more extensively and with much greater impact. The number of Indonesians in small towns and the countryside able to imagine themselves living a life style that is 'modern Indonesian' is manifestly larger today than three decades ago. Their life style may seem, to the Jakarta elite, a 'faded image'—a pale imitation—of Jakarta elite life style but—in the small towns and villages of Indonesia—it marks local elite status and sets them apart from others able to be less fully 'modern'" (1996:101–102). It seems apparent, then, that the situation on the ground is simultaneously much more diverse and homogeneous than implied by Schiller's terminology or description. Later in this chapter I make a distinction between an official and an autonomous domain of cultural practice in order to convey the idea that there are multiple intertwined layers of regional and national culture in which the peoples of the archipelago participate throughout their lives. Consequently, "national culture" in the sense in which I use it, as a supralocal identity, is not only the product of "cultural engineering" in its official guise but also a "cultural mix" that is influenced as much by globalization as it is by official rhetoric, as much by regional cultural dynamics as by trends emanating out of Jakarta. Thus it is not one or the other, but rather both, as indeed is the case with regional culture.

4. I am not suggesting, however, that members of rural communities are

totally isolated from the surrounding world. Certainly, since the advent of radio, newspaper, and, more recently, television, there are very few Balinese who have not been influenced by, or at least exposed to, external elements. My point is, rather, to indicate the primary locus of identity of these people.

5. See Sutton (1995) for a discussion of identities as different terms of identification. My use of "epistemic" refers to the different conceptual worlds that are associated with the use of specific languages as well as the specific contexts within which linguistic interaction takes place. Leigh (1991:34) develops this notion in her discussion of secondary schooling by arguing that the use of different languages demarcates distinct worlds—school and out-of school.

6. See Pemberton (1994b) and Errington (1997) for a discussion of this process as manifested in the logic of Taman Mini Indonesia Indah. See also Taylor (1994) for discussion of the *"nusantara* concept of culture" that is evident in the layout of Indonesian museums.

7. Zurbuchen cites the following statement from Chapter 18 of the "Third National Development Plan" (Repelita III): "Culture is closely tied to the national development now being implemented, because on the one hand development requires prerequisite cultural values that support development, while on the other hand development results in side effects whose resolution hopefully can be discovered by means of culture" (1990:133). As Zurbuchen points out, this view posits "culture as creating the conditions favorable for development and ironing out any difficulties arising along the way" (p. 133). Just as national culture needs to be created and nurtured, so too the conditions for national development need to be engineered to ensure success, through the government's nurturing of "harmonious patterns of culture that neither impede development nor destroy essential indigenous values" (p. 134).

8. Both Lindsay and Hughes-Freeland indicate the rationale behind combining the two in the one ministry. Lindsay writes: "Where societies stress an educative role for cultural forms (the arts, language, literature) this translates with ease to a national educative role for culture in forming national identity (including the fostering of a national language, for example). From building the person or building the kingdom, comes building the nation. Linking education and culture in a government ministry is a natural progression" (1995a:659). Similarly, Hughes-Freeland (1993) argues that culture *(kebudayaan)* in the ideology of nation building "is to bring order and civilization to the members of the many ethnic groups which comprise the Indonesian citizenry" (p. 89), so that in time "individual Indonesians [will] come to acquire the kind of selfhood, expectations, and aspirations which are regarded as the preconditions for development in New Order Indonesia" (p. 88).

9. This process has been well documented in the case of the popular dance form known as *tayuban*. For discussion of cases in Central Java see Widodo (1995) and Hughes-Freeland (1993); for East Java see Hefner (1987).

10. The problem with such an underlying rationale is that there already ex-

ists a preconceived idea of what is acceptable—a criterion that some performing arts traditions easily meet (for example, Balinese, Javanese, Sudanese [West Java]) while others need to be modified or revamped. "Still other arts show different qualities and impulses altogether," writes Yampolsky. "They celebrate wildness and irreverence, and encourage participants and spectators to let loose and be unruly. But these, performers quickly learn, are not characteristics that Depdikbud values. If an art form is to be approved by Depdikbud, it must disown such features and conform to the Depdikbud aesthetic" (Yampolsky 1995:712).

11. See, for instance, Acciaioli (1985). See also the references in note 13 for discussion of some of the ways in which local communities have responded to government intervention.

12. The term *"kampung"* can refer to a village as well as a district in an urban center. In cultural matters, the term is often employed in a disparaging way to refer to something that is rustic, uncouth, and unsophisticated.

13. For discussion of the responses of various ethnic groups to state intervention in their traditions see Acciaioli (1994), Aragon (1991–1992), Atkinson (1987), Brawn (1994), Forth (1994), Graham (1994), Guinness (1994), Hoskins (1987), Rodgers (1986, 1987), Sutton (1985a, 1985b, 1991), Tsing (1993, 1996), and Volkman (1984, 1987, 1990).

14. Even in the case of the stronger regional groups the situation is not straightforward, since it is often the cultural practices of urban elites that are regarded as the standard. See the work of Sutton (1991) and Hughes-Freeland (1993).

15. The former conservatories of music were known as Konservatori Karawitan (KOKAR). These secondary-level conservatories have now been replaced by Sekolah Menengah Karawitan/Kesenian Indonesia (SMKI), the "High School of Indonesian Music/Art." The present-day performing arts academies comprise Akademi Seni Tari Indonesia (ASTI), the "Academy of Indonesian Dance," in Bandung (West Java) and Akademi Seni Karawitan Indonesia (ASKI), the "Academy of Indonesian Music," in Padang Panjang (West Sumatra). The colleges comprise the tertiary-level STSI in Denpasar and Surakarta (Central Java), which replaced ASTI in the former and ASKI in the latter. The tertiary-level institute known as Institut Seni Indonesia (ISI) is located in Yogyakarta (Central Java). The focus of these institutions on either *karawitan* (indigenous musical forms that use a pentatonic scale) or *tari* (dance) is largely a matter of emphasis, as music, dance, and shadow puppetry have been taught by all. Use of the term *"seni"* (arts) in the titles of STSI and ISI encompasses a broad range including the visual, plastic, and dramatic arts as well as film and television.

16. See note 1 above.

17. The preamble to the decree that established ASTI explicitly emphasized its role in maintaining and developing a Balinese identity within the context of an Indonesian identity. By contrast, STSI's aims as expressed in the

early 1990s emphasize the creation and development of a national Indonesian identity without any mention of Bali.

18. Direktorat Jendral Kebudayaan.

19. Direktorat Jendral Perguruan Tinggi.

20. ASKI too was caught up in the restructuring of Depdikbud.

21. Jennifer Lindsay (pers. comm.).

22. Apart from a generally underdeveloped academic culture, other problems include lack of financial and material resources; excessive regulation, centralization, and bureaucratization; too many nonproductive staff members; lack of mobility for staff; and no effective social control or input from students. For detailed discussion of these issues see the papers by Harjono, Oey-Gardiner, Daroesman, and Nasoetion in Hill (1991). In the specific case of tertiary arts institutions, there is also the somewhat contradictory combination of bureaucracy and the arts: the former depends on control, order, rationalization, and centralization, while the latter relies on creativity, individual initiative, variety, and a degree of anarchy.

23. STSI's role in Bali is largely unchallenged as it is the only tertiary-level arts institution. Although a multitude of community-based performing groups, dance foundations, and various government agencies are involved in the performing arts, none has the prestige or resources of STSI. The recent establishment of the privately funded Agung Rai Museum of Art (ARMA) in Peliatan, however, may provide an alternative to STSI's dominance. ARMA has been active in sponsoring exhibitions and festivals featuring village-based practitioners.

24. The practice of having more than one instructor at a time is related to the fact that STSI has too many employees and insufficient work for them. This practice also ensures that if one teacher fails to turn up, there is a good chance that another will attend. See Oey-Gardiner (1991) and Harjono (1991) for discussion of this situation in other tertiary institutions.

25. Instructors frequently turned up late for class, left early, or even failed to attend at all. Moreover, the often large number of students militated against frequent repetition of the piece.

26. In Balinese, an actor-dancer is referred to as a *pragina* (or *juru igel*), a musician as a *juru gamel*, a shadow puppeteer as a *dalang*. The generic Indonesian term *"seniman,"* which refers to all artists and performers, has no Balinese equivalent.

27. Essentially the "leveling" effect of the system renders it unable to deal with such anomalies as the *seniman alam*. Since the incorporation of arts institutions into the national bureaucracy, all government servants in these institutions must possess formal qualifications equivalent to those held by members of other government departments. Since all teaching staff receive the same levels of pay and have to fulfill the same requirements for promotion, there is, in fact, little to differentiate members of STSI's teaching staff from nonteaching members.

28. Some village artists complained, for instance, that they had not received their honorarium. Others complained that it was not worth their while to travel all the way to Denpasar to teach at STSI—due to the expense involved, the time they would spend away from their own activities, and the feeling of not being valued once there.

29. The dictionary translation of the phrase is "obligatory (rural) social action internships for advanced university students," which although cumbersome does convey the intent of the program (Echols and Shadily 1989:300). The program is also quite distinct from other community service obligations *(pengabdian pada masyarakat)* that institutions are required to undertake.

30. This is not surprising inasmuch as some students might only know the STSI version. Moreover, they may be teaching to communities that have no dance or musical traditions of their own. The STSI style is often considered to be more prestigious and "up to date," particularly among younger community members, while the accompanying music is readily available on commercial cassette records. I am not aware of any official policy to popularize or disseminate the STSI style but would suggest, rather, that this occurs by default. As students might have learned a particular dance in a large group context, it is likely that they will, in turn, use that version to teach. The use of STSI versions also enables other people familiar with the style to take over the instruction. A major problem with STSI's KKN program is that students often feel that their assignment is to teach rather than to learn and assist. Students (and their teachers) easily fall into the role of being "experts" who are there to instruct. Consequently, without any sustained questioning of the philosophical basis underlying their intervention and its long-term effect on local practice, they may inadvertently work toward homogenizing existing diversity.

31. Requests for KKN from STSI can be made directly from a community or from the head of the regional *(kabupaten)* or provincial *(propinsi)* governments. The Community Outreach Center (Balai Pengabdian Masyarakat) at STSI determines the localities where, based on these requests and STSI's own needs, the program will be carried out. Generally there are more requests than can be met each year. Communities, however, can also request the assistance of staff members at any time. In such cases, staff members may spend a specified period assisting the community or else be available for assistance when required. It is this form of assistance that is most likely to result in the forging of long-term links.

32. For details about the murder case see the following reports that appeared in Bali's daily newspaper, the *Bali Post:* "Paranormal Dikerahkan Kades Abang Soongan Menghilang" (13 December 1991), "Mayatnya Ditemukan Terpotong Delapan" (15 February 1991), "Sepasang Suami-Istri Mengaku Membunuh" (18 February 1991), "Mahasiswi pun Menangis Potongan Mayat Ditemukan" (18 February 1991), and "Termasuk Pekerja Keras dan Ulet" (20 February 1991). The KKN program continued at Batur Tengah and finished with a closing ceremony on 15 February 1991. The major problem faced in

Batur Tengah was the general lack of interest. A member of the community who did participate in the program commented that the people of the area were just too busy making money to be concerned with such activities. This failure to inspire enthusiasm points to the folly of imposing a program from without that does not take into account local contexts. The Penelokan–Batur–Kintamani region, in this case, has never had the extensive performing arts tradition of the lowland areas; instead it has remained a stronghold of older ritual forms, most noticeably Gong Gede (an older-style gamelan ensemble) and Baris Gede (ceremonial Baris dance).

33. The following reports published in the *Bali Post* are critical of the entire program: "Kesan Jenuh terhadap KKN bukan Kesalahan Mahasiswa" (8 January 1991), "KKN: Apanya yang Salah?" (1 March 1991), "KKN Jenuh namun Perlu" (4 March 1991), "Dari Kampus Turun ke Kampung" (26 January 1997), "Komentar Tokoh Mahasiswa: Mendesak, Reorientasi KKN" (16 February 1997), "Prof. Dr. I. Wayan Bawa: Pelaksanaan KKN Ini Mubazir" (16 February 1997), and "Dr. IGN Gorda M.S.: Bukan Takut atau tidak, tetapi" (16 February 1997).

34. The lack of preparation seems to vary from year to year, depending on the individuals responsible for coordinating the program. The following newspaper reports in the *Bali Post* cite lack of preparation as the reason why Udayana University's permission to undertake KKN in 1996–1997 was canceled: "Gubenur Oka Tolak Usulan PR III Unud" (11 February 1997), "Soal Pembatalan KKN Mahasiswa Unud. Benarkah Ditunda karena Ditolak Gubenur?" (16 February 1997).

35. Prior to 1995, the examination was known as Ujian Seniman (Performer's Examination).

36. Music students are usually paired with a dance student. Consequently two students may be examined in one performance. As there are usually more dance than music students, not everyone is paired.

37. Of the three examinations I observed (1989–1990, 1990–1991, and the first round of 1994–1995), only six performances stood out each time as being of a high technical standard and combining traditional elements with new ones to produce, in effect, a piece that extends existing practice. The dominance of "tradition" in the performing arts cannot be underestimated. Modern theater groups and many promising choreographers, for example, face a considerable degree of audience indifference and, at times, antipathy toward their efforts.

38. Before the Sarjana Ilmu Seni degree was created, its predecessor reflected the candidate's specialization in a particular branch of the arts: Dance Artist (Seniman Seni Tari), Gamelan Artist (Seniman Seni Karawitan), and Shadow Puppet Artist (Seniman Seni Pedalangan). The Sarjana Ilmu Seni is the equivalent of the bachelor's degree awarded at Indonesian universities.

39. Sedana makes the following observation regarding his contemporaries: "What of the SMKI/STSI artist? After a degree has been earned, some grad-

uates take government positions, others become independent artists, and most try to do both. Who would not rather face a puppet screen at night than a desk in the morning? The dalang's social and religious responsibility and the higher compensation he enjoys become added incentives to choose performance over an office job. Although the graduates of formal training are few compared to the many village-trained dalang, a preliminary analysis of their current occupations is informative. Most graduates of pedalangan [shadow puppetry] at SMKI and STSI teach: one at elementary school, five at the high school level (three at SMKI itself), four at STSI. Two work at the government radio station (RRI). Only a handful are exclusively performing dalang" (1993:96).

40. Many of these students are often "tied" *(ikatan dinas)* to the institution before they graduate. They receive a degree of financial assistance while they complete their degrees and, after graduating, must serve *(mengabdi)* STSI in an honorary capacity until it is able to take them on as full-time staff members. This is one means by which STSI ensures their availability as future members of its teaching staff. It is also a way to establish patronage. Obligations to *seniman alam* are sometimes repaid by ensuring that their children are provided with employment.

41. In its thirty years of existence, the institution has had only three directors. The first was I Wayan Mertha Suteja (1967–1981)—one of a number of military appointments to government institutions during the early years of the New Order. Under current regulations, the position of director can be held for a maximum of two four-year terms. Bandem occupied the directorship of ASTI for the maximum of two terms, but the upgrading of the institution to STSI permitted his reappointment to the position for a further two terms. As the projected upgrading to an ISI did not occur by the end of his last term, he was ineligible to stand again. He has, however, been appointed to the directorship of ISI in Yogyakarta.

42. Tourism was previously combined in one ministry with post and telecommunications: Depparpostel (Departemen Pariwisata, Pos dan Telekomunikasi).

Chapter 9

The End of the World News: Articulating Television in Bali

Mark Hobart

A singular expression was being mooted about in Bali in the middle of 1997: *gumi suba wayah*, "the world is old." Slipped into conversations, it elicited responses from quiet recognition to enthusiastic endorsement. Balinese had not developed a genteel passion for geology; nor had they suddenly appreciated their past as a step from immature traditionality to the fulfillment of modernity.[1] The expression itself ("the world is old") is not new. It seems to have gained particular currency after the general elections in early 1997 because of people's sense of political stagnation. While the phrase mostly made sense in context, it is clearly *raos wayah* ("mature speech" or "indirect speech") as opposed to *raos nguda* ("immature speech"), where the reference is fully transparent. Because such idioms are much used by mature men and women when discussing complex or sensitive issues, the listener is required to be active, intelligent, and knowledgeable. One evening, therefore, I idly asked my Balinese companions the significance of this phrase. The ensuing discussion forms the substance of this chapter. "The world is old" turned out to be at once a diagnosis of the terminal, and irreversible, condition of society and a premonition of impending catastrophe. And television is deeply implicated.

Preamble

This chapter is about how Balinese engage with television in their lives and hence with the local, regional, and global, however vague or even incoherent we may find the referents of these terms. It would be wrong to categorize this study as simply one of "audience response." Such approaches reify media and divorce them from context. Moreover, such categories turn audiences into imaginary objects (Ang 1991; Hartley 1992a) whose workings are in principle fully determinate and determinable. As what audiences make of what they watch is arguably underdetermined, much work with audiences involves the multiple displacements of inferring the producers' intentions, imposing meanings upon programs, and imputing your reactions to others—steps that are even more questionable if you are working with people whose language, background, and viewing habits differ radically from your own. And finally, such categorizing abstracts what viewers may be thinking or feeling (or otherwise) from the circumstances under which they do so. In other words, I am interested in media such as television as *practices*. "Practice" has become a buzzword. Its main use these days is to supplement the palpable inadequacies of theory. By contrast I prefer to treat social life, following the later Michel Foucault, as practices (Hobart 1996). Apart from the untaxing activity of gawking at television programs, there are more active practices. Among these, notably, are commenting on, and theorizing, other practices—including watching television itself. Like other Indonesians, many Balinese I know both enjoy and are highly skilled at reflecting critically on what is happening about them in the world.

Before I turn to what was said, let me explain where I was, what I was doing, and who I was talking to that night. Since 1970, I have worked in a large settlement, known pseudonymously as Tengahpadang, in south central Bali. Once the settlement was a remote mountainous backwater, but today mass tourism and a boom in handicrafts have brought varying degrees of prosperity, the lure of wealth, new aspirations, and uncertainty. In 1980, so far as I know, no one in the village knew how to carve wood. By the late 1980s Tengahpadang was hailed in the guidebooks as "a traditional village of carvers." By then, apart from thirty or more daily tourist buses hurtling past the "art shops" that had sprung up, television had begun to have a major impact. More than 80 percent of Bali's theater companies (many casual or seasonal) disappeared during the 1980s as audiences demanded the best theater troupes on the island as seen on television. I have heard reflective Balinese argue that television has transformed life for the majority of people in Bali more than tourism and other, more ostensible, forms of modernization.

Almost every household in Tengahpadang now has at least one radio and a television set. Although poor families own black-and-white sets that receive only the state television channel (TVRI), more people now own color sets that can also receive five commercial channels and more than twelve satellite stations. (No one has yet bought a satellite dish in the settlement itself.) Such sets cost over half a million rupiahs at the time of writing ($200 or more) and the dishes more than a million ($500). Quite how the less-well-off pay for these luxuries is a question that exercises Balinese themselves. Much work—whether carving, sanding, and painting statues or making offerings and cooking—is compatible with watching, or at least listening to, television. Sets are increasingly turned on from morning to late at night.

My interest in television was aroused during a year's field research in 1988–1989 because people preferred to stay at home and watch television rather than drop in for a drink and a chat as they had in the past. When I could catch them, however, they would muse about television—

Figure 37. "Watching television while making offerings" cartoon by Surya Dharma.

a topic of immediate concern. My appreciation of the growing importance of mass media in Indonesia continued for some time in an equally contingent fashion. During the 1988–1989 field trip, a major topic of conversation involved the question of when a reputedly superb theater piece, performed and videotaped at the annual Bali Arts Festival, would be serialized on television. One day I dropped into the local station of TVRI to ask about this—only to discover that the tape had been recorded over because the station had neither the funds nor the facilities to store and preserve such broadcasts.

By a roundabout route, this problem led to a collaborative project—the Balinese Historical and Instructional Study Material Archive (BHISMA)—between the College of Performing Arts (STSI) in Bali and the School of Oriental and African Studies at the University of London, an arrangement that has been running continuously since 1990. Its purpose has been to record and transcribe television programs that Balinese themselves consider valuable as a record of their changing artistic and cultural activities. As Balinese come to define themselves self-consciously within Indonesia in terms of their "art" and "culture" (see Hough 1992; Picard 1990a, 1990b, 1996b; Chapters 1 and 8 in this volume), television has become an increasingly important medium.[2] My engagement, however, runs counter to the ideal of neutral scientific observers who remain aloof from (and have no effect on) the people they study. In running the BHISMA project, I am affecting both the object of study and the people who are caught up in it, even if how this actually works is less than clear. In any case, the "neutral observer" thesis always was a rather self-serving fantasy and singularly inappropriate to a postcolonial era. As John Hartley has remarked of media studies, it is far from evident what an objective account would look like—for scholars judge and intervene in the very nature of their activity, most certainly in media studies (1992b).

If we are untidily implicated in the lives of the people we work with and study, perhaps we should start by recognizing the inescapability of this implication. Not only does the family where I stay receive a significant part of its income from working for the project, for example, but my being there for at least two months each year over the last decade has altered in complex ways my relationship to the people I work with and (partly the same thing) my object of study. Visiting scholars remain in a world apart because they always can—and indeed do—disengage at will. How being engaged in people's lives affects the way I am treated and how I participate in discussions is hard for me to judge.

Obviously there are both drawbacks and advantages to knowing the people you work with for twenty years.

A key part of my research on television consists in working with a changing group of villagers whose main criterion of self-selection is that they like talking about the issues I am interested in and often do so among themselves when I am not there. Among the central figures are 'Gung 'Kak (Anak Agung Pekak), a well-known local actor who is related to the local court and still flourishing at ninety-one. His intellectual protagonist and spokesman is a former long-distance truck driver, ex-village headman, ex-hitman (occasionally my bodyguard), and part-time actor who, as his curriculum vitae suggests, is a man of many parts—the anthropologist's well-informed informant. These two were abetted by two close neighbors: a wealthy farmer (a devotee of shadow theater) and a poor flower seller (and wordsmith). Among the other regulars was the ex-headman's daughter-in-law, an actress-dancer who recently graduated with distinction from the College of Indonesian Performing Arts and the only one to have more than elementary school education. We meet after dinner, when the day's work is over. Separately I also work with three generations of women from one family: the young dancer just mentioned, her mother (who runs a small general grocery shop and was a fine singer in her day), and her grandmother, who still goes to market every day to trade in agricultural produce. How and where I work with them is determined by the demanding routine of women in Bali.[3] On the evening in question, just the old actor, the ex-headman, and the dancer had turned up.

If theatrical links seem to be a leitmotif, it is because, in this neck of the woods, actors tend to be the local intellectuals. (Priests are thought primarily fit for ceremonial matters.) Anthropology hinges more than most practitioners would like to admit upon engagement with local intellectuals and their practices. As a critical inquiry, however, ethnography involves its own distinctive interrogative and disciplinary practices. All too often the ethnographer produces a world peopled by subjects that are largely the products of these practices and bear precious little relation to the practices of the interlocutors. In Bali these practices are often highly dialogic and involve forms of complex agency (Hobart 1990, 1991). This is why I almost always work with groups of people. In the first instance, my interest is not how Balinese answer my questions but what kinds of questions they ask one another, what issues they consider important, how they talk and argue matters out, and when and why they agree or come to differ. When possible, only after

Figure 38. Satellite dish in a house among the rice fields. Photo: Richard Grant.

having a chance to reflect on what transpired, do I start to interrogate them to try to clarify the presuppositions they have made.

The End of the World News

On the evening of 3 July 1997, in the ex-headman's house after dinner, with a cassette recorder running, I asked what exactly was at issue when people said that the world was old. My question led to an animated conversation, lasting about an hour and a half. What follows are key passages, in translation, from these discussions. (The following night I returned to the theme and asked questions to which I turn later in the chapter.)[4]

EX-HEAD:	If you ask my opinion, if things carry on for a long time like this our grandchildren will be in difficulties if there isn't— what do you call it?
ACTOR:	Turmoil.
EX-HEAD:	Yes, that's it.
ACTOR:	If there isn't turmoil, so that everything starts afresh.
SELF:	What do you mean by "turmoil"?
EX-HEAD:	"Turmoil" means war.
ACTOR:	War.
SELF:	Could you explain a bit more? I haven't fully understood.
ACTOR:	It is everything turned upside down. Destruction.
DANCER:	Lots of people killed.
SELF:	But what's the use of a war?
EX-HEAD:	Its use is that everything starts all over again. After a fresh beginning things are ordered again. . . . You can't get, as you do now, people "buffaloing."
SELF:	What's "buffaloing"?
EX-HEAD:	It's a proverb: those who are already too big just get bigger.
ACTOR:	It's already too late.
EX-HEAD:	Ordinary people can do nothing.
ACTOR:	They can't lift a finger.
EX-HEAD:	For example, they're like tiny insects, they count for nothing. Even if I spoke up and said this or that, no one would pay any attention.
ACTOR:	They have no worth, those who are called "the poor." They are useless. No one believes them.
SELF:	Would the rich agree with you that it would be a good idea to have a war?
EX-HEAD:	Heavens, no. They'd be terrified.
DANCER:	They'd be frightened if there were a war.

ACTOR: They'd try to make sure that it wouldn't happen.

Ex-Head: Sure. The rich have never had it so good.

I then turned to an issue that various people had remarked on a year before: the overwhelming preponderance of programs and films celebrating the lifestyle of the wealthy. I asked why the lives of the poor were not shown much on television.[5]

ACTOR: As for the poor, they are of no use. The rich never think of actually talking with the poor. If possible, they keep as far away from them as they can—where the rich can talk among themselves about whatever. I don't think that the poor could succeed in speaking. Even if they did, as was said earlier, they are worth nothing, no one is listening.

EX-HEAD: They show the good life on television. They provide images of beautiful things, so that those without will strive for them. The only problem is that they can't succeed.

ACTOR: They haven't the wherewithal.

EX-HEAD: Yes, it's hard. Why? You can say . . . people these days, it's like advertisements. Why should government promote television the whole time and only broadcast what comes across as good? But what's bad is not, or is rarely, shown. I think you can say it's theory versus practice. The theory is fine. . . .

ACTOR: But the practice is a very far cry from that.

EX-HEAD: The practice is rotten. It is tantalizing the masses, goading them on, so that they will want to slave away.

ACTOR: So that they'll be joyful, for example, so that they will do what they're told is right.

EX-HEAD: Yes. But afterwards there is the practice, which is different. For example, consider people going on transmigration. They never show transmigrants starving. It's always people who . . .

ACTOR: Who are happy.

DANCER: "Successful"!

EX-HEAD: Just the ones who have made it. A lot of people have been duped that way.

They then turned to some of the "success stories" such as the growth of Indonesia's car manufacturing capacity and monumental projects.

EX-HEAD:	Now they keep on putting up these big buildings, don't they, 'Gung 'Kak? So that the masses feel good. Now if you ask me what do the masses get out of this, it's feeling—not what lies behind it. It's done like this so they feel happy. But the real good is for others. The feeling you get is sadness— you don't feel happy.
DANCER:	Those feelings are close. Now I feel happy if I get to watch television. I enjoy watching the programs. But the next day when you've got a kid who nags that he has got to have it just like on television, then you're sad again.

I then asked what they thought about the range of programs.

EX-HEAD:	If television is important, as it was just said to be, it is so that people don't think too much.
ACTOR:	About problems.
EX-HEAD:	About being angry. So they give you entertainment, don't they? You won't be confused and undecided. Watch television and very soon you'll stop feeling pissed off. Isn't that so, 'Gung 'Kak?
ACTOR:	That's how it's used.
EX-HEAD:	It's used to divert people's minds. So that they don't long for—so that they don't think about—anything else. So that you won't remember, you'll just forget yourself the whole time.

I then turned to a favorite theme in Bali: the "influence" *(pengaruh)* of television.[6]

SELF:	Can you oppose what's on television?
EX-HEAD:	As for opposing, there's no opportunity.
ACTOR:	You can't.
DANCER:	It's difficult.
ACTOR:	Because you can't . . . there is no opportunity to do so.
EX-HEAD:	What would you use?
ACTOR:	What would you use?
DANCER:	Against whom?

Ex-Head:	Whom am I going to oppose? That is why we beg for uproar now. I don't know who would bring it about. It would just explode . . . just be war.
Actor:	Apocalypse.
Ex-Head:	That's why there's no point in opposing.[7]
Actor:	I cannot oppose. Let me use an analogy.
Dancer:	It isn't that we can't succeed. We're reluctant.
Actor:	Reluctant? What's behind that is that we wouldn't succeed. It isn't reluctance. We'd fail. For example, suppose I translated my opposition into action. It would fail. Really, it's like preparing rice, isn't it? If you're going to cook, you winnow the paddy to get the hulled rice. But how do you get clean rice if the unhulled rice gathers into a pile?[8] Now, if it were just hulled rice, it would be easy. It would be fine for porridge. You could use it for cooking, couldn't you?
Self:	You can't oppose? Can you explain?
Ex-Head:	What's on television contains nothing to think about. It has no exemplary use. What can you emulate in it? There is nothing worth imitating. How do you set about opposing?
Actor:	You can't.
Ex-Head:	There are no ideas you can use to help formulate criticism. If people do evil, there is nothing upon which to build a counterargument.

A Few Universals

The analysis in the foregoing passages is remarkably subtle, sustained, and penetrating. It made me wonder what it is that academics add apart from codification, pontificating, polysyllables, and monologues. In anthropology at least, more theoretical sophistication is appropriated from their subjects than scholars care to admit.

From what little I know of media studies, what the commentators had to say echoes the approach favored by center-left academics. On one reading you might think the villagers had studied their media imperialism theory beforehand. We have a classic statement of the irreversible momentum and logic of capital with the reduction of most humans to units of labor: a class in, and not for, itself. This perspective is complemented by the bourgeoisie's fear of threats to its preeminence and the breakdown of reciprocal, or moral, relations between members of classes. Crucially the proletariat are alienated and silenced through the ideological use of mass media as opiates. Television emerges as the medium par excellence of domination—not least by depriving the masses of the means to criticize their fate. Finally there is the recognition of the impossibility of structural change without revolution. A less dogmatic interpretation might note that the main speakers are traditional intellectuals, whose former importance as opinion makers and the brains behind the premodern order has been irreversibly eroded by new species of organic intellectuals. New forms of good sense fit ill with traditional forms of common sense. By stressing the degree to which it relies on domination and ideological manipulation, such an interpretation might elaborate on the extent to which the commentators lament the loss of an earlier hegemonic order and question how far the new order (ironically the regime of President Suharto was known as the "New Order") manages to make itself hegemonic at all.

The problem with all such academic accounts is they apply so generally as to be uninformative. In most cases they tell us more about the preoccupations of their authors than those of their subjects. The former analysis rounds up all the usual suspects. Capital is organized and, like structure, is imbued with transcendental powers of agency and mind. Its metaphysics relies upon now-familiar dichotomies—traditional/modern, structure/ideology, determination/choice, matter/mind—as it does on the presumed superiority of the knower over the known. Contingency, indeterminacy, situatedness are articulated away. The central structures, forces, or agents are autonomous and self-determining. Such essentializing ignores the degree to which such entities are continually constituted by what is outside them (Laclau 1990a and 1996, after Derrida)—a problem that a great deal of time is spent denying through television.

A favored academic practice for dealing with indeterminacy and lack of closure is overinterpretation (Hobart in press). Were the commentators anticipating class revolution? Or, given Balinese penchant for reiterating what we might call Saivite-style thinking (Teeuw et al. 1969), were they trying out familiar eschatological presuppositions on new kinds of events? In fact, they did not use everyday Balinese expressions but Sanskrit and Kawi words replete with connotations.[9] In the term *"kali yuga,"* for example, translated as "apocalypse" in the last of the translated passages, *kali* is the final age *(yuga)* in which morality and order fall apart before destruction *(sengara)*—especially the periodic destruction of the universe at the end of a cycle of ages *(kalpa)* (Zoet-mulder 1982:1665).

Similarly, was the irreversibility of domination couched in the linear time of Euro-American (and Marxist) cosmology? Or was it part of a Balinese metaphysics of transformation *(matemahan)*? Earlier in the evening the commentators had described the process of differentiation as *rodan pedati,* "the turn of the cartwheel," by which what is up must go down and vice versa. Later they reviewed the reversal of family fortunes in the village over the last generations and concluded that cycles took about fifty years, spurred by disruptions such as the Dutch conquest, the Japanese occupation, or the coup in 1965. Contrary to determinate explanations (infrastructural, processual, or psychological), the commentators argued for *ganti,* "contingency."[10]

Fortunately this is not a problem—according to G. C. Spivak (1988). The subaltern cannot speak because of the constraints on her discursive positioning—a point the Balinese commentators argued on almost diametrically opposed grounds.[11] In fact it was precisely the a priori dismissal of anything they might say, without bothering to listen to it first, that exercised them. What the commentators had to say challenges elite claims to epistemic superiority, especially when this elite refuses to engage with those it purports to speak of (an example itself of denying the constitutive outside). In fact the villagers' stress on contingency, disjuncture, and antagonism is more theoretically subtle than the approaches that purport to explain them. Not only are these approaches antagonistic to other kinds of practices, they are condemned largely to ignore them. The old actor's remark about the rich not thinking about actually talking to the poor was not just an observation of social mores. As he noted later, it is a determination *not* to inquire, *not* to know. Fundamentally it is the denial of the dialogic nature of social life. The old actor was engaging in a philosophical critique of the nature of society and knowledge. Similarly the reference to images of beautiful things presupposes an acquaintance with Balinese ideas about how desire is fomented and how it must be disciplined if humans are to achieve a measure of agency and not become totally subject to others and their own appetites,[12] exemplified, for instance, in the widespread sale of productive land to purchase consumer goods, such as television sets, in Bali.

It is against this background that the repeated statements about the worthlessness of the poor make sense. As the old actor remarked: even rubbish can be burned as firewood. In earlier political formations, you might be politically insignificant subjects *(panjak, kaula, semut barak)*, but that did not encompass your other skills, abilities, or intelligence. The refusal to listen to others—and therefore recognize and engage them—is far more serious than treating people as mere labor power (something Balinese have been familiar with for a long time). It is to treat people not as agents or even subjects, but as objects. Television epitomizes the mutual disenchantment. People do not believe what the elite tell them, nor do the elite believe it themselves. It is mere manipulation.

Let me give two brief examples of the subtlety of the discussion. The ex-village head remarked that the only thing the masses get from grand projects is "a good feeling." The word he uses for this is *"suksema,"* one of the hardest words to gloss, even in Balinese. It connotes "subtle," "immaterial," "refined," and hence the feeling of accomplishing or being offered something good. It is deliberately ambiguous *(ngempelin)*. If listeners wish to infer material advantage, that is up to them. The reference is slightly veiled *(makulit)*. Indeed it is an exercise in mature speech *(raos wayah)*, which the undiscriminating listener or reader, like our imaginary leftish media studies' expert, takes as it appears instead of rethinking it critically. Remember the ex-village head's complaint about television programs: there is nothing to think about, or with.

Another point worth noting is the complexity of the subject position from which the older commentators speak. There is a refusal to unify, center, or essentialize oneself as an enunciating "subject" or universalize this into objective class interests. (The "you" I have inserted into the translation to avoid clumsiness was as absent as were references to "we" or "I" except as illocutionary modifiers.) There is an ironic distance by which the subject starts to elide with the object of its own knowledge. Clearly this is not a disavowal. Before using these extracts, I showed them to the commentators. They were rather pleased at what I had chosen. I asked if they felt the words were harsh or could be construed as deprecatory *(nyacadin)*. The ex-village head replied that things were so. It was not a matter of personal opinion. As he truly felt this to be the case, the words could not be deprecatory. Balinese categories of truth and slander are as distinctive as they are widely ignored by scholars.

Subjects or Agents?

A crucial section comes at the end of the last passage of the conversation. The ex-village head criticized much television programming because there was nothing to emulate. Then he added: "How do you set about opposing?" Without much twisting and turning, this is not a world that is appreciable only through the categories and mental processes of a universalizable knowing subject whether unified or split—the ghost in the television. Without something on which someone else has already started work, you cannot think or act. In emulating it, you change yourself. What you think, what you think with, and what you think about are not predetermined but the result of endless engagement. If you are flung into a world in which people do evil, you need the means—the thinking of others before you—to enable you to think at all, let alone be able to convey the results of your thinking.

In short, the commentators spoke of themselves as agents, or as victims, not as subjects. That is, they stressed action, its responsibilities and consequences, where you may command, go along with, or have action inflicted on you. They avoided talking about a pure consciousness as the source or object of actions, which transcended actions and events. Yet at the same time the commentators also presented people like themselves as subject to economic, political, and social forces over which they have little command. There is more at stake here than the ambiguity in the word "subject." (See Henriques et al. 1984:3; Williams 1983:308–312.)

To address this issue obliges me to refer to a series of discussions about television I held with another group of people three years ago (outlined in Hobart n.d.). The drift of the argument was that watching television is like standing near a water spout at a bathing place: you get whatever is about. (The term used was *"kena,"* to be the recipient of someone else's actions.) This may be for good or ill, but it affects who you become. (The law of *karma pala,* the effects of actions, being general, you are the products of your actions and what is done to you.) If you are not to be swept along passively, you have to be disciplined *(tegeg)* and learn from past example how to avoid what is bad and exercise self-restraint. This is no spartan or puritan code. I found Balinese open about their sexual arousal over attractive actors and actresses on television. Humans, after all, are comprised of antagonistic drives and dispositions *(triguna, triwarga),* not harmonious wholes.

I found it particularly interesting how people would talk of different kinds and degrees of engagement with television. These tended to a rough order: each stage commonly being a necessary, but by no means sufficient, condition for the next. First, you know something (for example, the news). You might also enjoy it *(seneng).* Most engagement

Figure 39. "Farmer watching McGyver" cartoon by Surya Dharma.

with television stops there. Sometimes, though, you feel for the characters or find yourself gripped by your own feelings *(marasa)*. Only
then are you likely to understand or appreciate what is at issue. The
word is *"ngaresep"*—at once active and passive, "to penetrate or infil-
trate into" and "to be penetrated or infiltrated." To appreciate is not
only to be changed, but to change. Finally, you may decide to act upon
(nelebang) whatever is the outcome for you. In practice, of course,
these distinctions are deployed more flexibly than a bald list suggests.
Media theorists tend to put much emphasis on television news as a
hegemonic device. (See, for example, Fiske 1989:289–308.) Not only
is the sort of knowledge involved superficial on this account, but most
Balinese are deeply skeptical about its accuracy. The relationship pre-
supposed between persons and images (indeed the lived world as a
whole) seems quite different from some media theorists' emphasis on
"identification" as the essential mode of mediation. It is also more
complicated and more subtle than the idea that viewers implicate and
extricate themselves at will (Fiske 1989:174–190) or the notion of
simple degrees of engagement and emulation (Smith 1995).[13]

It is at this point that television viewing practices in rural Bali begin
to have wider implications. One of the serious intellectual battles of
the twentieth century is over the nature of the human subject and its

epistemological implications. It is hard to imagine what media studies would look like without some more—or less—coherent set of presuppositions about the subject. What would link production with purpose, programs with meaning, images with content, or define viewing? An account of the subject has in effect to be universal (ahistorical and acultural) and a priori—and hence the plaything of ethnocentric fantasy. This seems to be one of the most vexed issues facing critical media studies. Such approaches are caught, as Foucault (1970) pointed out, in the circularity common to the human sciences of being both its own subject and object (see Habermas 1987).[14] An analysis of how people appreciate television in Bali offers a radical solution. It is not simply the familiar anthropological move of decentering the Western subject by positing another. It is to dispense with the subject entirely.

The Balinese commentators, however, worked with quite different presuppositions. First, the knower is neither superior to, nor radically ontologically different from, the known. Humans are the products of past practices: both what has been done to them and what they do. Television, as a major source of representations, is therefore important.[15] As people are continually interacting with their environment, notably other humans, often in groups, it makes little sense to postulate an atomized subject—whether as presocial homunculus, unitary consciousness, or fractured ideal state.[16] It follows that humans are not the only, or even the most important, agents (see Hobart 1990). In fact, the stress on agency in academic writings instantiates an elitist bias: most humans and groups spend more time being at least partly instruments or subjects of the decisions and actions of others—a point that the commentators elaborated at length. An analysis of television viewing is therefore as much an account of patiency as of agency.[17]

But are there no differences between what Balinese had to say about television in July 1997 and three years previously? The earlier comments seemed less pessimistic about the scope for agency or, perhaps better, active patiency: you could not by and large determine broadcasting schedules or content—although, in their own way, people like the young dancer (who has featured in various broadcasts as dancer, singer, and translator) did—but you could affect how they impacted on you, your family, and friends. The later account resonated more of abject patiency and objectivation. While they had a strong sense of the limits of their capacity to be heard, the commentators were aware in varying degree that their arguments reached a wider audience through me and were interested to see what I had selected for this chapter.

The next night I switched to direct interrogation about the differences in the two accounts. While this is one phase of anthropological inquiry, it runs the familiar risk of presuming the commentators to be unitary subjects, striving accurately to represent a stable world, independent of the circumstances of the questioning—precisely the abstraction the commentators challenged as theory divorced from practice. The differences turned out to be in large part situational: they depended on what had been discussed earlier and what was going on in society at large.

Can you avoid the "influence" of television? Yes, if you do not simply believe what you hear and see.[18] If you have begun to feel *(marasa, that precedes intellection)*, you can avoid ill effects—just as if you warn a child and it is sensitive to what you say, it will pay heed. Does that not contradict the hopelessness of opposition? No, you can oppose in your thoughts and feelings. But if whatever you are opposing does not know about it, the effects are rather limited! Like a grasshopper in a matchbox, it makes a lot of noise but does not achieve much.

What about advertisements? You can oppose them by not buying the product. It is much easier to oppose commercial companies than government, because the latter imposes law. If you fall for the blandishments of advertisers, it is your own fault. But doesn't the effectiveness of television wear off with time? The commentators agreed it was largely entertainment. What required lengthy discussion was the relationship of two contrary, and partly irreconcilable, ways in which Balinese talk about television. On the one hand, television cannot be all that important in the end because it is just an image *(lawat)*. On the other, its effects depend on the quality of thought behind the presentation and what you can make of it.

But surely refusing to engage—just enjoying—is a form of opposition? This question drew laughter. Of course it is. Television is like a parent telling off a child. The child just keeps quiet. What can you do? Turning off the set or switching channels is a form of opposition. Most people turn off both local and national news (Berita Daerah and Berita Nasional). If you want to find out what is actually going on, it is better to rely on the world news broadcasts (Dunia Dalam Berita) because the foreign news reports are likely to dissimulate less. With much hilarity, my companions started recounting recent occasions when they had switched off the TV during speeches by senior government figures.[19] By contrast, during the Gulf War and before the Indonesian general election, people had watched eagerly, trying to discern what was really going on.

Why then, I asked, was the tone of their account so different from the way they had talked three years ago? It is because nothing has changed for a long time. Like a new kind of food, at first it is great fun. But if you eat the same thing day in day out for years, you grow sick of it. After a long period of no change, without any explosion of activity *(makebiahan)* to follow, people conclude that what they are told is worthless *(tanpa guna)*. I suggested, therefore, that an implicit symmetry emerges: the rich and powerful consider what ordinary people have to say of no interest, while ordinary people dismiss what their leaders say as of no value. They agreed this was so.

Finally, the old actor made a passing remark that led to me intervene more directly. He noted that in the past, people had firmly believed their leaders *("Bapak kapracayain pisan dumun")*. I almost missed it, but the word they had used before for "believe" was *"ngega,"* not *"pracaya."* *"Ngega"* (*"ngugu"* in Low Balinese) implies both different truth conditions and an emotive relationship to the speaker's statement (Hobart 1985). *"Ngega"* suggests that speakers have demonstrable evidence for what they assert; *"pracaya"* implies something closer to an act of blind faith. In other words, the commentators were saying no one believed the poor, even though what they said was demonstrably true, but previously they had faith in their leaders.

I asked if television had reduced people's trust in their leaders now that they were visible and the relationship of their words and deeds could be monitored. Could it be, I suggested, that earlier leaders had been more like the gods: powerful yet remote? The old actor was particularly delighted with the analogy. Of course. "If Divinity were manifest, you would believe in It much less. If you can't encounter It, you believe that much more fervently."[20] Perhaps de-deifying their leaders has been one of television's most perduring effects in Bali.

Appendix: Transcripts of Commentaries

EX-HEAD: Yèn puniki yèn nah kamanah antuk tiang, mangkin sampun asapuniki kawèntenané. Yèn ngararis suwé-suwé asapuniki niki sakadi nah wènten cucu-cucu kènten jeg mèweh malih pidan.

SELF: Mmm.

EX-HEAD: Yèn 'ten puniki wènten sakadi napi wastané.

ACTOR: Wènten kali?

EX-HEAD: Enggih. Kènten.

ACTOR:	Yèn 'ten minab wènten kali mangda ngawit malih kawèntenané.
SELF:	Yèning ngaraos wènten kali. Napi kali?
EX-HEAD:	Kali punika yuda.
ACTOR:	Yuda.
SELF:	Dados nerangang malih akidik. Dèrèng ngaresep!
EX-HEAD:	Yèn kali punika nika yuda punika kènten.
ACTOR:	Kali sengaran jagat.
DANCER:	'Ten, akèh padem jatma kènten.
SELF:	Napi gunané wènten yuda?
EX-HEAD:	Yèn niki gunané wènten yuda puniki 'ten mangda napi wastané wènten pangawit malih.
SELF:	Nah.
EX-HEAD:	Enggih kènten. Yèn sampun wènten pangawit derika 'ten, madabdab malih. Nènten maresidang sakadi mangkin niki nah napi wastané nah sakadi anak makebo-keboan.
ACTOR:	Manuju-nujuan.
EX-HEAD:	Makebo-keboan artiné kènten. Niki.
SELF:	Napi makebo-keboan?
EX-HEAD:	Niki sasenggak makebo-keboan.
SELF:	Enggih.
EX-HEAD:	Ané kadung ageng jeg ageng.
ACTOR:	Ané kadunga.
EX-HEAD:	Alit jeg 'ten maresidang napi kènten.
ACTOR:	'Ten maresidang makikiganga . . .
EX-HEAD:	Nah yèn mangkin upaminipun. Yèn raosang puniki yèn nah rerehang wimba puniki rumasat jeg bebaosang gumatat-gumitit sané nènten maji kènten. Yadian puniki tiang ngaraos asapuniki-asapunika 'ten wènten anak rungu.
ACTOR:	'Ten.
SELF:	Sapunapi? Enggih.
ACTOR:	'Ten wènten guna ané bebaosan Sang Tiwas 'ten wènten gunané.
EX-HEAD:	'Ten wènten anak ngega.
ACTOR:	'Ten wènten anak ngega.

SELF:	Sapunapi Sang Sugih minab cocok ring baos Ktut, becik wènten yuda?
EX-HEAD:	Bih! 'Ten.
ACTOR:	'Ten.
DANCER:	'Ten.
EX-HEAD:	Jejeh.
DANCER:	Jejeh yèn anak sugih wènten yuda.
ACTOR:	Yèn anak sugih mangda makta jalan mangda nènten wènten.
EX-HEAD:	Enggih Sang Sugih niki paling becik mangkin kawèntenané kènten.

✹   ✹   ✹

ACTOR:	Yèn anak tiwas-tiwas anak 'ten wènten gunana. 'Ten wènten anak ngaraosang jagi mabebaosang ring Sang Tiwas Sang Sugih punika. Yèn dados antuk ipun mangda maedohan pisan, mangda niki sareng-sareng sané sugih-sugih mabebaosang sapuniki-sapunika. Sang Tiwas 'ten ja wènten nyidang ngaraos napi-napi yèn tiang ngamanahin. Yadian ngaraos kadi raosé wawu nènten maguna nènten wènten anak rungu . . .
EX-HEAD:	Sampun sané becik-becik sané sugih-sugih kènten èdèngang ring télévisiné, 'ten? Nyontohin niki mangda sané 'ten anu, mangda maresidang asapunika, 'ten kènten?
ACTOR:	Nah ento enyak kemu lakua.
EX-HEAD:	Enggih. Kuwanten niki maresidangé 'ten lakar anu.
ACTOR:	'Ten mampu.
EX-HEAD:	Enggih mèweh. Ngudiang? Anak cara mangkiné dados raosang puniki nah sakadi réklame 'ten kènten. Nah niki sampun napi mawinan puniki sakéng pemerintah puniki ngawèntenang télévisi puniki, ngararis puniki nah nyiarang puniki sané becik-becik kuwanten? Yèn sané kaon-kaon punika nènten, arang pisan kaèdèngang. . . . Yèn niki sampun minab nah maresidang ngaraosang puniki niki téori ring praktèk 'ten kènten. Enggih niki téorié puniki becik ja kènten.
ACTOR:	Praktèkné ejoh pesan.
EX-HEAD:	Praktèké puniki sané kaon 'ten kèntena. . . . Puniki sakadi

ngèdèngang sakadi nudut pikayun I Para Panjak puniki mangda enyak saat makarya 'ten kènten.

ACTOR: Kèto.

EX-HEAD: Èdèngin mangkin sané becik-becik iya 'ten enyak edot kènten.

ACTOR: Apang enyak iya girang, apang enyak iya upaminé malaksana ané madan saja.

EX-HEAD: Enggih. Kuwanten disampun praktèké nika tios 'ten kènten. . . . Upaminipun nah sakadi niki rerehang mangkin sakadi anak transmigrasi kènten. 'Ten naenin puniki anak sané jeg makenta niki ring transmigrasi puniki kaèdèngang. Jeg ngararis sampun anak sané. . . .

ACTOR: Suka.

DANCER: Suksés.

EX-HEAD: Sampun berhasil nika makanten. . . . Nika akèh anak nguluk-nguluk asapunika.

*   *   *

EX-HEAD: Jani lantasang gaénang wewangunang gedé-gedé 'ten kèntena 'Gung 'Kak. Apang I Rakyaté totoa artiné maan rasa ento kènten. Yèn niki I Para Panjak puniki sané kakeni-ang puniki yèn kamanah antuk titiang puniki rasa, nènten kasukseman kènten. . . . Mangkin kakaryanin asapuniki-asa-punika marasa seneng. Sakéwanten kasuksemané anak tios kènten. . . . Rasa jeg polih rasa sebet punika, 'ten ja polih rasa lianga kènten.

DANCER: Madampingan artiné. Jani iraga demen rasa liang maan ma-balih télévisi, demen hatié nepukin siaran. Suba kèto buin mani enyak ada panak nagih lantesang meli kèto cara di TVé, buin sebet.

*   *   *

EX-HEAD: Yèn télévisi puniki utama ja naler puniki sakadi nah kènten sampun sakadi baosé wawu puniki. Mangda nènten bes banget pikayuné.

ACTOR: Kaméwehan.

EX-HEAD: Gedeg. Niki kaicèn hiburan 'ten asapunika. Niki 'ten akèh, ah!, jeg inguh kenehé sing karuan-karuan, mabalih TV endèn ajahan apang enyak hilang pedih basangé. 'Ten kènten 'Gung 'Kak.

ACTOR: Nah! Ento suba anggona anu.

Ex-Head: Nah! Anggianga panyelimur pikayun ento kènten. Mangda nènten kayun, nènten kantun mikayunin, indik sané tiostiosan. Mangda jeg engsap lantesang ring raga lantesang.

✻ ✻ ✻

SELF: Maresidang ngalawan punika sané munggah ring télévisi?

EX-HEAD: Bèh! Yèn indik ngalawané nika, nika sampun 'ten wènten galah.

ACTOR: 'Ten nyidang.

DANCER: Mèweh.

ACTOR: Sahantukan 'ten nyidangé, 'ten wènten galah pacang iraga.

EX-HEAD: Napi anggiang?

ACTOR: Napi anggiang?

DANCER: Ring sira?

EX-HEAD: Ring sira tiang puniki pacang ngalawan? Mawinan puniki wènten pinunas puniki mangda jeg wènten kali sen niki kènten. Yèn sampun wènten kali puniki 'ten sira sané ngeranang nika 'ten uningin. Sampun jeg plug jeg iyeg kènten.

ACTOR: Kaliyuga.

EX-HEAD: Nika kohné ngalawan.

ACTOR: Ngalawané iraga sing suba nyidang. Nah, jani anggon pratiwimba, sing kèto?

DANCER: Sing ja sing nyidang. Ngakoh.

ACTOR: Ngakoh. Pokokné api anu sing suba lakar nyidang. Sing ja ngakoh. Jeg sing nyidang api bakal iraga malaksana upaminé lakar ngalawan, sing nyidang. Cendekné cara anaké anu cara baasé, sing kèto? Ané lakar jakan. Jani indangin ditu baasé ento alih jijih-jijihné. Amun apa ada jijih yèn onyang punduhang ento jijihné. Jani, yèn suba dadi baas yèn baas lonto abesik, sing èlah suba. Patut anggon bubuh—anggon jakan, sing kèto?

SELF: 'Ten maresidang ngalawan? Dados nerangang punika.

EX-HEAD: Nah, 'ten madaging pitutur—'ten madaging pangelèmèk. Napi sané pacang tulad punika? 'Ten wènten punika sané pacang tulad. 'Ten maresidang ngalawan napi.

Actor: Sing nyidang.

Ex-Head: 'Ten wènten lawat-lawat anggiang pacang anggiang ngalawan. Yèn anak sané makarya corah sapuniki antuk ngalawan 'ten wènten.

Notes

1. Like many other Indonesians, Balinese are struggling to articulate contemporary economic and social transformations, using the imagery and vocabulary of the modern and modernity in distinctive ways (Vickers 1996b).

2. The project is run jointly with Professor Made Bandem, until 1997 director of STSI (Indonesian College of Performing Arts, Denpasar), and in collaboration with the Center for Documentation of Balinese Culture and the Faculty of Arts, Udayana University, Bali. Today we have over 1,500 hours of high-quality broadcasts recorded on S-VHS tape in a small, special dehumidified studio built in Tengahpadang. In recognition of its educational importance, Indonesian State Television has granted us permission to digitize and reproduce the collection's materials for research and teaching purposes. I am grateful to the British Academy Committee for Southeast Asian Studies and to SOAS for providing much of the funding for this project between 1990 and 1995 and to Felicia Hughes-Freeland, University College, Swansea, and Alan Bicker and John Bousfield, University of Kent at Canterbury, for their help and support at different stages of the project.

3. The ex-headman's son (that is, the dancer's husband), a high school teacher, is the main person employed by the project to record and transcribe broadcasts, although both the ex-headman and the dancer have been paid at various times to oversee the project and help with transcription of theatrical terms and idioms. One could argue that the people present that evening were not typical; that, despite the young woman's presence, this was about elderly males ideologizing; that my presence and the fact that they knew me well and were responding to what they thought I expected of them made them articulate in a way they would not otherwise have done. There is obviously something in these observations from sociology of knowledge. Reducing people to functions of their subject positions, however, is a familiar form of essentializing and determinism: treating them as producers of behavior to be explained and not as thinkers in their own right. Over the last three years in different parts of Bali, I have heard almost all the points made by the discussants being

put forward to me or to others by women and men of different ages and social backgrounds.

4. I have tidied up the text in two important respects. First, I have extrapolated sections from the discussion (breaks are indicated by asterisks in the appendix). Second, such conversations are so dialogic that they are hard to read. In the English I have omitted many interjections, reiterations by other people, and so on. They remain in the Balinese original in the appendix.

5. The poor appear, of course, in television in stereotyped roles, as caricatures rather than characters (reminiscent of Stuart Hall's remarks (1990) about the roles permitted to blacks in Britain and America).

6. I put the word in quotes for two reasons. First, it is an Indonesian word that is often used to split off Indonesian "influence" as bad. Second, in English the word is a fudge: it conveniently bypasses the need to think critically about the relationship in question.

7. The expression *"ngakoh"* is poignant. It suggests the pointlessness of doing anything. At the Third International Balinese Studies Workshop held in Sydney in 1995, Anak Agung Gede Santikarma delivered a paper entitled "Koh ngomong" ("What's the Point in Saying Anything?")—which is now, as people pointed out to me with delight, the name painted on the side of a local bus in Bali.

8. What can decent people do if scum are on top? There is a further implied image that harks back to the previous theme. The broken grains that move centrifugally outward are little valued and thrown to chickens for fodder. That is the fate of ordinary decent people these days.

9. "Kawi" is a Balinese term that designates various distinct but interrelated literary idioms.

10. So much for Lévi-Strauss' thesis (1966) of premodern thought as overdeterministic. How are we to decide between interpretations?

11. If one looks at Spivak's practice, not her tendentious theoretical claims (see Ram 1993), a quite different picture emerges. Her analysis of Indian Hindu *sati* is embarrassingly simple-minded and ill informed. Happily "the subaltern" is a sufficiently elastic category, in Spivak's hands, to eliminate anyone who might disagree. Interestingly, the actor and ex-headman in Tengahpadang could be viewed as subalterns if you make a rather different reading of Gramsci's distinction between the masses and subalterns, whose task precisely is to articulate the hegemony of the dominant group to the masses.

12. If Foucault thought it necessary to devote two volumes of *The History of Sexuality* (1978) to exploring radical discursive differences in earlier European eras, perhaps we should not unthinkingly impose our own commonsense ideas on others' good sense.

13. There is now a vast academic suturing industry, driven especially by an idealist union of textual studies with idiosyncratic readings of Lacan, which is in the business of textualizing action and universalizing the imaginary viewer. The questions—"what is all this effort attempting to articulate?" or, less often

considered, "what is being disarticulated here?"—are far more interesting than the results of their theorizings.

14. Any knowledge about the human subject presupposes the subject who does the knowing, with the same subject reappearing as both judge and limiting condition.

15. But less important than lived events, according to most Balinese I have talked to.

16. Henriques et al. (1984) provide an excellent critique of the first two options and their variants. I do not know of a really good critique of the Lacanian recension of the subject. Williamson (1992) is useful on the narrative teleology of the Lacanian account. Fink, as a Lacanian analyst, undermines much of the a priorism of grand theorizing using extrapolations from selected texts of Lacan as the springboard to universalistic claims (1995). He points out that theory in psychoanalysis is an aid to, and revisable through, therapeutic practice.

17. The words "patient" and "patiency," borrowed from Collingwood (1942), have an unfamiliar ring to modern ears. They have the advantage, however, of being part of the vocabulary of action and avoid the massive ambiguities of the term "subject" in English (see Williams 1983).

18. A point that runs counter to Eipper's somewhat Ricoeurian appeal for trust in authority to counter the hermeneutics of suspicion (1996). The commentators have, I think, adequately addressed such arguments.

19. Because commercial channels are required to broadcast simultaneously the news put out by state television, which is part of the Indonesian Ministry of Information, you cannot simply switch channels, but must either put up with it or turn the set off. That the families I know tend to leave the set on during Muslim or Christian religious broadcasts, but either switch the news off or the sound down, may be more informative than the news itself.

20. "Yen nyidang manggihin Batara, kapracayaan kirang. Yen sing tepuk, kerengan kapracayaan."

Glossary

ABRI Angkatan Bersenjata Republik Indonesia; the Indonesian Armed Forces.

adat Tradition; local customary law and institutions.

agama Religion; in contemporary Indonesia the term is officially restricted to those religions claiming to be monotheistic and universalist.

Agama Bali Hindu The "Hindu Balinese religion"; the name of Balinese religion promoted by the periodical *Surya Kanta*.

Agama Hindu Bali The "Balinese Hindu religion"; the name of Balinese religion defended by the periodical *Bali Adnjana*.

anak jaba "People outside"; Sudra or commoners as opposed to the *triwangsa*.

ASKI Akademi Seni Karawitan Indonesia; the Academy of Indonesian Music.

ASTI Akademi Seni Tari Indonesia; the Academy of Indonesian Dance, founded in Denpasar in 1967.

ATBM Alat Tenun Bukan Mesin; a treadle loom (the term is Indonesian).

babad Historical/genealogical text.

Bali Adnjana Periodical published in Singaraja between 1924 and 1930 by the Santi organization; it became the mouthpiece of the aristocrats after the establishment of *Surya Kanta*.

Bali Aga See Wong Bali Aga.

banjar Residential village ward.

Baris Male warrior dance.

barong Term for a range of large masks, often in dragon, lion, or human form, animated by spiritual beings.

batik Cloth printed by applying wax in a desired pattern to seal it from the dye.

Bhawanagara Periodical published in Singaraja between 1931 and

291

1935 by the Kirtya Liefrinck-Van der Tuuk, a Dutch foundation dedicated to the preservation of traditional Balinese literature.

BHISMA   Balinese Historical and Instructional Study Material Archive.

Bhujangga Waisnawa   A prominent *jaba* clan.

bisama   Sacred ancestral message; religious stipulation of PHDI having moral force for Hindus.

BNR   Bali Nirwana Resort.

bos   Boss.

BPPLA   Badan Pelaksana Pembina Lembaga Adat; Agency for the Development of Customary Institutions.

budaya; kebudayaan   Culture; *kebudayaan* is a neologism of Sanskrit origin whose root *(budaya)* pointed to the development of a person's reason or character before taking on the meaning of "culture."

cagcag   Traditional backstrap loom.

camat   District head.

cokorda   Title of the aristocratic Satria Dalem clan, the highest Satria grouping.

dalang   Shadow puppeteer.

Depdikbud   Departemen Pendidikan dan Kebudayaan; the Department of Education and Culture.

desa   Village; customary *(desa adat)* or administrative *(desa dinas)* unit.

Dikti   Direktorat Jenderal Perguruan Tinggi; the Directorate General of Higher Education.

dinas   Service, official, agency; from the Dutch *dienst,* "service."

Djatajoe   Periodical published in Singaraja between 1936 and 1941 by the Bali Darma Laksana organization.

DPRD   Dewan Perwakilan Rakyat Daerah; the Provincial House of Representatives.

dwifungsi   "Dual function" (of the army) in civil and military action.

dwijati   "Twice-born"; refers to a *sulinggih* priest.

endek   Single-weft *ikat* made on treadle looms.

FCHI   Forum Cendekiawan Hindu Indonesia; the Indonesian Hindu Intellectuals Forum, established in Jakarta in 1991.

FMHB   Forum Mahasiswa Hindu Bali; the Forum of Balinese Hindu Students.

Galungan-Kuningan   Main festive period in the Balinese calendar.

Gambuh   Classical dance-drama.

Golkar   Golongan Karya; the government's Functional Groups party.

GWK   Garuda Wisnu Kencana; the "Golden Garuda Monument" project.

hukum   Law; religious (Muslim) law as opposed to customary law (*adat*).

hukum adat   "Customary law"; Indonesian rendering of the Dutch word *"adatrecht"*; the etymology of these two words originally placed them in opposition to each other.

ICMI   Ikatan Cendekiawan Muslim Indonesia; the Indonesian Muslim Intellectuals Association, established in 1990.

ikat   Cloth made using a tie-dye technique.

ISI   Institut Seni Indonesia; the Institute of Indonesian Arts.

jaba   See *anak jaba*.

kabupaten   Regency; administrative division of a province.

kamben   Wraparound cloth worn by both men and women.

kamben bek   Two half-pieces of cloth, with gold supplementary-weft thread running the full length, which are sewn together to make a wraparound.

Kebalian   "Balineseness"; the Balinese cultural, ethnic, and religious identity.

Kebangkitan Hindu   "Hindu Awakening"; refers to the recent upsurge in Hinduism evinced by the Balinese intelligentsia faced with the growing assertiveness of Islam in Indonesia.

kebiar   A style of dance and accompanying gamelan music.

kebudayaan daerah   "Regional culture"; the acknowledged cultural manifestations deemed representative of a province and expected to contribute to the building of the national Indonesian culture; see also *budaya*.

kerajaan   Kingdom; the domain controlled by a palace.

kesaktian   Invisible spiritual power or efficacy.

keterbukaan   "Openness"; a phrase used since 1989 to refer to a more liberal climate of political expression.

KKN   Kuliah Kerja Nyata; compulsory community service internship for tertiary students in Indonesia.

KODAM   Komando Daerah Militer; Regional Military Command. The chief commander is called Panglima KODAM.

KOKAR Konservatori Karawitan; the Conservatory of Traditional Music, founded in Denpasar in 1960.

Listibiya Majelis Pertimbangan dan Pembinaan Kebudayaan Daerah Propinsi Bali; the Consultative and Promotional Council for Balinese Culture, founded in Denpasar in 1966.

mabakti (Voluntary) devotional acts.

Majapahit An East Javanese Hindu empire from the thirteenth to fifteenth centuries from which Balinese nobility claim descent.

Margapati *Kebiar*-style dance depicting a character study of a young man.

MPLA Majelis Pembina Lembaga Adat; the Council for the Development of Customary Institutions, established in 1979 under the aegis of the governor's office to reinforce and reform the role of customary institutions in the province of Bali; the steering committee of BPPLA.

Mpu Dwijendra Fifteenth-century Javanese priest and progenitor of Bali's Brahmana clan.

nabe Priestly consecrator.

negara State; term used by Clifford Geertz to denote the nineteenth-century Balinese state constituted by ritual dramaturgy rather than orthodox technologies of power.

niskala Invisible, subtle, of the spiritual world.

nyepi Lowland festival of the new year *(nyepi pemerintah)* with many local variants *(nyepi desa)*.

Pancasila The Five Principles of official Indonesian state ideology.

Pande A prominent *jaba* clan.

Panyembrama Modern dance used to welcome guests.

papanen Warp beam.

Parisada See PHDI.

pariwisata budaya "Cultural tourism"; Bali's official tourism policy, which utilizes Balinese culture to attract tourists while employing the revenues generated by tourism to preserve and promote Balinese culture.

Pasek A prominent *jaba* clan; there are several branches of this clan, such as the Pasek Sapta Resi.

PDI Partai Demokrasi Indonesia; the Indonesian Democratic Party.

pedanda Brahmana priest.

pemangku Temple priest.

pembangunan   Social and economic development.

Pendet   Ceremonial dance for females.

Pesta Kesenian Bali   Bali Arts Festival; an annual event launched by the governor in 1979 to preserve and promote the Balinese "cultural arts."

PHD; PHDI   Parisada Hindu Dharma Indonesia; the Indonesian Hindu Council, founded in Denpasar in 1959 as the official liaison body between the Balinese Hindu congregation and the Indonesian Ministry of Religion.

PKI   Partai Komunis Indonesia; the Indonesian Communist Party.

PKK   Pembinaan Kesejahteraan Keluarga; the Family Welfare Movement of Indonesia.

plaspas   Inaugural purification ritual.

PNI   Partai Nasionalis Indonesia; the Indonesian Nationalist Party.

PPP   Partai Persatuan Pembangunan; the United Development Party.

PRD   Partai Rakyat Demokratik; the Democratic People's Party.

punggawa   District chief during the precolonial and colonial periods.

puputan   "Finishing" through willed death of ruler and retinue; act of resistance to colonial rule, as in Puputan Badung (1906), Puputan Klungkung (1908), and Puputan Margarana (1946).

puri   Royal palace; noble house.

pusaka   Heirloom regalia.

Repelita   Rencana Pembangunan Lima Tahun; the five-year plans.

rsi bhujangga   Priest from the Bhujangga Waisnawa clan.

saput   Short wraparound cloth worn over *kamben* by men.

Sarjana Ilmu Seni   Bachelor of Arts.

Satria   One of the three status groups of the nobility; see *triwangsa* and *warna*.

SDSB   Sumbangan Dana Sosial Berhadiah; the state-sponsored lottery.

semangat   Enthusiasm, energy, spirit.

seni budaya   "Cultural arts"; culture as art.

seni; kesenian   Art; the root word *"seni"* meant "fine," "refined," before becoming understood in the modern sense of "art."

seniman   Artist, performer.

seniman alam   Village artist; "natural" artist.

slendang   Waist sash worn by women.

SMKI   Sekolah Menengah Karawitan Indonesia; the High School of Traditional Indonesian Music, founded in 1979 to replace KOKAR.

songket   Supplementary-weft *ikat* using golden threads; brocade.

sri mpu   Priest from the Pande or Pasek clans.

stabilitas   (Political) stability.

STSI   Sekolah Tinggi Seni Indonesia; the College of Indonesian Arts, founded in 1988 to replace ASTI.

Sudra   Commoners, one way of referring to non-*triwangsa;* see also *anak jaba* and *warna.*

sulinggih   "Twice-born" priest.

Surya Kanta   Periodical published in Singaraja between 1925 and 1927; also the journal of the eponymous commoners' association.

Taman Mini Indonesia Indah   Beautiful Indonesia-in-Miniature Park, located on the outskirts of Jakarta, opened in 1977.

tirta   Sanctified water.

topeng   Improvised dance-drama based on historical incidents.

Tri Dharma Perguruan Tinggi   The Threefold Tasks of Tertiary Education Institutions.

triwangsa   The "three peoples"; the Balinese nobility made up of the three upper casts (Brahmana, Satria, Wesia) as opposed to the commoners *(anak jaba).*

udeng   Headdress worn by men.

ulu apad   Village assembly of mountain communities ranked in order of seniority, with a council of paired elders at the head.

warga   *Jaba* clan organization.

warna   Status categories; Balinese hierarchical system comprising the Brahmana, Satria, Wesia, and Sudra *(anak jaba).*

Werdi Budaya   The Art Center founded in Denpasar in 1976.

Wong Bali Aga   Bali Aga, the Balinese people of the mountains; the "original inhabitants."

YLBHI   Yayasan Lembaga Bantuan Hukum Indonesia; the Indonesian Legal Aid Foundation.

References

Abdullah, T.

1966   "*Adat* and Islam: An Examination of Conflict in Minangkabau."
        Indonesia 2:1–24.

1971   *Schools and Politics: The Kaum Muda Movement in West Sumatra.*
        Ithaca: Modern Indonesia Project, Cornell University.

1972   "Modernization in the Minangkabau World: West Sumatra in the
        Early Decades of the Twentieth Century." In *Culture and Politics
        in Indonesia,* edited by C. Holt, pp. 179–245. Ithaca: Cornell
        University Press.

Acciaioli, G.

1985   "Culture as Art: From Practice to Spectacle in Indonesia." *Can-
        berra Anthropology* 8(1–2):148–174.

1994   "What's in a Name? Appropriating Idioms in the South Sulawesi
        Rice Intensification Programme." *Social Analysis* 35:39–60.

Adam, A. B.

1995   *The Vernacular Press and the Emergence of Modern Indonesian
        Consciousness (1855–1913).* Ithaca: Southeast Asia Program, Cor-
        nell University.

Adams, K. M.

1995   "Making-up the Toraja? The Appropriation of Tourism, Anthro-
        pology, and Museums for Politics in Upland Sulawesi, Indonesia."
        Ethnology 34(2):143–153.

Aditjondro, G.

1995a   "Bali and Balim: The Politics of Representation and Exclusion in
        Two Tourist Destinies in the Indonesian Political Realm."
        Keynote Address presented at the Third International Bali Studies
        Conference, University of Sydney, 3–7 July.

1995b   "Bali, Jakarta's Colony: Social and Ecological Impacts of Jakarta-
        Based Conglomerates in Bali's Tourism Industry." Working Paper

58. Perth: Asia Research Centre on Social, Political, and Economic Change, Murdoch University.

Agung, A. A. G.
1991   *Bali in the 19th Century.* Jakarta: Yayasan Obor Indonesia.

Agung, A. A. Gd. P.
1972   "Lahirnja idee-idee pembaharuan dalam organisasi sosial di Bali."
        Basis 21(6):183–189.
1974   "Perobahan Sosial dan Pertentangan Kasta di Bali Utara,
        1924–1928." M.A. thesis, Universitas Gadjah Mada, Yogyakarta.

Alexander, P. (ed.)
1989   *Creating Indonesian Cultures.* Oceania Ethnographies 3. Sydney:
        Oceania Publications.

Anandakusuma, Sri Reshi
1966   *Pergolakan Hindu Dharma.* Denpasar: Balimas.

Anderson, B. R. O'G.
1972   "The Idea of Power in Javanese Culture." In *Culture and Politics
        in Indonesia,* edited by C. Holt, pp. 17–76. Ithaca: Cornell Uni-
        versity Press.
1983   *Imagined Communities: Reflections on the Origin and Spread of
        Nationalism.* London: Verso.
1990a   "Language, Fantasy, Revolution: Java 1900–1945." *Prisma*
        50:25–39.
1990b   *Language and Power: Exploring Political Cultures in Indonesia.*
        Ithaca: Cornell Univerity Press.
1991   *Imagined Communities: Reflections on the Origin and Spread of
        Nationalism.* Rev. ed. London: Verso.
1998   "A Javanese King Talks of His End." *Inside Indonesia* 54
        (April–June):16–17.

Ang, I.
1991   *Desperately Seeking the Audience.* London: Routledge.

Antweiler, C.
1993   "South Sulawesi: Towards a Regional Ethnic Identity?" Paper pre-
        sented at the conference on Nationalism and Ethnicity in South-
        east Asia, Humboldt University, Berlin.

Appadurai, A., and C. A. Breckenridge
1988   "Why Public Culture?" *Public Culture* 1(1):5–9.

Aragon, L.
1991–   "Revised Rituals in Central Sulawesi: The Maintenance of Tradi-
1992   tional Cosmological Concepts in the Face of Allegiance to World
        Religion." *Anthropological Forum* 6(3):371–384.

Arntzenius, J. O. H.
1874   *De derde Balische Expeditie in Herinnering gebracht.* The Hague: Belinfante.

Aspinall, E.
1996   "What Happened Before the Riots?" *Inside Indonesia* 48:4–8.

Atkinson, J. M.
1987   "Religions in Dialogue: The Construction of an Indonesian Minority Religion." In *Indonesian Religions in Transition,* edited by R. S. Kipp and S. Rodgers, pp. 171–186. Tucson: University of Arizona Press.

Atmaja, J. (ed.)
1988   *Puspanjali: Persembahan untuk Prof. Dr. Ida Bagus Mantra.* Denpasar: Kayumas.

Atmadja, N. B.
1987   "Surya Kanta Sebagai Perkumpulan Sempalan dan Gagasannya Dalam Mewujudkan Kemajuan dan Kesempurnaan Masyarakat Bali (1925–1927)." Unpublished research report, Universitas Udayana, Singaraja.

The Australian

Badudu, J. S., and S. M. Zein
1994   *Kamus Umum Bahasa Indonesia.* Jakarta: Pustaka Sinar Harapan.

Bagus, Gst. Ng.
1969   *Pertentangan Kasta dalam Bentuk Baru pada Masjarakat Bali.* Denpasar: Universitas Udayana.
1972   *A Short Note on the Modern Hindu Movements in Balinese Society.* Denpasar: Universitas Udayana.
1975   "Surya Kanta: A *Kewangsaan* Movement of the *Jaba* Caste in Bali." *Masyarakat Indonesia* 2(2):153–162.
1991   "Bali in the 1950s: The Role of the Pemuda Pejuang in the Balinese Political Process." In *State and Society in Bali: Historical, Textual, and Anthropological Aproaches,* edited by H. Geertz, pp. 199–212. VKI 146. Leiden: KITLV.
1996   "The Play 'Woman's Fidelity': Literature and Caste Conflict in Bali." In *Being Modern in Bali: Image and Change,* edited by A. Vickers, pp. 92–114. Monograph 43. New Haven: Yale University Southeast Asia Studies.

Bakhtin, M. M.
1986   "From Notes Made in 1970–71." In *Speech Genres and Other Late Essays,* edited by C. Emerson and M. Holquist, pp. 132–158. Austin: University of Texas Press.

Bakker, F. L.
1993   *The Struggle of the Hindu Balinese Intellectuals: Developments in Modern Hindu Thinking in Independent Indonesia.* Amsterdam: VU University Press.

Bakker, J. B.
1937   "Goederenbalans en Belastingdruk van de Afdeeling Zuid-Bali." *Koloniaal Tijdschrift* 26:287–294.

Bali Adnjana
1924–   Singaradja: Perkoempoelan Santi.
1930

Bali Post

Barber, C. C.
1979   *A Balinese-English Dictionary.* 2 vols. Aberdeen: University of Aberdeen Library.

Barnes, R. H.
1996   "The Power of Strangers in Flores and Timor." Paper presented at the conference on Hierarchization: Processes of Social Differentiation in the Austronesian World, International Institute for Asian Studies, Leiden, 17–19 April.

Bateson, G.
1973   "Bali: The Value System of a Steady State." In *Steps to an Ecology of Mind: Collected Essays in Anthropology, Psychiatry, Evolution, and Epistemology,* pp. 80–100. St. Albans: Paladin.

Bateson, G., and M. Mead
1942   *Balinese Character: A Photographic Analysis.* New York: New York Academy of Sciences.

Batubara, C.
n.d.   "Indonesia in the New Order." Unpublished paper.

Baum, V.
1973   *A Tale from Bali.* Kuala Lumpur: Oxford University Press. Originally published in 1937.

Benda, H. J.
1962   "Non-Western Intelligentsia as Political Elites." In *Political Change in Underdeveloped Countries: Nationalism and Communism,* edited by J. H. Kautsky, pp. 235–251. New York: Wiley.

Benda-Beckmann, F. von, and K. von Benda-Beckmann
1988   "*Adat* and Religion in Minangkabau and Ambon." In *Time Past, Time Present, Time Future: Perspectives on Indonesian Culture: Essays in Honour of Prof. P. E. de Josselin de Jong,* edited by H. J. M. Claessen and D. S. Moyer, pp. 195–212. Dordrecht: Foris.

Benería, L. (ed.)
1982   *Women and Development: The Sexual Division of Labor in Rural Societies.* New York: Praeger.

Benjamin, W.
1969   "Theses on the Philosophy of History." In *Illuminations,* translated by Harry Zohn. New York: Schocken.

Bhadra, Wy.
1953   *Treaty tentang Agama Hindu Bali.* Singaradja: Kantor Penerangan Agama Propinsi Sunda-Ketjil.

Bhakti
1952–   Singaradja: Badan Penerbit Bhakti.
1954

Bhawanagara
1931–   Singaradja: Kirtya Liefrinck–Van der Tuuk.
1935

Biersack, A. (ed.)
1991   *Clio in Oceania: Toward a Historical Anthropology.* Washington: Smithsonian Institution Press.

Black, S., and W. A. Hanna
1973   *Guide to Bali.* Singapore: Apa Productions.

Boon, J. A.
1977   *The Anthropological Romance of Bali, 1597–1972: Dynamic Perspectives in Marriage and Caste, Politics and Religion.* Cambridge: Cambridge University Press.
1979   "Balinese Temple Politics and the Religious Revitalization of Caste Ideals." In *The Imagination of Reality: Essays in Southeast Asian Coherence Systems,* edited by A. L. Becker and A. A. Yengoyan, pp. 271–291. Norwood: Ablex.
1986   "Between-the-Wars Bali: Re-reading the Relics." In *The History of Anthropology,* vol. 4: *Romantic Motives,* edited by G. W. Stocking, pp. 218–247. Madison: University of Wisconsin Press.

Bosch, F. D. K.
1932   "Een ontoelaatbaar experiment." *De Stuw* 3(17):205–207.
1933   "Bali en de zending." *Djawa* 13(1):1–39.

Boserup, E.
1970   *Women's Role in Economic Development.* London: Allen & Unwin.

Bourdieu, P.
1994   "Structures, Habitus, Power: Basis for a Theory of Symbolic Power." In *Culture/Power/History: A Reader in Contemporary Social Theory,* edited by N. Dirks, G. Eley, and S. Ortner, pp. 154–199. Princeton: Princeton University Press.

Branson, J., and D. Miller
1988   "The Changing Fortunes of Balinese Market Women." In *Development and Displacement: Women in Southeast Asia,* edited by G. Chandler, N. Sullivan, and J. Branson, pp. 1–16. Monash Papers on Southeast Asia, no. 18. Clayton (Victoria): Centre of Southeast Asian Studies, Monash University.

Brawn, D. M.
1994   "Immanent Domains: Cultural Worth in Bone, South Sulawesi." *Social Analysis* 35:84–101.

Breman, J.
1988   *The Shattered Image: Construction and Deconstruction of the Village in Colonial Asia.* Comparative Asian Studies, no. 2. Dordrecht: Foris.

B[roek], H. A. van den
1835   "Verslag nopens het Eiland Bali." *De Oosterling: Tijdschrift bij Uitsluiting Toegewijd aan de Verbreiding der Kennis van Oost-Indië* 1:158–236.

Budiman, A.
1998   "Friend or foe?" *Inside Indonesia* 54 (April–June):18–19.

Carter, P.
1987   *The Road to Botany Bay: An Essay in Spatial History.* London: Faber.

Cartland, B.
1979   *Lovers in Paradise.* London: Severin House.

Casey, M.
1989   "Women and Work in Silungkang, Minangkabau." Ph.D. dissertation, University of London.

Certeau, M. de
1984   *The Practice of Everyday Life.* Berkeley: University of California Press.

Chandler, G., N. Sullivan, and J. Branson (eds.)
1988   *Development and Displacement: Women in Southeast Asia.* Monash Papers on Southeast Asia, no. 18. Clayton (Victoria): Centre of Southeast Asian Studies, Monash University.

Chatterjee, P.
1986   *Nationalist Thought and the Colonial World: A Derivative Discourse.* London: Zed Books.

Chen, K.-H.
1996   "Post-Marxism: Between/Beyond Critical Postmodernism and

Cultural Studies." In *Stuart Hall: Critical Dialogues in Cultural Studies,* edited by D. Morley and K.-H. Chen, pp. 309–325. London: Routledge.

Cohen, I. J.
1989   *Structuration Theory: Anthony Giddens and the Constitution of Social Life.* Houndmills (Hampshire): Macmillan.

Cohen, M.
1994   "God and Mammon: Luxury Resort Triggers Outcry Over Bali's Future." *Far Eastern Economic Review,* 26 May, pp. 28–33.

Cole, W. S.
1983   "Balinese Food-Related Behavior: A Study of the Effects of Ecological, Economic, Social, and Cultural Processes on Rates of Change." Ph.D. dissertation, Washington University.

College of Indonesian Arts
1988   "Information Brochure." Denpasar: Sekolah Tinggi Seni Indonesia.

Collingwood, R. G.
1938   *The Principles of Art.* Oxford: Clarendon Press.
1940   *An Essay on Metaphysics.* Oxford: Clarendon Press.
1942   *The New Leviathan; or Man, Society, Civilization, and Barbarism.* Oxford: Clarendon Press.

Comaroff, J., and J. Comaroff
1992   "The Long and the Short of It." In *Ethnography and the Historical Imagination,* edited by J. Comaroff and J. Comaroff, pp. 95–126. Boulder: Westview.

Connor, L. H.
1982   "In Darkness and Light: A Study of Peasant Intellectuals in Bali." Ph.D. dissertation, University of Sydney.
1983   "Healing as Women's Work in Bali." In W*omen's Work and Women's Roles: Economics and Everyday Life in Indonesia, Malaysia, and Singapore,* edited by L. Manderson, pp. 53–72. Monograph 32. Canberra: Development Studies Centre, Australian National University.
1996   "Contesting and Transforming the Work for the Dead in Bali: The Case of *Ngaben Ngirit.*" In *Being Modern in Bali: Image and Change,* edited by A. Vickers, pp. 179–211. Monograph 43. New Haven: Yale University Southeast Asia Studies.

Conrad, J.
1992   "Karain: A Memory." In *The Complete Short Fiction of Joseph Conrad,* vol. 1: *The Stories,* edited by S. Hynes, pp. 62–99. London: Pickering.

Covarrubias, M.
1972   *Island of Bali.* Kuala Lumpur: Oxford University Press. Originally published in 1937.

Crawfurd, J.
1820   "On the Existence of the Hindu Religion in the Island of Bali." *Asiatick Researches* 13:128–170.

Creese, H.
1997   "In Search of Majapahit: The Transformation of Balinese Identities." Working Paper 101. Clayton (Victoria): Centre of Southeast Asian Studies, Monash University.

Cribb, R. (ed.)
1990   *The Indonesian Killings of 1965–66: Studies from Java and Bali.* Monash Papers on Southeast Asia, no. 21. Clayton (Victoria): Centre of Southeast Asian Studies, Monash University.

Crystal, E.
1974   "Cooking Pot Politics: A Toraja Village Study." *Indonesia* 18:119–151.

Cunningham, C. E.
1965   "Order and Change in an Atoni Diarchy." *Southwestern Journal of Anthropology* 21:359–382.
1989   "Celebrating a Toba Batak National Hero: An Indonesian Rite of Identity." In *Changing Lives, Changing Rites: Ritual and Social Dynamics in Philippine and Indonesian Uplands,* edited by S. D. Russell and C. E. Cunningham, pp.167–200. Michigan Studies of South and Southeast Asia, no. 1. Ann Arbor: Center for South and Southeast Asian Studies, University of Michigan.

Damai
1953–   Denpasar: Jajasan Kebaktian Pedjuang.
1956

Danandjaja, J.
1980   *Kebudayaan Petani Desa Trunyan di Bali.* Jakarta: Universitas Indonesia Press.

Daroesman, R.
1991   "Staff Development in Indonesian State Universities." In *Indonesia Assessment 1991,* edited by H. Hill, pp. 106–119. Political and Social Change Monograph 13. Canberra: Australian National University.

Davis, M.
1992   *City of Quartz: Excavating the Future in Los Angeles.* New York: Vintage.

Descombes, V.
1991   "Apropos of the 'Critique of the Subject' and of the Critique of This Critique." In *Who Comes After the Subject?*, edited by E. Cadava, P. Connor, and J.-L. Nancy, pp. 120–134. London: Routledge.

Dherana, Tj. R.
1982   *Garis-garis Besar Pedoman Penulisan Awig-awig Desa Adat.* Denpasar: Mabhakti.

Diantari, P.
1990   "Gerakan Pembaruan Hindu: Studi Tentang Perkembangan Pemikiran Intelektual Hindu di Bali Tahun 1925–1958." M.A. thesis, Universitas Udayana.

Dick, H.
1990   "Further Reflections on the Middle Class." In *The Politics of Middle Class Indonesia,* edited by R. Tanter and K. Young, pp. 63–70. Monash Papers on Southeast Asia, no. 19. Clayton (Victoria): Centre of Southeast Asian Studies, Monash University.

Dinas Pendidikan dan Kebudayaan
1986   *Sejarah Bali.* Denpasar: n.p.

Dirks, N. B.
1990   "History as a Sign of the Modern." *Public Culture* 2(2):25–32.
1992   (ed.) *Colonialism and Culture.* Ann Arbor: University of Michigan Press.
1994   "Ritual and Resistance: Subversion as a Social Fact." In *Culture/Power/History: A Reader in Contemporary Social Theory,* edited by N. Dirks, G. Eley, and S. Ortner, pp. 483–503. Princeton: Princeton University Press.

Djatajoe
1936–   Singaradja: Bali Darma Laksana.
1941

Dove, M. R. (ed.)
1988   *The Real and Imagined Role of Culture in Development: Case Studies from Indonesia.* Honolulu: University of Hawai'i Press.

Dyer, R.
1992   *Only Entertainment.* London: Routledge.

Echols, J., and H. Shadily
1989   *Kamus Indonesia Inggris.* 3rd ed. Jakarta: Gramedia.

Edmondson, J. C.
1992   *Bali Revisited: Rural Economy, Intergenerational Exchanges, and*

the Transition to Smaller Family Sizes, 1977–1990. Denpasar: Universitas Udayana.

Eipper, C.
1996   "Ethnographic Testimony, Trust and Authority." *Canberra Anthropology* 19(1):15–30.

Eiseman, F. B.
1990   *Bali: Sekala and Niskala.* Vol. 1: *Essays on Religion, Ritual, and Art.* Singapore: Periplus.

Errington, S.
1983   "The Place of Regalia in Luwu." In *Centres, Symbols and Hierarchies: Essays on the Classical States of Southeast Asia,* edited by L. Gesick, pp. 194–241. New Haven: Yale University Press.
1997   "The Cosmic Theme Park of the Javanese." *RIMA* 31(1):7–35.

Etienne, M.
1980   "Women and Men, Cloth and Colonization: The Transformation of Production Distribution Relations Among the Baul (Ivory Coast)." In *Women and Colonization,* edited by M. Etienne and E. Leacock, pp. 214–238. New York: Praeger.

Evans-Pritchard, E. E.
1963   "Social Anthropology: Past and Present." In *Essays in Social Anthropology,* pp. 13–28. Glencoe: Free Press. Originally published in 1950.

Fabian, J.
1983   *Time and the Other: How Anthropology Makes Its Object.* New York: Columbia University Press.

Fatah, R. E. S.
1994   "Gerakan Protes Massa dan Demokratisasi." *Prisma* 4:3–22.

Fink, B.
1995   *The Lacanian Subject: Between Language and Jouissance.* Princeton: Princeton University Press.

Fiske, J.
1989   *Television Culture.* London: Routledge.

Flierhaar, H. te
1941   "De Aanpassing van het Inlandsch Onderwijs op Bali aan de Eigen Sfeer." *Koloniale Studiën* 25:135–159.

Florida, N.
1995   *Writing the Past, Inscribing the Future.* Durham: Duke University Press.

Foley, S.
1987   "The Ecological Transition in Bali." Ph.D. dissertation, Australian
            National University.

Forge, A.
1980   "Balinese Religion and Indonesian Identity." In *Indonesia: Aus-
            tralian Perspectives,* edited by J. J. Fox et al., pp. 221–233. Can-
            berra: Research School of Pacific Studies, Australian National
            University.

Forth, G.
1994   "'Post' Modernism: Issues of Meaning, Cultural Objectification
            and National-Local Distinctions in an Eastern Indonesian Com-
            munity." *Social Analysis* 35:44–156.

Foster, R.
1991   "Making National Cultures in the Global Ecumene." *Annual Re-
            view of Anthropology* 20:235–260.

Foucault, M.
1970   *The Order of Things: An Archaeology of the Human Sciences.* Lon-
            don: Tavistock.
1978   *The History of Sexuality.* 3 vols. Translated from the French by
            R. Hurley. London: Allen Lane.

Foulcher, K.
1990   "The Construction of an Indonesian National Culture: Patterns
            of Hegemony and Resistance." In *State and Civil Society in In-
            donesia,* edited by A. Budiman, pp. 301–320. Clayton (Victoria):
            Centre of Southeast Asian Studies, Monash University.

Fox, J. J.
1987   "The House as a Type of Social Organisation on the Island of
            Roti." In *De la Hutte au Palais: Sociétés "à maison" en Asie du
            Sud-Est insulaire,* edited by C. Macdonald et al., pp. 171–178.
            Paris: CNRS.
1994   "Installing the 'Outsider' Inside: An Exploration of an Austrone-
            sian Cultural Theme and Its Social Significance." Paper presented
            at the First International Symposium on Austronesian Cultural
            Studies, Universitas Udayana, 14–16 August.

Friederich, R. Th. A.
1849–   "Voorlopig Verslag van het Eiland Bali." *Verhandelingen van het
1850   Bataviaasch Genootschap voor Kunsten en Wetenschappen* 22:1–63;
            23:1–57.

Geertz, C.
1963   *Peddlers and Princes.* Chicago: University of Chicago Press.

| 1964 | "'Internal Conversion' in Contemporary Bali." In *Malayan and Indonesian Studies Presented to Sir Richard Winstedt*, edited by J. Bastin and R. Roolvink, pp. 282–302. Oxford: Oxford University Press. |

1980   *Negara: The Theatre State in Nineteenth-Century Bali.* Princeton: Princeton University Press.

1990   "'Popular Art' and the Javanese Tradition." *Indonesia* 50:77–94.

Geertz, H. (ed.)

1991   *State and Society in Bali: Historical, Textual, and Anthropological Approaches.* VKI 146. Leiden: KITLV Press.

Geertz, H., and C. Geertz

1975   *Kinship in Bali.* Chicago: University of Chicago Press.

Giddens, A.

1984   *The Constitution of Society: Outline of the Theory of Structuration.* Berkeley: University of California Press.

1991   "Structuration Theory: Past, Present, and Future." In *Giddens' Theory of Structuration: A Critical Appreciation*, edited by C. Bryant and D. Jary, pp. 1–29. London: Routledge.

Gillis, J. R. (ed.)

1994   *Commemorations: The Politics of National Identity.* Princeton: Princeton University Press.

Ginarsa, Kt., et al.

1979   *Bhujangga Dharma.* Denpasar: Eka Bhuwana Suta.

Gonda, J.

1973   *Sanskrit in Indonesia.* New Delhi: International Academy of Indian Culture. Originally published in 1952.

Goodman, N.

1968   *Languages of Art.* Indianapolis: Bobbs-Merrill.

Goris, R.

1932   "Bali sebagai Padang Pekerdjaan oentoek Berbagai-bagai Pengetahoean." *Bhawanagara* 1(12):191–192; 2(1):8–9; 2(4):50–53; 2(5):75–79; 2(6):87–90.

1933   "De strijd over Bali en de Zending: De waarde van Dr. Kraemer's boek." Batavia: Minerva.

1954   *Prasasti Bali: Inscripties voor Anak Wungçu.* 2 vols. Lembaga Bahasa dan Budaja, Fakultet Sastra dan Filsafat, Universitas Indonesia. Bandung: N. V. Masa Baru.

1984   "Holidays and Holy Days." In *Bali: Studies in Life, Thought, and Ritual*, pp. 113–129. Dordrecht: Foris. Originally published in 1960.

n.d.   *Contemporaneous Religious Phenomena in Bali.* n.p.

Goris, R., and P. L. Dronkers
1952   *Bali: Atlas Kebudajaan—Cults and Customs—Cultuurgeschiede-nis in Beeld.* Jakarta: Government of the Republic of Indonesia.

Gosa, M.
1986   "Peranan Parisada Hindu Dharma Dalam Perkembangan Agama Hindu di Bali 1958–1985." M.A. thesis, Universitas Udayana, Denpasar.

Graham, P.
1994   "Rhetorics of Consensus, Politics of Diversity: Church, State, and Local Identity in Eastern Indonesia." *Social Analysis* 35:122–143.

Greenberg, J. B.
1995   "Capital, Ritual, and the Boundaries of the Closed Corporate Community." In *Articulating Hidden Histories: Exploring the Influence of Eric R. Wolf,* edited by J. Schneider and R. Rapp, pp. 67–81. Berkeley: University of California Press.

Grijns, M.
1987   "Tea-Pickers in West Java as Mothers and Workers." In *Indonesian Women in Focus,* edited by E. Locher-Scholten and A. Niehof, pp. 104–119. Dordrecht: Foris.

Grijns, M., et al. (eds.)
1994   *Different Women, Different Work: Gender and Industrialisation in Indonesia.* Aldershot (England): Avebury.

Grijp, P. van der, and T. van Meijl (eds.)
1993   "Politics, Tradition, and Change in the Pacific." *Bijdragen tot de Taal-, Land-, en Volkenkunde* 149(4). [Special issue.]

Guermonprez, J.-F.
1987   *Les Pandé de Bali: La Formation d'une "Caste" et la Valeur d'un Titre.* Publications de l'École Française d'Extrême-Orient, vol. 142. Paris: École Française d'Extrême-Orient.
1990   "On the Elusive Balinese Village: Hierarchy and Values Versus Political Models." *Review of Indonesian and Malaysian Affairs* 24(2):56–89.

Guinness, P.
1994   "Local Society and Culture." In *Indonesia's New Order,* edited by H. Hill, pp. 267–304. St. Leonards (NSW): Allen & Unwin.

Gullick, J. M.
1988   *Indigenous Political Systems of Western Malaya.* London: Athlone.

Habermas, J.
1987   *The Philosophical Discourse of Modernity: Twelve Lectures.* Translated by F. Lawrence. Cambridge: Polity Press.

Hacking, I.
1990   *The Taming of Chance.* Cambridge: Cambridge University Press.

Hadiz, V. R.
1994   "Challenging State Corporatism on the Labor Front: Working Class Politics in the 1990s." In *Democracy in Indonesia, 1950s and 1990s,* edited by D. Bourchier and J. Legge, pp. 190–203. Monash Papers on Southeast Asia, no. 31. Clayton (Victoria): Centre of Southeast Asian Studies, Monash University.

Haferkamp, H., and N. J. Smelser
1992   "Introduction." In *Social Change and Modernity,* edited by H. Haferkamp and N. J. Smelser, pp. 1–33. Berkeley: University of California Press.

Hall, S.
1980a   "Race, Articulation, and Societies Structured in Dominance." In *Sociological Theories: Race and Colonialism,* pp. 305–345. Paris: UNESCO.
1980b   "Encoding/Decoding." In *Culture, Media, Language: Working Papers in Cultural Studies, 1972–79,* edited by S. Hall et al., pp. 128–138. London: Unwin Hyman.
1989   "Ideology and Communication Theory." In *Rethinking Communication,* vol 1: *Paradigm Issues,* edited by B. Dervin et al., pp. 40–52. London: Sage.
1990   "The Whites of Their Eyes: Racist Ideologies and the Media." In *The Media Reader,* edited by M. Alvarado and J. O. Thompson, pp. 7–23. London: British Film Institute.
1996   "On Postmodernism and Articulation: An Interview with Stuart Hall." In *Stuart Hall: Critical Dialogues in Cultural Studies,* edited by D. Morley and K.-H. Chen, pp. 131–150. London: Routledge.

Handler, R., and J. Linnekin
1984   "Tradition, Genuine or Spurious." *Journal of American Folklore* 97(385):273–290.

Hanna, W. A.
1976   *Bali Profile: People, Events, Circumstances (1001–1976).* New York: American Universities Field Staff. Reprint, Banda Nair: Rumah Budaya, 1990.

Hanson, A.
1989   "The Making of the Maori: Culture Invention and Its Logic." *American Anthropologist* 91(4):890–902.

Harjono, J.
1991   "Higher Education: A Word from the Classroom." In *Indonesia Assessment 1991*, edited by H. Hill, pp. 155–162. Political and Social Change Monograph 13. Canberra: Australian National University.

Hartley, J.
1992a   "The Real World of Audiences." In *Tele-ology: Studies in Television*, edited by J. Hartley, pp. 119–125. London: Routledge.
1992b   "Tele-ology." In *Tele-ology: Studies in Television*, edited by J. Hartley, pp. 3–20. London: Routledge.
1996   *Popular Reality: Journalism, Modernity, Popular Culture*. London: Arnold.

Harvey, D.
1990   *The Condition of Post-Modernity: An Enquiry into the Origins of Cultural Change*. Cambridge, Mass.: Blackwell.

Hauser-Schäublin, B.
1995   "Temples and Tourism: Between Adaption, Resistance, and Surrender?" Paper presented at the Third International Bali Studies Workshop, University of Sydney, 3–7 July.

Hauser-Schäublin, B., et al. (eds.)
1991   *Balinese Textiles*. London: British Museum Press.

Hearman, V.
1996   "A Day with Indonesia's Radical Student Organization." *Inside Indonesia* 48:8–9.

Hefner, R. W.
1985   *Hindu Javanese: Tengger Tradition and Islam*. Princeton: Princeton University Press.
1987   "The Politics of Popular Art: *Tayuban* Dance and Culture Changing East Java." *Indonesia* 43:75–96.
1990   *The Political Economy of Mountain Java: An Interpretive History*. Berkeley: University of California Press.
1993   "Islam, State, and Civil Society: ICMI and the Struggle for the Indonesian Middle Class." *Indonesia* 56:1–35.

Heider, K. G.
1991   *Indonesian Cinema: National Culture on Screen*. Honolulu: University of Hawai'i Press.

Henriques, J., et al. (eds.)
1984   *Changing the Subject: Psychology, Social Regulation, and Subjectivity*. London: Methuen.

Heyzer, N.
1986   *Working Women in South-East Asia: Development, Subordination,*

and Emancipation. Milton Keynes (England): Open University Press.

Hilbery, R. (ed.)
1979   *Reminiscences of a Balinese Prince, Tjokorda Gde Agung Sukawati.* Southeast Asia Paper 14. Honolulu: University of Hawai'i Press.

Hill, D.
1994   *The Press in New Order Indonesia.* Asia Paper 4. Perth: University of Western Australia Press in association with Asia Research Centre on Social, Political, and Economic Change.

Hill, H. (ed.)
1991   *Indonesia Assessment 1991.* Political and Social Change Monograph 13. Canberra: Australian National University.

Hirst, P., and G. Thompson
1996   *Globalization in Question: The International Economy and the Possibilities of Governance.* Cambridge: Polity Press.

Hoadley, M. C., and M. B. Hooker
1981   *An Introduction to Javanese Law: A Translation of and Commentary on the Agama.* Tucson: University of Arizona Press.

Hobart, M.
1985   "Anthropos Through the Looking-Glass: Or How to Teach the Balinese to Bark." In *Reason and Morality,* edited by J. Overing, pp. 104–134. London: Tavistock.
1986   "Thinker, Thespian, Soldier, Slave? Assumptions About Human Nature in the Study of Balinese Society." In *Context, Meaning, and Power in Southeast Asia,* edited by M. Hobart and R. H. Taylor, pp. 131–156. Ithaca: Cornell Southeast Asia Program.
1990   "The Patience of Plants: A Note on Agency in Bali." *Review of Indonesian and Malaysian Affairs* 24(2):90–135.
1991   "Criticizing Genres: Bakhtin and Bali." *Bulletin of the John Rylands University Library of Manchester* 73(3):195–216.
1996   "Ethnography as a Practice, or the Unimportance of Penguins." *Europaea* 2(1):3–36.
1997   "The Missing Subject: Balinese Time and the Elimination of History." *Review of Indonesian and Malaysian Affairs* 31(1): 123–172.
n.d.   "Rich Kids Can't Cry: The Subject of Television in Bali." Unpublished paper.
in press "As They Like It: Overinterpretation and Hyporeality in Bali." In *Interpretation and Context,* edited by R. Dilley. Oxford: Berghahn

Hobsbawm, E., and T. Ranger
1983   *The Invention of Tradition.* Cambridge: Cambridge University Press.

Hoëvell, W. R. van
1848   "Recent Scientific Researches on the Islands of Bali and Lombok." *Journal of the Indian Archipelago and Eastern Asia* 2:151–159.

Hooker, V. M. (ed.)
1993   *Culture and Society in New Order Indonesia.* Kuala Lumpur: Oxford University Press.

Hooyer, G. B
1895   *De Krijgsgeschiedenis van Nederlandsch-Indië van 1811 tot 1894.* The Hague: De Gebr. van Cleef.

Hooykaas, C.
1973   *Religion in Bali.* Leiden: Brill.
1974   *Cosmogony and Creation in Balinese Tradition.* The Hague: Nijhoff.
1976   "Dukuh as a Balinese Priest: A Sociological Problem." *Southeast Asian Review* 1:3–15.

Hoskins, J.
1987   "The Headhunter as Hero: Local Traditions and Their Reinterpretation in National History." *American Ethnologist* 14(4): 605–622.

Houben, V. J. H., H. M. J. Maier, and W. van der Molen (eds.)
1992   *Looking in Odd Mirrors: The Java Sea.* SEMAIAN 5. Leiden: Vakgroep Talen en Culturen van Zuidoost-Azië en Oceanië, Rijksuniversiteit te Leiden.

Hough, B.
1992   *Contemporary Balinese Dance Spectacles as National Ritual.* Working Paper 74. Clayton (Victoria): Centre of Southeast Asian Studies, Monash University.

Howell, J. D.
1978   "Modernizing Religious Reform and the Far Eastern Religions in Twentieth Century Indonesia." In *Spectrum: Essays Presented to Sutan Takdir Alisjahbana on His Seventieth Birthday,* edited by S. Udin, pp. 260–276. Jakarta: Dian Rakyat.
1982   "Indonesia: Searching for Consensus." In *Religions and Societies: Asia and the Middle East,* edited by C. Caldarola, pp. 497–548. Berlin: Mouton.

Hughes-Freeland, F.
1993   "Golèk Mènak and Tayuban: Patronage and Professionalism in Two Spheres of Central Javanese Culture." In *Performance in Java and Bali: Studies of Narrative, Theatre, Music, and Dance,* edited by B. Arps, pp. 88–120. London: School of Oriental and African Studies, University of London.

Inden, R.
1976   *Marriage and Rank in Bengali Culture*. Berkeley: University of California Press.

Indonesia Business Weekly

Inside Indonesia

Jakarta Jakarta

Jakarta Post

Java Bode

Jenkins, D.
1998   "Vanishing Regime." *Sydney Morning Herald*, 18 April, p. 41.

Jayasuriya, S., and Kt. Nehen
1989   "Bali: Economic Growth and Tourism." In *Unity and Diversity: Regional Economic Development in Indonesia Since 1970*, edited by H. Hill, pp. 331–348. Singapore: Oxford University Press.

Jolly, M.
1992   "Specters of Inauthenticity." *Contemporary Pacific* 4(1):49–72.

Jolly, M., and N. Thomas (eds.)
1992   "The Politics of Tradition in the Pacific." *Oceania* 62(4). [Special issue.]

Joseph, R.
1987   *Worker, Middlewomen, Entrepreneur: Women in the Indonesian Batik Industry*. Bangkok: Population Council.

Kaaden, W. F. van der
1938   "Nota van Toelichtingen betreffende het in te stellen Zelfbestuurend Landschap Gianjar." Unpublished document.

Kahn, J. S.
1993   *Constituting the Minangkabau: Peasants, Culture, and Modernity in Colonial Indonesia*. Oxford: Berg.

Kahn, J. S., and F. L. K. Wah (eds.)
1992   *Fragmented Vision: Culture and Politics in Contemporary Malaysia*. Asian Studies Association of Australia Southeast Asia Publication 22. Sydney: Allen & Unwin.

Kasiri, J., and S. Nubaiti
1992   "Hindu pun Bertuhan Satu." *Tempo*, 15 February, p. 103.

Keesing, R. M.
1989   "Creating the Past: Custom and Identity in the Contemporary Pacific." *Contemporary Pacific* 1(1–2):19–42.

Keesing, R. M., and R. Tonkinson (eds.)
1982   "Reinventing Traditional Culture: The Politics of Kastom in Island Melanesia." *Mankind* 13(4). [Special issue.]

Kelurahan Ubud
1983   *Monografi Ubud*. Photocopied typescript.

Kemp, J.
1988   *Seductive Mirage: The Search for the Village Community in Southeast Asia*. Comparative Asian Studies 3. Dordrecht: Foris.

Kipp, R. S.
1993   *Dissociated Identities: Ethnicity, Religion, and Class in an Indonesian Society*. Ann Arbor: University of Michigan Press.

Kipp, R. S., and S. Rodgers (eds.)
1987   *Indonesian Religions in Transition*. Tucson: University of Arizona Press.

Klinken, G. van
1994   "Sukarno's Daughter Takes Over Indonesia's Democrats." *Inside Indonesia* 38:2–4.

Kol, H. H. van
1903   *Uit onze Koloniën: Uitvoerig Reisverhaal*. Leiden: A. W. Slijthoff.
1914   *Driemal dwars door Sumatra en Zwerftochten door Bali*. Rotterdam: W. J. and J. Brusse.

Kompas

Konta, A. A. Ng. A.
1977   *Puputan Badung: Bandana Pralaya*. Denpasar: A. A. Alit Konta, Puri Dangin Kawwi.

Korn, V. E.
1925   "Bali is apart . . . is fijner bezenuwd dan eenig ander deel van Indië." *Koloniaal Tijdschrift* 14:44–53.
1932   *Het Adatrecht van Bali*. The Hague: Naeff. Originally published in 1924.

Kraemer, H.
1932   "Het eenig-toelaatbaar experiment." *De Stuw* 3(18):219–223.
1933a "Repliek op 'Bali en de Zending'." *Djawa* 13(1):40–77.
1933b "De strijd over Bali en de Zending: Een studie en een appel." Amsterdam: H. J. Paris.

Kusuma, B.
1994   "The McDonaldisation of Bali." *Inside Indonesia* 41:9–10.

Kutoyo, S., et al.
1977– *Sejarah Kebangkitan Nasional (1900–1942) Daerah Bali*. Proyek
1978   Penelitian dan Pencatatan Kebudayaan Daerah. Jakarta: Pusat Penelitian Sejarah dan Budaya.

Laclau, E.
1977   *Politics and Ideology in Marxist Theory.* London: New Left Books.
1990a   "New Reflections on the Revolution of Our Time." In *New Reflections on the Revolution of Our Time,* edited by E. Laclau, pp. 3–85, London: Verso.
1990b   "The Impossibility of Society." In *New Reflections on the Revolution of Our Time,* edited by E. Laclau, pp. 89–92. London: Verso.
1996   "Universalism, Particularism, and the Question of Identity." In *The Politics of Difference: Ethnic Premises in a World of Power,* edited by E. N. Wilmsen and P. McAllister, pp. 45–58. London: University of Chicago Press.

Laclau, E., and C. Mouffe
1985   *Hegemony and Socialist Strategy: Towards a Radical Democratic Politics.* London: Verso.

Lanfant, F., J. B. Allcock, and E. M. Bruner (eds.)
1995   *International Tourism: Identity and Change.* London: Sage.

Langenberg, M. van
1986   "Analysing Indonesia's New Order State: A Keywords Approach." *Review of Indonesian and Malaysian Affairs* 20(2):1–47.

Lansing, S. J.
1983   *The Three Worlds of Bali.* New York: Praeger.
1991   *Priests and Programmers: Technologies of Power in the Engineered Landscape of Bali.* Princeton: Princeton University Press.

Larson, G. J.
1987   "Introduction to the Philosophy of Samkhya." In *Samkhya: A Dualist Tradition in Indian Philosophy,* edited by G. J. Larson and R. S. Bhattacharya, pp. 3–103. Princeton: Princeton University Press.

Leach, E. R.
1954   *Political Systems of Highland Burma: A Study of Kachin Social Structure.* London: Bell.

Lefebvre, H.
1991   *The Production of Space.* Translated by D. Nicholson-Smith. Oxford: Blackwell.

Leigh, B.
1991   "Making the Indonesian State: The Role of School Texts." *Review of Indonesian and Malaysian Affairs* 25(1):17–43.

Lev, D.
1990   "Intermediate Classes and Change in Indonesia: Some Initial Reflections." In *The Politics of Middle Class Indonesia,* edited by R. Tanter and K. Young, pp. 25–43. Monash Papers on Southeast

Asia, no. 19. Clayton (Victoria): Centre of Southeast Asian Studies, Monash University.

Lévi-Strauss, C.
1966   *The Savage Mind.* London: Weidenfeld & Nicholson.

Liddle, R. W.
1989   "The National Political Culture and the New Order." *Prisma* 46:4–20.
1990   "The Middle Class and New Order Legitimacy." In *The Politics of Middle Class Indonesia,* edited by R. Tanter and K. Young, pp. 49–52. Monash Papers on Southeast Asia, no. 19. Clayton (Victoria): Centre of Southeast Asian Studies, Monash University.

Liefrinck, F. A.
1890   "Bijdrage tot de kennis van het eiland Bali." *Tijdschrift Bataviaasch Genootschap* 33:233–427.

Lindsay, J.
1995a   "Cultural Policy and the Performing Arts in Southeast Asia." *Bijdragen tot de Taal-, Land-, en Volkenkunde* 152(4):656–671.
1995b   "The Currency of Cultural Exchange: Australia-Indonesia." In *Intercultural Exchange Between Australia and Indonesia,* edited by B. Hough and B. Hatley, pp. 54–63. Annual Indonesia Lecture Series, no. 18, Monash Asia Institute. Clayton (Victoria): Monash University.

Lindsey, T.
1997   *The Romance of K'tut Tantri and Indonesia: Texts and Scripts, History and Identity.* Kuala Lumpur: Oxford University Press.

Lindstrom, L., and G. M. White (eds.)
1993   "Custom Today." *Anthropological Forum* 6(4). [Special issue.]

Linnekin, J.
1991   "Inside, Outside: A Hawai'ian Community in the World-System." In *Clio in Oceania: Toward a Historical Anthropology,* edited by A. Biersack, pp. 165–204. Washington: Smithsonian Institution Press.

Linnekin, J., and L. Poyer (eds.)
1990   *Cultural Identity and Ethnicity in the Pacific.* Honolulu: University of Hawai'i Press.

Listibiya
1973   *Pola Dasar Kebijaksanaan Pembinaan Kebudayaan Daerah Bali.* Bali: Majelis Pertimbangan dan Pembinaan Kebudayaan Daerah Propinsi Bali.

Locher-Scholten, E.
1987   "Female Labor in Twentieth Century Java: European Notions—

Indonesian Practice." In *Indonesian Women in Focus,* edited by E. Locher-Scholten and A. Niehof, pp. 77–103. Dordrecht: Foris.

Locher-Scholten, E., and A. Niehof (eds.)
1987   *Indonesian Women in Focus.* Dordrecht: Foris.

Mackie, J., and A. MacIntyre
1994   "Politics." In *Indonesia's New Order: The Dynamics of Socio-Economic Transformation,* edited by H. Hill, pp. 1–53. Sydney: Allen & Unwin.

MacRae, G. S.
1992   "Tourism and Balinese Culture." M.Phil. thesis, University of Auckland.
1995   "Ubud: Cultural Networks and History." Paper presented at the Third International Bali Studies Workshop, University of Sydney, 3–7 July.
1998a   "Economy, Ritual and History in a Balinese Tourist Town." Ph.D. dissertation, University of Auckland.
1998b   "Ritual Networks in South Bali: Geographical Form and Historical Process." *Review of Indonesian and Malaysian Affairs* 32(1):110–143.
n.d.   "BNR: A Symbolic Critique of the Limits of Tourism?" Unpublished paper.

Magenda, B. D.
1988   "Ethnicity and State-Building in Indonesia: The Cultural Base of the New Order." In *Ethnicity and Nations: Processes of Interethnic Relations in Latin America, Southeast Asia, and the Pacific,* edited by R. Guidieri, F. Pellizi, and S. J. Tambiah, pp. 345–361. Austin: Rothko Chapel.

Mahaudiana
1968   *Babad Manggis Gianyar.* Gianyar (Bali): Thaman.

"Mailrapport."
1914   No. 1360. Ministry of Colonies Archives, Algemeen Rijksarchief, The Hague.
1916   Nos. 1655 and 1703. Ministry of Colonies Archives, Algemeen Rijksarchief, The Hague.
1917   Nos. 1104, 1201, 1281, 1451. Ministry of Colonies Archives, Algemeen Rijksarchief, The Hague.

Majelis Pembina Lembaga Adat [MPLA]
1990   *Mengenal dan Pembinaan Desa Adat di Bali.* Denpasar: Majelis Pembina Lembaga Adat Daerah Tingkat I Bali.
1993   "Hasil-Hasil Pesamuhan Majelis Pembina Lembaga Adat, Daerah Bali, 26 February 1993." Unpublished report.

Malaka, T.
1991   *From Jail to Jail.* Vol. 2. Translated and edited by Helen Jarvis. Southeast Asia Series, no. 83. Athens: Ohio University Center for International Studies.

Manderson, L. (ed.)
1983   *Women's Work and Women's Roles: Economics and Everyday Life in Indonesia, Malaysia and Singapore.* Monograph 32. Canberra: Development Studies Centre, Australian National University.

Marriott, M.
1976   "Hindu Transactions: Diversity Without Dualism." In *Transaction and Meaning,* edited by B. Kapferer, pp. 109–142. Philadelphia: ISHI.

Mauss, M.
1990   *The Gift: The Form and Reason for Exchange in Archaic Societies.* London: Routledge.

McBeth, J.
1993   "Lottery Lament: Government Backs Down in Face of Rising Public Protest." *Far Eastern Economic Review,* 9 December, p. 22.

McLuhan, M.
1968   *War and Peace in the Global Village.* New York: McGraw-Hill.

McLuhan, M., and Q. Fiore
1967   *The Medium Is the Massage.* Harmondsworth (Middlesex): Penguin.

McLuhan, M., and B. R. Powers
1989   *The Global Village: Transformations in World Life and Media in the 21st Century.* New York: Oxford University Press.

McVey, R. T.
1979   "The Enchantment of the Revolution: History and Action in an Indonesian Communist Text." In *Perceptions of the Past in Southeast Asia,* edited by A. Reid and D. Marr, pp. 340–358. Singapore: Heinemann.
1994   "The Case of the Disappearing Decade." In *Democracy in Indonesia, 1950s and 1990s,* edited by D. Bourchier and J. Legge, pp. 3–15. Monash Papers on Southeast Asia, no. 31. Clayton (Victoria): Centre of Southeast Asian Studies, Monash University.
1996   "Building Behemoth: Indonesian Constructions of the Nation-State." In *Making Indonesia,* edited by D. S. Lev and R. McVey, pp. 11–25. Ithaca: Cornell Southeast Asia Program.

Mies, M.
1982a   "The Dynamics of the Sexual Division of Labor and Integration of

Rural Women into the World Market." In *Women and Development,* edited by L. Benería, pp. 1–28. New York: Praeger.

1982b   *The Lace Makers of Narsapur: Indian Housewives Produce for the World Market.* London: Zed Books.

Mihardja, A. K. (ed.)
1948   *Polemik Kebudayaan.* Jakarta: Pustaka Jaya.

Milner, A. C.
1982   *Kerajaan: Malay Culture on the Eve of Colonial Rule.* Tucson: University of Arizona Press.
1995   *The Invention of Politics in Colonial Malaya: Contesting Nationalism and the Expansion of the Public Sphere.* Cambridge: Cambridge University Press.

Mirsha, Gst. Ng. Rai
1975   *Puputan Badung (Kutipan dan Terjemahan Lontar Bhuwana Winasa).* Denpasar: Panitia Peringatan Hari Ulang Tahun Puputan Badung.
1979   *Brosur Patung Pahlawan Puputan Badung.* Denpasar: Panitia Penyusun Rencana Pembangunan Monumen Puputan Badung.

Mitchell, T.
1988   *Colonizing Egypt.* Berkeley: University of California Press.

Mohamad, G.
1993   "*Pasemon*: On Allusion and Illusions." *Menagerie* 2:119–135.
1997   "Citizens Organise Themselves." *Inside Indonesia* 51:5.

Moir, H.
1980   "Economic Activities of Women in Rural Java: Are the Data Adequate?" Occasional Paper 20. Canberra: Development Studies Centre, Australian National University.

Monier-Williams, M.
1956   *A Sanskrit-English Dictionary.* Oxford: Oxford University Press. Originally published in 1899.

Monografi Desa "Singarsa"
1982   Denpasar: n.p.
1989   N.p. Mimeograph.

Morley, D.
1992   *Television, Audiences and Cultural Studies.* London: Routledge.

Nakatani, A.
1995a   "Contested Time: Women's Work and Marriage in Bali." Ph.D. dissertation, Oxford University.
1995b   "Transgressing Boundaries: The Changing Division of Labor in the Balinese Weaving Industry." *Indonesia Circle* 67:249–272.

1995c   "Divisions Within: Changing Women's Work in the Balinese Hand-Weaving Industry." *Journal of Sophia Asian Studies* 13:185–206.

1997   "Private or Public?: Defining Female Roles in the Balinese Ritual Domain." *Tonan Ajia Kenkyu* 34(4):722–740.

Nasoetion, A. H.

1991   "Indonesian Higher Education: Improving Input to Improve Output Quality." In *Indonesia Assessment 1991,* edited by H. Hill, pp. 58–76. Political and Social Change Monograph 13. Canberra: Australian National University.

Needham, R.

1980   *Reconnaissances.* Toronto: University of Toronto Press.

Nourse, J. W.

1994   "Textbook Heroes and Local Memory: Writing the Right History in Central Sulawesi." *Social Analysis* 35:102–121.

Oey-Gardiner, M.

1991   "Policy-Making in Higher Education and Implications for Equity." In *Indonesia Assessment 1991,* edited by H. Hill, pp. 77–95. Political and Social Change Monograph 13. Canberra: Australian National University.

Office of Strategic Services

1945   "Programs of Japan in Java and Bali: FCC Stations from December 1941 to May 15, 1945, and from OSS Sources, Honolulu." Unpublished report.

Ong, A.

1987   *Spirits of Resistance and Capitalist Discipline: Factory Women in Malaysia.* Albany: State University of New York Press.

Padmawati, P.

1982   "Pertumbuhan Perkoempoelan Shanti di Singaraja Antara Tahun 1921–1924." B.A. thesis, Universitas Udayana.

Pangdjaja, I. B. (ed.)

1991   *Bali Arts Festival: Pesta Kesenian Bali.* Denpasar: Cita Budaya.

Panyarikan, Kt. S.

1982–   *I Gusti Ngurah Rai.* Jakarta: Proyek Inventarisasi dan Dokument-
1983   asi Sejarah Nasional, Departemen Pendidikan dan Kebudayaan.

Parisada Hindu Dharma [PHD]

1967   *Upadeça tentang Ajaran-ajaran Agama Hindu.* Denpasar: Parisada Hindu Dharma.

1970   *Pokok-pokok Sejarah Perkembangan Parisada Hindu Dharma.* Denpasar: Parisada Hindu Dharma.

Parker, L.
1992a   "The Creation of Indonesian Citizens in Balinese Primary Schools." *Review of Indonesian and Malaysian Affairs* 26(1):42–70.
1992b   "The Quality of Schooling in a Balinese Village." *Indonesia* 54:95–116.

Pelras, C.
1962   "Tissages Balinais." *Objects et Mondes* 2(4):215–240.

Pemberton, J.
1994a   *On the Subject of "Java."* Ithaca: Cornell University Press.
1994b   "Recollections from 'Beautiful Indonesia': Somewhere Beyond the Postmodern." *Public Culture* (6):241–262.

Pendit, Ny. S.
1995   *Hindu Dalam Tafsir Modern.* Denpasar: Yayasan Dharma Naradha.

Perret, D.
1995   *La Formation d'un Paysage Ethnique: Batak et Malais de Sumatra Nord-Est.* Paris: École Française d'Extrême-Orient.

Picard, M.
1990a   "'Cultural Tourism' in Bali: Cultural Performances as Tourist Attractions." *Indonesia* 49:37–74.
1990b   "Kebalian Orang Bali: Tourism and the Uses of 'Balinese Culture' in New Order Indonesia." *Review of Indonesian and Malaysian Affairs* 24:1–38.
1993   "'Cultural Tourism' in Bali: National Integration and Regional Differentiation." In *Tourism in South-East Asia,* edited by M. Hitchcock, V. T. King, and M. J. G. Parnwell, pp. 71–98. London: Routledge.
1995   "Cultural Heritage and Tourist Capital: Cultural Tourism in Bali." In *International Tourism: Identity and Change,* edited by M. F. Lanfant, J. B. Allcock, and E. M. Bruner, pp. 44–66. London: Sage.
1996a   "Dance and Drama in Bali: The Making of an Indonesian Art Form." In *Being Modern in Bali: Image and Change,* edited by A. Vickers, pp. 115–157. Monograph 43. New Haven: Yale University Southeast Asia Studies.
1996b   *Bali: Cultural Tourism and Touristic Culture.* Singapore: Archipelago Press.
1997   "Cultural Tourism, Nation Building, and Regional Culture: The Making of a Balinese Identity." In *Tourism, Ethnicity, and the State in Asian and Pacific Societies,* edited by M. Picard and R. E. Wood, pp. 181–214. Honolulu: University of Hawai'i Press.

Pitana, Gd.
1992   "Daya Dukung Bali terhadap Kepariwisataan (Aspek Sosial-
           Budaya)." In *Pembangunan Bali Berwawasan Budaya,* edited by
           I Gst. Ng. Bagus et al., pp. 62–70. *Journal of Udayana University.*
           [Special issue.]
1994   (ed.) *Dinamika Masyarakat dan Kebudayaan Bali.* Denpasar: B. P.
1995   "Kepariwisataan Indonesia: Pencermatan dari Gatra Sosial-Bu-
           daya." In *Indonesia dalam Transisi,* edited by G. H. Sofyan, pp.
           218–237. Jakarta: Halmahera.
1998   "In Search of Difference: Origin Groups, Status and Identity in
           Contemporary Bali." Ph.D. dissertation, Australian National
           University.

Poffenberger, M., and M. S. Zurbuchen
1980   "The Economics of Village Bali: Three Perspectives." *Economic
           Development and Cultural Change* 29:91–133.

Popular Memory Group
1982   "Popular Memory: Theory, Politics, Method." In *Making His-
           tories: Studies in History-Writing and Politics,* edited by R. John-
           son et al., pp. 205–252. London: Hutchinson in association
           with the Centre for Contemporary Studies, University of
           Birmingham.

Powell, H.
1930   *The Last Paradise.* London: Jonathan Cape.

Prakash, G.
1990   "Writing Post-Orientalist Histories of the Third World: Perspec-
           tives from Indian Historiography." *Comparative Studies in Society
           and History* 32:383–408.

"Prasasti Pande Besi"
n.d.   Manuscript 1133/10. Gedong Kirtya, Singaraja.

Pratiknyo, H.
1992   "Bali's Traditional Identity Eroded Due to Super-Rapid Tourist
           Growth." *Jakarta Post,* 14 August, p. 8.

Prisma

Proyek Inventarisasi dan Dokumentasi Sejarah Nasional
1985   *Seminar Sejarah Nasional IV: Sub Tema Pendidikan Sejarah.*
           Jakarta: Departemen Pendidikan dan Kebudayaan, Direktorat Se-
           jarah dan Nilai Tradisional.

Punyatmadja, I B. O.
1970   *Pancha Çradha.* Denpasar: Parisada Hindu Dharma Pusat.

Purwita, I.
1993   *Upacara Mediksa*. Denpasar: Upada Sastra.

Putra, A. A. P. O.
1989   "Perkumpulan Bali Darma Laksana: Sebuah Organisasi Sosial di
        Bali, 1936–1942." M.A. thesis, Universitas Udayana.

Raffles, T. S.
1817   *The History of Java*. London: Black, Parbury & Allen.

Ram, K.
1991   *Mukkuvar Women: Gender, Hegemony and Capitalist Transforma-
        tion in a South Indian Fishing Community*. London: Zed Books.
1993   "Too 'Traditional' Once Again: Some Poststructuralists on the
        Aspirations of the Immigrant/Third World Female Subject." *Aus-
        tralian Feminist Studies* 17:5–28.

Ramage, D. E.
1994   "Pancasila Discourse in Suharto's Late New Order." In *Democ-
        racy in Indonesia, 1950s and 1990s*, edited by D. Bourchier and J.
        Legge, pp. 156–167. Monash Papers on Southeast Asia, no. 31.
        Clayton (Victoria): Centre of Southeast Asian Studies, Monash
        University.

Ramseyer, U.
1977   *The Art and Culture of Bali*. Oxford: Oxford University Press.
1987   "The Traditional Textile Craft and Textile Workshops of Sidemen,
        Bali." *Indonesian Circle* 42:3–15.

Ramseyer, U., and M. L. Nabholz-Kartaschoff
1991   "Songket: Golden Threads, Caste and Privilege." In *Balinese Tex-
        tiles*, edited by B. Hauser-Schäublin et al., pp. 33–50. London:
        British Museum Press.

Ramstedt, M.
1992   "Indonesian Cultural Policy in Relation to the Development of
        Balinese Performing Arts." In *Balinese Music in Context*, edited by
        D. Schaareman, pp. 59–84. Forum Ethnomusicologicum 4. Win-
        terthur: Amadeus.

Redfield, R.
1953   *The Primitive World and Its Transformation*. Ithaca: Cornell Uni-
        versity Press.

Reid, A.
1979   "The Nationalist Quest for an Indonesian Past." In *Perceptions of
        the Past in Southeast Asia*, edited by A. Reid and D. Marr, pp.
        281–298. Asian Studies Association of Australia Southeast Asia
        Publication Series. Singapore: Heinemann.

1988   *Southeast Asia in the Age of Commerce: The Lands Below the Winds.*
           New Haven: Yale University Press.

Reuter, T. A.
1996   "Custodians of the Sacred Mountains: The Ritual Domains of
           Highland Bali." Ph.D. dissertation, Australian National Univer-
           sity.

Rhodius, H., and J. Darling
1980   *Walter Spies and Balinese Art.* Zutphen: Terra.

Robinson, G. B.
1995   *The Dark Side of Paradise: Political Violence in Bali.* Ithaca: Cor-
           nell University Press.

Robinson, K.
1988   "What Kind of Freedom Is Cutting Your Hair?" In *Development
           and Displacement: Women in Southeast Asia,* edited by G. Chan-
           dler, N. Sullivan, and J. Branson, pp. 111–128. Clayton (Victo-
           ria): Monash University.
1997   "History, Houses, and Regional Identities." *Australian Journal
           of Anthropology* 8(1):71–88.

Robison, R.
1990   *Power and Economy in Suharto's Indonesia.* Manila: Journal of
           Contemporary Asia.

Rodgers, S.
1986   "Batak Tape Cassette Kinship: Constructing Kinship Through the
           Indonesian Mass Media." *American Ethnologist* 13(1):23–42.
1987   "City Newspapers in the Creation of a Batak Political Heritage."
           In *Cultures and Societies of North Sumatra,* edited by R. Carle, pp.
           189–220. Berlin: Dietrich Reimer Verlag.
1987–   "A Batak Antiquarian Writes His Culture: Print Literacy and So-
1988   cial Thought in an Indonesian Society." *Journal of the Stewart
           Anthropological Society* 17(1–2):99–120.
1993   "Batak Heritage and the Indonesian State: Print Literacy and the
           Construction of Ethnic Cultures in Indonesia." In *Ethnicity and
           the State,* edited by J. D. Toland, pp. 147–176. New Brunswick:
           Transaction.

Rogers, B.
1980   *The Domestication of Women: Discrimination in Developing Soci-
           eties.* London: Kegan Paul.

Roseberry, W.
1989   *Anthropologies and Histories: Essays in Culture, History and Polit-
           ical Economy.* New Brunswick: Rutgers University Press.

Roxborough, I.
1979   *Theories of Underdevelopment.* London: Macmillan.

Rubinstein, R.
1996   "Allegiance and Alliance: The Banjar War of 1868." In *Being Modern in Bali: Image and Change,* edited by A. Vickers, pp. 38–70. Monograph 43. New Haven: Yale University Southeast Asia Studies.

Ruiter, T., and H. Schulte Nordholt
1989   "The Village Revisited: Community and Locality in Southeast Asia." *Sojourn* 4(1):127–134.

Sahlins, M.
1976   *Culture and Practical Reason.* Chicago: University of Chicago Press.
1985   *Islands of History.* Chicago: University of Chicago Press.
1993   "Goodbye to Tristes Tropes: Ethnography in the Context of Modern World History." *Journal of Modern History* 65(1):1–25.

Sailendri
1996   "Megawati: 'Why Not a Woman President?'" *Inside Indonesia* 48:2–3.

Sajogyo, P.
1984   "A Conceptual Framework for Understanding Women's Work and Women's Role in Family Welfare and in Rural Development." Draft report.

Sarjadi, S.
1996   *Kaum Pinggiran—Kelas Menengah: Quo Vadis?* Jakarta: Gramedia.

Sastra, Gd. S.
1994   *Konsepsi Monotheisme Dalam Agama Hindu.* Denpasar: Upada Sastra.

Sastrodiwiryo, S.
1994   *I Gusti Anglurah Panji Sakti, Raja Buleleng 1599–1680.* Denpasar: Kayu Mas.

Schiller, A.
1997   *Small Sacrifices: Religious Change and Cultural Identity Among the Ngaju of Indonesia.* New York: Oxford University Press.

Schiller, J.
1996   *Developing Jepara in New Order Indonesia.* Clayton (Victoria): Monash Asia Institute.

Schulte Nordholt, H.
1981   "Negara: A Theatre State?" *Bijdragen tot de Taal-, Land-, en Volkenkunde* 137:470–476.

1986   *Bali: Colonial Conceptions and Political Change, 1700–1940: From Shifting Hierarchies to "Fixed Order."* Rotterdam: Erasmus University.

1988   "The Quest for Life." Paper presented at the Annual Conference of the Society for Balinese Studies, Denpasar, 29–31 July.

1991a   "Temple and Authority in South Bali, 1900–1980." In *State and Society in Bali: Historical, Textual and Anthropological Approaches,* edited by H. Geertz, pp. 137–163. VKI 146. Leiden: KITLV Press.

1991b   *State, Village, and Ritual in Bali.* Amsterdam: VU University Press.

1994   "The Making of Traditional Bali: Colonial Ethnography and Bureaucratic Reproduction." *History and Anthropology* 8(1–4): 89–127.

1996   *The Spell of Power: A History of Balinese Politics, 1650–1940.* Leiden: KITLV Press.

Schwartz, H. J. E. F.
1900   "Aanteekeningen omtrent het Landschap Gianjar." *Tijdschrift voor het Binnenlands Bestuur* 19:166–189.

Schwarz, A.
1994   *A Nation in Waiting: Indonesia in the 1990s.* Sydney: Allen & Unwin.

Scott, J. C.
1977   *The Moral Economy of the Peasant: Rebellion and Subsistence in Southeast Asia.* New Haven: Yale University Press.

1985   *Weapons of the Weak: Everyday Forms of Peasant Resistance.* New Haven: Yale University Press.

Sears, L. J.
1996   *Shadows of Empire: Colonial Discourse and Javanese Tales.* Durham: Duke University Press.

Sedana, Ny.
1993   "The Education of a Dalang." [Edited by Kathy Foley.] *Asian Theatre Journal* 10(1):81–100.

Sekolah Tinggi Seni Indonesia
1993   "Pedoman Perkuliahan: Sekolah Tinggi Seni Indonesia, Denpasar." Internal document.

Sellato, B.
1990   "Indonesia Goes Ethnic—Provincial Culture, Image, and Identity: Current Trends in Kalimantan." Paper presented at the Conference on Centers and Peripheries in Insular Southeast Asia, CNRS-DEVI, Paris.

Seminar
1971   *Hasil Keputusan Seminar Pariwisata Budaja.* Denpasar: Daerah Bali.

Seminar Sejarah Nasional III
1982–   *Panel Sejarah Lokal.* Jakarta: Proyek Inventarisasi dan Doku-
1983   mentasi Sejarah Nasional, Departemen Pendidikan dan Kebu-
           dayaan, Direktorat Sejarah dan Nilai Tradisional.

Sen, K.
1994   *Indonesian Cinema: Framing the New Order.* London: Zed Books.

Setia, Pt.
1992   (ed.) *Cendekiawan Hindu Bicara.* Denpasar: Yayasan Dharma
            Naradha.
1993a   *Kebangkitan Hindu Menyongsong Abad Ke-21.* Jakarta: Pustaka
            Manik Geni.
1993b   (ed.) *Suara Kaum Muda Hindu.* Jakarta: Yayasan Dharma Nu-
            santara–FCHI.
1994   (ed.) *Dialog Nyepi 1916 Çaka: Umat Beragama dan Persatuan
            Bangsa.* Jakarta: Panitia Bersama Dharma Çanti Hari Raya Nyepi
            Tahun Çaka 1916.

Shills, E.
1962   "The Intellectuals in the Political Development of the New States."
            In *Political Change in Underdeveloped Countries: Nationalism and
            Communism,* edited by J. H. Kautsky, pp. 195–224. New York:
            Wiley.

Siasat
1950s   Jakarta: n.p.

Simpen, I W.
1958   *Sedjarah Perang Keradjaan Badung menentang Kaum Pendjajah
            Belanda sedjak Tahun 1920 sampai 1908.* Denpasar: Pustaka
            Balimas.

Skeat, W. W.
1965   *Malay Magic: An Introduction to the Folklore and Popular Reli-
            gion of the Malay Peninsula.* London: Frank Cass. Originally pub-
            lished in 1900.

Slack, J. D.
1996   "The Theory and Method of Articulation in Cultural Studies."
            In Stuart Hall: *Critical Dialogues in Cultural Studies,* edited by
            D. Morley and K.-H. Chen, pp. 112–127. London: Routledge.

Smart, A.
1993   "Gifts, Bribes and *Guanxi*: A Reconsideration of Bourdieu's So-
            cial Capital." *Cultural Anthropology* 8(3):388–408.

Smith, M.
1995 *Engaging Characters: Fiction, Emotion, and the Cinema.* Oxford: Clarendon Press.

Smyth, I. A.
1993 "A Critical Look at the Indonesian Government's Policies for Women." In *Development and Social Welfare: Indonesia's Experiences Under the New Order,* edited by J.-P. Dirkse, F. Hüsken and M. Rutten, pp. 117–130. Leiden: KITLV Press.

Soebadio, H.
1985 *Cultural Policy in Indonesia.* Paris: UNESCO.

Soebandi, J. G. M. K.
1991 *Bhisama Para Leluhur Pasek (Maha Gotra Pasek Sanak Sapta Rsi).* Denpasar: Yayasan Adhi Sapta Kerthi.

Solyom, B.
1995 "The Museum Bali: The Significance of Its Colonial Past in Contemporary Bali." Paper presented at the Third International Bali Studies Conference, University of Sydney, 3–7 July.

Spivak, G. C.
1988 "Can the Subaltern Speak?" In *Marxism and the Interpretation of Culture,* edited by C. Nelson and L. Grossberg, pp. 271–313. Basingstoke: Macmillan.

Standing, H.
1991 *Dependence and Autonomy: Women's Employment and the Family in Calcutta.* London: Routledge.

Statistik Bali
1991 Denpasar: Kantor Statistik Propinsi Bali.

Stivens, M.
1996 *Matriliny and Modernity: Sexual Politics and Social Change in Rural Malaysia.* Women in Asia Publication Series. St. Leonards (NSW): Allen & Unwin.

Stoler, A.
1977 "Class Structure and Female Autonomy in Rural Java." *Signs* 3(1):74–89.

Stuart-Fox, D. J.
1987 "Pura Besakih: A Study of Balinese Religion and Society." Ph.D. dissertation, Australian National University.

Suara Pembaruan

Suardika, Wy., and E. Warijadi
1996   "Pelestarian Budaya Bali dan Kelas Menengah." *Nusa Tenggara,*
         21 January.

Subagyo, W.
1991   *Pengrajin Tradisional di Daerah Propinsi Bali.* Jakarta: Depart-
         men Pendidikan dan Kebudayaan.

Sudhartha, Tj. R., et al. (eds.)
1993   *Kebudayaan dan Kepribadian Bangsa.* Denpasar: Upada Sastra.

Sudibya, Gd.
1994   *Hindu menjawab Dinamika Zaman.* Denpasar: B. P.

Sugriwa, I Gst. B.
1954   "Tjeramah Agama terhadap Rombongan Mahasiswa pada tgl. 19
         Oktober 1953 dibalai Masjarakat Denpasar." *Bahasa dan Budaja*
         2(6):40–45.
1957   *Kitab Babad Pasek.* Denpasar: Pustaka Balimas.

Sujana, N. N.
1988   "Orang Bali Semakin Kehilangan Kebaliannya." *Bali Post,* 3 De-
         cember, p. 7.

Supartha, Ng. O.
1994   *Karya Dirghayusa Bhumi di Pura Dalem, Desa Adat Bresela.* Bre-
         sela (Bali): Panitia Karya Dirghayusa Bhumi, Desa Adat Bresela,
         Kecamatan Payangan, Kabupaten Daerah Tingkat II, Gianyar.
1996   *Karya Agung Dirghayusa Bhumi di Pura Dalem Kauh di Bhumi
         Janggala Kusara.* Tegallalang (Bali): Panitia Pelaksana Karya
         Agung Dirghayusa Bhumi di Pura Dalem Kauh, Banjar Pejengaji
         dan Banjar Gagah, Desa Adat Tegallalang, Kabupaten Daerah
         Tingkat II, Gianyar.

Supartha, Wy. (ed.)
1994a   *Hak Asasi Manusia Dalam Hindu.* Jakarta: Pustaka Manik Geni.
1994b   *Memahami Aliran Kepercayaan.* Denpasar: B. P.

Supomo, S.
1979   "The Image of Majapahit in Later Javanese and Indonesian Writ-
         ing." In *Perceptions of the Past in Southeast Asia,* edited by A. Reid
         and D. Marr, pp.171–185. Asian Studies Association of Australia
         Southeast Asia Publication Series. Singapore: Heinemann.

Suratiyah, K., et al.
1991   *Pembangunan Pertanian dan Peranan Wanita di Pedesaan Yo-
         gyakarta dan Bali.* Yogyakarta: Pusat Penelitian Kependudukan,
         Universitas Gajah Mada.

Surpha, Wy.
1986   *Eksistensi Desa Adat di Bali dengan diundangkannya Undang-undang No. 5 Th. 1979. (Tentang Pemerintahan Desa)*. Reprint, Denpasar: Upada Sastra, 1992.

Surya Kanta
1925–   Singaradja: Perkoempoelan Surya Kanta.
1927

Sutton, R. A.
1985a   "Commercial Cassette Recordings of Traditional Music in Java: Implications for Performers and Scholars." *World of Music* 27(3): 23–43.
1985b   "Musical Pluralism in Java: Three Local Traditions." *Ethnomusicology* 29(1):56–85.
1991   *Traditions of Gamelan Music in Java: Musical Pluralism and Regional Identity*. Cambridge: Cambridge University Press.
1995   "Performing Arts and Cultural Politics in South Sulawesi." *Bijdragen tot de Taal-, Land-, en Volkenkunde* 151(4):672–699.

Swellengrebel, J. L.
1960   "Introduction: Some Religious Problems of Today." In *Bali: Studies in Life, Thought, and Ritual*, pp. 68–76. The Hague: Van Hoeve.

Sydney Morning Herald

Tambiah, S. J.
1985   A Reformulation of Geertz's Conception of the Theatre State. In *Culture, Thought and Social Action: An Anthropological Perspective*, edited by S. J. Tambiah, pp. 252–286. Cambridge, Mass.: Harvard University Press.

Tanter, R., and K. Young (eds.)
1990   *The Politics of Middle Class Indonesia*. Monash Papers on Southeast Asia, no. 19. Clayton (Victoria): Centre of Southeast Asian Studies, Monash University.

Taussig, M.
1980   *The Devil and Commodity Fetishism*. Chapel Hill: University of North Carolina Press.
1987   *Shamanism, Colonialism, and the Wild Man: A Study in Terror and Healing*. Chicago: University of Chicago Press.

Taylor, P. M.
1994   "The *Nusantara* Concept of Culture: Local Traditions and National Identity as Expressed in Indonesia's Museums." In *Fragile*

Traditions: Indonesian Art in Jeopardy, edited by P. M. Taylor, pp. 71–90. Honolulu: University of Hawai'i Press.

Teeuw, A., et al.
1969   *Siwaratrikalpa of Mpu Tanakung.* Bibliotheca Indonesica 3. The Hague: Nijhoff.

Tempo

Thomas, N.
1994   *Colonialism's Culture: Anthropology, Travel and Government.* Princeton: Princeton University Press.

Tickell, P.
1994   "Free from What? Responsible to Whom? The Problem of Democracy and the Indonesian Press." In *Democracy in Indonesia, 1950s and 1990s,* edited by D. Bourchier and J. Legge, pp. 192–198. Monash Papers on Southeast Asia, no. 31. Clayton (Victoria): Centre of Southeast Asian Studies, Monash University.

Titib, M.
1993   "Sulinggih yang Berwawasan Esoterik dan Cara Mempersiapkannya." *Aditya* 3:33–40.

Toer, P. A.
1990   *Footsteps.* Translated by M. Lane. Victoria: Penguin. Originally published in 1985.

Tooker, D. E.
1996   "Putting the Mandala in Its Place: A Practice-Based Approach to the Spatialization of Power on the Southeast Asian Periphery— The Case of the Akha." *Journal of Asian Studies* 55(2):323–358.

Truong, T.-D.
1990   *Sex, Money and Morality: Prostitution and Tourism in South-East Asia.* London: Zed Books.

Tsing, A. L.
1993   *In the Realm of the Diamond Queen: Marginality in an Out-of-the-Way Place.* Princeton: Princeton University Press.
1996   "Telling Violence in the Meratus Mountains. In *Headhunting and the Social Imagination in Southeast Asia,* edited by J. Hoskins, pp. 184–215. Stanford: Stanford University Press.

Tuuk, H. N. van der
1897–   *Kawi-Balineesch-Nederlandsch Woordenboek.* 4 vols. Batavia:
1912   Landsdrukkerij.

University of Auckland
1994   "Advertisement for Lecturer in Social Anthropology."

V.30 May 1917, no. 37
>   Ministry of Colonies Archives, Algemeen Rijksarchief, The Hague.

V.3 June 1913, no. 45, IIIC9
>   Ministry of Colonies Archives, Algemeen Rijksarchief, The Hague.

Valeri, V.
1991   "The Transformation of a Transformation: A Structural Essay on an Aspect of Hawai'ian History (1809–1819)." In *Clio in Oceania: Toward a Historical Anthropology,* edited by A. Biersack, pp. 101–164. Washington: Smithsonian Institution Press.

Verdery, K.
1996   "Wither 'Nation' and 'Nationalism'?" In *Mapping the Nation,* edited by G. Balakrishnan, pp. 226–234. London: Verso.

Vickers, A.
1987   "Hinduism and Islam in Indonesia: Bali and the Pasisir World." *Indonesia* 44:31–58.
1989   *Bali: A Paradise Created.* Ringwood (Victoria): Penguin.
1996a   (ed.) *Being Modern in Bali: Image and Change,* edited by A. Vickers. Monograph 43. New Haven: Yale University Southeast Asia Studies.
1996b   "Introduction." In *Being Modern in Bali: Image and Change,* edited by A. Vickers, pp. 1–36. Monograph 43. New Haven: Yale University Southeast Asia Studies.

Vignato, S.
1998   *Les Hindouistes de Sumatra-Nord: Une étude comparée chez les Tamouls et les Karo en Indonésie.* Ph.D. dissertation, EHESS, Paris.

Volkman, T. A.
1984   "Great Performances: Toraja Cultural Identity in the 1970s." *American Ethnologist* 11(1):152–169.
1985   *Feasts of Honor: Ritual and Change in the Toraja Highlands.* Urbana: University of Illinois Press.
1987   "Mortuary Tourism in Tana Toraja." In *Indonesian Religions in Transition,* edited by R. S. Kipp and S. Rogers, pp. 161–167. Tucson: University of Arizona Press.
1990   "Visions and Revisions: Toraja Culture and the Tourist Gaze." *American Ethnologist* 17(1):91–110.

Vollenhoven, C. van
1928   *De Ontdekking van het Adatrecht.* Leiden: Brill.

Wagner, R.
1975   *The Invention of Culture*. Englewood Cliffs: Prentice-Hall.

Walkerdine, V.
1990   "Video Replay: Families, Films and Fantasies." In *The Media Reader*, edited by M. Alvorado and J. O. Thompson, pp. 339–357. London: British Film Institute.
1996   "Popular Culture and the Eroticization of Little Girls." In *Cultural Studies and Communication*, edited by J. Curran, D. Morley, and V. Walkerdine, pp. 323–333. London: Arnold.

Warna, Wy., et al.
1990   *Kamus Bali-Indonesia*. Denpasar: Dinas Pendidikan Dasar Propinsi Dati I Bali.

Warren, C.
1993   *Adat and Dinas: Balinese Communities in the Indonesian State*. Kuala Lumpur: Oxford University Press.
1994   *Centre and Periphery in Indonesia: Environment, Politics and Human Rights in the Regional Press (Bali)*. Working Paper 42. Perth: Murdoch University Asia Research Centre.
1995   "The Garuda Wisnu Kencana Monument Debate: Environment, Culture, and the Discourses of Nationalism in Late New Order Bali." In *Kulturen und Raum: theoretische Ansätze und empirische Kulturforschung in Indonesien*, edited by B. Werlen and S. Wälty, pp. 377–390. Zurich: Ruegger.
1998a   "Tanah Lot: The Cultural and Environmental Politics of Resort Development in Bali." In *Reclaiming Resources: The Political Economy of Environment in Southeast Asia*, edited by P. Hirsch and C. Warren, pp. 229–261. London: Routledge.
1998b   "Whose Tourism? Balinese Fight Back." *Inside Indonesia* 54 (April–June):24–25.

Weede, H. M. van
1908   *Indische Reisherinneringen*. Haarlem: H. D. Tjeenk Willink.

Weinstock, J. A.
1981   "Kaharingan: Borneo's 'Old Religion' Becomes Indonesia's Newest Religion." *Borneo Research Bulletin* 13(1):47–48.

Weitzel, A. W. P.
1859   *De Derde Militaire Expeditie naar het Eiland Bali in 1849*. Gorinchem: J. Noorduyn.

White, B.
1991   *Studying Women and Rural Non-Farm Sector Development in West Java*. Working Paper B-12, West Java Rural Non-Farm Sector Research Project. The Hague: Institute of Social Studies.

Wiana, Kt.
1993   *Bagaimana Umat Hindu menghayati Tuhan.* Jakarta: Pustaka Manik Geni.
1995   "Veda dalam Penerapannya." *Pustaka Hindu Raditya* 1:38–71.

Wiana, Kt., and R. Santeri
1993   *Kasta dalam Hindu: Kesalahpahaman Berabad-abad.* Denpasar: Yayasan Dharma Naradha.

Widminarko
1989   "Pendapat Pembaca Bali Post tentang Kebalian Orang Bali." *Forum Diskusi* sponsored by *Bali Post*, Denpasar.

Widodo, A.
1995   "The Stages of the State: Arts of the People and Rites of Hegemonization." *Review of Indonesian Malaysian Affairs* 29(1–2):1–36.

Wiener, M. J.
1994   "Object Lessons: Dutch Colonialism and the Looting of Bali." *History and Anthropology* 6(4):347–370.
1995a   *Visible and Invisible Realms: Power, Magic, and Colonial Conquest in Bali.* Chicago: University of Chicago Press.
1995b   "Doors of Perception: Power and Representation in Bali." *Cultural Anthropology* 10(4):1–37.
n.d.   "Disciplining Balinese Ritual in the Indonesian Nation-State." Unpublished paper.

Wieringa, S.
1985   *The Perfumed Nightmare: Indonesian Women's Organizations After 1950.* Subseries on Women's History and Development, Working Paper 5. The Hague: Institute of Social Studies.

Wijaya, Ny.
1990   "Dari Agama Bali Menuju Hindu Dharma: Studi Tentang Konflik Sosial di Bali 1913–1959." Unpublished research report, Universitas Udayana, Denpasar.

Wikan, U.
1990   *Managing Turbulent Hearts: A Balinese Formula for Living.* Chicago: University of Chicago Press.

Williams, L.
1997   "Jakarta's New Rich: Push for Clean Homes, Not Clean Politics." *Sydney Morning Herald*, 26 April, p. 17.
1998   "Defiant Soeharto Tells His Nation: No Reform for Five Years." *Sydney Morning Herald*, 2 May, p. 23.

Williams, R.
1977   *Marxism and Literature.* Oxford: Oxford University Press.

1983   *Keywords: A Vocabulary of Culture and Society.* London: Flamingo.

Williamson, D.
1992   "Language and Sexual Difference." In *The Sexual Subject: A Screen Reader in Sexuality,* pp. 107–125. London: Routledge.

Wiryatnaya, U., and J. Couteau (eds.)
1995   *Bali di Persimpangan Jalan.* 2 vols. Denpasar: NusaData Indo-Budaya.

Wolf, D. L.
1992   *Factory Daughters: Gender, Household Dynamics, and Rural Industrialization in Java.* Berkeley: University of California Press.

Wolf, E.
1957   "Closed Corporate Communities in Mesoamerica and Central Java." *Southwestern Journal of Anthropology* 13:1–18.
1982   *Europe and the People Without History.* Berkeley: University of California Press.

Wolters, O. W.
1982   *History, Culture, and Region in Southeast Asian Perspectives.* Singapore: Institute of Southeast Asian Studies.

Worsley, P.
1972   *Babad Buleleng: A Balinese Dynastic Genealogy.* Bibliotheca Indonesica 8. The Hague: Nijhoff.

Wouden, F. A. E. van
1968   *Types of Social Structure in Eastern Indonesia.* The Hague: Nijhoff. Originally published in 1935.

Yampolsky, P.
1995   "Forces for Change in the Regional Performing Arts of Indonesia." *Bijdragen tot de Taal-, Land-, en Volkenkunde* 151(4): 700–725.

Zoete, B. de, and W. Spies
1973   *Dance and Drama in Bali.* Kuala Lumpur: Oxford University Press. Originally published in 1938.

Zoetmulder, P. J.
1982   *Old Javanese-English Dictionary.* 2 vols. KITLV. The Hague: Nijhoff.

Zurbuchen, M. S.
1990   "Images of Culture and National Development in Indonesia: The Cockroach Opera." *Asian Theatre Journal* 7(2):127–150.

Contributors

The Editors

Linda H. Connor teaches anthropology at the University of Newcastle, NSW, Australia. Awarded a Ph.D. from the University of Sydney in 1982, she has carried out extensive field research in Bali over the last two decades and has written extensively on traditional healing and religious transformation in contemporary Bali. With Timothy and Patsy Asch, she is the author of *Jero Tapakan: Balinese Healer* (Cambridge University Press, 1986; Ethnographies Press, 2nd ed., 1996), as well as a number of ethnographic films on Balinese healing and cremation ceremonies.

Raechelle Rubinstein is an Australian Research Council fellow attached to the Department of Southeast Asian Studies at the University of Sydney. She has a Ph.D. (1990) and a Diploma of Museum Studies (1992) from the University of Sydney and has been a scholar of Bali for more than two decades. Her areas of specialization include Balinese and Kawi language and literature, as well as Balinese history and music. Her publications include *Beyond the Realm of the Senses: The Balinese Ritual of Kekawin Composition* (KITLV Press, in press).

The Contributors

Mark Hobart is Senior Lecturer in Anthropology with reference to Southeast Asia at the School of Oriental and African Studies, University of London. He has a special research interest in philosophical issues in anthropology and comparative media studies and has spent many years carrying out research in Bali, including extensive documentation of contemporary television genres. He is the editor of *An Anthropological Critique of Development: The Growth of Ignorance* (Routledge, 1993).

Brett Hough is a lecturer in the Department of Anthropology and Sociology at Monash University, Melbourne, Australia. He spent two years in Bali studying Balinese mask dancing at the College of Indonesian Arts, and in the village of Batuan, and is writing a Ph.D. dissertation on the performing arts in Bali.

Graeme MacRae trained initially as an architect and worked in this and other fields while studying anthropology in Australia and New Zealand. His Ph.D. dissertation on economy, ritual, history, and tourism in Bali was completed at the University of Auckland in 1997. Since then he has been a lecturer in social anthropology at Massey University, Albany, New Zealand.

Ayami Nakatani received her D.Phil. from the University of Oxford in 1995 and now teaches anthropology at Okayama University in Japan. Her dissertation focused on the changing conditions of Balinese women's labor in a rural hand-weaving industry. Her current research interests include the study of textile and garment factory workers in Indonesia and Japan.

Michel Picard is a research fellow at the French National Center of Scientific Research (CNRS). He has spent many years studying the implications of international tourism for Bali and is the author of *Bali: Cultural Tourism and Touristic Culture* (Archipelago Press, 1996) and co-editor of *Tourism, Ethnicity, and the State in Asian and Pacific Societies* (University of Hawai'i Press, 1997), as well as numerous other publications on tourism in Bali. He is currently pursuing research on Balinese society with the Laboratoire Asie du Sud-Est et Monde Austronésien (LASEMA).

I Gde Pitana has recently completed a Ph.D. at the Research School of Pacific and Asian Studies, Australian National University, and is teaching rural sociology in the Faculty of Agriculture, Udayana University, Bali. His research in Bali embraces the new political movements contesting the authority of Bali's traditional elite.

Thomas A. Reuter has a Ph.D. in anthropology from the Australian National University (1996). He was a lecturer in the Ethnological Institute at the University of Heidelberg, Germany, before taking up an Australian Research Council postdoctoral fellowship at the University of Melbourne. His research for his dissertation focused on the culture and identity of Bali Aga groups, and he pursues ongoing research in Bali on the topics of ritual alliance and temple networks as well as the politics of marginalization and ethnicity.

Putu Suasta is a graduate of the Faculty of Political and Social Science, Gadjah Mada University, Yogyakarta, Indonesia, and has an M.A. from Cornell University. He manages a landscape architecture firm in Bali and is a media commentator and active participant in current debates about Bali's future.

Margaret J. Wiener is an assistant professor in the Department of Anthropology at the University of North Carolina at Chapel Hill and has a Ph.D. (1990) from the University of Chicago. She has carried out extensive ethnohistorical research in the Klungkung region of Bali. Her publications include *Visible and Invisible Realms: Power, Magic, and Colonial Conquest in Bali* (University of Chicago Press, 1995).

Index

Page numbers in *italics* refer to illustrations, tables, and maps.

	DATE DUE		